THE INDIAN REFORM LETTERS OF

HELEN HUNT JACKSON, 1879–1885

The Indian Reform Letters of Helen Hunt Jackson, 1879–1885

EDITED BY

Valerie Sherer Mathes

UNIVERSITY OF OKLAHOMA PRESS : NORMAN

BY VALERIE SHERER MATHES

Helen Hunt Jackson and Her Indian Reform Legacy (Austin, Tex., 1990; Norman, 1997)
(ed.) *The Indian Reform Letters of Helen Hunt Jackson, 1879–1885* (Norman, 1998)

This book is published with the generous assistance of The Kerr Foundation, Inc.

Library of Congress Cataloging-in-Publication Data

Jackson, Helen Hunt, 1830–1885.
The Indian reform letters of Helen Hunt Jackson, 1879–1885 /
edited by Valerie Sherer Mathes
p.   cm.
Includes bibliographical references and index.
ISBN 0-8061-3090-3 (alk. paper)
1. Jackson, Helen Hunt, 1830–1885—Correspondence.   2. Jackson,
Helen Hunt, 1830–1885—Political and social views.   3. Women
authors, American—19th century—Correspondence.   4. Women social
reformers—United States—Correspondence.   5. Indians of North
America—Civil rights—California.   6. Ponca Indians—Government
relations.   I. Mathes, Valerie Sherer, 1941–   .   II. Title.
PS2108.A44   1998
818'.409—dc21
[B]   98-2507
CIP

The paper in this book meets the guidelines for permanence and durability of the
Committee on Production Guidelines for Book Longevity of the Council on Library
Resources, Inc. ∞

1 2 3 4 5 6 7 8 9 10

I SHALL BE FOUND WITH "INDIANS" ENGRAVED ON MY BRAIN WHEN I AM DEAD. — A FIRE HAS BEEN KINDLED WITHIN ME, WHICH WILL NEVER GO OUT. —

WHAT I WANT TO DO NOW IS TO WRITE A LITTLE BOOK — SIMPLY & CURTLY A RECORD OF OUR BROKEN TREATIES — & CALL IT "A CENTURY OF DISHONOR" —

HELEN HUNT JACKSON TO CHARLES DUDLEY WARNER, DECEMBER 21, 1879

Contents

Illustrations

Acknowledgments

MY JOURNEY WITH HELEN HUNT JACKSON BEGAN IN 1979 AND HAS TAKEN ME TO the mountains of Colorado Springs, the deserts of southern California, and the towns of New England—places where Jackson lived. This journey has been a long one, and Jackson has been a lively companion.

There are many who have supported me in this effort; I am sincerely indebted to the staff of the various archives and libraries that house Jackson materials. On a more personal level, I am most indebted to Pamela Herr, co-editor of *The Letters of Jessie Benton Frémont*, who shared her editorial skills with me, read and reread the manuscript, and helped me search for the more elusive bits and pieces needed to complete the notes. I am also indebted to Phil Brigandi, historian of the Ramona Pageant in Hemet, California, who read the manuscript and offered invaluable suggestions. Others who provided assistance include Professor Joe Gordon of Colorado College, Professor Richard Lowitt of the University of Oklahoma, Gloria Helmuth, editor of the HHJ Fan Club Newsletter, and Don Beilke, chairman of the English Department at City College of San Francisco. Any and all omissions or errors are my responsibility.

Editorial Comments

THE LETTERS

Because this collection of letters by Helen Hunt Jackson revolves around her passion for Indian reform, some lengthy passages that do not relate to Indians have been deleted. However, other passages that strongly reflect her personality, her relationship with her husband, or the monetary value of her literary works have been included. Her letters are presented as she wrote them, with as little editorial intrusion as possible. Jackson's inconsistent use of commas and apostrophes has not been corrected. Finally, her continual use of the dash has been reproduced because it reflects this vibrant, compassionate, dynamic woman, whose writing style was quick and intense. One can almost visualize the dash as a flourish of her hand when talking.

Abbreviations that might be confusing and a few misspelled names have been completed or corrected in square brackets. To avoid confusion in Jackson's lengthy letters to the editors, her brackets have been changed to parentheses. Her spellings of various Indian villages and names have been followed.

These letters, written to over forty individuals and various newspapers between the fall of 1879 and Jackson's death in 1885, represent approximately one-third of the letters from this period that I collected. Four different types of letters are presented in this volume. The majority were written, signed, mailed, and eventually found their way into various archives and libraries. The rest were published in books about Jackson or in newspapers as letters to the editor or were drafts that were never sent. In the first two instances, the originals are no longer extant. In transcribing the drafts, my intent was to provide a readable document reflecting the intensity of Jackson's passion for Indian reform.

The letters are divided into two distinct sections: those relative to Jackson's Ponca reform activity, which resulted in the publication of *A Century of Dishonor* in 1881, and those relative to her work among the Mission Indians of southern California, which resulted in the publication of *Ramona* in 1884. An introduction precedes each section.

THE NOTES

Letter recipients and individuals mentioned in letters are identified only once. To refresh the reader's memory, identifications and brief biographies are referenced in the index on the page where the individual is first mentioned.

Because Jackson was a prominent nineteenth-century author, her friends in the literary world were often easy to identify. However, in cases where she mentioned only a last name, identification has been more difficult and in a few cases impossible. Wherever possible, material from newspaper accounts has been added to flesh out the notes and give readers additional sources to consult.

Most articles and books are cited in the notes in abbreviated form. For the full citation, see the bibliography. Book reviews, some magazine articles, and all newspaper articles that are cited fully in the notes are not included in the bibliography.

SYMBOLS FOR ARCHIVAL SOURCES

CLU	Research Library, University of California, Los Angeles, California
CoCC	Tutt Library, Colorado College, Colorado Springs, Colorado
CSdHi	San Diego Historical Society, San Diego, California
CSf	San Francisco Public Library, San Francisco, California
CSmH	Huntington Library, San Marino, California
CtHT-W	Watkinson Library, Trinity College, Hartford, Connecticut
CtNhHi	Library, New Haven Colony Historical Society, New Haven, Connecticut
CU-B	Bancroft Library, University of California, Berkeley, California
DLC	Manuscript Division, Library of Congress, Washington, D.C.
MA	Amherst College Library, Amherst, Massachusetts
MAJ	Jones Library, Amherst, Massachusetts
MeB	The Library, Bowdoin College, Brunswick, Maine
MH	Houghton Library, Harvard University, Cambridge, Massachusetts
MHi	Massachusetts Historical Society, Boston, Massachusetts
MnHi	Minnesota Historical Society, St. Paul, Minnesota
NjP	The Library, Princeton University, Princeton, New Jersey
NN	New York Public Library, New York, New York
NN-B	Henry W. and Albert A. Berg Collection of English and American Literature, New York Public Library, New York, New York
NNC	Butler Library, Columbia University, New York, New York
NNPM	Pierpont Morgan Library, New York, New York

NNSII   Staten Island Institute of Arts and Sciences, Staten Island, New York

ViU   Alderman Library, University of Virginia, Charlottesville, Virginia

Collections without a designated symbol:

Hampton University, Hampton, Virginia

Seaver Center for Western History Research, Los Angeles County Museum of Natural History, Los Angeles, California

OTHER SYMBOLS USED

AL   Autograph letter
ALS   Autograph letter, signed
HHJ   Helen Hunt Jackson
P-M   Personal-Miscellaneous
WSJ   William Sharpless Jackson
[ ]   Word, date, or phrase supplied to clarify or correct.
[?]   Conjectural reading or conjectural identification of an addressee.
[. . .]   Illegible word or phrase.
. . .   Parts of published letters omitted by printed source or parts of original letters omitted by editor because of irrelevance to Jackson's Indian crusade.

PART ONE

The Ponca Cause and the Writing of
A Century of Dishonor

Introduction

A Century of Dishonor

THIS MORNING, THE FIRST THING THAT CAME INTO MY MIND AS I WAKED, . . .
— AS POWERS USED TO COME IN THE OLD DAYS — WERE THE WORDS "A
CENTURY OF DISHONOR" — AS IF SOME ONE SPOKE THEM ALOUD IN THE ROOM
— I CANNOT SHAKE THEM OFF — !
            HELEN HUNT JACKSON TO WILLIAM SHARPLESS JACKSON,
                        DECEMBER 19, 1879

"I BEGIN TO HAVE A HALF SUPERSTITIOUS FEELING ABOUT THIS IRRESISTIBLE impulse I feel to say especial words & phrases — as if they were put into my mind from outside," wrote Helen Hunt Jackson to her husband, William Sharpless Jackson, one mid-December day in 1879 from her Boston hotel room. A prominent nineteenth-century author, Jackson had only recently embarked on a crusade to awaken the public to the wrongs Indians suffered because of inept federal policies. "I write these Indian things in a totally different way from my ordinary habit of composition — I write these sentences . . . as *fast* as I can write the words,"[1] she remarked to Will, who had already expressed some criticism of his wife's newest endeavor. Three days later she confided to him: "Every hour my feelings grow intenser on this subject — & I feel more & more *impelled* to work for the cause."[2]

Marriage to Will Jackson, a prominent Colorado Springs banker and businessman, had provided Jackson for the past four years with the emotional and financial support that she needed. No longer forced to earn her own way, she could write on subjects that she was passionate about rather than on topics that sold well. By 1879 she was already well known. Under the initials "H.H." or pseudonyms such as "No Name," "Rip Van Winkle," "Marah," and "Saxe Holm," her articles as well as her fiction and poetry appeared in the *Atlantic Monthly*, *Nation*, *Christian Union*, *Hearth and Home*, *St. Nicholas*, *Independent*, *Scribner's Monthly Magazine*, and others. She had written more than a dozen books, and Ralph Waldo Emerson "heartily praise[d]" her work, describing her

Helen Hunt Jackson. (Courtesy of Jones Library, Inc., Amherst, Mass.)

as the "greatest American woman poet." He carried an 1870 newspaper clipping of one of her poems inside the front cover of his notebook.[3] Despite Emerson's praises, Jackson is best known today not for her poetry, but for *A Century of Dishonor*, an indictment of the government's Indian policy, and *Ramona*, her protest novel, both results of this "irresistible impulse."

Between 1879 and her death in 1885, Jackson devoted her energies to the Indian cause. She spent months away from her husband, traveling by train across the continent, living in hotel rooms in New York City, Boston, Washington, D.C., Los Angeles, and San Francisco, researching, writing, and at times demanding that editorial friends and acquaintances publish or read her articles written to awaken the public to the mistreatment of the Indians. Furthermore, she toured various California Mission Indian villages, initially for material for her *Century Magazine* articles and later as an official agent for the Department of the Interior.

Born Helen Maria Fiske on October 14, 1830, in Amherst, Massachusetts, to Deborah Waterman Vinal Fiske and Nathan Welby Fiske, an Amherst professor, she was a rebellious child. She had lost both of her parents by the time she was seventeen and, at thirty-five, had lost her husband, Edward Bissell Hunt, a West Point engineer and army officer, as well as their two sons, Murray and Warren Horsford. To assuage her grief and to supplement a small income, she turned to writing.

When Jackson embarked upon her Indian work, she joined the ranks of hundreds of middle- and upper-class men and women who eventually transformed the federal government's Indian policy. However, she was atypical of most of these reformers, who were part of a strong evangelical Protestant movement that included a good portion of the American elite.[4] Devoted Christians, they would have been critical of Jackson, who had forsaken the severe Congregationalism of her family and, rather than attending weekly church services, much preferred her Sunday carriage rides through the peaceful Colorado Springs countryside, accompanied at times by her husband.[5] Her fellow Indian reformers were anti-Catholic, whereas Jackson presented a sympathetic picture of the Franciscan missionaries in California.

Jackson was less interested in assimilation of the American Indians and more interested in the protection of their land rights and adherence to treaty provisions. In a November 20, 1879, letter to the editor of the *New York Daily Tribune*, she asked: "Has the Indian any rights which the white man is bound to respect?"[6] By the time of her death in August 1885, national Indian associations were just beginning to implement their acculturation and Indian rights protection programs; the Dawes Severalty Act, an attempt to end communal land ownership and substitute private property ownership through land allotment in severalty, was still two years from passage. Had she lived longer, one can only speculate whether she, too, would have been swept along with other reformers in demanding acculturation and private ownership of land.

Jackson worked alone, like a muckraker, ferreting out bits and pieces of neglect, fraud, or treaty violations as she researched in New York's Astor Library. Pressuring her wide circle of literary acquaintances, she succeeded in publishing initially in New York and Boston newspapers, later in popular magazines, and finally in book form, while other reformers engaged in petition drives, wrote pamphlets suggesting policy changes, or sponsored a lobbyist who worked the halls of Congress. Thus her one-woman crusading journalistic approach differed from that of the missionary-minded reformers, who worked within the confines of such organizations as the Women's National Indian Association, founded in 1879, and the Indian Rights Association, founded in 1882, or participated annually in the Lake Mohonk Conference of the Friends of the Indians, founded in 1883 as a forum for discussing various reform ideas.[7]

The catalyst that threw Jackson into the arena of Indian reform was the forcible removal of the Poncas from their 96,000-acre reservation in the southeastern corner of Dakota Territory. They were driven to desolate Indian Territory as a result of a bureaucratic error in which their lands were mistakenly included in the Great Sioux Reservation of 1868. Repeated attacks by the more aggressive Sioux resulted in congressional appropriations in 1876 to relocate the Poncas for their safety. Although many tribal members, including Chief Standing Bear, opposed this move, newly appointed secretary of the interior Carl Schurz, busy acquainting himself with the details of running his department, chose to follow the previous administration's decision and allowed the removal to proceed under the direction of Inspector Edward C. Kemble. By mid-May 1877 the Indians were in Indian Territory. That fall Standing Bear and other headmen met with President Rutherford B. Hayes and Secretary Schurz in Washington, D.C. The Indians' request either to return to their old reservation or to join their Omaha kin in Nebraska was denied.

Standing Bear could only watch helplessly as 160 of his people, including his only remaining son, died of malaria and other diseases. On the night of January 2, 1879, the old chief headed north with the body of his son, accompanied by a small party of followers, to bury the boy in the land of his birth. Often befriended and fed by white settlers, the Poncas traveled for ten weeks before reaching the Omaha reservation in March, where they were welcomed by Chief Joseph La Flesche and given land to settle and cultivate.

Standing Bear, with his family. (Special Collections, Tutt Library, Colorado College Library, Colorado Springs)

General George Crook, commander of the Department of the Platte, on orders of Secretary Schurz, dispatched troops to arrest the Poncas for leaving without permission. The Indians, too weak to be returned to Indian Territory, were temporarily detained at Fort Omaha on March 27. Critical of the government's Indian policy and disturbed by the cruelty of the arrest, Crook conferred with *Omaha Herald* assistant editor Thomas Henry Tibbles. The two men had earlier worked together to publicize the general's views on Indian policy.[8] An interview with Standing Bear and others left both men deeply moved by the hardships the Poncas had endured.

Tibbles convinced John L. Webster, an Omaha lawyer, to draw up a writ of *habeas corpus* preventing the return of the Poncas to Indian Territory. At Webster's request, Tibbles approached Andrew Jackson Poppleton, chief attorney of the Union Pacific Railroad, to assist. While the two lawyers organized their case, Tibbles wrote editorials to alert the public to the condition of the Poncas and assisted in organizing the Omaha Ponca Indian Committee, composed of Omaha ministers and interested citizens.

During the two-day trial of *Standing Bear v. Crook*, Nebraska district court judge Elmer S. Dundy declared the Indian a legal "person" with a right to sue for a writ of *habeas corpus* in federal court. Once the Poncas were freed, Tibbles resigned his editorial post and organized a six-month lecture tour to eastern cities to generate support and raise money both to restore lost lands legally and to determine the legal status of the American Indian before the Supreme Court.[9] The group included Tibbles, Standing Bear, nineteen-year old Francis La Flesche (also known as "Woodworker"), an Omaha Indian, and his twenty-five-year-old sister Susette or "Bright Eyes."[10]

From the beginning Susette had been personally involved in the plight of the Poncas. White Swan, a Ponca chief, was her father's half-brother. She and Joseph had conferred with Ponca chiefs prior to removal, had visited the tribe during the removal process, had attended the trial, and, at the request of the Omaha Committee, had visited White Swan in Indian Territory in May 1879 to learn if the government was correct in its assertion that the Poncas were happy in their new home. Susette, educated at the Elizabeth Institute for Young Ladies in Elizabeth, New Jersey, was well prepared for her new role as Standing Bear's interpreter. The appearance onstage of the graceful Indian girl and the older dignified chief was a crowd pleaser.

After a journey on a Boston and Albany Railroad coach, Standing Bear and his party arrived on October 29 at the Tremont House in Boston, where they were greeted by Mayor Frederick O. Prince and other dignitaries. That evening a well-attended public reception was held at the Horticultural Hall. Residents opened their hearts and their purses to the visiting delegation, and the Boston Indian Citizenship Committee was organized to fight for the rights of the Poncas and other tribes. The personal interest of Delano A. Goddard, editor of the *Boston Advertiser*, Massachusetts governor Thomas Talbot and lieutenant governor John D. Long, and Massachusetts senator Henry L. Dawes, as well as prominent citizens like Henry Wadsworth Longfellow, Oliver Wendell Holmes, Sr., and the Reverend Edward Everett Hale, a member of the Society for

Frank and Susette La Flesche on tour with Standing Bear. (L164, 43, Nebraska State Historical Society)

Propagating the Gospel among the Indians, assured success. Numerous receptions were scheduled at local churches, the Merchants' Exchange, Faneuil Hall, and the Music Hall. In addition, the Goddards and publisher Henry Houghton opened their homes to the delegation, and Houghton gave Standing Bear and Susette a tour through every room of the busy Riverside Press.

Unfortunately, no letter has yet been found in which Helen Hunt Jackson describes her first meeting with Standing Bear.[11] However, on November 18 she asked *Hartford Courant* editor Charles Dudley Warner to reprint an article on the Poncas she had just written for the *Independent*, a New York weekly. About the same time, she visited Tibbles at his Boston hotel, showing him the article.[12] In his memoirs, Tibbles described Jackson as throwing "every ounce of her own strong influence into the scale in dealing with members of Congress, senators, editors, and writers." He believed her help was essential for the success of the cause.[13]

Jackson's article was only the beginning. On November 20, 1879, she wrote the first of many letters to the *Tribune* editor, relating the story of Standing Bear, the Ponca removal, and the Indians' need to raise money to regain their lost lands through the courts. Her initial writings had been driven by her moral outrage at the Ponca removal; by mid-December, as she learned more, she also began quoting from official government documents she found in the Astor Library.

After more than a month in Boston, the Ponca delegation arrived at the Fifth Avenue Hotel in New York City on December 5; that night they were invited to the home of Josiah M. Fiske, a prominent merchant, who along with former Boston mayor William H. Lincoln was in charge of the Poncas' schedule.[14] Others opened their homes to the Indian delegation, including Professor Vincenzo Botta and his wife, Anne Charlotte Lynch Botta, a close friend of Jackson.[15] Various receptions and meetings followed.

New York, however, was not as supportive as Boston; less money was collected. Jackson, who was living at the Brevoort House in the city, remarked to Warner on December 14 that "New York does not care for [the Poncas]" and complained that the *Tribune* and editor Whitelaw Reid did not defend them,[16] though the newspaper had already printed two of her letters to the editor and various articles by staff reporters.

The December 15 publication of her letter to the *Tribune* editor and an editorial, directing readers to it, forced Jackson to apologize to Reid. Quoting from Secretary Schurz's 1878 annual report, in her letter Jackson posed ten questions regarding the Indians. Still concerned about the Poncas, she noted that the secretary's assertion that they were content and acclimated to Indian Territory was incorrect. Instead, the Poncas were waiting like exiles while Standing Bear tried to obtain additional legal redress. She also introduced the public to a new concern, the White River Utes of Colorado, and inquired if readers were aware of the Utes' present condition.[17]

Now personally maligned, Secretary Schurz could no longer remain silent. Already well-sensitized by extensive coverage of Standing Bear's tour in both Boston and New York, Schurz immediately telegraphed a rebuttal. His letter, addressing each of Jackson's ten questions, appeared in the December 19 *Tribune*. The Utes were suffering, he commented, because the government contractor had failed to deliver their supplies. Tried and convicted, the contractor was now imprisoned. Schurz conceded that the Ponca situation was a mistake; the orders for their removal had been enacted before he assumed office, but since then both he and Indian commissioner Ezra A. Hayt had been attempting to compensate them.[18]

Reading Schurz's rebuttal, Jackson wrote William Hayes Ward, editor of the *Independent*, that she was "wild with delight."[19] "What glory to have Schurz answer me by telegraph," she confided to Warner. "I had hardly hoped I could do anything for the Indians. Now I see that I can."[20] Inspired by Schurz's response, on December 23 she wrote another letter to the *Tribune*, answering the secretary point by point.[21]

On January 9, 1880, Jackson wrote directly to Schurz, enclosing excerpts from the letter of a Boston woman willing to contribute the remainder of the money needed to prosecute a suit to regain Ponca lands. Jackson inquired if Schurz approved of such a suit and, if not, if he would be willing to explain his reasoning.[22] The secretary, answering on January 17, explained that Indian tribes could not sue the government or any state in federal courts. He suggested that money collected should go toward improving Indian schools. Schurz believed that the solution to Indian landholding was legislation transferring tribal ownership to individual ownership, enabling them to "hold their lands by the same title by which white men hold theirs, and . . . [with] the same standing in the courts, and the same legal protection of their property."[23]

Their private letters were printed in the *Boston Advertiser*, at Schurz's request, and the *Tribune*, at Jackson's request. The public interest generated by their publication prompted the *New York Times* on February 21, 1880, to review them in a lengthy editorial. The *Times* praised Jackson while criticizing Schurz for opposing the Indians' attempt to gain legal redress through the courts and for suggesting instead that the solution was individual land ownership in severalty. It was regrettable, remarked the editor, that the secretary did not adequately show "how the giving to an Indian of 160 acres of land can clothe him with civil rights which he does not now possess," rights which the secretary "thinks that the courts cannot give him."[24]

This public debate between Secretary Schurz and Helen Hunt Jackson was inevitable, given their strong personalities and the charged atmosphere surrounding the Ponca removal. Jackson's tenacity made her a formidable opponent. According to her fellow author and mentor, Thomas Wentworth Higginson, "where her sympathy went," Jackson "was ready to give all she had, — attention, time, trouble, money, popularity, reputation, — and this with only too little thought of the morrow." As a consequence, her ardent sympathies brought both great joy and peril and "often involv[ed] misconception, perplexity, and keen disappointment to herself and to others." Sometimes she was "impulsive in her scorn of mean actions."[25] Obviously she must have viewed the tragic Ponca removal, carried out under orders from Schurz, as a "mean action."

As a liberal Republican reformer, Secretary Schurz's goal was to end incompetence and corruption in his department, not to defend policies of previous administrations or to debate the government's Indian policy. Although he took no action to reverse the Ponca removal, in his first official report in 1878 he had publicly "set forth the wrong done to the Poncas." Commissioner Hayt had concurred. The bill presented by the Interior Department on February 3, 1879, to compensate the Poncas for their losses had failed to pass Congress.[26] As the Indians became acclimated to their new home and their living conditions appeared to improve, both Schurz and Hayt believed they should remain in Indian Territory, a conclusion supported by the Board of Indian Commissioners in its 1879 report,[27] but not by Tibbles and Jackson.

The fact that Schurz's practical policies differed from those of Jackson and other eastern philanthropists was not the only driving force in this controversy. Following the abolition of slavery, Indian rights had became the new humanitarian cause. Boston and New York philanthropists, who had raised money for the Ponca legal fund, opposed Schurz, who believed that the money could be better spent elsewhere. Sides were taken, and on February 24, 1881, the *Nation* published "The Schurz Mystery," examining the quarrel between the Boston philanthropists and Schurz. The *Nation* concluded that the more it examined the different points of view, "the more unaccountable . . . [the] intensity of feeling . . . seemed."[28]

Both Jackson and Schurz felt compelled to defend themselves, Jackson through her letters to the editors, and Schurz in open letters to Governor John D. Long,[29] Senator Henry L. Dawes,[30] and former Indian inspector Edward C. Kemble, who as the field official in charge of the Ponca removal had accompanied Standing Bear and nine other headmen in 1877 to Indian Territory to select a new home. During December 1879 and January 1880, Schurz and Kemble defended their positions. Having personally explained to Schurz that the Poncas bitterly opposed removal, Kemble remarked that now the secretary was placing the blame for the removal on subordinates and on the Indians. Succinctly, Kemble declared: "Mr. Schurz could have stopped the whole business, had he been so disposed."[31]

Before she had undertaken her intensive research into the history of the government's dealings with the Indians, Jackson had, as she said, been "an enthusiastic admirer" of Carl Schurz. However, as she searched through official records, she became suspicious of his motives. In almost identical letters in early March to Oliver Wendell Holmes and Henry Wadsworth Longfellow, she remarked that Schurz had developed "such malignity towards innocent people, and such astounding and wholesale lying" that true friends of the Indians should denounce him and his methods.[32] As late as the fall of 1884, she still harbored ill will, remarking to interior secretary Henry Teller, a fellow Coloradoan, that Schurz was a "hypocrite" and that she prayed daily that he would not be "rewarded" with another cabinet position.[33]

While Jackson and Schurz sparred through letters, and Tibbles kept the public alerted to the controversy, in early February 1880 a Senate committee chaired by Iowa's Senator Samuel J. Kirkwood began a formal investigation. Agents, inspectors, prominent clergymen, and Indians testified. Late in the month, Jackson wrote her sister, Annie: "I cannot but think that I have already accomplished something in the way of rousing public attention to the outrageous injustice of our treatment of those poor creatures —."[34]

But Jackson's work had only begun. In late December 1879 she shifted her attention to the Utes, many of whom lived in Colorado. During the early 1870s, new mineral strikes in Colorado had resulted in the inevitable flood of prospectors onto Ute land. Although the Indians had reluctantly given up one-quarter of their reservation, following statehood in 1876, Colorado residents began a campaign to remove the Utes to Indian Territory. Living in Colorado Springs at the time, Jackson had to be aware of this confrontation between residents and the Utes, but she was not yet drawn to the Indian cause. That changed, however, when she met Standing Bear and Susette La Flesche in 1879 and was exposed to the human side of the Indian question.

Therefore, from her Boston hotel room she now wrote in defense of the Utes. Her husband, Will, must have heard some criticism of her pro-Indian views from local Colorado residents, because on December 29 she assured him that she was not writing "as a sentimentalist" but only presenting to the public "verbatim reports officially authenticated."[35] Several months later, proud of his wife's accomplishments, he described a letter that appeared in the March 3, 1880, *Tribune* as a "controversial weapon, worth all [she] ever did before."[36] Although Will Jackson may have disagreed with his wife's increasingly activist role, his Quaker upbringing, which viewed women as equals with the same privileges in the church as men, would no doubt have caused him to support her anyway. In addition, the Jacksons respected each other's work. Writing to a friend shortly before she married Will, she noted: "I trust him to the *core*, which is what I have seldom felt of any man."[37]

Using documents sent her by Henry Teller, then a Colorado senator, Jackson wrote about broken Ute treaties in a January 2, 1880, letter to the *Tribune*. She was especially interested in the White River Utes of Colorado, who on September 29, 1879, had murdered agent Nathan C. Meeker. Secretary Schurz was withholding their rations, and the tribe was slowly starving to death. Siding with the Indians, she blamed not only the government's failure to remove white trespassers from their reservation, but specifically the arbitrary policies of the murdered agent.[38]

To elicit sympathy for the Utes, in early February 1880 the *Tribune* published "The Starving Utes: More Questions for the People by 'H.H.,'" in which she recounted the activities of the Third Colorado Volunteers, who, under Col. John M. Chivington, had attacked Black Kettle's peaceful band of Cheyenne and Arapaho Indians in Colorado in 1864.[39] On February 6, writing from Washington, D.C., William Newton Byers, founder and former editor of the Denver, Colorado, *Rocky Mountain News*, responded in much the same vein as Schurz; a spirited public exchange of letters resulted.

Byers accused Jackson of ignoring the causes of the Sand Creek Massacre while dramatizing the current condition of the Utes. He claimed that the Indians at Sand Creek were not under government protection and furthermore had murdered over fifty Colorado citizens and had stolen livestock worth hundreds of thousands of dollars, evidence of which had been found in their camp following Chivington's attack. Therefore, Byers smugly remarked, "Colorado soldiers have again covered themselves with glory." A twenty-year resident of the area, Byers believed that the recent Ute attacks had been deliberately planned and that by withholding their supplies, an action that Jackson had criticized, Secretary Schurz was simply obeying the law.[40]

Using testimony from various investigations of the massacre as well as Interior Department reports, Jackson's February 22 reply presented evidence that the Cheyennes and Arapahoes had indeed been under government protection and had committed no depredations.[41] Byers disagreed. Furthermore, he refused to accept Jackson's claim that only a dozen White River Utes were guilty. Finally, to exonerate the people of Colorado from blame for Sand Creek, he remarked that his state had been denied a fair hearing.[42] Jackson, after discovering over 220 pages of official testimony, replied on March 3, 1880, that a military commission investigating the Sand Creek massacre had held hearings for seventy-three days both in Denver and at Fort Lyon and that Chivington had notified the commission that he had no more witnesses in his defense.

After the debate with Byers, Jackson continued her research, locating materials for more *Tribune* letters and prose pieces for the *Independent*.

"Another Indian Story: The Massacre of the Cheyennes" in the January 1, 1880, issue was her account of a small band of Northern Cheyennes confined in 1878 to Fort Robinson, Nebraska, who—facing inevitable return to Indian Territory—escaped, were pursued, and were shot down. "How the Indians Were Moved," her detailed article on the Ponca removal, appeared on February 5. "One of the Early Indian Removals," her history of the peaceful Christian Delaware and Mohicans who were removed to Philadelphia in 1763 for their safety, appeared on May 20. "The Conestoga Massacre," an account of an attack by frontier ruffians upon peaceful Conestoga Indians of Pennsylvania in 1763, was published on June 3. "The Gnadenhutten Massacre of 1782," detailing the attack by Pennsylvania militiamen on a peaceful Moravian mission of Delawares in central Ohio, appeared on June 24. On July 8 the *Independent* published "The Reward of Loyalty to the United States Government" on the condition of the Caddo Indians, formerly of Texas. Finally, "The End of a Century of Dishonor," detailing the fate of the Cherokees after their removal to Indian Territory, was published on January 13, 1881.

In between her *Tribune* letters, her articles in the *Independent*, and her March 1880 *Scribner's Monthly* article, "The Wards of the United States Government," Jackson completed a book-length manuscript on May 5, 1880. Months earlier she had confided to Warner that she wanted to write "simply & *curtly* a *Record* of our broken Treaties — & call it '*A Century of Dishonor.*'" She intended this work to be factual not sentimental. "I never so much as dreamed what we had been guilty of," she concluded.[43] To William Hayes Ward she confided that "all the heart & soul I possess" had gone into this book.[44] She signed a contract guaranteeing her ten percent of royalties with Harper & Brothers on May 21, 1880,[45] and worked closely with her friend Moncure D. Conway, minister, abolitionist, and author, to have it published simultaneously in England.

Thoroughly exhausted from her intensive seven-month research project, she left the proofreading to Thomas Wentworth Higginson and joined friends in Europe. Upon receiving a letter full of newspaper clippings about her "beloved Indians" from her friend Anne Charlotte Lynch Botta, Jackson thanked her "a hundred times" and remarked that "nothing puts the Indians out of my mind, except that I know there is nothing to be done this summer." Otherwise she would not have been content to travel to Europe. "In the autumn I will take hold again, unless William Jackson objects." She concluded, "I propose to 'fight it out on that line' until something is accomplished."[46] Upon her return in October she did exactly that, concentrating her efforts on the appendix of *A Century of Dishonor*. The Reverend Henry B. Whipple,

Episcopal bishop of Minnesota, an Indian advocate in his own right, agreed to write the preface, while Julius H. Seelye, president of Amherst College, who had been active in the Ponca struggle, agreed to prepare the introduction. Meanwhile her letters to the editors continued.

By December Jackson had begun to see evidence that her efforts were successful. She informed Reid that her *Tribune* articles and the newspaper's editorials were really aiding the Indian cause. Furthermore, a committee from Boston was looking into the fraud of the "pretended petition," signed on October 25, 1880, by the Poncas in Indian Territory, in which they relinquished all rights to their Dakota lands, requesting in return a title to their new home. In addition, a committee of bishops, clergymen, and laypeople appointed by the Episcopal Convention was to monitor congressional action during the coming winter. Members of the Women's National Indian Association were gathering petition signatures, and meetings discussing the "Indian question" were held in numerous cities.[47] Unknown to Jackson, President Rutherford B. Hayes had become aware of the gravity of the situation. On December 8, 1880, he wrote in his diary: "A great and grievous wrong has been done to the Poncas."[48]

Shortly thereafter, Hayes appointed a special commission composed of Generals George Crook and Nelson A. Miles and two civilians, William Stickney of the Board of Indian Commissioners and Walter Allen of the Boston Committee, to confer with the Poncas living in both Indian Territory and the Dakotas.[49] Reacting strongly against the composition of this commission, in December 1880 Jackson encouraged Senator Dawes not to let the committee proceed as it stood. Because Schurz had organized it, she was certain that "not a man in it can be absolutely trusted not to be either hoodwinked or influenced, except Gen. Crook."[50] Not only was she displeased with the commission's membership, but she was afraid that Schurz intended to "*bully*, or intrigue, or bayonet" a bill through, thereby not allowing the Poncas the right of selecting either Indian Territory or Dakota as their permanent home.[51]

Jackson's letters in December increasingly reflected her contempt for Secretary Schurz. In February 1881 she traveled to Washington, D.C., and witnessed his participation in congressional hearings. She wrote to Warner that she would never forget the "malignity & craft of [his] face — never. — It was a study. I could *paint* it, if I knew how to paint. —"[52]

At the end of January the Ponca commission recommended that the Indians be allowed to choose whichever reservation they preferred. In March 1881 Congress appropriated $165,000 for losses sustained during their removal; and in May Commissioner Hiram Price authorized the distribution of

$10,000 to Standing Bear's group in Dakota because it was the more destitute of the two.[53]

In early January 1881 Jackson had received a printer's proof of *A Century of Dishonor* and read it fondly, "but with some terror," she noted to Warner. "I don't know what they'll do to me."[54] At personal expense, she sent copies to each congressman. But neither Congress nor the public responded enthusiastically, although some reviews were better than her wildest hopes, and Schurz had not yet attacked her. Nevertheless, she remained suspicious, afraid Schurz might have something brewing.[55] Later she concluded, "My book did not sell — but somehow it stirred things — for you see books, pamphlets, & mag[azine] articles are steadily pouring out on the subject. . . . The world moves. —"[56]

A Century of Dishonor was reviewed in major newspapers and magazines. Martha Le Baron Goddard, wife of the editor of the *Boston Advertiser*, praised Jackson for "confining herself with remarkable and praiseworthy reserve to the unimpeachable facts of the official records,"[57] while the *Nation* reviewer, although describing the book as "very interesting and valuable," believed it would cause "disunion" instead of solidarity among philanthropists. The reviewer regretfully noted that it would be an "obstacle to the fair trial of Mr. Schurz's plan" of allotment of land in severalty.[58]

Even Jackson's own husband was ambivalent in his praise. Although he thought the book would sell, the style was such that it would not "clutch the average reader." Only those concerned with the "Indian Question" would be interested, finding it a "very attractive & carefully prepared work on a question that so little has heretofore been written about in a . . . condensed shape." He did commend her for writing such a clear and forceful first chapter defining Indian land title.[59]

Although *A Century of Dishonor* did not become a bestseller, it did lay the groundwork for Jackson's next Indian crusade, for the Mission Indians of southern California. Her work on behalf of the Poncas and others had acquainted the public with the deplorable condition of the American Indians and was read with interest by humanitarian reformers, who would take up her crusade. Even more importantly, her months of research at the Astor Library, her letters to the editors, and her controversies with both Secretary Carl Schurz and former editor William N. Byers gave her the determination and the skills necessary to defend the Mission Indians.

Commissioned in the spring of 1881 by *Harper's Magazine* to write four articles on California, Jackson made preparations to head west with her husband. Suffering from chronic bronchitis for over a month, she eagerly looked forward to the mild climate, which she fondly remembered from her May 1872

California trip. In March 1881 she informed Warner that her "bronchial tubes smack their mouths at the thought of the soft air," noting that New York's climate was fit only for "bears & tigers."[60] But Jackson was not to make that California journey. When unforeseen business demands forced her husband to remain in Colorado and she was unable to find anyone to accompany her, she declined the *Harper's* offer and returned home to Colorado Springs in June. Continually driven by her Indian interest, the Jacksons traveled to New Mexico twice to visit old Pueblo villages and watch Indian dancing.[61]

1. For quotations, see HHJ to WSJ, Dec. 16, 1879, below. The Jacksons were married in a Quaker ceremony in Oct. 1875. The most complete biographical treatment of HHJ is Odell, *Helen Hunt Jackson*. See also Mathes, *Helen Hunt Jackson and Her Indian Reform Legacy*; Mathes, "Helen Hunt Jackson: A Legacy of Indian Reform"; and Mathes, "Helen Hunt Jackson as Power Broker."

2. HHJ to WSJ, Dec. 19, 1879, below.

3. Emerson, *The Journals and Miscellaneous Notebooks of Ralph Waldo Emerson, 1866–1882*, pp. 98, 105; and Dorr, "Emerson's Admiration of 'H.H.'"

4. The best introduction to this subject is Prucha, *American Indian Policy in Crisis: Christian Reformers and the Indian, 1865–1900*.

5. For her "anti church going habits," see HHJ to Joseph Benson Gilder, May 20 and June 3, 1885 (NN, P-M [HHJ]).

6. Justice [H.H.] to the Editor of the *Tribune*, Nov. 20, 1879, below (hereinafter the *New York Daily Tribune* is cited as the *Tribune*).

7. For the Women's National Indian Association, see Wanken, "Woman's Sphere and Indian Reform: The Women's National Indian Association, 1879–1901"; and Mathes, "Nineteenth-Century Women and Reform: The Women's National Indian Association." For the Indian Rights Association, see Hagan, *The Indian Rights Association: The Herbert Welsh Years, 1882–1904*; and for Lake Mohonk, see Burgess, "The Lake Mohonk Conference on the Indian, 1883–1916."

8. Crook's June 19, 1879, letter to Tibbles had been published on Oct. 10, 1879, in the *Tribune*, p. 2, as "General Crook's Letter." See also Tibbles, *Buckskin and Blanket Days*, pp. 193–98; and King, "A Better Way: General George Crook and the Ponca Indians," pp. 242–47.

9. See Jackson (H.H.), *A Century of Dishonor: A Sketch of the United States Government's Dealings with Some of the Indian Tribes*; and Tibbles, *The Ponca Chiefs: An Account of the Trial of Standing Bear*. See also Hayter, "The Ponca Removal"; Clark, "Ponca Publicity"; Mathes, "Helen Hunt Jackson and the Ponca Controversy"; Mathes, "Helen Hunt Jackson and the Campaign for Ponca Restitution, 1880–1881"; and Mardock, "Standing Bear and the Reformers."

See also "The Trials of a Tribe: The Two Sides of the Ponca Indian Story," *Boston Daily Advertiser* (hereinafter cited as *Boston Advertiser*), Aug. 23, 1879, p. 1, and "The Other Side: Statements of White Eagle and Standing Bear," p. 2. For a letter to the editor by Standing Bear through an interpreter, see "The Man from Washington,"

Independent, Jan. 1, 1880, p. 3. Editorials in the *NY Times* include "Indian Civil Rights," May 21, 1879; "Civil Rights in Acres," Feb. 21, 1880; "The Wronged Poncas," Dec. 19, 1879; and "The President and the Indians," Feb. 3, 1881, reprinted in Hays, *A Race at Bay: New York Times Editorials on "the Indian Problem," 1860–1900,* pp. 35–37, 37–40, 221–23, and 248–50.

10. Wilson, *Bright Eyes: The Story of Susette La Flesche, an Omaha Indian;* Green, *Iron Eye's Family: The Children of Joseph La Flesche,* pp. 97–121, 568–81; and Green, "Four Sisters: Daughters of Joseph La Flesche."

11. Odell, *Helen Hunt Jackson,* p. 153, notes that HHJ first heard the Poncas in early Nov.; however, Banning, *Helen Hunt Jackson,* p. 144, cites Oct. 29, 1879, though with no supporting evidence. On Nov. 1, 1879, the Ponca delegation had tea at the home of the Goddards, who were friends of HHJ; on Nov. 10 they spoke at the Horticultural Hall with Oliver Wendell Holmes present; and on Nov. 15 they were given a concert by the Fisk University singers at the Berkeley Street Church. HHJ could have attended any or all of these public forums. See respectively, "The Poncas," *Boston Advertiser,* Nov. 3, 11, and 17, 1879, pp. 3, 1, and 1.

12. See HHJ to Warner, Nov. 18, 1879, below. The article was "Standing Bear and Bright Eyes," *Independent* (Nov. 20, 1879): 1–2.

13. Tibbles, *Buckskin and Blanket Days,* p. 216. Tibbles, in "Anecdotes of Standing Bear," p. 274, wrote that HHJ traveled with them "for some weeks." There is no supporting evidence from HHJ's letters.

14. "Arrival of the Ponca Indians," *Tribune,* Dec. 6, 1879, p. 2.

15. See Wright, *My New York,* pp. 247–48.

16. HHJ to Warner, Dec. 14, 1879, below.

17. HHJ to the Editor of the *Tribune,* Dec. 11, 1879, below.

18. "Mr. Schurz on Indian Affairs: The Secretary Replies to the Letter of H.H., in the Tribune," *Tribune,* Dec. 19, 1879, p. 1. See also Schurz to Edward Atkinson, Nov. 28, 1879, and to E. Dunbar Lockwood, Apr. 1, 1880, in Schurz, *Speeches, Correspondence and Political Papers,* 3:485, 505. Trefousse, *Carl Schurz: A Biography,* p. 247, describes Schurz's actions in the Ponca affair as "inept," while Nevins, "Helen Hunt Jackson, Sentimentalist v. Realist," pp. 271–74, defends Schurz.

19. HHJ to Ward, Dec. 20, 1879, below.

20. HHJ to Warner, Dec. 21, 1879, below; see also HHJ to Reid, Dec. 20, 1879, below.

21. HHJ to the Editor of the *Tribune,* Dec. 23, 1879, below.

22. HHJ to Schurz, Jan. 9, 1880, below.

23. Schurz to HHJ, Jan. 17, 1880, in *A Century of Dishonor,* p. 362, and in Schurz, *Speeches, Correspondence and Political Papers,* 3:498.

24. "Civil Rights in Acres," *NY Times,* Feb. 21, 1880, p. 4, reprinted in *A Century of Dishonor,* p. 368; and Hays, *A Race at Bay,* pp. 37–40.

25. All quotations in Higginson, *Contemporaries,* pp. 164–65.

26. Schurz to Edward Atkinson, Nov. 28, 1879, in Schurz, *Speeches, Correspondence and Political Papers,* 3:485 (quotation); see "The Poncas," in *Annual Report of the Commissioner of Indian Affairs to the Secretary of the Interior for the Year 1879,* p. xiv (hereinafter cited as *Annual Report of the Commissioner, 1879*). Some of the more revelant newspaper articles include "Secretary Schurz's Report," Dec. 2, 1880; "The

Ponca Case," Dec. 6, 1880; and "Secretary Schurz's Apology," Dec. 24, 1880, all in the *Tribune*, pp. 1, 4, 4, respectively.

27. Board of Indian Commissioners (BIC), *Eleventh Annual Report for the Year 1879*, p. 13. See also "Indian Affairs: The Red Man Improving in Civilization and Generally Living a Peaceful Life," *Tribune*, Nov. 28, 1879. This board was established by President Ulysses S. Grant in 1869. Members, nominated by various Protestant denominations, were authorized to exercise joint control with the Interior Department in the purchase and inspection of goods and disbursement of funds.

28. "The Schurz Mystery," *Nation* 31 (Feb. 24, 1881): 125. Between Feb. 2 and Aug. 25, 1881, numerous Ponca-related articles appeared in the *Nation*. For a reprint, see Adams, *The Letters of Mrs. Henry Adams, 1865–1883*, pp. 489–503.

29. Written in response to sympathetic speeches on behalf of the Poncas by Governor Long and others at Tremont Temple in Boston on Dec. 3, Schurz to Long, Dec. 9, 1880, can be found in Schurz, *Speeches, Correspondence and Political Papers*, 4:50–78. See also "Wrongs of the Poncas: Defence by the Secretary of the Interior against Charges Made at a Recent Meeting at Boston," *Tribune*, Dec. 13, 1880, p. 1.

For Long's reply, see "The Poncas Defended: Governor Long Replies to Secretary Schurz—a Clear and Emphatic Arraignment," Dec. 21, 1880, p. 1; and "Secretary Schurz's Apology," Dec. 24, 1880, p. 4, both in the *Tribune*.

30. A Dawes speech had "made certain reflections on the conduct of the Interior Department." See Schurz to Dawes, Feb. 7, 1881, in Schurz, *Speeches, Correspondence and Political Papers*, 4:91–114 (quotation on p. 91).

31. "A Few Words with Mr. Schurz: By Col. E. C. Kemble, Late Indian Inspector," Jan. 15, 1880, pp. 5–6 (quotation on p. 5); see also "The Removal of the Poncas: By the Hon. Carl Schurz, Secretary of the Interior," Jan. 1, 1880, p. 1, both in the *Independent*.

32. HHJ to Longfellow, Mar. 2, 1881, below, and to Holmes, Mar. 2, 1881, MH, Holmes Papers. The Holmes letter has been reprinted in Mathes, "Helen Hunt Jackson and the Campaign for Ponca Restitution, 1880–1881," pp. 36–40.

33. HHJ to Teller, Nov. 27, 1884, below.

34. HHJ to Ann Scholfield (Fiske) Banfield, Feb. 29 [1880], below.

35. HHJ to WSJ, Dec. 29, 1879, below.

36. HHJ to Reid, Mar. 3, 1880, below.

37. HHJ to Charlotte Cushman, July 29, 1875, DLC, Charlotte Cushman Papers.

38. HHJ to the Editor of the *Tribune*, Jan. 2, 1880, below.

39. HHJ to the Editor of the *Tribune*, Jan. 31, 1880, below.

40. Byers to the Editor of the *Tribune*, Feb. 6, 1880, printed as "'The Starving Utes': A Reply to Questions by 'H.H.,'" *Tribune*, Feb. 22, 1880, p. 5; reprinted in *A Century of Dishonor*, pp. 346–50.

41. HHJ to the Editor of the *Tribune*, Feb. 22, 1880, below.

42. Byers to the Editor of the *Tribune*, Feb. 24, 1880, printed as "The Sand Creek Massacre: A Card from William N. Byers in Reply to 'H.H.'s' Letter to Tuesday's *Tribune*," *Tribune*, Feb. 27, 1880, p. 5; reprinted in *A Century of Dishonor*, pp. 356–57.

43. Both quotations from HHJ to Warner, Dec. 21, 1879, below; see also HHJ to Ward, Jan. 21. 1880, and Jan. 27 [1880], below.

44. HHJ to Ward [mid-March–early April 1880], below.

45. Agreement between Mrs. Helen Jackson and Harper & Brothers for the Publication of "A Century of Dishonor," May 21, 1880, NNC, Special Manuscript Collection, Harper Brothers.

46. HHJ to Botta, July 30, 1880, MAJ, HHJ Papers.

47. HHJ to Reid [Nov. 30, 1880] and [Dec. 1, 1880], both below.

48. Hayes, *Diary and Letters of Rutherford Hayes: Nineteenth President of the United States*, 3:629.

49. See Schurz to Dawes, Feb. 7, 1881, Schurz, *Speeches, Correspondence and Political Papers*, 4:104–11.

50. HHJ to Dawes [Dec. 10, 1880], below. See also HHJ to Dawes [Dec. 23, 1880] and Dec. 30, 1880, both below.

51. HHJ to Warner, Feb. 12 [1881], below.

52. HHJ to Warner, [ca. Feb. 21, 1881], below; see also HHJ to Lyman Abbott [Feb. 21, 1881], below.

53. Price to Delano A. Goddard, May 31, 1881, DLC, Dawes Papers.

54. HHJ to Warner, Jan. 6 [1881], below.

55. HHJ to Warner [ca. Feb. 21, 1881], below.

56. HHJ to Warner, Oct. 31, 1882, below.

57. Goddard, "A Century of Dishonor," p. 573; see also Friend, "Helen Hunt Jackson: A Critical Study," pp. 234–43.

58. "A Century of Dishonor," *Nation* 32 (Mar. 3, 1881): 152.

59. WSJ to HHJ, Jan. 31, 1881, CoCC, WSJ I, box 1, fd. 5.

60. HHJ to Warner [Mar. 3, 1881], below.

61. HHJ to Higginson, July 22, 1881, and HHJ to Thomas Bailey Aldrich, Aug. 19, 1881, MH, Higginson Field Book and Aldrich Papers.

TO CHARLES DUDLEY WARNER

New York
Nov. 18, 1879
Brevoort House

Dear Mr. Warner —

To prove to you that I am the most imprudent woman alive, I shall ask you to do something for me — no less a thing than to reprint in your paper an article in this weeks Independent about the Ponca Indians.[1] It is only one whole side of the Independent & a little more — and it is thrillingly interesting. Will you do it? — Do help, and don't be funny about the Indians. They are right & we are wrong — and the one chance the race has for freedom and right — and our one chance for decency as a nation in our treatment of them, is just now, in this movement toward the courts, by the Poncas. —

I wish you would write something about them, as you did about the Doe in the Adirondacks![2] There is no telling what you might accomplish by it. You might even prick through to Carl Schurz's[3] heart. — I am going to try to set Gail Hamilton[4] on the track. I did not expect ever to desire to lead her to unsling her vulgar tomahawk; but she can get at things nobody else can — and if she could once be roused on the question, her "dinging" would do good.

Mr. Jackson and I have been saying every day "we must go up or over and take tea with the Warners" — we have been to Boston & back twice — but there has never been a day when he could spare a minute, and now I am afraid he is chained tight here by the hour; but after he goes back to Col[orado] Dec. 1st, I shall come and stay a day with you, if you want me — and mean time — perhaps you will be here. Mrs. Runkle[5] — whom I have not yet seen — wrote me that you might possibly come this week. — I hope so and that Mrs. Warner will come too — we shall be here for two weeks yet —: with hearty love to you both,

Your audacious friend
Helen Jackson

P.S. If youre "agin" the Indians, dont mention the subject when we meet.

ALS (Charles Dudley Warner Collection, Watkinson Library, Trinity College, Hartford, Connecticut; hereinafter cited as CtHT-W, Warner Collection).

Charles Dudley Warner (1829–1900), a well-known writer and poet, became co-editor of the *Hartford Courant* in 1867. He was also a contributing editor of *Harper's*, 1884–98, and with his brother, George H. Warner, edited the *Library of the World's Best Literature* (1896–97) in thirteen volumes.

Charles Dudley Warner, editor of the *Hartford Daily Courant*, ca. 1874. (Harriet Beecher Stowe Center, Hartford, Conn.)

1. A reference to "Standing Bear and Bright Eyes," HHJ's *Independent* article on Ponca removal.

2. Warner, "A-Hunting of the Deer," was a poignant story of a doe attempting to protect her fawn from hunters.

3. German-born Carl Schurz (1829–1906) emigrated to the United States in 1852 and joined the Republican Party as a liberal reformer. He worked for the *Tribune* as a Washington correspondent and served as a senator from Missouri. In 1877 he was appointed secretary of the interior by Rutherford B. Hayes.

4. Mary Abby Dodge ("Gail Hamilton"; 1833–96), active in the abolition crusade and the women's movement, wrote for the *Atlantic Monthly, Congregationalist, Tribune,* and *Independent.*

5. Lucia Isabella Gilbert Calhoun Runkle (1844–1923), called "Bertie" by HHJ, wrote editorials for the *Tribune* and articles for *Harper's*. Her second husband, Cornelius A. Runkle, was the *Tribune* counsel.

TO CHARLES DUDLEY WARNER

Wed.

Nov. 19 [1879]

Dear Mr. Warner —

Here it is. If you reprint it — will you kindly separate, the Extracts, from my article?[1] My article ends with the appeal for money — and I had intended to append the Extracts to it, by a sentence as if from the Editor, to this effect. —

"In this communication the following Extracts will be seen to have significance and interest." — Mr. Ward[2] forgot to send me the proof — and the Extracts did not arrive till the last minute; so the only wonder is that it was not worse botched than it is.

Yours truly ever

Helen Jackson

ALS (CtHT-W, Warner Collection).

1. Warner introduced HHJ's article, "Standing Bear and Bright Eyes," with a short editorial, reprinting all but the first few paragraphs in the *Hartford Courant*, Nov. 25, 1879, p. 1. The extracts, which were not included, were from "The Trials of a Tribe: The Two Sides of the Ponca Indian Story," *Boston Advertiser*, Aug. 23, 1879, pp. 1–2. This lengthy article included statements by both Interior Secretary Schurz and Standing Bear as well as extracts from the 1878 Ponca Indian Agency report from Indian Territory.

2. William Hayes Ward (1835–1916), a graduate of Amherst College and Andover Theological Seminary, served as pastor of several Congregational churches in Kansas before accepting a position on the editorial staff of the New York *Independent* in 1868. He remained associated with this weekly until his death, first as associate editor, 1868–70, as superintending editor, 1870–96, and finally as editor, 1896–1913.

TO THE EDITOR OF THE *TRIBUNE*

[November 20, 1879]

To the Editor of The Tribune.

SIR: The story of Standing Bear, the Ponca Chief, now in Boston asking aid to enable his tribe to recover their lands, is a striking illustration of the working of our Indian policy. Our last treaty with the Poncas, made in 1865, read thus: "In consideration of the military services and of other lands ceded to the

United States, the Government of the United States, cede and reliquish all title and interest in the following described territory." Then follows the description of certain townships and sections upon which they established themselves. They had five hundred acres under cultivation, had built one hundred and fifty houses and were living quietly on their farms, when they were visited by the Inspector [Kemble][1] and told that they must remove to the Indian Territory, where the President would give them other lands and pay them for those they were to leave, and that if they did not like the new lands they should be allowed to communicate directly with him. After great persuasion, ten chiefs of the tribe were induced to make the journey of 1,000 miles to the Indian Territory. They found the lands sterile and the water bad, and they declined to remain. Every effort short of imprisonment was made to prevent their escape. They were refused money, and the services of the interpreter whom they had themselves paid. It was midwinter when they started to return to their homes; they travelled on foot, subsisted on the dried corn which they found in the fields, and slept under hay stacks or such cover as they could find. After a journey of fifty days they reached the Otoe Reservation,[2] and when they entered the Agent's room they left the prints of their feet in blood upon the floor. Meanwhile the Inspector had telegraphed that the chiefs had run away, and requested that no aid should be afforded them. The friendly Otoes, notwithstanding, received them kindly, and furnished each one with a pony, and after a journey of four days more they reached their homes, where the Inspector—who did not walk—had already arrived. The troops were called in, whatever could be moved was packed in wagons, and although they preferred to die rather than to go, they were hurried off. Many died on the way, and after 150 of the tribe and all the horses and cattle were dead, Standing Bear and thirty of his people, men, women and children, escaped. After a journey of three months' they reached the Omaha Reservation,[3] weak, sick and starved. The Omahas gave them land and they were hastening to plant and plough it when they were again arrested, to be driven back to the Indian Territory by military force. Halting near Omaha City on their way they were visited by Mr. Tibbles,[4] a lawyer and the editor of an Omaha paper, who listened to their tragic story and by a happy inspiration applied to Judge Dundy[5] for a writ of habeas corpus, which was granted, and they were set free. This simple process gives an entirely new aspect to the Indian question, and what the Government, the philanthropist, the Indian Bureau and agents even have not been able to grapple with successfully, the law may decide; and reduced to its lowest terms, the question is just this: "Has the Indian any rights which the white man is bound to respect?" We may answer this inquiry in the case of the negro affirmatively—after some delay, it is true. Standing Bear seeks also a response, and asks pecuniary aid to enable him to appeal to the courts to restore to his people the lands unconditionally ceded to them by the United States, from which they have been so unjustly and barbarously expelled.[6]

The Right Rev. Robert Clarkson,[7] Bishop of Nebraska, is chairman of the Western Committee for the relief of this tribe, and the Rev. A. F. Sherris,[8] of Omaha, treasurer. Mayor Prince[9] is chairman of the Boston Committee, and Eben Jordan[10] treasurer. Contributions may be sent to any one of these gentlemen.

JUSTICE.

New-York. Nov. 20. 1879.

Printed in the *Tribune*, Nov. 24, 1879, p. 5, as "Standing Bear and the Poncas: The Story of Their Hardships and Sufferings Retold—An Appeal for Aid in Their Efforts to Recover Their Lands."

1. Edward C. Kemble (1828–86), field official in charge of the Ponca removal, came to California in 1846 and served as editor of the *California Star* (San Francisco), 1847–48, before establishing the *Placer Times* and the *Alta California*. In the 1870s he became one of the first Indian inspectors hired to make routine investigations of Indian agencies. He later moved to New York and worked as assistant manager of the Associated Press office in New York City.

2. The Oto reservation was located on the Big Blue River on the Kansas-Nebraska border.

3. The Omaha Reservation was located on the Missouri River in eastern Nebraska. The Omahas and Poncas belonged to the same linguistic family and often intermarried.

4. Thomas Henry Tibbles (1838–1928) was an itinerant Methodist preacher before becoming a reporter on the *Omaha Daily Bee* and later on the *Omaha Daily Herald*. In 1881 he married Susette La Flesche, an Omaha Indian woman who had served as Standing Bear's interpreter. Tibbles continued his interest in reform, was active in the Populist movement, and became the party's vice-presidential candidate in 1904. In 1905 he wrote his autobiography, *Buckskin and Blanket Days*.

5. Elmer Scipio Dundy (1830–96) served in the Nebraska territorial legislature until his appointment in 1863 as a territorial federal judge. In 1868 he was appointed a United States district judge for Nebraska and served until his death.

6. In late March 1877 a Ponca Indian delegation had visited the *Niobrara Pioneer*, in Knox County, Nebraska, informing the newspaper staff that they had been deceived by the government. See "A Ponca Pow-Wow," Mar. 29, 1877, p. 8; "The Poncas Desert," Mar. 8, 1877, p. 1; "Removal of the Poncas," Apr. 5, 1877, p. 4; "Swindled Poncas," Apr. 5, 1877, p. 1; "The Ponca Treaty," Apr. 12, 1877, p. 8; and "The Poncas Must Go," May 3, 1877, all in the *Niobrara Pioneer*.

7. Episcopal clergyman Robert Harper Clarkson (1826–84) served as rector of St. James Church in Chicago before becoming missionary bishop of Nebraska and Dakota in 1865.

8. Canadian-born Alvin F. Sherrill (b. 1843) became pastor of the First Congregational Church in Omaha in 1870. After serving for eight years, he moved to Atlanta, Georgia. The *Tribune* typesetter misread HHJ's handwriting, spelling the name "Sherris."

9. A Harvard graduate and a lawyer, Frederick Octavius Prince (1818–99) served his state in both legislative houses, 1851–56, before becoming mayor of Boston in 1877; he served as mayor again, 1879–81.

10. Eben Dyer Jordan (1822–95), founder of Jordan Marsh & Company, was a prominent Boston merchant and humanitarian. He served on the Boston relief commission, which aided the victims of the 1872 Chicago fire, supported the peace jubilees of 1869 and 1872, and established a free evening school for his employees.

TO THE EDITOR OF THE *TRIBUNE*

[December 6, 1879]

To the Editor of The Tribune.

SIR: There will be published this week, by Messrs. Lockwood, Brooks & Co., Boston, a little book with the title, "The Ponca Chiefs: an Indian's attempt to appeal from the tomahawk to the courts."[1] This book gives a full history of the robbery of the Ponca tribe of Indians, with all the papers filed and evidence taken in the "Standing Bear" habeas corpus case, and the full text of Judge Dundy's celebrated decision, with some suggestions toward a solution of the Indian question. The book has this dedication, written by Wendell Phillips:[2] "To the people of the United States—those who love liberty and intend that this Government shall protect every man on its soil, and execute justice between man and man—this narrative, with an introduction written by an Indian girl, of the wrongs suffered at the hands of the Government by the Poncas, in consequence of which one-third of the tribe have died within the last eighteen months, and the rest have endured and still endure cruel and wasting oppression, is respectfully dedicated as a fair specimen of the system of injustice, oppression and robbery which the Government calls its 'Indian policy': which has covered it with disgrace as incompetent, cruel, faithless, never keeping its treaties, and systematically and shamelessly violating its most solemn pledges; has earned the contempt and detestation of all honest men, and the distrust and hate of the Indian tribes.—Wendell Phillips."

The introduction is written by "Inshtatheamba," "Bright Eyes,"[3] a girl of the Omaha tribe, who is acting as interpreter for the Ponca Chief, Standing Bear, in his appeals to the people for money to enable his tribe to bring the suits necessary to recover the lands of which the United States government has robbed them. Bright Eyes was educated in Elizabeth, New-Jersey, and has been a teacher on the Omaha Reservation for some time. She speaks English with quaint simplicity and force, which are the results of her familiarity with the English written by William Shakespeare; a little copy of Shakespeare's Plays which she drew as a prize at school, being the only book of value which she possesses.

In this introduction is the following sentence: "It is a little thing, a simple thing, which my people ask of a Nation whose watchword is liberty, but it is endless in its consequences. They ask for their liberty, and law is liberty." When I read this sentence I said to Mr. Tibbles, the friend and champion of the Poncas, who accompanies them: "Did Bright Eyes really write that sentence herself?" "Every word of the introduction," he said, "just as it stands. I was astonished at it when I read it, and I looked up at her and said, 'How did you get at that? What makes you say law is liberty?'

"She was sitting by the window; she pointed to the people going up and down the street, and said, 'I see it here. I see all people coming and going as they like; they can go to Europe if they like; that is being free; and it is because they have law to take care of them that they can go.'"

What writer on political economy has made a stronger or better argument than this? And what could be more profoundly touching than the thought of this Indian girl herself liable to arrest at any moment, as a "ward" of the United States Government, absent without cause from the "reservation" appointed for her tribe—sitting at her window, looking out on the hurrying city crowds, and thinking, not of the gayety, the beauty, the novelty of the spectacle, but simply, "I see all people going, coming, as they like; that is being free!"

Shall we give to this long wronged race the "liberty" for which they ask— the "liberty of law"?

                                                                              H.H.

New-York, Dec. 6. 1879.

Printed in the *Tribune*, Dec. 9, 1879, p. 5, as "An Appeal for the Indians: Full History of the Wrongs of the Ponca Tribe—Bright Eyes on Law and Liberty."

1. Written by Thomas Henry Tibbles using the pseudonym Zylyff, this book was reprinted as Tibbles, *The Ponca Chiefs: An Account of the Trial of Standing Bear.*

2. Wendell Phillips (1811–84) was active in the abolition movement and served as president of the American Anti-Slavery Society. Following emancipation, he fought for political and legal rights for women, blacks, and industrial laborers.

3. Susette La Flesche (1854–1903), eldest daughter of Joseph La Flesche, the last Omaha chief, was educated at Elizabeth Institute for Young Ladies. She returned to the reservation and taught school before joining the Standing Bear tour as interpreter. She became an outspoken critic of the government's Indian policy and, following her

marriage to Tibbles, wrote numerous articles and editorials and participated in the crusade for free silver and populism.

TO WHITELAW REID

Dec. 7, 1879.

Dear Mr. Reid

Think how much I must have wanted a thing done, to seek you out on your own hearth stone, to ask it! — Will you print the enclosed article for me?[1] — and in a good conspicuous place? I say "for me" — I mean, for the Poncas. — And if not, will you send it back to me tomorrow — so that I may try some other harder hearted Editor? —

And will you print for me, under my signature a short article called "Eight Questions for the American People"?— being a condensed statement of a few Indian grievances, all tersely put — and authenticated by references to official reports — the form being as follows "How many of our people know that? x x &c &c.["][2] — Send me word at the Brevoort House: — or perhaps you will return my call!

Yours truly
Helen Jackson

ALS (Papers of Whitelaw Reid, Reel 151, Library of Congress, Washington, D.C.; hereinafter cited as DLC, Reid Papers).

Whitelaw Reid (1837–1912) wrote for country newspapers until he joined the *Tribune* in 1868. He served as managing editor, 1869–1905, resigning to assume the post of American ambassador to Great Britain, a position he held until his death.

1. Probably a reference to her Dec. 6 letter to the *Tribune*, above, reviewing *The Ponca Chiefs.*

2. Probably a reference to her Dec. 11, 1879, letter to the *Tribune*, below. In its final version there were ten not eight questions. As published, this letter carried the date Dec. 11, 1879, at the bottom, although HHJ referred to it in both her Dec. 7 and Dec. 9 letters.

TO WHITELAW REID

Tuesday Eve
Dec 9, 1879
Brevoort House

Dear Mr. Reid:

I construe your silence into assent, and send you that paper I spoke of.[1] I hope you will want to print it, and give it a conspicuous place. — The questions

Whitelaw Reid, editor of the *New York Tribune*. (Library of Congress)

should be printed in large type — headed — the comments in fine type in brackets. — In this way it will not take up much room.

Thank you for printing the other communication. I am sure you must have been touched by the quotation from Bright Eyes' introduction. —[2]

Do go and see them — and do write an Editorial for them —and do go to the meeting on Friday evening at Steinway Hall.[3]

Yours truly,

Helen Jackson

P.S. Every assertion I make in this article is made on trustworthy authority. The figures of the Govt's indebtedness to the Utes I had from Mr. Teller[4] himself, and the story of the supplies lying a year at Rawlings, I had from the Head Clerk of the Indian Bureau [William M. Leeds].[5] —

H.J.

of course — if you do not print this,
I would be glad of it as soon as possible
to try elsewhere.

ALS (DLC, Reid Papers).
Reid wrote the following on the letter: "Mr. Hassard = This is from Helen Hunt who is a little bit crazy, I am afraid, on the Ponca question. We printed one letter from her on Tuesday. Please let me have your opinion about this tonight. WR." John Rose Greene Hassard (1836–88) worked with editor George Ripley on the *New American Cyclopaedia* as well as serving as reporter for the *Tribune*. In 1865 he became editor of the *Catholic World*, but he returned to the *Tribune* the following year, making his most important contribution as an essayist and music critic.

1. See note 2, HHJ to Reid, Dec. 7, 1879, above.

2. A reference to her Dec. 6 letter to the *Tribune*, above.

3. For an account of this meeting, see "Wrongs of the Indians," *Tribune*, Dec. 13, 1879, p. 5.

4. Henry Moore Teller (1830–1914) practiced law in Colorado before becoming president of the Colorado Central Railroad in 1872. Elected to the U.S. Senate in 1876, he resigned in 1882 to became Chester A. Arthur's secretary of the interior, the first westerner to hold this position. He returned to the Senate in 1885, serving four terms.

5. William M. Leeds was an investigator in Indian Territory for the Board of Indian Commissioners until his appointment as chief clerk in 1877. In 1878 he temporarily served as acting commissioner of Indian affairs; he left his clerkship in 1879.

TO WILLIAM HAYES WARD

Brevoort House
Wed. Am.
[ca. December 10, 1879]

Dear Mr. Ward —

I have not had time to get down & see you — If the Cheyenne Massacre[1] is in this weeks Ind[ependent] — please send me *20* copies this PM, here — (*not* in wrappers) — I shall cut this article out and mail it. — Send C.O.D. — if the office can't spare them, I am going to send them far & wide. *Do* make time to go to the Fifth Av. [Hotel] & see Standing Bear & Bright Eyes —Everything promises splendidly — hope you saw my letter in the Tribune yesterday —[2]

— Great haste yrs —

H.J. —

P.S. The Breakfast[3] was a grand success — the atmosphere of the occasion could not be described in words.

Have you any more copies of the Standing Bear article.[4] If so, I would like two.

ALS (Helen Hunt Jackson manuscripts, HM 13978, Henry E. Huntington Library, San Marino, California; hereinafter cited as CSmH, HHJ MSS).

1. "The Massacre of the Cheyennes" finally appeared in the *Independent*, Jan. 1, 1880, pp. 2–3.

2. A reference to her Dec. 6, 1879, letter to the *Tribune*, above.

3. Oliver Wendell Holmes's seventieth birthday breakfast was held on Dec. 3 at the Hotel Brunswick in Boston by the publishers of the *Atlantic*. Those in attendance included Charles Dudley Warner, Thomas Bailey Aldrich, Ralph Waldo Emerson, Mark Twain, Francis Parkman, Harriet Beecher Stowe, and Louisa May Alcott. See "The Holmes Breakfast," *Boston Advertiser*, Dec. 3, 1879, p. 1, and "Honoring Dr. Holmes," *Tribune*, Dec. 4, 1879, p. 5.

4. A reference to HHJ's "Standing Bear and Bright Eyes."

TO THE EDITOR OF THE *TRIBUNE*

[December 11, 1879]

To the Editor of The Tribune.

SIR: I. How many of the American people know that for any white man, other than the one licensed Reservation trader, to sell anything to, or buy anything from, an Indian on a Reservation, is an offense punishable by a fine of $500 and the forfeiture of all his merchandise?

This law, it is said, was made for the protection of the Indian. To believe this is to compliment the law makers' humanity at the expense of their common sense. The operation of this law on the Omaha Reservation last Summer, for instance, was to make it impossible for an Omaha Indian to get more than 40 cents a bushel for his wheat at a time when the open market price for wheat was 90 cents a bushel.[1]

II. How many of the American people know that it is declared in section 2,079 of Chapter II, under Title xxviii of the Revised Statutes of the United States, that,

"No Indian nation or tribe within the territory of the United States shall be acknowledged or recognized as an independent nation, tribe or power, with whom the United States may contract by treaty."

III. How many of the American people believe that this statute is known and understood by the Indians who "cede lands" to the United States, "in consideration of" other lands, or sums of money?

IV. How many of the American people know that "Indians living on Reservations have in general the right to cut hay for the use of their livestock, but are invested with no proprietorship in such spontaneous products of the soil as will authorize them to charge and receive compensation for hay cut and used by white persons thereto duly empowered by the Government of the United States." Annual Report of the Indian Commissioner for 1878. P. 69.

Under the operation of this law the white man can (and does) cut wood, and sell it, to steamboats going up the Missouri River, for instance; can cut it wherever on the reservation he and the agent please; and the Indians on whose land these "spontaneous products," the trees, have grown, are powerless. Under the operation of this law 1,800 cords of wood were cut down last Winter on the Ponca Reservation, and sold to army contractors by order of Mr. Hayt,[2] Commissioner of Indian Affairs.

V. How many of the American people know that if an Indian on a reservation raises a flock of sheep he cannot sell the wool, neither can the agent sell the wool and give the money to the Indian. The agent must sell the wool and turn the proceeds into the United States Treasury.

(How many farmers in Vermont or Massachusetts would become, or continue industrious, hard working and contented, under such conditions as these?)

VI. How many American people know that an Indian cannot be legally prosecuted or punished for an offence committed against an Indian? In two years the Winnebagoes stole over 100 ponies from the Omahas, and passed the ponies along to the white men who had hired them to steal them. When one of the Omaha Chiefs who had lost several valuable ponies and knew where some of them were (in white men's possession), applied to the Agent for redress, the Agent said he didn't know of any way for him to get them but to steal them back again.

VII. How many of the American people will be able to believe this—than an Indian "may kill an Indian woman without excuse or provocation, and he thereby violates no Federal law. If he marries, instead of killing her, having a former wife living, he is subject to arraignment, trial and punishment by the Courts of the United States for bigamy." Annual Report of the Indian Commissioner for 1878, P. 61.

In the Annual Report of the Indian Commissioner for 1876, p. 9, we read as follows: "We have within our midst 275,000 people, the least intelligent portion of our population, for whom we provide no law either for their protection or for the punishment of crimes committed among themselves. Civilization, even among white men, could not long exist without the guarantees which law alone affords."

VIII. How many of the American people know that when the Nez Percé Indians, under Chief Joseph,[3] surrendered to General Mills [Miles][4] in 1877 on the express condition that they should be taken back to Idaho in the Spring, they were taken to a place in the Missouri River bottom so unhealthy, that "after the arrival of Joseph and his band in the Indian Territory," (not in Idaho, where they had been promised they should go) "the bad effect of their location at Fort Leavenworth manifested itself in the prostration by sickness at one time of 260 out of the 410"; and "within a few months" in the death of "more than one-quarter of the entire number." Annual Report of the Indian Commission for 1878. Page 33. (Was Andersonville[5] much worse than this?)

IX. How many of the American people know anything about the true situation and experience of the White River Utes,[6] of whom the Hon. Carl Schurz says in his recent most able and most ably worded annual report, that they have "no just cause of complaint"? Let us see.

"The situation of the White River Ute Agency is the worst possible in all respects, unless it should be the intention to keep the Indians as National paupers. It is accessible for training [teaming] only two months in the year. The soil is not good, and why the location was chosen at all for an Indian Agency is a profound mystery."[7]

Report of the Agent. See Annual Report of the Indian Commissioners for 1878. P. 41.

So much for the situation. Now let us see what they were to do there. The requisition asked for by the Indian Bureau and appropriated by Congress for the White River Ute Agency (see Annual Report of Indian Commissioners for 1878. P. 299), covers just "34 per cent" of their substance. The remaining "66 per cent" they are expected to get for themselves by "hunting, fishing and root-digging." (See same page of report.)

We will say nothing about "root digging;" roots being "spontaneous productions of the soil," there might be some question about the Indians' title to even them; but there are probably not enough "roots" in the White River Agency to be worth talking about. As to "fishing"—there are serious geographical objections to the White River Utes getting much of a living by that. "Hunting" remains. Well and good.

It is a standing order of the Indian Bureau that no reservation trader is to sell ammunition to an Indian! Sixty-six per cent of his living the White River Ute is to get by "hunting or fishing and root-digging." Now, let us see what success he has had in getting hold of that "34 per cent" of his subsistence which is to be furnished him by the Government.

The annual supplies for these Utes for the fiscal year ending 1877 lay in a store-house at Rawlings, Wyoming, one whole year. During this time these Utes, spite of their legitimate occupations of "fishing and root-digging," spite of a good deal of illegitimate "hunting" with ammunition not bought from the Government trader, were starving—not simply suffering hunger—starving, dying for want of food. Some of the chiefs went with their own wagons to Rawlins, asked, begged, implored for some of the food in this storehouse. They had come 200 miles to get it. They had left their women and children starving for want of it. It was their own. It was refused to them. Nobody there had legal right to give it to them; and they went back without it.

We have seen how the Government has treated these Utes in the matter of lands, and of subsistence; now let us see how it has treated them in the matter of money.

After the Bruno [Brunot] Treaty of 1873[8] with them, no payment was made to them for three years, the yearly sum due them by the treaty being $25,000. To-day, what with this interest money, and other indebtedness, it is estimated by persons familiar with the facts and figures that the government owes them over $100,000.

"No just cause for complaint."

Mr. Teller, Senator from Colorado, has been making for two years unwearied, but vain, efforts to induce the Commissioner of Indian Affairs to take the steps necessary for the payment of this money. Mr. Teller has warned the Department repeatedly that a Ute war would surely break out before long if this money was not paid.

X. How many of the American people know anything of the present condition and present feelings of the Ponca Indians, of whom this same ably worded report by the Secretary of Interior says that they are now content and acclimated in their new home in the Indian Territory, and that "the Department has done all that was in its power to indemnify them for the wrong done them," and that it is an open question whether it is worth while to make any effort to restore to them the lands of which they were robbed, because it would be "a mere vindication of a right to a piece of land."

Yes; that is all it would be. But a great many men have laid down their lives for just such a "mere vindication of a right to a piece of land." It is astonishing the hold a "mere" "piece of land" can get on a man's affections. Men have deserted in face of the certainty of being shot to get a look at a "mere" "piece of land," and have died of homesickness for a "mere" "piece of land." No race in the world except the Swiss has ever shown a stronger love of the "mere" "land" than the race to which the Honorable Secretary of the Interior belongs. No poets have so immortalized their "Fatherland" as have the poets of his own country. It was a strange phase for a German to use; but he has used it and it is likely to be remembered. It is a "precedent" somewhat startling in an official document, treating of a case of indisputable and confessed robbery. Official though it be, however, it stands for nothing more than the Secretary's private opinion, the Secretary's individual standard, the Secretary's peculiar estimate of the relative significance and importance of ownership and possession.

The simple truth is in regard to the Poncas at present in the Indian Territory that they are not contented and never will be. They are waiting with the straining fear and hope of exiles for the result of the effort now being made by their Chief Standing Bear to secure legal redress for their wrongs, and restoration of their stolen lands. White Eagle,[9] their head chief, has sent word, by a runner, within three months, that he can keep them quiet, he thinks, till Spring; but he can promise no longer.

"Big Snake," Standing Bear's brother was shot dead, by United States soldiers, only a month ago, for endeavoring to escape, and stir up others to escape with him.[10]

It is marvelous what an effect it has on a man, sometimes, just to remove him by force from one "mere" "piece of land" which he loves and calls "home" to another which he hates so that he would rather die than stay in it. Even in the official documents of the Department of the Interior we find touching records of the sorrowing of these Indians. The words bring to mind some of the words written about captives as far back as the days of Jeremiah.[11]

"There is a restless, discontented feeling pervading the whole tribe. They seem to have lost faith in the promises of the Government, and often say that the 'Great Father' has forgotten them; by the time he again remembers them none will be left to receive what he has promised them." Report of the Agent for the Poncas.[12] Annual Report of Ind[ian] Com[missioner] for 1878, p. 65.

It cannot be too strenuously urged upon the attention of the people at this time, that the appeal of these Ponca Indians to the Supreme Court will, if successful, do for the Indian race precisely what the Emancipation act did for the negro. When the Omaha lawyers served a writ on the Army officer [General George Crook],[13] holding Standing Bear and his band as prisoners, and commanded him to "show cause" why he held them prisoners, the United States District-Attorney endeavored to have the writ dismissed on the grounds that Indians stand as wards to the Government, as minors to parents or guardians, and no attorney could appeal for an Indian unless authorized to do so by the Indian Bureau. Judge Dundy, with a burst of indignant eloquence, declared that there was no man living, white, black or red, who could not come into his court, and he set Standing Bear and his band free. They are the only free Indians in the United States to-day, except a few in some of the Eastern States, who are under the protection of State laws.

How have the eyes of the American people been so long blinded to this evident and flagrant oppression? It has been ably said by Governor Seymour:[14] "Every human being born upon our Continent, or who comes here from any quarter of the world, whether savage or civilized, can go to our courts for protection, except those who belong to the tribes who once owned this country. The cannibal from the islands of the Pacific, the worst criminals from Europe, Asia or Africa can appeal to the law and Courts for their rights of person and property; all save our native Indians, who, above all, should be protected from wrong." Will the American people allow this wrong to continue?

H.H.

New-York, Dec. 11, 1879.

Printed in the *Tribune*, Dec. 15, 1879, p. 5, as "The Indian Problem: Questions for the American People, Propounded by 'H.H.'" Warner reprinted this letter in the *Hartford Courant*, Dec. 22, 1879, p. 1.

Reid, in a brief editorial note in "The News This Morning," p. 4, directed readers to "peruse" HHJ's letter on the following page. Secretary Schurz responded to each one of HHJ's questions in a detailed telegram to the *Tribune*; see "Mr. Schurz on Indian Affairs: The Secretary Replies to the Letter of H. H. in the *Tribune*," *Tribune*, Dec. 19, 1879, p. 1.

1. This letter prompted Charles P. Morgan, an Omaha Indian who served as interpreter, to write the *Tribune* protesting that the Omaha Indians were under no restraints to sell their wheat. "I know much more about the management and their privileges than any of their Agent's enemies," he concluded. See "A Denial from the Omaha Agency," *Tribune*, Jan. 11, 1880, p. 5.

2. Ezra A. Hayt (1823–1902) served on the Board of Indian Commissioners, 1874–77. In 1877 he was appointed commissioner of Indian affairs, but served only twenty-eight months. Leeds was his chief clerk.

3. Chief Joseph (1840–1904), a leader of the nontreaty band of Nez Percés from northeastern Oregon, led his people on a thirteen-hundred-mile flight to Canada, pursued by military troops under General Oliver O. Howard and Colonel Nelson A. Miles. Captured by Miles, Joseph and his people temporarily settled on a reservation in southeastern Kansas, later moved to Indian Territory, and eventually returned to the Northwest, with half going to Idaho and the remainder to central Washington. Joseph's band never returned to their original home in the Wallowa Valley of northeastern Oregon.

4. Nelson Appleton Miles (1839–1925), a Civil War officer, fought the Plains Indians during the 1870s and the Apaches, including Geronimo, in the 1880s.

5. Established in Georgia in 1864, Andersonville was the largest Confederate military prison. At one time it housed over thirty thousand Union soldiers, of whom over twelve thousand died.

6. The White River Ute Agency in western Colorado served the northern bands of Utes. The ever encroaching mining frontier and the failure of the government to deliver goods and services promised in the treaties made peace impossible to maintain.

7. Congressional legislation of May 3, 1878, established a Ute commission that concluded that the location of the White River Agency was unsuitable.

8. In 1871 Congress ended the formal treaty-making process with Indian tribes, replacing it with bilateral agreements, negotiated with tribes but ratified by both houses of Congress instead of only by the Senate. Therefore the Brunot Treaty was an agreement with the Utes under Chief Ouray. See Prucha, *American Indian Treaties*, pp. 313–16.

9. White Eagle visited Washington, D.C., twice, in Nov. 1877 and in Dec. 1880, to plead the case of his tribe before government officials.

10. Big Snake, who was accused of threatening Agent William H. Whiteman and stirring up trouble, was shot by soldiers attempting to arrest him at Fort Reno in Oct. 1879. For a brief account, see "The Poncas," *Boston Advertiser*, Nov. 3, 1879, p. 4. After Senator Henry L. Dawes insinuated that the government had plotted Big Snake's death, Secretary Schurz addressed an open letter to Dawes, placing a copy on the desk of each senator. For the text see Schurz, *Speeches, Correspondence and Political Papers*, 4:91–114.

11. A reference to the book of the prophet Jeremiah in the Old Testament, in which Jerusalem fell and the Jews were exiled to Babylon.

12. William H. Whiteman, appointed Ponca agent on June 15, 1878, described the Poncas as "good Indians," superior to any other tribe he had ever met. See *Annual Report of the Commissioner, 1878*, p. 65.

13. General George Crook (1828–90) fought Indians in the Pacific Northwest before serving in the Civil War. He commanded the Department of Arizona in 1871, was assigned to the Department of the Platte, 1875–81, and was reassigned to Arizona, where he spend four years pursuing the Apaches. During the remainder of his life, Crook spoke out against government Indian policy. See King, "'A Better Way': General George Crook and the Ponca Indians."

14. Horatio Seymour (1810–86) was twice elected governor of New York. HHJ is quoting from a July 8, 1879, statement by Seymour that appeared in "Indians and the Law," *Boston Advertiser*, July 29, 1879, p. 2.

TO THE EDITORS OF THE *NEW YORK EVENING POST*

[December 14, 1879]

To the Editors of the Evening Post.

A small paper-covered book[1] of only one hundred and forty-six pages has recently been put forth through Lockwood, Brooks & Co. by the friends of the Ponca Indians, whose story it tells. It contains a history which might be expanded into volumes—a history which every American citizen must blush to read—the history of the faithlessness and cruelty of the United States government toward the tribe of Ponca Indians. These Indians had been always peaceable, industrious, friendly and faithful. They had rendered to our army officers valuable military service in times of war with hostile Indians.

"In consideration of" these faithful services and "of other lands ceded to the United States," the United States government "ceded and relinquished" to them a tract of land in Dakota, and agreed "to protect the Poncas in the possession." This same tract of land the United States government afterward, "by an inadvertence," ceded to the Sioux, and, by way of righting this wrong and atoning for this "inadvertence," appropriated on the 15th of August, 1876, $25,000 "for the removal of the Poncas to the Indian Territory." President Seelye[2] of Amherst College secured the insertion in that Appropriation bill of the clause "provided the Poncas consent." His humane provision was not worth the paper it was written on. The Poncas would not consent. They never did consent. They were taken to the Indian Territory by military force. They did not fight; they killed no United States soldiers on the way; and that is the reason that most of the people of the United States never knew anything about the matter at all.

The story of how a United States inspector named Kemble and a Protestant Episcopal clergyman named Hinman[3] went to the Poncas, told them they must move, took the ten Ponca chiefs down to the Indian Territory to examine the new lands, and then, when they refused to accept the lands, left them there, penniless, unable to speak a word of the language, to find their way back as best they could, one thousand miles, to their old home, is too long to tell here. It is told in the little book referred to above. It is a story that will never die out of the history of the United States. Neither will the story of the final removal of the tribe; how when the chiefs, after their return, had exhausted every device which helplessness has at its command; when they had telegraphed to the President and got no answer; when they had offered the greedy men all the money promised by the government to the tribe if they would only leave them in their homes; when they had locked up their houses and fled to the woods and hid rather than be carried away—when they had tried, as I say, every device which helplessness can try, they gave up. They stood by, hopeless and helpless, while the soldiers took their farming implements and their furniture out of their houses and piled it up in a big warehouse, loading into wagons such few things as could be conveniently carried. I do not know whether the Poncas marched behind or before the soldiers, but they were at the point of the bayonet, either way. They were told that if they did not go they would be shot; and they would have been.

The horrors of that journey cannot be told. Cattle died; horses died; women and children died, and before they had been six months in the unhealthy Indian Territory one hundred and fifty-eight of the tribe were dead.

Then Standing Bear with thirty of his people ran away. The soldiers overtook them, arrested them, and on their way back to the Indian Territory with them halted at Omaha. Here an Omaha editor, Mr. Tibbles, and two Omaha lawyers, Mr. Webster[4] and Mr. Poppleton,[5] determined to test the question of the legality of compelling these Indians by force to return to that Indian Territory. By a writ of *habeas corpus* they were brought into the District Court of the United States for the District of Nebraska, and set free by the judge of that court. His name is Dundy. Will not the name of Judge Dundy stand by the side of that of Abraham Lincoln in the matter of emancipation acts?

The government attorney, the Honorable G. M. Lambertson,[6] made an argument, five hours long, "ingenious and eloquent," to prove than an Indian was not entitled to the protection of the writ of *habeas corpus*, "not being a person or citizen under the laws."

Judge Dundy took several days to consider the case, and gave a decision which strikes straight to the root of the whole matter—a decision which, when it is enforced everywhere by the highest legal tribunal of our land, will take the ground out from under the feet of a horde of unscrupulous and heartless thieves who have been robbing, oppressing and maddening the Indians for so long a term of years that to try to unmask and expose their processes or to make clean their methods is a task before which good men, nay, whole denominations of good men, have given up disheartened and worn out.

It is a task, however, which the American people would rise up in indignation and demand from their Representative in Washington if the true facts of the case could once be got before them. But the American people do not know the facts in the case. Probably to ninety-nine out of a hundred of them it would be a new, an astounding and well-nigh incredible statement that no attorney may or can appear for an Indian until he is authorized to do so by the government! That, until this decision of Judge Dundy, it has been held that even our bulwark of *habeas corpus*, which shelters, as Governor Seymour has most eloquently said, even "the cannibal from the islands of the Pacific, the worst criminals from Europe, Asia or Africa," if they choose to avail themselves of it, cannot be extended to an Indian.

How long would any man in New York city keep his house, his land, his money, if he were legally disqualified from bringing any suit against a man or men who might rob him?

How safe would women and children be in New York, in the houses of husbands and fathers, who, no matter what outrage befell wife or child, could hold no man legally responsible for his acts?

Juries have again and again acquitted of the charge of murder men who have killed seducers and adulterers, men who have killed burglars, men who have killed "in self-defense" those who committed assaults on them; and this in spite of the fact that to all these men who killed in hot haste of either resentment or terror there was open the law, if they had waited; the law, with a prison and a gallows.

Shall we wholly forget this when we call the Indian a murderous savage because he uses his tomahawk? When Standing Bear found that by the decision of Judge Dundy he was really a free man, and could go where he pleased, he made a speech which I think should be printed and laid on the desk of every Representative and Senator in the American Congress. He said after a most touching expression of gratitude to the lawyers who had pleaded his cause:

> "Hitherto when we have been wronged we went to war to assert our rights and avenge our wrongs. We took the tomahawk. We had no law to punish those who did wrong; so we took our tomahawks and went to kill. If they had guns and could kill us first it was the fate of war. But you have found a better way. You have gone into the court for us: and I find that our wrongs can be righted there. Now I have no more use for the tomahawk. I want to lay it down forever."

Uttering these words with eloquent impressiveness the old chief, stooping down, placed the tomahawk on the floor at his feet; then, standing erect, he folded his arms with native dignity and continued:

> "I lay it down. I have no more use for it. I have found a better way."

Stooping again and taking up the weapon he placed it in Mr. Webster's hands and said:

> "I present it to you as a token of my gratitude. I want you to keep it in remembrance of this great victory which you have gained. I have no further use for it; I can now seek the ways of peace."

All the profits from the sale of the little book published for the purpose of laying facts before the people will be devoted to securing, through the processes of law, the recovery of the lands taken from the Poncas and to settling the question once for all, and once and forever, by a decision of the Supreme

Court, whether or not the life and property of an Indian can be protected by law.

The chairman of the western committee for the receipt of these funds is Bishop Clarkson of Nebraska. The chairman of the committee in Boston is Mayor Prince of that city.

A committee will soon be appointed in New York, and Standing Bear himself is now at the Fifth Avenue Hotel. He is accompanied by Bright Eyes and her brother Wood-Worker,[7] two educated Omaha Indians who act as interpreters for him. The party is in charge of Mr. T. H. Tibbles, the faithful champion who was the means of rescuing Standing Bear and his party at Omaha.

To hear Standing Bear tell his own story interpreted by Bright Eyes is, if possible, more touching than to read it. If he could go, or if the book which tells his story could go into every American home, there would be a swift and mighty revulsion of American sentiment upon the "Indian Question." For this Ponca case is but one of hundreds. It differs from the rest only in two particulars: First, that the government had made with the Poncas a treaty so specific and so technical in wording that their title would hold good in any court in the land. The seizure of their lands, therefore, was a more flagrant crime, a more unquestionable robbery than the government has ever committed in moving other tribes with whom they have made treaties riddled with loopholes for evasions—loopholes which Indians could not see.

The benefit—if it be a benefit—of this difference between the Ponca treaty and other Indian treaties we can give to the government in our estimate of the morality of its course in breaking them.

Secondly, the Ponca case differs from most of the rest in the fact that the Poncas did not fight; they submitted hopelessly, and went to their death without resistance. If they had resisted they would have been shot down, as the Cheyennes were last winter.[8] And if they cannot get back their homes, if they cannot get from the Supreme Court their legal freedom, they will, no doubt, wish they had resisted, and had been shot down, Who would not?

H.H.

New York, December 14, 1879.

Printed in the *NY Evening Post*, Dec. 17, 1879, p. 1, as "The Story of the Poncas: A Vigorous Rehearsal of a Shameful Tale—What Wrongs Have Been Done in the Name of the American People to a Peaceful Tribe—The Chivalric Interference of Omaha Men and Its Results—A Ponca Chief's Suggestive Speech—An Appeal for Right and Laws."

1. A reference to *The Ponca Chiefs* by Tibbles.

2. Julius H. Seelye (1824–95) served as pastor of the First Dutch Reformed Church in Schenectady and taught at Amherst College before his election in 1874 to the House of Representatives, where he was a member of the Indian Affairs Committee. He served as the fifth president of Amherst College, 1877–90.

Seelye strongly believed in Indian citizenship. For his opinions see "Indians and the Law," July 29, 1879, p. 2, and "Indian Rights: A Boston Audience Speaks in Faneuil Hall," Dec. 3, 1879, p. 1, both in the *Boston Advertiser*.

3. Samuel Dutton Hinman (1839–90) was the first Episcopal missionary to the Sioux Indians. He established the Mission of St. John at the Lower Sioux Agency in Redwood County, Minnesota, worked among the Indians at Fort Snelling, and was assigned to the Santee Sioux Agency in Nebraska in 1866.

The *Niobrara Pioneer* on Feb. 15, 1877, p. 4, while noting that Hinman was in Indian Territory to help the Poncas select a new reservation, wrote: "This 'exemplary' Christian missionary humbug is at the head of the whole business, and, with the aid of whiskey in high places and Hiawathas in low places, has a wonderful influence with the heads of the Indian Department at Washington."

4. John Lee Webster (b. 1847) established a law practice in Omaha, Nebraska, in 1871, serving as general counsel for the water district, the Wabash Railroad, and the Omaha & Council Bluffs Railway system. He also was a state legislator.

5. Andrew Jackson Poppleton (1830–96), a member of Nebraska's first territorial legislature, served as chief attorney of the Union Pacific Railroad for a quarter of a century.

6. Genio Madison Lambertson (1850–1902), who moved to Lincoln in 1874 from Indiana, was appointed United States district attorney for Nebraska in 1878, serving eight years. During the 1880s he was assistant secretary of the treasury under Benjamin Harrison.

7. Woodworker or Francis La Flesche (1857–1932) was a son of Omaha chief Joseph La Flesche. He had a twenty-six-year career with the Bureau of American Ethnology, during which he collaborated with ethnologist Alice Cunningham Fletcher on a history of the Omaha Indians.

8. After participating in the Battle of the Little Big Horn in 1876, the Northern Cheyennes surrendered and were sent to the Southern Cheyenne and Arapaho reservation in Indian Territory, where they suffered from disease, starvation, and homesickness. Some three hundred Cheyennes led by Dull Knife and Little Wolf fled in 1878. Dull Knife and his party headed for Fort Robinson, surrendered, and were imprisoned. During a desperate escape, one-third died.

TO CHARLES DUDLEY WARNER

Brevoort House [New York City]
Friday, Dec. 14 1879

Dear Mr. Warner:

I was on the point of writing to you to say that I would stop tomorrow on my way to Boston, & pass a night with you, when Mrs. Botta[1] told me that

Mrs. Warner had been in town a week. — I feel myself much aggrieved that she did not keep *your* promise to me, that she would let me know as soon as she came that I might go and see her. — Mrs. Botta did not even know where she was staying — so I have no clue — except that Mrs. B[otta] was under the impression that it was in one of the square houses near the Everett. — Even on that slender clue, I believe I would have started, if I had known sooner. — Give my love to her and tell her so. —

I go to Boston & Cambridge — for two visits — return here on the 27*th* or 28*th* & go to Mrs. Bottas to await Mr. Jackson who will be here by the 1*st* of Jan. Then we shall establish ourselves again at this house or the Berkeley — for a month or two. — I am determined to have my dislike of New York crystallize into a morbid mania, at this rate. I didn't know I could dislike it any more than I began by doing. —

The Poncas have come — New York does not care for them. I have walked, talked, written & spent myself all in vain — The Tribune will not say a word for them — Reid does not wish to make an enemy anywhere, this year. He wants to go to England. I hope he will never get anything he wants — When I see you I will tell you strings of things about it all. I am going to write an article for Scribner about the Indians — that is some comfort. Roswell Smith[2] asked me to do it — said it would be a "card," for them! So I bring my sentiment to market to be sold as it were, dead in the shambles, to make money for a Philistine — I wish you edited the Tribune & the Scribner's Mag[azine] and all the country newspapers from Maine to Georgia. — I saw Mr. Ripley[3] today & tried to interest him in Tibbles' book which is just out. — As soon as he discovered the drift of the thing, he began to retire and pull up his bridges; and said that the Tribune must be a "unit" — &c &c — & that even in the literary dept, nothing would be "allowed" which mitigated against the policy of the paper.— He called Mr. Reid the "autocrat of all the Russias" —and was very genial and kind, and I forgave him a good deal in consideration of his being shut up there with Mrs. Ripley[4] — a woman who would make either a murderer or an imbecile of me in three days, — even now and what effect she would produce on me at three score and ten I cannot conceive. —

If you think of anything to tell me, you can send to Roberts Bros — till the 27*th* but I can't stop at Hartford on the way back because I have but just time for the visits as it is — and I have promised Mrs. Botta to be here for New Years Day. — That shows that I have softening of the brain —.

Yours disheartenedly
Helen Jackson

ALS (CtHT-W, Warner Collection).

1. A longtime friend of HHJ, Anne Charlotte Lynch Botta (1815–91) was a poet and the wife of Italian scholar Vincenzo Botta. Her salon was a gathering place for the New York literati.

2. Roswell Smith (1829–92) joined with Josiah Gilbert Holland and Charles Scribner to established *Scribner's Monthly* in 1870. Holland became editor-in-chief and Richard Watson Gilder managing editor. In 1881, when Holland sold his interest to Smith, *Scribner's Monthly* became the *Century Illustrated Monthly Magazine*.

3. George Ripley (1802–80) was a Unitarian minister as well as a founder of *Dial* magazine and Brook Farm. Beginning in 1849, he served as literary critic for the *Tribune* for thirty-one years. He was a founder of *Harper's New Monthly Magazine* in 1850 and served as editor of its literary department.

4. Ripley married Louisa A. Schlossberger, a German widow thirty years his junior, in 1865.

TO WHITELAW REID

[December 14, 1879]

Dear Mr. Reid

Did you receive my article "A few questions for the American People"?[1]

I had been hoping as it did not appear, that you were going to print it in the Sunday Tribune — but as it is not there, I began to fear that it did not reach you, for I asked you to return it to me immediately if you could not use it.

The Scribners have asked me to prepare an article for the March No. of Scribners,[2] on the same general subject — and I am not sure but I would better save all my ammunition for that one shot. Do you think that it would weaken my Scribners article at all, to have had much of its substance appear before in the Tribune article? I ask you this honestly, because I believe your heart to be in sympathy with the cause, though I see to my great regret, that it has been determined that the Tribune shall ignore it. — If you would only see Mr. Tibbles once, and talk with him, I believe you would disregard every other consideration except the one great moral obligation of helping these Poncas to their rights — no matter what reflection might be involved upon the Secretary of the Interior. — Mr. Tibbles tells me, he has tried in vain to be permitted to see you. —

— Will you please send word by the bearer, if you intend to use my article — and if not — can you return it to me tonight? I go to Boston tomorrow.

Yours very truly

Helen Jackson

Brevoort House
Sunday, Morn. Dec 14, 1879.

ALS (DLC, Reid Papers).
1. A reference to HHJ's Dec. 11 letter to the *Tribune*, above.
2. A reference to "The Wards of the United States Government," which included a detailed history of Chief Joseph and the Nez Percé war.

TO WHITELAW REID

Monday, Morn
15 Dec., 1879

Dear Mr. Reid —

I take back every hard thing I have said about the Tribune this past week[1] — Bless you — now will you follow it up? —Will you see Mr. Tibbles? Will you call attention to the meetings?

— I want twenty five copies of this mornings Tribune sent to me care Roberts Bros, Boston —

tonight — I go by the boat — & will be glad to find them there tomorrow morning — Whatever these Tribunes cost, I will pay if the bill is sent in the parcel — or they can be sent C.O.D. to Mr. Niles,[2] for me "by order of 'H.H.'" —

Yours remorsefully & gratefully
Helen Jackson

I shall be back here at N[ew] Years — at Mrs. Bottas & hope to see you then —

ALS (DLC, Reid Papers).
1. Reid not only published her Dec. 11 letter on Dec. 15 but wrote an editorial calling attention to it.
2. Thomas Niles (1825–94), partner, manager, and editor at Roberts Brothers of Boston, developed the "No Name" Series to which HHJ contributed. He also discovered Louisa May Alcott and edited her writing.

TO WILLIAM SHARPLESS JACKSON

Boston
Tuesday Eve.
Dec. 16 — 1879

Dearest one —

I came by boat last night — had a most curious interview at the Brevoort just before leaving with that Rev. Smith[1] who made all the trouble between Tibbles & party & their Agent. — Mr. Goddard[2] says he is probably a little crazy. I thought so while he was talking with me. — Mr. Ward of the

William Sharpless Jackson was Helen Hunt Jackson's second husband. (Special Collections, Colorado College Library)

Ind[ependent] was on board & we had a capital talk all the eve — & in the cars this AM. — I never saw so much of him before. He is an interesting old fox, —
— Boat was late — I did not reach Mrs. Hunts³ till nine o'clock: stopped at Roberts for letters. —
. . . .

The Transcript[4] tonight copies my Tribune letter entire — with a tremendous endorsement of it — I do believe it is going the country through. Mr. Goddard & Mrs. Goddard[5] have been here this evening — & Mr. G[oddard] is going to copy it — He says "it is a splendid paper"! — Will, do you know I begin to have a half superstitious feeling about this irresistible impulse I feel to say especial words & phrases — as if they were put into my mind from outside! — I know — if my own consciousness is any evidence of anything, that I write these Indian things in a totally different way from my ordinary habit of composition — I write these sentences — which would ordinarily cost me much thought & work, to get them so condensed — as *fast* as I can write the words. — Goodnight — Dearest one — I kiss your eyes. —

. . . .

AL (WSJ Family Papers I, box 1, fd. 7, Special Collections, Tutt Library, Colorado College, Colorado Springs, Colorado; hereinafter cited as CoCC, WSJ I). Non-Indian-related paragraphs, including two about the weather, have been deleted.

William Sharpless Jackson (1836–1919), a Pennsylvania Quaker, had served as treasurer of the Lake Superior and Mississippi Railroad before moving to Colorado and assuming a position with the Denver and Rio Grande Railroad. In 1876, a year after he became Helen Maria Fiske Hunt's second husband, he formed an association with the El Paso County Bank. He was a founder and director of the Denver National Bank, a trustee of Colorado College, and a court-appointed receiver and later president of the Denver and Rio Grande Railroad.

1. B. P. Smith from Brookline wrote "The Indian's Cause: Further Light on the Present Status of the Tribes," *Boston Advertiser*, Aug. 27, 1879, p. 1. There is, of course, no definitive way to know if this is the same Smith, but a mutual interest in the Ponca cause is a link.

2. Delano A. Goddard (1831–82), editor of the *Boston Advertiser*, was a strong supporter of the Poncas. In a Nov. 29, 1879, editorial commenting on Secretary Schurz's recently released annual report, Goddard remarked that the indemnity given the Ponca Indians was inadequate and the "chiefs . . . are right in protesting against it." "Unhappily," he concluded, "an Indian's word counts for little against the great men of the land."

3. A close friend of HHJ, Mrs. William Hunt, the former Louisa Dumeresq Perkins, married the noted artist William Morris Hunt (1824–79) in 1855. The Hunts lived in Germany and France and eventually settled in Boston.

4. HHJ's Dec. 11, 1879, *Tribune* letter appeared in the *Boston Evening Transcript* on Dec. 16, 1879, p. 3.

5. Martha Le Baron Goddard (d. 1888) married Delano A. Goddard in 1863 while he was working at the *Worcester Spy*. She wrote for the *Spy* and, after they moved to Boston, continued to write a weekly letter for the paper in addition to assisting her husband at the *Boston Advertiser*. She was a book reviewer and poet.

TO WILLIAM SHARPLESS JACKSON

Friday Morn.
Dec 19. 1879
405 Beacon St. [Boston]

Dearest Will

Our first snow storm! It feels as if winter were coming, but dear me — how mild & warm it is by side of the cold weather in Col[orado] last winter.

Yesterday, I worked all the morning here: went to the Pub[lic] Lib[rary] & looked over Documents on Ind[ian] Affairs till 4:30 —

. . . .

I had a most profoundly interesting afternoon in the Lib[rary] —I came out bowed down with a sense of our national disgrace: — how little has been known & still less realized of our treatment of the Indians —

This morning, the first thing that came into my mind as I waked, almost before I waked — as powers used to come in the old days — were the words "A Century of Dishonor" — as if some one spoke them aloud in the room — I cannot shake them off —! nor the impulse to write a small book, by that title, telling sharply & succinctly, the whole story of the century's record of our dealings with the Indians — would it not be a good thing & would it not help rouse the nation to a sense of the infamy with which we are covering ourselves! How does the idea strike you? — I do not mean a minute & exhaustive history, of course — that would be a years hard work — or even more — but a short history — I think I could do it in three months or less: I believe it would be a noble work to do: — to do this I should have to work at the East — of course — in *N. York* or Boston — Now if it is likely that you are going to have to be, say half of the next four months here, — is it not, on many accounts, the best possible thing for me to undertake? —

I feel *"led"* towards it. Every hour my feelings grow intenser on this subject — & I feel more & more *impelled* to work for the cause. Are there indications of a reality? or not? — How do they impress you? — If favorably — work your own plans towards arrangements which will favor it —You thought you would be likely to be in N. York five or six weeks now; after Jan. 1st — If you would then return to C[olorado] only for an interval say, a month — & then come back again to the East, it would seem all natural & right for me to remain quiet here to await you, as I am doing now. — It seems to me that what with your interests with Caleb[1] & your interests in N. York, you have about as many irons in the fire *here*, as there! — & it is clear, that so far as my "irons in the fire" are concerned both fire & irons are here! —

— All this Indian business I should have known nothing of, at home — & even if I had — could not have consulted authorities. — I can hardly tell you the praise I am getting for the manly method in which I have stated things — the quiet tone — the repression: all this is part of the inspiration which is at work on me — for it is not my temperament to work that way. —

Of course if you think it on the whole wiser for you to plan to spend a good part of the next four or five months at the East, you will prefer to shut the house up — especially as it may be that you will make so much money in the course of the winter that you will feel that we can take a three months journey — say June July & August — if I should do this great piece of work, between Jan. & May — a total change & rest — & some lighter work like letters, for the summer, would be the best possible thing —Eng. Scotland Wales & Ireland as we have so often planned. — Darling — how does this all strike you? Remember —it is only suggestions — and remember always that I wish you to decide your plans so far as is possible just as you would, if you had not me to think of — whatever it is your own preference to do — I want you to do — & I will then do my best to fall in with all — & do all I can for you in the way you wish me to. — This I think you know — but I cannot repeat it too often, for the impulse of my heart towards you, my beloved one. — In all the whole course of my life, I have never had any experiences like those of the past two months — have never felt such a sense of being in the hands of powers & events I could neither resist nor understand. — Nothing happens in any human life for *nought*:

—It may be that I am being wrought upon for some purpose, to some end that I do not dream of! — who knows! Perhaps you are, also. Perhaps we may both yet walk as a [. . .] on a plane, which we have not even seen, now. — If great wealth is to be put into your hands, that is only another new element, new force to mould us, and to enable us to mould others. — Goodbye my dearest one — I wish I could have talked all this over with you with my arms around your neck & kissing you between every two words — but if I had, I do not think you would have known any better than you do now, that I am always — first above all things —

Your own loving Peggy, —

. . . .

ALS (CoCC, WSJ I, box 1, fd. 4). Irrelevant portions of this letter have been deleted.
    1. Probably a reference to WSJ's brother Caleb.

TO THE EDITOR OF THE *NEW YORK TIMES*

[ca. December 19–20, 1879]

To the Editor of the New-York Times.

Ever since the days when traitors bickered among themselves over the parting of the raiment of Stephen,[1] disputes among thieves have been common, and thieves have been unjust to each other. It would be a strange thing if greed could ever be fair in the partition of spoils: and the dishonester the spoils the fiercer the fight always.

But it has been reserved for the Forty-sixth American Congress to give to the world the most notable spectacle yet of this kind of quarreling. In a recent debate in the House, Mr. Belford, Representative from Colorado,[2] spoke with great fervor in favor of the bill providing for the removal of the Utes from that State. The opposition which this bill had met with at the hands of some of the Representatives from the Middle and Western States seemed to arouse Mr. Belford's keenest resentment. The telegraphic report of his speech says he "turned upon the Representatives of Iowa, Illinois, Michigan, and the other Western States, and in the most impressive manner declared that every one of those States had been stolen from the Indians, and it ill befitted those Representatives to preach morality and plead for the observance of treaties with the Indians." He "strode over to the Democratic side of the chamber, and defied the Representatives of a State which had driven the Cherokees from its borders, to protest against the spoiliation of the Utes." No wonder the scene was said to be "almost dramatic." Dramatic, indeed! A very tragedy of dishonor. Did the Representative from Colorado realize—could he possibly be made to realize—the hideousness of his logic?

Year after year for nearly a century the United States Government has broken treaty after treaty with the Indian tribes. Therefore, it may as well go on breaking treaties. Ohio, Illinois, Michigan, Iowa, and the rest of the Western States have all had their share of the stolen lands, reaped their proportion of the benefit of the broken treaties. The Indians cannot help themselves. "We have in 250 years wasted their numbers from 2,500,000 down to 250,000, a waste of numbers equal to all their children born to them in the last 250 years." We have taken absolute ownership of 3,232,936,351 acres of their land, leaving to all the tribes collectively only 97,745,009 acres of ground. Hardly a State in the Union but has been "receiver" of some of these stolen goods. Shall Colorado alone be left out in this distribution of other people's possessions? If Iowa, Illinois, Michigan, Georgia, and the rest have had their millions of acres apiece, shall Colorado go without? It is not any worse to steal in 1879 than it was in 1838 or in 1800. Hold your tongues, and let Colorado have her chance. What business have retired thieves, who have got all they want, to cry "Stop thief" at the back of the young one, who is just on the point of seizing his first booty? There is a directness or consecutiveness in this chain of reasoning—a ghastly justice, too, more's the pity. But it is a justice only half just, after all; a justice which is its own executioner, slain by its own pleadings. Will no man rise up on the floor of the House of Representatives to hold up this reasoning in the light of the scorn it deserves? To show this Forty-sixth Congress the chance it has to do at least one thing toward the redemption of the perjured name of the United States Government? Because we have broken more than 400 treaties, is it, therefore, no shame to break another? Nay, it is all the greater shame. Treacheries repeated pile up infamy by a hideous geometrical ratio. The poison of baseness, of treacherousness, of cruelty is in a nation's character as in a man's, like certain poisons in the body, cumulative. Unsuspected and unobserved, the slow process of dying goes on, till the one fatal moment, after which it is too late for any cure, and death is inevitable.

H.H.

Printed in the *NY Times*, Dec. 30, 1879, p. 2, as "Fair Play among Thieves."

The following editorial note appeared at the bottom: "See minority report of Joint Committee appointed by the two houses of the Forty-fourth Congress to consider the expedience of transferring the Indian Bureau to the War Department." Originally part of the War Department, the Bureau of Indian Affairs had been transferred to the Department of the Interior in 1849. Increased Indian hostilities during and after the Civil War provoked an attempt to transfer the bureau back to military control. Humanitarian reformers, desirous of continuing civilian control, successfully prevented such a transfer. Priest, *Uncle Sam's Stepchildren: The Reformation of United States Indian Policy, 1865–1887*, devotes a chapter to this issue, pp. 15–27.

1. Probably a biblical reference to Stephen, the first Christian martyr, who was cast out of the city and stoned. The cloaks of his attackers were laid at the feet of Saul, who would later take the name of Paul.

2. A reference to James Burns Belford's speech of Dec. 18, 1879, as quoted from "'Must the Utes Go' under Debate: A Passionate Speech by Mr. Belford of Colorado—the Indians Find Able Defenders—the House Very Much Roused by the Debate," *Tribune*, Dec. 19, 1879, p. 1. See also "The Ute Indians: The Proposed Removal to Another Reservation," *Boston Advertiser*, Dec. 19, 1879, p. 1.

Belford (1837–1910) practiced law and served in the Indiana state legislature before his appointment in 1870 as associate justice of the Supreme Court of Colorado. He served Colorado in the United States Congress, 1876–85, and then retired to practice law in Denver.

TO WHITELAW REID

Boston
Dec. 20. 1879
Sat Eve

Dear Mr. Reid,

If ever you want anything done that I can do, ask me! — I was grateful to you for your first Editorial note[1] calling attention to my "questions" but how much more grateful I am for this second one,[2] — pointing out, as I could not do, for myself, the feebleness and sophistry of Schurz's reply.

I am profoundly flattered by his thinking it worth while. I have hardly dared to hope that I could do anything for the Indians; but now I begin to hope I can and I do not mean to "let go" so long as there is a stone left to turn.

I am boiling over with wrath at our Colorado Representative Belford: — will you not write an Editorial on him — or may I? What a subtle bareness in his logic! — what an infamy to go on the records of our Congress.

My authority for that statement about the Indian's flock of sheep was Mr. Leeds, Ex-head clerk of the Ind. Bureau removed by Hayt. — Is it worth while to make a short paragraph of a few points in the Secretarys letter? — I will enclose one — print it if you can & think best. —

Don't you mean also to give the Poncas an Editorial? Just think how it would help them. —

Yours truly
Helen Jackson

Care:
Roberts Bros. Boston.
P.S. Sunday morn.
Dear Mr. Reid — Before I went to bed last night, I was forced to write these three papers. — I suppose I am infatuated to think that you will want them; but I shall be glad if you do: and if you do not, is it asking too much to ask you to return them to me, the two Editorials. Of course the reply to the Secretary cannot be made elsewhere than in the Tribune.[3] I have telegraphed to you for twenty five copies of his letter — & shall mail it with every copy I mail of my own. He has simply doubled the value of my paper to the cause of the Indians. — In case you print this reply, I want twenty five copies of that also and I will mail all three together, to some of the prominent men in Washington — N. York — Boston — & a few country ministers. —

I am "boiling down" my article for the March Scribners into seven pages. — It is to be called "The United States Wards" or the United States

"Government Wards" — which is better? — Take a minute to think, and tell me. —

H.J.

ALS (DLC, Reid Papers).

Reid wrote the following on the letter: "Mr. Hassard = What is your judgment about this? Incline to print Helen Hunt's reply to Schurz at once, but don't feel like letting her into the editorial columns. W.R." Hassard wrote: "I would print the reply to Schurz; but I think the editorials are too spasmodic. JH."

1. A reference to an item in "The News This Morning," *Tribune*, Dec. 15, 1879, p. 4, which alerted readers to HHJ's Dec. 11, 1879, letter. Reid ended his editorial: "The record of Indian wrongs and oppressions which this Nation is steadily making, day by day, will make hideous reading for posterity."

2. "The string of pungent questions" presented by "H.H." had disturbed Schurz, Reid wrote in his *Tribune* editorial on Dec. 19, p. 4, as he called attention to the secretary's response, which was silent on several points raised by HHJ.

3. The *Tribune*, on Dec. 28, printed HHJ's reply to Schurz's Dec. 19 letter. Although Dec. 23 was printed at the bottom of this reply, it is apparent from this Dec. 20 letter to Reid, and her Dec. 21 letter to Warner, that she had already sent her response to Reid. Why Dec. 23 was printed on the bottom of her letter is unknown; possibly the date was misread in the Tribune office during typesetting.

TO WILLIAM HAYES WARD

Boston
Dec. 20 — 1879

Dear Mr. Ward —

Mr. Goddard of the Daily Advertiser says, that Kembles paper[1] in the main *substantiates* Standing Bear's story — I think so too! — and if I had time would show it. — I am sorry you did not read it more closely & compare it with the other. If you had, you would not have written that Editorial note. —[2]

I have written to Tibbles, and asked him to work up a few words, the points touched on — & I am sure you will not refuse to print it. Because Standing Bear is an Indian, is no reason he should be called a liar in public print, & no chance given him to prove he is not! — I know of few things proving more stingingly the feeling in even kind men towards the Indian than the fact that Kemble did not hesitate to write, & you did not hesitate to print, the words "falsehoods" &c, &c. in this connection. Kemble would not have used them, nor you printed them of a white man who would bring a suit! — There are ten

witnesses for Standing Bear — all the chiefs told the *same* story — If you will
only go & see Bright Eyes, you will believe it.

Yrs. ever —

H.J.

P.S. Sat. Eve.—

I have just seen Sec. Schurz' telegraphic reply to me![3] I am almost wild with
delight — Is the man a blockhead? Does he suppose he has helped his cause?
As Whitelaw Reid says in his sarcastic Editorial Note

How many American people will be satisfied with an explanation like
that.—[4]

For fear you have not yet read my paper in the Trib. I enclose it to you.

For the statement about the sheep I had the authority of a former Head
Clerk in the Ind. Bureau! — Mr. Leeds — You see the Sec. does not define
what constitutes an "Agency flock of sheep." — nor alludes to the fact that any
Agent can "empower" any white man or men, to cut wood &c. —

This is all delightfull — will all help. —

I am much grieved about this article[5] — you will not *let* anything delay it
again will you? And do give it a place on the front page? I shall want 25 copies
of it — to send to Washington & elsewhere. I am not going to "let go" yet. My
article in Scribner's is going to be scorching.

ALS (CSmH, HHJ MSS, HM 13977).

1. In "The Story of the Poncas: By Col. E. C. Kemble," *Independent* (Dec. 18,
1879): 4–5, Kemble, who had been in charge of the Ponca removal, presented his
version. He described Standing Bear's story as "fiction, invented to cover their bad
faith and shortcomings."

Kemble's letter was of wide interest. In a lengthy front-page article, "Our Poncas'
Claim: The Inspector Kemble and Secretary Schurz's Positions," the *Niobrara Pioneer*
on Jan. 6, 1880, quoted from the *Springfield Republican* review of the letter. Also, a
Boston Advertiser, Dec. 20, 1879, p. 2, editorial note concluded: "It is due to Colonel
Kemble to say that his letter is written in good spirit, and that he confesses that, as it
has turned out, the removal of the Poncas was a grievous wrong."

2. In the Dec. 18, 1879, *Independent*, p. 15, Ward described Kemble as a "trustworthy Christian gentleman" sympathetic to the attempt to regain Ponca land—a
reference, no doubt, to Kemble's membership on the Protestant Episcopal Church's
Domestic Missions Board. Most early Indian inspectors were chosen from the
membership of various denominational mission boards as part of President Grant's
attempt to reform Indian policy.

3. "Mr. Schurz on Indian Affairs: The Secretary Replies to the Letter of H. H. in
the Tribune," *Tribune*, Dec. 19, 1879, p. 1, was the telegraphic response to HHJ's Dec.
11 letter.

4. Reid ended his Dec. 19 editorial with this statement.

5. Ward published her next article, "The Massacre of the Cheyennes," in the Jan. 1, 1880, issue, pp. 2–3. If this is the article she is referring to, he did not print it on the front page as she requested.

TO CHARLES DUDLEY WARNER

Boston
Sunday.
Dec. 21. 1879

Dear Mr. Warner—

What glory to have Schurz answer me by telegraph — I had hardly hoped I could do anything for the Indians. Now I see that I can. And was not Reid's Editorial note superb?

" 'How many American people' will be satisfied with an explanation like this"! —

I have ordered 25 copies of the Sec.s letter & shall mail it with my answer everywhere. It simply doubles the value of mine. — I have also sent Reid a short paper "a few points in the Sec.s reply to the letter of H.H."[1] — which I hope he will print. —

Kemble also is out with a letter, which Mr. Goddard says "while it seems to deny, really substantiates Standing Bear's story" —

I shall be found with "Indians" engraved on my brain when I am dead. — A fire has been kindled within me, which will never go out. —

What I want to do now is to write a little book — simply & *curtly* a *Record* of our broken Treaties— & call it "*A Century of Dishonor*" —

If Mr. Jackson is going to be half of the time for the next four months at the East, I can stay here the whole of it, if he is willing, & do this work — & get the book out in May. —Will it not be worth while? —

You understand — no sentiment — no prattle of suggestion — a bare record of facts in fewest possible words. I never so much as dreamed what we had been guilty of. —

Print the Sec.s reply & my letter — & call attention to the weakness of his phrases — do. — & "go for" that scoundrel Belford with his "logic of infamy." I'll make you a present of that title. —

Love to Mrs. Warner —

Yours always aff[ectionately] —
H.J.

Roberts Bros. —
till the 27th, — after that — 25 W. 37th St. New York

ALS (CtHT-W, Warner Collection).
1. A reference to HHJ's Dec. 23 letter to the *Tribune,* below.

TO THE EDITOR OF THE *TRIBUNE*

[December 23, 1879]

To the Editor of The Tribune.

SIR: *First*—The Secretary does not say that the reservation trader would give the Omaha Indians the market prices for their wheat last Summer. If he would, why did the Indians carry their wheat to Sioux City to sell? And why was the trader informed that if he trusted the Omahas on account of their wheat "he would have to rely entirely on their honor to secure his pay."

Second—The Secretary says: "It will scarcely be considered a hardship when persons duly empowered by the Government cut hay on Indian reservations or use the products of the soil that are not used by the Indians for the use of the Indian agencies or military posts." To whom does the "soil" of the Indian reservations belong?—to the United States Government, or to the Indians to whom it has been "ceded and relinquished" in consideration of other lands by them given up? The Secretary farther says: "Admitting that white men do cut down wood on some of these reservations and sell it to steamboats on the Missouri River—but the white men doing this have to steal it in order to get it. The law does not authorize them to take it." Suppose the agent who is "duly empowered by the Government" sees fit to connive with the white men who cut down this wood? The law makes it impossible for the Indian to interfere. He has "no proprietorship in the wood."

Third—The Secretary says that it is not true that if an Indian on a Reservation raises a flock of sheep he cannot sell the wool, neither can the agent sell the wool, and give the money to the Indian. The money must be turned into the United States Treasury. This statement in the letter of H.H. was made on the authority of a former head clerk of the Indian Bureau. The Secretary says that "when a flock of sheep belongs to the agency," the money for the wool of such a flock is "accounted for to the Government" by the agent, under the head of "miscellaneous receipts," and paid into the Treasury. This would be more satisfactory if it had been explained how and "when" flocks of sheep "belong to the agency," and if it is even specified in treaties giving Reservations to Indians, that the Government reserves the right of sheep raising on tracts therein included.

Fourth—The Secretary says that "H.H. should have added" to her question: "How many American people know that an Indian cannot be legally prosecuted or punished for an offence committed against an Indian?" the statement that "this Department has been endeavoring for a considerable time to induce Congress to pass an act putting Indians under the protection as well as under the restraints of law." Why should H.H. have stated that? What has it to do with the present fact to which H.H.'s question pointed?

Fifth—The Secretary says that "H.H. ought to have added" to the account of the sufferings of the Utes when their yearly supplies were held one whole year in a storehouse in Rawlings, Wyoming, and refused to them, though they were literally starving, "that the failure to supply the Utes arose from the delinquency of a transportation contractor, who has since been prosecuted by this Department, tried, convicted, and sentenced to the Penitentiary, where he is now serving his time." Why ought H.H. "to have added" this? What difference does this make to the Utes who starved? The statement of the Utes' sufferings was not made to show that the Government does not prosecute dishonest contractors, when it happens to find them out, but to show that the Utes had had in years past some "just cause of complaint." So, also, in regard to the arrears of money said to be due from our Government to the Utes; and if Senator Teller's significantly-worded resolution of inquiry "whether any money be due to the Utes?" brings out an open statement of the truth in regard to the pecuniary relations of the United States Government with the tribe, the information will be indeed "useful" to all interested in these matters.

Sixth—The Secretary says that "the present Secretary of the Interior and Commissioners of Indian Affairs were the first persons to bring the wrongs inflicted on the Poncas to public notice." They were among the first. The first, however, was A. F. Tibbles,[1] and Messrs. Webster and Poppleton, of Omaha, when they applied for a writ of habeas Corpus to rescue Standing Bear and his band from the United States soldiers, who held them under arrest. The letter of the present Secretary of the Interior, published in the *Boston Daily Advertiser*, of August 23, 1879, was one of the next noticeable instrumentalities in bringing the "wrongs inflicted on the Poncas to public notice." And one of the most noticeable statements in this letter was the following:

> The buildings of the Poncas, which consisted of log cabins on the margin of the river, were turned over to the Spotted Tail Indians.[2] There never were more than sixty of these cabins, and many of them had been washed away by the rain before the Poncas left.

In this connection it will be "useful" to quote from the official documents of the Department of Interior the following statement:

In May last, D. H. Jerome,[3] of the Board of Indian Commissioners, Lieutenant-Colonel Lugenbeel,[4] 1st Infantry, U.S.A., and I. H. Hammond,[5] Superintendent of Indian Affairs for Dakota Territory, were appointed a commission to select locations for the new Red Cloud and Spotted Tail Agencies. For the former, the site chosen is the Yellow Medicine and Missouri Rivers. For the latter, the old Ponca Reserve was decided upon, where the Agency dwellings, storehouses, 150 Indian houses, and 500 acres of cultivated fields, left vacant by the Poncas, offer special advantages for present quarters.—(Report of Indian Commission[er], 1877, p. 18).

Boston, Dec. 23, 1879.   H.H.

Printed in the *Tribune,* Dec. 28, 1879, p. 5, as "The Wrongs of the Indians: 'H.H.' Takes Up Mr. Schurz's Reply: A Few Noticeable Points in the Statement of the Secretary of the Interior." This letter was a rebuttal to Schurz's comments in the Dec. 19, 1879, *Tribune.* A Dec. 30, 1879, *Hartford Courant* editorial called attention to HHJ's letter by quoting it briefly.

1. A. F. Tibbles should read T. H. Tibbles, another example of HHJ's difficult handwriting.

2. Spotted Tail Indians were those Sioux (Lakotas) living at the Spotted Tail agency. Spotted Tail (1823–81), recognized by 1866 as head chief of the Brulé Sioux, became a proponent of peace following a year's detainment at Fort Leavenworth. In 1878 he and his followers settled down at the Spotted Tail agency at Rosebud Creek.

3. David H. Jerome (1829–96) served on the Board of Indian Commissioners, 1876–81. He was governor of Michigan, 1881–83, and was appointed to the Cherokee Commission in 1889, authorized to negotiate for lands in Indian Territory. Ultimately more than fifteen million acres were acquired with his assistance.

4. Pinkney Lugenbeel (d. 1886), who graduated from the military academy in 1835, served as a lieutenant colonel in the First Regiment, 1867–80, at which time he became a colonel with the Fifth Infantry.

5. It is not I. H. Hammond but John H. Hammond who was appointed as superintendent of the Dakota Superintendency on April 5, 1878.

TO WHITELAW REID

Boston,

Dec. 26 — 1879

Dear Mr. Reid,

I don't believe you often receive a letter from the writer of a rejected article saying that he thinks you were quite right in rejecting it, do you? — very well. You have such a letter now — On reading over my little papers, I only wonder I did not know better than to think you would say them editorially. I must say such things as these under my own name if at all: — my "belief" is "too strong," no doubt for any newspapers policy (or perhaps propriety?) — but it is not "too strong" for a motive power of work — with one any less strong, I would sink down disheartened.

When I come back to New York, I shall hope to have a long talk with you again about these matters. — Things are pouring in before me from all sides, since that letter.[1] —

Of course you understood that that article in reply to Schurz,[2] I did not send to be printed under my initials — only as a communication, either without signature — or with any you choose — or, if you only would — as the Tribune's own comments on Schurz's letter. —

Yours truly,
Helen Jackson

ALS (DLC, Reid Papers).
1. Probably a reference to her Dec. 11 *Tribune* letter, above.
2. A reference to her Dec. 23 *Tribune* letter, above.

TO THE EDITOR OF THE *TRIBUNE*

[December 26, 1879]

To the Editor of The Tribune.

SIR: "The Utes must work for a living or get out of the way." —*General Sherman,*[1] *at the New England Dinner in New York December 22.*

In the official report of the Indian Bureau for the year 1877 can be read the following statistics:

In the year 1877 the White River Utes owned 1,250 head of cattle, 20 mules, and 3,000 horses. They sold $15,000 worth of skins and furs, they built 20 rods of fence: they cut 30 cords of wood; they sawed 57,000 feet of lumber; they cut 10 tons of hay; they raised 25 bushels of vegetables; they are recorded as earning 66 per cent of their subsistence.

The Utes at the Los Pinos Agency[2] owned 100 head of cattle, 25 mules and 6,000 horses; they sold $6,000 worth of skins and furs; they cut 100 cords of wood; they sawed 12,816 feet of lumber; they raised 200 bushels of vegetables, 20 bushels of oats and barley and 20 bushels of wheat; they broke 20 new acres of land; they are reported as earning 45 percent of their subsistence.

The Southern Utes are entered on this table, "showing agricultural implements, stock, productions and sources of subsistence of the different Indian tribes," as earning the whole 100 per cent of subsistence by "hunting, root digging and fishing." No issue of Government rations whatever.

"Work for a living or get out of the way."

H. H.

Printed in the *Tribune*, Dec. 29, 1879, p. 1, as "The Utes Must Work."

1. William Tecumseh Sherman (1820–91) served in the Mexican American and Civil Wars and commanded the Division of the Missouri, which included the Great Plains, 1866–69. Critical of the Bureau of Indian Affairs, he favored the return of Indian control to the Department of War. Until his retirement in 1883, Sherman continued to influence western military policy.

Sherman's quote is from a speech reprinted on the editorial page of the Dec. 24, 1879, *Boston Advertiser*, p. 2.

2. The northern Ute bands were represented by the White River Agency, while the three southern bands belonged to the Los Pinos Agency.

TO WILLIAM SHARPLESS JACKSON

Boston. Dec. 26, 1879

Dearest Will —

Your letter of Dec. 20 is at hand. It made me feel blue at first — but I am so sure that your sense of justice is strong — that I gird up my loins with the hope of yet influencing you to feel warmly with me on this Indian business.

First I will answer some of the sentences in your letter. —You say "I am sorry you are printing anything in Tibbles Book". — I can't imagine what you mean — Is it my bad writing which has given you that idea! — I have not written a word in Tibbles Book. — I have written a notice of it, which was published in the Eve. Post — & has waked up that paper so that it has had two good Editorials since on the general subject. —

2*d* You say I am "going open mouthed after the Secretary of the Interior!" —

If you *read* my "Questions" I dont see how you could say such a thing. I have never so much as mentioned his name! — I have never made the slightest attack on the *Dept.* even! — It is only on the laws — *the Government* position towards the Indian. — If Sec. Schurz & Hayt were angels, they could not have the Indians properly treated, while the laws are as they are. —

You say *I* am "berating" him as a worthless scoundrel! — I am strongly inclined to think he is a dishonest — or at any rate a dishonest *minded* man: — an expression which he uses in an Official Document given to the Country at large is proper matter of comment & criticism: — I do not think an honest minded man would have used that expression.

"Mere vindication of a right to a title to a piece of land." — but I treated of it only in reference to the Poncas — & I have never yet written one word bordering on a "personal attack" on the Sec. — & I never shall. Merely as a matter of policy I should not — & certainly as a matter of taste.

So far from the Tribune's not doing anything about the Indian question —
they have published two of the sharpest possible Editorial notes first endorsing
my paper — & then holding up the Secretary's reply to the ridicule it deserved,
and asking "How many American People will be satisfied with such
explanations as these!"

You say

"Now will you & Tibbles take charge of the Indian Bureau? You & Tibbles
would make a nice mess of it if you had the matter in charge"! — Do you think
that is fair argument? logical? —Because I am not able — as I most certainly
am not, to "outline" or even *conceive* of a proper & detailed system for the
management of 250,000 Indians — is that any reason why I should not be
qualified to protest against *broken* treaties — cruel massacres — & unjust laws.
— A woman does not need to be a statesman, to know that it is base to break
promises — to oppress the helpless — ! —

You say "for myself I am giving no attention to the Indian Question." —
That is really the secret of all your feeling about it. You feel much as *I* felt four
months ago. — If you had read the evidence which I have read, *mostly in
Official* Reports in this last month, I believe you would feel more strongly even
than I do! — & above all, you would *never* say such a thing as you say in this
letter[.]

"The Indian will never get my sympathy until he will work honestly &
industriously for a living, which I have but little faith of his ever doing." — That
is true of *only a* part of the Indians — & not of *any single* tribe that has had any
thing *like* a chance! — How much would *you* work, if Government could pull
you up at any minute & carry you to Indian Territory! — if men could *steal* all
you owned & you couldn't sue them? —

Spite of this, there are *dozens* of tribes who are working —some who are
even manufacturing — the *Choctaws*[1] took a prize for cotton last year! — I tell
you Will when I get a lot of such sharp salient *facts* as these, all collated & set
together, you will be more astonished than you have ever been yet. I am
incredulous myself, all the while, as I come on fact after fact about these
people. —

You say I have got the reputation of being "excited" on this matter, — I *am*
stirred to the core with a great & solemn indignation — not against any *man*, or
men — in particular — but against the whole position & action of our Government — for one whole Century! & I profoundly believe that the time has come
when the whole thing is going to be *righted* — not this year — or perhaps next
— but a new feeling is "in the air" — & new agencies are at work — & the
people are going to be reached. — Congress can right the thing — slowly —

but it can be done, — the only thing that is clear to me, is that nothing ever can be right, for the Indian, so long as he has no protection of the law, & the glaring inconsistency of bringing him to trial for *murder*, in courts which would refuse to try a white man for murder of *him*, is grotesque. —

You say "keep cool! keep cool" — right my darling — that is just what I *do* keep, my *brain*. Mr. Hale² — Gen. Armstrong,³ Mr. Goddard — *all* said I had not written a word a "cool headed man might not have written"! — Mr. Hale said, when he read my article, he leaned back in his chair, & said aloud "Nunc dimittis," (that is the beginning of the Latin chant "now let me depart") —

Gen. Armstrong wants me to come to Hampton, & says he will take me to Washington if I want to go there! — Of course, a paper written about Hampton, showing how well the Indians *work & learn*, would have great importance now. —

Dear heart — by virtue of your organization, you ought to be as strong for *justice* to the Indians, as you were for *justice* to the Negro. — Don't let the wicked & selfish atmosphere of the present Colorado talk about the Utes, warp your native instinct for justice. —

I can't write a word, or words, with any heart, if you are not going to feel *with* me, in it all. — & I do feel as earnest & solemn a "call" as ever a human being felt to — work for this cause. —

—So much in re Indians!

—My cold is better today. I can speak aloud, though in notes like a crow's. — Dr. Nichols⁴ thinks I may be able to go to N. York on Tues. — or Wed. — if the weather is good — I am hoping you will not arrive till Thursday — I know you will be so disappointed not to find me here — & above all to find that I am ill. —

I am very apprehensive that I am not going to be free from this bronchial trouble at all, this winter. It is an ugly customer. — You remember I told you last winter it was a serious thing, to have four attacks of almost bronchitis one after the other. —

I hope very much that there will be an apartment for us at either the Berkeley or Grosvenor. — If I am to be shut up in the house most of the time, it will make it much less intolerable, if I can have a pleasant sitting room — & in fact, it will be almost a necessity for my work, if I go on with this Indian research & writing for I shall see a great many people with whom I do not want to talk in public parlors. —

I shall see among others the wife & daughter of a *former* Agent of the White River Utes. Mr. Hale has sent their letters to me. — They are going to be present at the trial of those Utes they say, *whenever* it is, to see that the

Interpreter *tells the truth* (What the Utes say!) — Suppose you & I were to be
tried for life in Russia without one English speaking person near us, except a
hostile Interpreter! — and what a token of real good in even those poor Utes,
that these women who lived among them are eager to come forward for their
help now.[5] —

Goodbye dearest one — I do hope you will not be long in N. York without
me. — Love to Mrs. Botta & the Prof. —

Your own Peggy. —

. . . .

ALS (CoCC, WSJ I, box 1, fd. 7). The latter portion of this letter, about HHJ
buying clothing for her husband, has been deleted.

　　1. The Choctaws originally lived in the Southeast but were removed in the 1830s
and resettled in Indian Territory.

　　2. Edward Everett Hale (1822–1909), a noted writer, served as minister of the
South Congregational Church in Boston for forty-three years.

　　3. Samuel Chapman Armstrong (1839–93) led black troops during the Civil War,
was appointed an agent of the Freedmen's Bureau, and founded the Hampton Normal
and Industrial Institute in 1868. Hampton Institute not only educated black students
but educated Indian students from 1879 to 1923.

　　4. Dr. Charles Fessenden Nichols (b. 1846) graduated with a medical degree
from Harvard. He practiced homeopathic medicine in Boston and edited the *New
England Medical Gazette*. He was friendly not only with Jackson but with other
reformers such as Wendell Phillips and Edward Everett Hale.

　　5. A commission established by Secretary Schurz, who was eager to achieve a
peaceful solution following Ute hostilities, met at Los Pinos Agency to examine
witnesses during Nov. and Dec. 1879. Ultimately twelve Utes were charged with
murder and kidnapping and ordered to face trial. Only one was held in custody for a
year at Fort Leavenworth; the remainder were never arrested. In early 1880 the White
River Utes agreed to move to the Uintah Reservation in Utah, while the rest of the
Utes moved to southwestern Colorado. See Utley, *Frontier Regulars: The United States
Army and the Indian, 1866–1891*, pp. 339–42.

TO WHITELAW REID

Boston
Sat AM
Dec 27 — 1879

Dear Mr. Reid,

　　If you use the extracts I sent you last night in regard to the Utes,[1] please
omit the last quotation of the "Southern Utes." — I see on studying the detailed
report, that it was a new agency — only just then organized — & though the

Indians for whom it was provided, must have been self supporting — up to that
date, they were "wild Indians" in N. Mexico chiefly — and it was stupid to put
it down in the Tabular page as carrying 100 per cent of subsistance — But I do
not wish to leave a loophole of attack on a single assertion. So I will say nothing
about the "Southern Utes" — only the "Los Pinos" — and "White River". —
But I would like to add to the paper the enclosed sheet. —

Yours truly
Helen Jackson

ALS (DLC, Reid Papers).
1. HHJ is referring to her Dec. 26 letter to the *Tribune*, above.

TO WILLIAM SHARPLESS JACKSON

Mon. Morning.
Dec. 29. 1879 —

Dearest Will —

Your line of Dec. 23*rd* is just at hand. I am partly relieved — & partly sorry
to hear that you will not be in N. York till tomorrow, for I was depending on
your Decision as to what to do about coming to Mrs. Bottas. — I hope you will
get there tomorrow, & telegraph to me immediately. I do not believe I can
come any way before Thursday. —

I have not the least idea of touching on the question of the Ute Massacre.[1] I
know nothing about it. — But the Question of the U.S. keeping its treaties with
the Utes is another thing. — — & You are entirely mistaken in saying that the
White River Utes had no interest in that money — if Gov. P[itkin][2] told you so,
it only shows that he like everybody else does not take trouble to investigate.

I have the Articles of the Treaty here! — in the Official Rep. of Ind.
Com[missioner] for 1873. — & the whole account of the Council, — Meetings
opened by prayer every day by Brunot[3] the Com[missioner] — a good man I
don't doubt. — & the poor Utes so encouraged because he "asked the Great
Spirit to help!" —

The treaty is with the Chiefs of the "Confederated bands of the Ute
Nation" — "the Tabeguache, Muache, Capote, Weeminuche, Yampa, Grand
River & Uintah bands of the Ute Nation." — of these, the "Grand River,
Yampa, & Uintah bands are at the *White River* Agency & the others at *Los
Pinos*"! — So much for Governor Pitkin's knowledge of facts!

Dear you may be sure of one thing that I am not writing — & shall not
write *one word* as a sentimentalist! Statistical Records — verbatim reports

officially authenticated, are what I wish to get before the American people: —
& are all which are needed, to rouse public sentiment. — The ignorance of
everybody on the subject is simply astonishing — my own included — till six
weeks ago, & even now I am only beginning. —

Molly[4] writes that there is a possible chance of an apartment there — for us
— & I am so delighted — that would seem _home_. — Mean time however — the
rooms are engaged for Wed. at the Brevoort — so we can go there. Goodbye —
Just wait till I kiss you. —

Your loving Peggy. —

Article 5*th* of the Brunot Treaty with the Utes (all the tribes enumerated) —
All the provisions of the treaty of 1868 not altered by this agreement shall
continue in force & the following words from article two of said treaty, viz "The
United States now, _solemnly agree_ that no persons except those herein authorized to do so, & except such officials agents & employees of the Govt. as may
be authorized to enter upon Indian Reservations in discharge of duties
enjoined & by law shall _ever be permitted_ to pass over settle upon or reside in the
territory described in the article," except as herein otherwise worded are hereby
expressly reaffirmed —

ALS (CoCC, WSJ I, box 1, fd. 7).

1. Appointed White River agent in 1878, Nathan C. Meeker (1817–79)
attempted to introduce extensive agricultural practices despite strong objections
from the Indians. His call for military support brought troops, who were attacked
upon entering the reservation. Then the Utes killed Meeker and eight others and
took Meeker's wife and daughters captive. For his daughter's account, see "The
Story of Josephine Meeker: The Massacre of the Agency and the Adventures of the
Women and Children—Scenes in Camp and on the Trail—Their Treatment While in
Captivity—Graphic Pictures of Indian Camp Life," _Boston Advertiser_, Oct. 31, 1879,
p. 2.

2. Frederick W. Pitkin (1837–86), a native of Connecticut, moved to Colorado for
his health. He served as governor of the state, 1878–82. He later moved to Pueblo,
where he practiced law.

3. Felix R. Brunot (1820–98) was a Pittsburgh industrialist and philanthropist. In
1869 he was appointed to the Board of Indian Commissioners, shortly thereafter
becoming board chairman. For the next five years he visited western tribes, including
the Utes, and wrote articles and letters bringing the plight of the Indians to public
attention.

4. Molly (Mary Walbridge) was the widow of Washington Hunt, former New York
governor and brother of HHJ's first husband, Edward Bissell Hunt. See HHJ to
Whipple, Oct. 29, 1880, below.

TO WHITELAW REID

Boston,
Dec. 30. 1879

Dear Mr. Reid,

I see I was too late with my change of the paragraph. "Work for a living,"
&c. — also with my request about signature. —Never mind: — only this —

If anybody from Washington telegraphs that I'm an ignorant fool to have
said that the Utes at the Southern Ute Agency earned 100 per ct. of their living
— won't you please make a short & clear little Editorial note stating that before
the paragraph in question was printed I had sent to the Tribune a correction —
saying that I had discovered by the Agency Reports that I had made the
mistake?

This, not for me! but that the weight of what I am going to keep on saying
may not be lessened by my having made a blunder.

I can't imagine why the figures should have been put under the heading as
they were, in the Table: — It would mislead anyone not studying with great
care: — no — anyone not used to statistical tables of that sort. — I did study
with great care. My one dread is of making any accusation that is not fortified
by unanswerable evidence.

Senator Teller has sent me some valuable Doc[uments] & I am going to
prepare a short statement of the treaties broken, with the Utes — & the
Reports from them for the last six years.[1] —

I am looking day after day after day with "hope deferred," for your ringing
Editorial on the general Indian question. When I think what an almost incalculable power you would have, to mould public sentiment — & influence the
action of Congress — nay of the Supreme Court too, — I wonder why the
Lord lets you keep silent.

Yours truly
Helen Jackson

P.S. And moreover — the bands of wild Utes which were to be collected at
that Southern Ute Agency must have been earning their own living such as
it was, for they were said to be "wild," moving about down in New Mexico
chiefly —

— What the govt wanted to get them together for but then I don't know
unless to make a new place for an A[gent] —

ALS (DLC, Reid Papers).
1. See HHJ to the Editor of the *Tribune*, Jan. 2, 1880, below.

TO THE EDITOR OF THE *TRIBUNE*

[January 2, 1880]

To the Editor of The Tribune.

SIR: There might have been added to the old fable of the wolf in sheep's clothing a supplement, setting forth how there came a time when the wolf had grown so big that no sheepskin would have covered him; and when he tried to get into one, both sheep and shepherds laughed at his efforts. This is suggested by the report from Washington that the United States' last treaty with the Utes is now to be "examined carefully," to see whether any one of its articles requires the tribe to give up for punishment murderers of white men. Why does the Government concern itself about there being or not being any such provision in this treaty? What obligation does the Government recognize in any treaty with Indians? Has the Government fulfilled one article of its treaties with the Utes? Why this masquerade in sheepskin?

Some extracts from the United States' last treaty with the Utes will not be out of place here. The treaty was made in 1873, between Felix R. Brunot, Commissioner for the United States, and the chiefs, headmen and men of the "confederated bands of the Ute Nation." By this treaty the Utes sold back to the United States a part of the reservation heretofore conveyed to them by the United States. The bounds of this reservation were mentioned, and a special stipulation was added that "if any part of the Uncompahgre Park shall be found to extend south of the north line of said described country, the same is not intended to be included therein, and is hereby reserved and retained as a portion of the Ute Reservation." The treaty says that the Indians shall have the right to hunt on these lands "so long as the game lasts and the Indians are at peace with the white people."

The third article is:

The United States agree to set apart and hold as a perpetual trust for the Ute Indians a sum of money, or its equivalent in bonds, which shall be sufficent to produce the sum of $25,000 per annum; which sum of $25,000 per annum shall be disbursed or invested at the discretion of the President, or as he may direct, for the use and benefit of the Indians, annually forever.

The fifth article of this treaty is:

All the provisions of the Treaty of 1868 not altered by this agreement shall continue in force, and the following words from Article II, of said treaty, viz: "The United States now solemnly agree that no persons except those herein authorized to do so, and except such officers, agents and employees of the Government as may be authorized to enter upon Indian reservations in discharge of duties enjoined by law, shall ever be permitted to pass over, settle upon or reside in the territory" described in the article, "except as herein otherwise provided," are hereby expressly reaffirmed, except so far as they applied to the country herein relinquished.

The council at which this treaty was made lasted seven days. The meetings were opened each day with prayer by Mr. Brunot, and the Indians were much impressed by the fact that the "Great Spirit" had been asked "to help."

The Commissioners say in their report:

The only advantages we had in the negotiations were the oft-tested friendship of the Utes for the whites, and their earnest desire to do all that would in their opinion tend to perpetuate and strengthen a reciprocal feeling by the whites for them, and the fact that not a single white person was present during the council except those connected with the Commission or the Agency.

The country ceded contains about four millions of acres, and is rich in mineral deposits.

The chiefs were unwilling to sell any of their land, and they refused to give up a rod of farming land. They said:

We will soon need all the farming land on our reservation, as the time is not far distant when the Utes will have to give up hunting and take to farming and stock-raising as the whites do.

They also said that the lines of their reservation were being changed continually and had not been adhered to since the last treaty. Said Ouray:[1]

It is changing them all the time, taking a little now and a little again, that makes trouble. You said you do not know anything in regard to these lines (the old ones), and it may be the same in regard to lines you make. Thus do many men talk about it to us; they say they are going to have the lines as they want, whether the Utes like it or not. It is common talk, every one tells it to the Utes. * * * With you it is different. You talk in the name of the Great Spirit. We understand that, and think it right and ought to have great weight.

(All the above extracts are from the official report of the Commissioner of Indian Affairs for 1876.) In the same report we read on page 94:

The fact that for two years the presence of miners on the reservation was well known, and that the frequent complaints of the Indians were disregarded, led them to distrust the promises of the Government.

Also:

> The southern boundary line of the reservation was also a considerable distance north of the natural boundary line which the Indians assert was given them at the time of the Treaty of 1868, and that the mistake was not theirs is probable, from the fact that an actual survey located in New-Mexico, some distance below the northern boundary line, towns that had been prior to it claimed as being in Colorado.

Secretary Schurz says, in the *NEW-YORK TRIBUTE* of December 18, that he found "that Indians are very well acquainted with the laws of the United States touching them particularly, and with the treaties made with their tribes."

We have then, from official records, the fact that from 1868 to 1873 the Government had failed to keep its promise to keep white men off the Ute Reservation, and that the Utes had considered themselves cheated by the Government in the matter of boundary lines.

In 1874 we find the agents of the Utes reporting that they are much dissatisfied because of the nonfulfilment of the terms of the treaties. In 1875 dissatisfaction is on the increase. Settlers are pushing in on these lands, and they have received "no payment for the lands given up," for which they were to have had, it will be remembered, $25,000 annually forever. The agent of the Los Pinos Agency says, in 1875:[2]

> It is possible that even now, two years after the cession of land was agreed to, an offer of the delayed compensation may pacify the Indians and make them contented to surrender what they much value. It is more likely that a year ago such an offer would have answered the purpose. It has been impossible for me to give the Utes any reason for this long delay on the part of the Government which they consider satisfactory. They now declare that they will not receive any compensation till the boundary line is settled.

In 1876 the agent writes:

> I am not at all surprised that the Utes still feel very much aggrieved in regard to the Brunot agreement, both because it is not what they understand it to be at the time (the boundaries fixed by it including much farming as well as mining land), and because they received no pay under it, while the country ceded has become occupied more and more, and now contains several thousand white people.

In 1877 the agent[3] writes again of still further trouble from squatters on the reservation. The Uncompahgre Park, which it was especially stipulated by the treaty should belong to the Utes, was being settled by white men. The Government ordered them off, but did not enforce its order. From the White River Agency the agent writes:[4]

> No clothing, blanket, tent or implement or utensil of any kind, has been issued at this agency for nearly two years; no flour, except once, fifteen pounds to a family, since last May (three months). In addition to the usual proportion of their subsistence which the Indians provide for themselves—66 per cent—they have had this deficiency to make up.

In 1878 the Government wished to have some more of the Utes' land, and another Commission was sent out to treat with them. The report of this Commission is full of humiliating statements:

> (The Indians) insisted that they had been overreached in the agreement of 1873; that they intended to sell nothing but the minerals; that the Government had not complied with the agreement; that they understood that a large sum of money was to be paid to the Utes yearly, and that so far as they were concerned they had received nothing. They absolutely declined to go into a general council, said they would not go to White River to live, did not wish to part with their present possessions, and asked that the Government should pay what it had promised.

These were the Muache, Capote and Weeminuche bands. "One great difficulty," this Commission says, "in negotiating with the confederated bands of Utes consists in the fact that they hold the reservation in common, and yet, as between themselves, they have by common consent made partition of the territory, and utterly refuse to come together for conference."

Later, the chiefs of the Weeminuche, Capote and Muache bands of Utes sent to the Commissioners a written statement that they would sell their part of the reservation on three conditions. The fourth was: "That the $80,000 now due us be paid before our settling on the new territory to be occupied by us."

This paper was not incorporated in the agreement, but the Commissioner of Indian Affairs, in his report of the whole transaction, says:

> That they expected compensation for the lands so ceded by them is fully apparent from an examination of the report of the Commission, with its accompanying documents. It is shown thereby that at first they declined to entertain any proposition looking to a further cession of any portion of their territory. Afterward, however, by a paper signed on the 28th of August, 1878, herewith, they consented to remove from their present reservation, and agreed to sell the same at a price to be fixed by the Commission and the Utes. *While this was not carried into the agreement subsequently made*, it shows the views and feelings of the Indians on the subject.

The *treaties* are mine. The Government sent some presents to the Indians, over $800 worth. In regard to these the Commission reports:

It was with considerable difficulty that they were induced to receive the presents. * * * The money they requested me to return to the Great Father, or pay the expense of a delegation to Washington with it. They declined to receive it, as it had not been given them when promised. They evidently feared that it was a ruse to purchase the Uncompahgre Park, in regard to which they declined to treat.

A complete list is given of these presents, and the receipt of each individual Indian for each article he received. Some of the items in the list of presents seem trivial factors in the conducting of negotiations with "confederated bands" of a "nation" which is to be held strictly to terms and visited with penalities as other nations would be.

"Pocket-knives," "sewing cotton," "canned peaches," "prunes" and "candy"; sixty pounds of candy. It cost $18. It did not go very far "among so many," for there were seventy-two of the Utes, and as "Sapanavero," the chief, had ten pounds, and "Billy," "Tom" and "Colorado Chiquita," one pound each, the rest had only three-quarters of a pound apiece. But they signed these sixty-eight receipts for it, each by "X his mark."

"Examine the treaty carefully," and after we have examined carefully, let us ask ourselves whether the only resource left to the United States Government now, by means of which it can satisfy the ends of justice in regard to twelve Indian men guilty of murder and rape, is to make war upon four thousand men, women and children who not only have done us no wrong, but have been for ten years thus patient and long-suffering under the wrongs we have done to them.

H.H.

Boston, Jan. 2, 1880.

Printed in the *Tribune,* Jan. 19, 1880, p. 2, as "The Case of the Utes: A Few More Points by 'H.H.': 'Examine the Treaty Carefully'—An Examination Shows—Some Suggestions as to the Honor and Advantage of Resorting to War." An editorial note on p. 4 called the reader's attention to this letter.

1. Ouray (ca. 1820 or ca. 1833–80), who negotiated his first treaty with the government in 1863, was a spokesman for the seven bands of Ute: the three northern bands (Grand River, Yampa, and Uintah); the three southern bands (Mouache, Capote, and Wiminuche); and his own band, the Tabeguache of western Colorado. A spokesman for Ouray and Charles Adams, a former Ute agent personally selected by Secretary Schurz as a special agent of the Interior Department, succeeded in obtaining the release of the women hostages. Ouray and Adams served on a commission to

investigate the outbreak, and later the Ute leader traveled to Washington, D.C., to sign an agreement moving the Utes to Utah.

2. Henry F. Bond, appointed on May 20, 1874, served at Los Pinos until Sept. 1876.

3. Williard D. Wheeler became the Los Pinos agent in Sept. 1876 and served until Dec. 1877.

4. Edward H. Danforth was appointed on May 8, 1874, as agent at White River.

TO THE EDITOR OF THE *TRIBUNE*

[January 3, 1880]

To the Editor of The Tribune.

Sir: The readers of THE TRIBUNE will perhaps remember the following paragraph in Secretary Schurz's communication to THE TRIBUNE of December 18:[1]

H. H. asks: "How many of the American people know that, if an Indian on a reservation raises a flock of sheep, he cannot sell the wool; neither can the agent sell the wool and give the money to the Indian. The agent must sell the wool and turn the proceeds into the United States Treasury?" I admit that not many of the American people know this. Neither does H.H., for it is not true. When a flock of sheep belongs to the agency, and the wool is sold, then the money received is accounted for to the Government by the agent under the head of "miscellaneous receipts," and paid into the Treasury.

Also THE TRIBUNE readers may remember this paragraph in my reply:

This statement in the letter of H.H. was made on the authority of a former head clerk in the Indian Bureau. The Secretary's reply would be more satisfactory if it had been explained "how" and "when" flocks of sheep "belong to the agency," and if it is ever specified in treaties giving reservations to Indians that the Government reserves the right of sheep-raising on tracts therein included.

Within the past week there has come to me from beyond the Mississippi this narrative of a flock of sheep which was sold by the agent of the Yankton Indians[2] last year. It appears to be a striking illustration of the manner in which flocks of sheep "belong" to "agencies."

A few years ago sheep husbandry was begun among the Yankton Indians, in Dakota, by the Rev. John G. Gasmann,[3] their agent. He bought some sheep, paying for them "from a fund he had accumulated out of the savings made from time to time from the Indians' supplies. The sheep were kept on the Indians' land; fed with their grass in Summer; in Winter with grass cut, dried and put up at their expense. Shepherds were hired to take care of the sheep, and paid for from the Indian annuity funds. Two looms were secured, and a white woman employed to teach the Indian women how to weave. Some strong 'linsey' was manufactured by them, very pretty in pattern and well adapted to the manufacture of warm and durable dresses. Mr. Gasmann's plans, however, for carrying on or enlarging this industry were not encouraged by the Indian Bureau. He resigned his position as agent in April, 1878. His successor, Major I. W. Douglas,[4] on reaching the Yankton Agency, had his attention brought to this flock of sheep by the chiefs and head-men assembled in council. They then, and ever after, claimed these sheep as their own property, as belonging to them, and not to the Government. They complained that they were deriving no benefit from them whatever, and wished that the sheep might be sold or exchanged for oxen and cows, which they very much needed."

Major Douglas approved of this suggestion. Major W. I. Pollock,[5] the Dakota Superintendent of Indian Affairs, agreed with him, and wrote at once to the Commissioner of Indian Affairs a strong and pressing letter in favor of the sale of the sheep. The Summer passed away, and the Commissioner would not, or could not, come to any conclusion in the matter. "The sheep were fat and in fine condition to be sold, and many parties in Nebraska and Iowa had written Major Douglas in the mean time about their sale, or exchange for cattle.

"At last to bring the matter to an issue, Major Douglas telegraphed to the Commissioner to send him his conclusion about the sale; because upon that conclusion depended the cutting, hauling and putting up, or not, of 200 tons of hay for the sheep's Winter feeding. No reply was ever received to this telegram.

"At the last moment the hay was therefore cut and put up, and the old sheds repaired as well as possible for protecting the sheep another Winter, though the labor and expense attending all this was really needed for other industries at the agency."

In September a great fire swept over a large tract of the sheep's Winter range, destroying the grass. A very severe Winter followed; the scab appeared on the flock, and many sheep died. But by great care, and feeding the sheep with bran and ground barley (all bought with money out of the Indians' annuity funds), the flock was brought out in fair condition in the Spring.

"On the last day of April Major Douglas's resignation as agent took effect. His successor was Major Gardner,[6] Special Indian Agent. Under him the sheep were shorn in time; and by him—it is understood, under orders from the Commissioner—the sheep were sold, in a body, to one person, without publicly advertising them for sale, or allowing other parties to bid for them, who were ready and anxious to buy them in whole or in part. They were sold for $1,800, and the whole proceeds of their sale and the sale of the wool, rightfully belonging to the Yankton Indians, were returned to the United States Treasury. "It is reported on good authority that when these sheep were sold, one party who had been watching for their purchase for many months stood ready to give $2,800 for them."

The Commission which is presently to investigate Commissioner Hayt's methods and management of Indian affairs may be able to ascertain whether this account is in all particulars true.[7] They may also be able to find out whether it is true, as has been reported, that Howard White,[8] agent for the Winnebagoes, was compelled last Spring by explicit orders from the Indian Bureau to buy seed wheat at $1.10 a bushel, when he could readily have bought it at 62 cents. (Wheat, moreover, which was full of cockles, and ought not to have been bought at any price.)

Boston. Jan. 3, 1880. H.H.

Printed in the *Tribune*, Jan. 8, 1880, p. 2, as "Letters from the People: 'H.H.' Replies Again to Mr. Schurz: Fuller Details of a Transaction Which Any Investigation of Indian Affairs Ought to Cover." An editorial note, drawing attention to this letter, appeared on p. 4 of the same issue.

1. A reference to "Mr. Schurz on Indian Affairs: The Secretary Replies to the Letter of H.H. in the Tribune," *Tribune*, Dec. 19, 1879, p. 1.

2. One of the regional divisions of the Sioux.

3. John G. Gasmann was appointed agent at Yankton in the Dakota Superintendency on Feb. 23, 1872. On Apr. 25, 1877, he became the Santee Sioux (or Dakota) agent in Nebraska.

4. This should read Major John W. Douglas. Douglas replaced Gasmann at Yankton on March 28, 1878.

5. This should read Major W. J. Pollock. William J. Pollock was appointed to head the Dakota Superintendency on Feb. 21, 1878. The superintendency was discontinued in June when Pollock was appointed as a special agent.

6. Major Robert S. Gardner was on duty at Yankton beginning May 16, 1879. On Aug. 31, 1879, he was assigned as special agent to the Fort Berthold Agency in North Dakota; and on June 16, 1880, he was the special agent at the Otoe Agency in southern Nebraska.

7. Accused of mismanagement, Hayt underwent congressional investigations in late 1879 and early 1880, first by the Senate looking into the 1878 Northern Cheyenne flight from Indian Territory and later by a House committee investigating the White River Ute uprising. A scandal at the San Carlos Apache Agency in Arizona involving his son was the final straw, and Secretary Schurz removed Hayt from office on Jan. 29. See Meyer, "Ezra A. Hayt 1877–1880," in Robert Kvasnicka and Herman J. Viola, eds., *The Commissioners of Indian Affairs, 1824–1977*, pp. 155–66.

In early Jan. 1880 General Clinton Bowen Fisk announced in the *Tribune* that he intended to bring charges against Hayt before the Board of Indian Commissioners.

Both Hayt and Fisk defended their positions on Jan. 13, 15, and 16 in the *Tribune*, pp. 1, 5, and 5, respectively. In a Jan. 30 editorial on Hayt, p. 4, the *Tribune* editorial staff noted that there "can be no question that the Indian service will gain by his withdrawal." See also "Mr. Hayt's Removal," Jan. 31, 1880, p. 1; and "Cause of Mr. Hayt's Removal," Feb. 2, 1880, p. 1, both in the *Tribune*. Hayt, in a lengthy letter to the editor published on Feb. 11, defended his position and described Fisk's role as "highly dishonorable from the beginning." This prompted the editorial staff to remark that it would not help Hayt's position to "abuse" Fisk publicly, p. 4.

8. Howard White, a New Jersey Hicksite Quaker, was appointed Winnebago agent on June 9, 1869, serving until the agency was consolidated with the Omaha Agency in 1879. He served as the new Omaha and Winnebago agent until July 1880.

TO THE EDITOR OF THE *NEW YORK TIMES*

[early to mid-January 1880]

To the Editor of the New-York Times.

Will the committee of investigation of charges against Mr. Hayt explain the schedule of supplies on page 23 of his report for 1878, when, in order to prove that the Northern Cheyennes were not and could not have been starving, as they claimed, he calculates beef at three pounds gross, and gives the quantity of beef which was dealt out to the Indians as 1,242,208 pounds, and the quantity to which they were entitled as 1,026,840 pounds?

As each three pounds gross includes one and a half pounds of hide, hoofs, horns, entrails, and refuse, (or the 50 per cent. "tare" which is deducted when the animals are purchased,) which are improperly put down as beef, there should be deducted from the quantity of beef dealth out 621,104 pounds, and from the quantity due 513,420 pounds, thus making a difference between the quantity of beef due the Indians and the quantity dealth out to them of only 107,684 pounds, instead of 215,368 pounds. But a difference of only 107,684 pounds on the articles of beef would have proved that their total supply must have been at least 52,953 pounds short, whereas by the Commissioner's schedule, he was enabled to make it appear that there was a surplus of 54,731 pounds. The hides of beeves slaughtered at Indian agencies "belong to the agencies." When they are sold by the agent the money for them must be paid into the Treasury. It seems hardly fair to call them "beef" and ration them as subsistence for the Indians.

H.H.

Printed in the *NY Times*, Jan. 16, 1880, as "Delusive Beef."

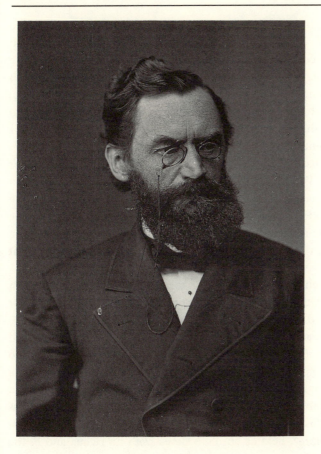

Carl Schurz, secretary of
the interior, 1877–81.
(Library of Congress)

TO CARL SCHURZ

New York, Friday, Jan. 9th, 1880.

To the Secretary of the Interior:

Dear Sir,—I have received from a Boston lady a letter which has so important a bearing on the interests of the Poncas that I take the liberty of asking you to read and reply to the following extracts. I send them to you with the writer's permission:

"In Boston most of those who are likely to give most largely and feel most strongly for the Indians have confidence in Secretary Schurz. They think that so far he has shown himself their friend, and they feel unprepared to help any plan with regard to the Indians which he opposes. The greatest service which could be rendered to the Indian cause at present would be given, therefore, by some one sufficiently interested to obtain an answer who would write to Secretary Schurz, and request him, on the part of the Indians, either to aid them by publicly and cordially endorsing this effort of the Poncas to secure their legal rights in the courts, or else to give his reasons against this attempt, in so clear a form that one could understand them. If there are good reasons, there can be no ground for keeping them secret, and the public has a right to know them. If not, no man can call himself a friend of the Indians who throws cold water on the present interest of the public in this matter.

"Secretary Schurz has already stated that it was not worth while to sue for the Ponca lands, as the Poncas are better off where they now are; but Secretary Schurz cannot deny that it is worth ten times $10,000 to prove that if the Government seizes land given to the Indians forever by solemn compact, the latter can by the courts recover it. Secretary Schurz has also said that a bill to give the Indians land in severalty is already before Congress. If he wishes that bill to pass he must know that it is only by help of the people that ignorance, apathy, and greed which are accountable for the shameful record of the past can be overcome; and that, whatever his sentiments toward these particular Poncas, he cannot afford to throw aside the interest they have excited.

"For a hundred years the Indians have been the victims of fraud and oppression on the part of the Government. Will anything put an end to it but to give the Indians the legal right to protect themselves? Promises and plans will not do it, for who can assure their performance? Secretary Schurz's position is a strange one, and the public are waiting and watching to see what it means. It is possible that he is satisfied to have 250,000 human beings, with valuable possessions (however uncivilized), held as absolute slaves, with no rights, and at the mercy of a government like ours, whose constant changes, to say the least, render most improbable the wise, equitable, and humane treatment he recommends in his report—and when the distance of the Indian from the personal interests of all but those States which have a personal interest in possessing his lands makes the assistance of Congress in such treatment still more unlikely? I cannot but believe that he has allowed himself to be driven into an opposition he does not really feel; and that he will yet have the magnanimity to forget any criticism on his own acts, and take the lead with those who would try to give the Indians a permanent defence against the vicissitudes of party and the greed of men.

"I will not forget to add that if the three thousand and odd hundreds of dollars needed to complete the ten thousand required to pay the costs of the Ponca suits cannot be raised in the great city of New York, I will myself guarantee to raise it in Boston in twenty-four hours if Secretary Schurz will openly endorse the plan."

The matter stands, therefore, in this shape: If you can say that you approve of the Poncas bringing the suits they wish to bring for the recovery of their lands, all the money for which they ask can be placed in their hands immediately. The writer of the above letter assured me that she would herself give the entire sum if there were any difficulty in raising it. If you do not approve of the Poncas bringing these suits, or making an effort to bring them, are you willing to give the reasons of your disapproval? It would be a great satisfaction to those Boston friends of yours whose action in this matter turns solely on your decision, if these reasons could be stated in clear and explicit form.

Yours respectfully,

Helen Jackson

Printed in *A Century of Dishonor*, pp. 359–61.

Schurz's response of Jan. 17, 1880, appears in *A Century of Dishonor*, pp. 361–63; and in Schurz, *Speeches, Correpondence and Political Papers*, 3:496–99.

TO WHITELAW REID

[January 12, 1880]

Dear Mr. Reid,

Can you not possibly put in my "Examine the Treaty Carefully" — tomorrow morning?[1] It seems to me that this is the precise moment when a word could be said for *innocent* Utes, with great effect — just as the public is aroused by Schurz's high handed outrage in treating them like prisoners in Washington.

Gen. Fisk[2] says "we must score one for Tibbles for that manly protest against Schurz's conduct in refusing the Utes a chance to tell their story." — Can't the Tribune agents in Washington compel him to allow them to see at least Ouray? — The Secretary is complaisant enough to the Tribune Reporters when he wants to say something himself! —

Now, when will you come to breakfast? Mrs Botta begs that you will set your own day as before, and I beg that you will set it soon, and come. I was sorely disappointed the other day. —Can't you come Wednesday.

Yours truly
Helen Jackson. —

Mon Eve.

January 12, 1880

ALS (DLC, Reid Papers).

1. A reference to HHJ's Jan. 2, 1880, letter to the editor, above, which did not appear in the *Tribune* until Jan. 19.

2. Clinton Bowen Fisk (1828–90), a distinguished brigadier-general of volunteers during the Civil War, founded Fisk University in 1866 to educate freedmen. He was appointed by President Grant to the Board of Indian Commissioners in 1874 and in 1881 became board president, a position he held until his death.

TO CHARLES DUDLEY WARNER

25 W. 37th St.
Thurs. Am.
Jan 15 — 1880

Dear Mr. Warner —

Note the telegraphic news in the Tribune this AM[1] — that the Sec. of the Int.[,] Com. of Ind. Affairs — & members of the Board of Ind. Comm[issioners] —decided that the interests of the govt. would be best met by buying *Texas* cattle for the Indian Territory, "because Kansas & Missouri cattle, would not *live in Indian Territory*"!

Do write a scathing ed. on that![2] — Even cattle couldnt live there! — taken from a climate so nice as Kansas.

Of course it's a lie told to cover up the fraudulent purchase of cattle — but never mind, they've said it.

I'd give a thousand dollars to have access to a newspaper at this minute. I can't make Reid print my things — & I am chafing under the misery of not saying half I want to.—

But I am going soon to buckle down to serious work! — we shall go to the Brevoort next Tuesday. —

Mrs. Botta has a reception for me on Mon. Eve. next. — can't you come & bring Mrs. Warner? — Do —

Yrs in greatest haste
H.J.

ALS (CtHT-W, Warner Collection).
1. A reference to "Iregular Purchase of Cattle," *Tribune*, Jan. 15, 1880, p. 5.
2. Warner's editorial appeared in the *Hartford Courant*, Jan. 19, 1880, p. 2. He ended it: "If it is true that *cattle* from Kansas cannot live in the territory, how is it about the Indians who have been sent down there!" He suggested that Schurz "would better get out a lantern and look around."

TO THE EDITOR OF THE *TRIBUNE*

[January 15, 1880]

To the Editor of The Tribune.

SIR: Here are two noticeable opinions from the Department of the Interior on the subject of removals to the Indian Territory in 1877 and 1878. They seem of special interest now:

> Experience has demonstrated the impolicy of sending Northern Indians to the Indian Territory. To go no further back than the date of the Pawnee removal,[1] it will be seen that the effect of a radical change of climate is disastrous, as this tribe alone in the first two years lost by death over 800 out of its number of 2,376. The Northern Cheyennes have suffered severely, and the Poncas who were recently removed from contact with the unfriendly Sioux, and arrived there in July last, have already lost 36 by death, which by an ordinary computation would be the death rate for the entire tribe for a period of four years.
>
> In this connection I recommend the removal of all the Indians in Colorado and Arizona to the Indian Territory.—(Annual report of Commissioner Hayt on Indian Affairs for 1877). Page 6.

In the telegraphic news from Washington, printed in THE TRIBUNE of January 15, we read, under the head of "Irregular Purchase of Cattle":

> Commissioner Hayt says in regard to the matter that the contract was awarded after due consideration between representatives of the Board of Indian Commissioners, the Secretary of the Interior and himself, the decision being that the best interests of the Government would be served by the purchase of Texas cattle. Among the influences which operated to bring about the decision was the representation made by the Indian Office, after advertisement had been made, that Missouri and Kansas cattle could not live in Indian Territory.

H.H.

New-York, Jan. 15, 1880.

Printed in the *Tribune,* Jan. 16, 1880, p. 5, as "About Removing Northern Indians."

1. Subject to continued attack by the Sioux, the Pawnees of Nebraska in open council agreed to remove to Indian Territory. The initial removal began in the winter of 1873, with the main party following in the fall of 1874.

TO WHITELAW REID

16 Jany, 1880

Dear Mr. Reid,

I know you are fast coming to abbor me: — and you do not mean to come and see me — but I hope in spite of that — you will let me ask these questions in tomorrows Tribune?[1] and let the Ed[itorial] Head[ing] man put a little sign band to show where it is?

Has there ever been such a high handed outrage on the part of the Interior Dept. before? I think never. —

— As for the Committee of the Indian Board,[2] — if only I could see you, and tell you about Mr. Barstow[3]— — He is Hayt's *sworn* ally — he said to a friend of mine, "nothing under Heaven could make me believe anything against Mr. Hayt."

"What nothing? No nothing! No evidence in the World."

He is a stove manufacturer & the Poncas alone had 150 of his stoves!

He had a relative here in the grocery business who sells supplies to the Indian service —

"Expenditure supervised" by Indian Commissioners. —

Yours truly

Helen Jackson

P.S.— If you cannot find room for these questions — and for the "Examine the Treaty Carefully"[4] (which has been waiting now nearly three weeks —) will you send them back to me? If I *can't* say them in the Tribune, I must try the next best thing — but that "next best," is a long way off. —

ALS (DLC, Reid Papers).

1. Reid published her Jan. 16 letter, below, the following day.

2. A reference to the Board of Indian Commissioners.

3. A wealthy stove manufacturer, Amos Chafee Barstow (b. 1813) was mayor of Providence, Rhode Island, served in the state assembly, and was Speaker of the House in 1870. In 1875 he was appointed to the Board of Indian Commissioners, serving as chairman, 1879–80. His friendship with Hayt dated back to their mutual service on the board.

Quoting from a letter written by Barstow in the *Congregationalist*, a *Boston Advertiser* editorial on Nov. 6, 1879, p. 2, criticized the Rhode Islander for not supporting legal rights for the Indians. Barstow immediately requested that the entire letter be reprinted. The paper complied, and on Nov. 8, 1879, p. 4, published Barstow's rebuttal, the letter in the *Congregationalist*, and an editorial calling attention to both. Despite this apparent middle ground, the *Advertiser* made sure its readers were aware of its support for the Indian cause.

4. A reference to HHJ's Jan. 2, 1880, letter to the editor, above, which was not printed until Jan. 19.

TO THE EDITOR OF THE *TRIBUNE*

[January 16, 1880]

To the Editor of The Tribune.

Sir: *First*—How many of the American people believe that the truth was told to the NEW-YORK TRIBUNE reporter, a few days ago, when he was informed that the Ute Indians, now in Washington, could not be seen by any one because they needed "rest and recuperation" after their long journey?[1]

Second—How many of the American people believe that the Interior Department has a right "to suppress all information in regard to the Indians," as the NEW-YORK TRIBUNE reporter telegraphs, "it seems to be their intention" to do?

Third—How many of the American people—having committed no crime, have gone to Washington of their own free accord—would submit to being "kept at their hotel under guard," as the Chief Ouray and his companions are reported to be?

Fourth—Is there no power which can put a stop to this high-handed oppression? Will the press of the country submit to this outrage? This defiance of their rights, as the representatives of the people and the channels on which the people depend for information of current events?

Will the people themselves submit to this last and most flagrant violation on the part of the Government of the individual's "inalienable right" of "personal liberty?"

H.H.

New-York, Jan. 16, 1880.

Printed in the *Tribune*, Jan. 17, 1880, p. 5, as "The Indian Troubles: A Few More Questions for the American People."

1. The *Tribune* informed its readers that Secretary Schurz had secluded the Ute chiefs, thus preventing any communication between them and the outside world. However, in "The Utes in Washington," *Tribune*, Jan. 13, 1880, p. 1, Secretary Schurz described Ouray and his companions as a delegation and assured the public that they "would be treated as such." See also "The Ute Chiefs Secluded," Jan. 12; "The Utes in Washington," Jan. 16; and "The Ute Chiefs," Jan. 17, 1880, all in the *Tribune*, pp. 1, 5, and 1, respectively. In a lengthy editorial, "The Indians at Washington," the *Tribune* on Jan. 23, p. 4, noted that if Ouray were shut up in his hotel, he might be more easily induced to give up tribal land in Colorado. "If these people are to be swindled out of

their land, let us swindle them openly, as we have done before, without the disguise of any such small tricks and dramatic secrecy."

TO THOMAS WENTWORTH HIGGINSON

[January 17, 1880]

. . . .

I have done now, I believe, the last of the things I had said I never would do; I have become what I have said a thousand times was the most odious thing in life, — "a woman with a hobby." But I cannot help it. I think I feel as you must have felt in the old abolition days. I cannot think of anything else from night to morning and from morning to night. . . . I believe the time is drawing near for a great change in our policy toward the Indian. In some respects, it seems to me, he is really worse off than the slaves; they did have in the majority of cases good houses, and they were not much more arbitrarily controlled than the Indian is by the agent on a reservation. He can order a corporal's guard to fire on an Indian at any time he sees fit. He is "duly empowered by the government."

Excerpted in Higginson, *Contemporaries*, pp. 155–56; Higginson, "Mrs. Helen Jackson ('H.H.')," p. 254; and Davis and Alderson, *The True Story of "Ramona": Its Facts and Fictions, Inspiration and Purpose*, pp. 80–81.

Thomas Wentworth Higginson (1823–1911) was active in the abolition movement and became colonel of the first black regiment in the Union Army. Resigning in 1864, he returned to New England, spending the remainder of his life writing magazine articles, history, novels, and biographies. He served in the Massachusetts state legislature, 1880–81.

TO THE EDITOR OF THE *TRIBUNE*

[January 18, 1880]

To the Editor of The Tribune.

SIR: This is the difference in the United States between murdering a white man and murdering an Indian:

Henry Harris, a Winnebago in good standing, an industrious man and a successful farmer, was employed by Joseph Smith, a white man, to cut wood on his land in Dakota County, a short distance north of the reservation. While alone and thus engaged, on the 29th of last January, Harris was shot through the heart with a rifle ball. I had his dead body taken before the coroner of the county, and at the inquest held before that officer, it was shown to the satisfaction of the jury, that rendered a verdict in accordance therewith, that the Indian came to his death at the hands of one D. Balinska, who had been for many years leading a hermit's life on a tract of land that he owned adjoining the reservation, and who had threatened Harris's life a few months before, when they quarrelled about damages for corn destroyed by Balinska's horse. There being snow on the ground at the time of the murder, Balinska was tracked from his home to the place where, under cover, he did the shooting; and his shot-pouch, containing a moulded ball of the same weight as the one cut from the body of the Indian, was found near by and identified. Notwithstanding this direct evidence which was laid before the Grand Jury of Dakota County, that honorable body was unwilling to find a "true bill"; for the reason, as I understand, that it was only an Indian that was killed, and it would not be popular to incur the expense of bringing the case to trial. This is but another illustration of the difficulty of punishing a white man for a wrong committed against an Indian. I need hardly say that the Indians, when comparing this murder with that of a white man committed eight years ago by five of their young men, who, upon less direct evidence, were sentenced to imprisonment in the State Penitentiary for life, are struck with the wonderful difference in the application of the same law to whites and Indians.—(Report of the Agent on the Winnebago Agency; see Annual Report of the Secretary of the Interior for 1878, page 596.)[1]

Would it be worth while to ask the Government to combine with its efforts to apprehend the murderers of Mr. Meeker some attention to D. Balinska, the murderer of Henry Harris?

H.H.

New-York, Jan. 18, 1880.

Printed in the *Tribune*, Jan. 25, 1880, p. 5, as "A Small Matter to Murder an Indian: 'H.H.' Scores Another Point."
   1. Howard White was the Winnebago agent; see HHJ to the *Tribune* editor, Jan. 3, 1880, note 8.

TO WILLIAM HAYES WARD

Brevoort House
Wed. Eve.
Jan 21, 1880

Dear Mr. Ward,

I have just received a note enclosing your cheque for $25 for the "Cheyenne Massacre" — but making no allusion to the payment for the Holmes poem.[1]

Are the publishers really going to decline to pay for that poem, — which I brought to you a week beforehand — and you accepted, at the price I asked — $25, — with the distinct mention in our conversation that I brought it to you, because as your paper came out on Thursday morning, it would have it as soon as any of the Boston papers could print it — & before any New York papers? — It was not printed here till the *next* evening in the Post: —

I do not see on what grounds they can refuse to fulfil the arrangement which you had made with me — and I certainly think that it was worth something to the Independent to print that poem Thursday morning. However if they are unwilling — on this representation of mine — to pay it, let it go. —

Please send me a copy of last weeks Ind[ependent]. I have tried at every bookstall in this part of the town & could not get one. — I hear Kemble is out again in it and very severe on the Secretary.[2] — I hope you have seen all my papers in the Tribune & Times. I am hard at work — & am just ready to set about a still harder task, ie. the writing of the history in short of the Govts dealings with the Indians for the last 100 years. — It will be a solid three months work at least.[3]

We were sorry not to see you on Mon. Eve. Standing Bear & Bright Eyes were there — & if you had heard Standing Bears speech, you would have taken his word against Kemble's any day!

— I wish you could come up & see me — Send me word the day beforehand, & come up & take your lunch with me any day. It's only minutes by the Elevated R. R. — (Station at 8th St.)

Yours truly

Helen Jackson

ALS (CSmH, HHJ MSS, HM 13979).
1. HHJ had written this poem for Oliver Wendell Holmes's seventieth birthday.
2. "A Few Words with Mr. Schurz: By Col. E. C. Kemble," was published in the Jan. 15, 1880, *Independent*, pp. 5–6.
3. A reference to HHJ's research in the Astor Library for *A Century of Dishonor*.

TO CARL SCHURZ

Brevoort House, New York, Thursday, Jan. 22d, 1880.

Hon Carl Schurz:

DEAR SIR,—Your letter of the 17th instant is at hand. If I understand this letter correctly, the position which you take is as follows: That there is in your opinion, and in the opinion of the lawyers whom you have consulted on the subject, no way of bringing before the courts the suits for the prosecution of which money has been and is being contributed by the friends of the Poncas; that the reason you do not approve of this movement is that "it is evidently idle to collect money and to fee attorneys for the purpose of doing a thing which cannot be done." This is the sole reason which I understand you to give for discountenancing the collection of money for these suits. Am I correct in this? And are we to infer that it is on this ground and no other that you oppose the collection of money for this purpose? Are we to understand that you would be in favor of the Poncas recovering their lands by process of law, provided it were practicable?

You say, also, that you hope I will "concur" in your "recommendation that the money collected for taking the Ponca case into the courts should be devoted to the support and enlargement of our Indian schools." May I ask how it would be, in your opinion, possible to take money given by thousands of people for one specific purpose and use it for another different purpose? You say, "Had the friends of the Indians who are engaged in this work first consulted lawyers on the question of possibility, they would, no doubt, have come to the same conclusion." Had the friends of the Indians engaged in this work, and initiated this movement without having consulted lawyers, it would have been indeed foolish. But this was not the case. Lawyers of skill and standing were found ready to undertake the case; and the matter stands therefore to-day precisely as it stood when I wrote to you on the 17th instant. All the money which is thought to be needed for carrying the Ponca case before the courts can be raised in twenty-four hours in Boston, if you can say that you approve of the suits being brought. If your only objection to the movement is the one objection which you have stated, namely, that it would be futile, can you not say that, if lawyers of standing are ready to undertake the case, you would be glad to see the attempt made in the courts, and the question settled? If it is, as you think, a futile effort, it will be shown to be so. If it is, as the friends and lawyers of the Poncas think, a practicable thing, a great wrong will be righted.

You say that "to settle them (the Indians) in severalty, and give them by patent an individual fee-simple in their lands," will enable them to "hold their lands by the same title by which white men hold theirs," and that "then they will, as a matter of course, have the same standing in the courts and the same legal protection of their property." May I ask you if any bill has been brought before Congress which is so worded as to secure these ends?[1] My only apology for troubling you again is my deep interest in the Indians, and in the Ponca case especially.

Yours truly,
Helen Jackson

Printed in *A Century of Dishonor*, pp. 363–64; and Schurz, *Speeches, Correspondence and Political Papers*, 3:499–500.

1. In Schurz to HHJ, Jan. 26, 1880, in *A Century of Dishonor*, p. 366; and Schurz, *Speeches, Correspondence and Political Papers*, 3:503, the secretary replied that such bills were now before Congress. He added: "I trust we shall obtain the desired legislation during the present session of Congress."

The Indians' practice of communal land ownership was viewed as a hindrance to their individualization and assimilation. On Jan. 12, 1880, Nebraska's Senator Alvin Saunders introduced a general allotment bill, but it and similiar ones failed until the passage in 1887 of the Dawes Severalty Bill, sponsored by Henry Laurens Dawes. Reservation lands were parceled out in allotments of 160 acres or less in the hopes of turning the Indians into farmers. The reform failed; the Indians lost millions of acres of land and engaged in less farming than before.

TO AMELIA STONE QUINTON

Brevoort —

Jan 27 — 1880

Dear Miss Quinton —

Do send me 6 more petitions & tracts.[1]

I have got four more people who promise to get 100 each — & I want to send one to the John Hopkins University — & to Fisk University —

You would better send me *ten* —I can use them all. — Next week I'll try myself in Cambridge to get all the Harvard faculty. — If we can say we have the Presidents of Colleges &c. — it will be a good thing. —

Yrs ever —

H.J.

I think I'll get 2000 in all.— "H.H."

ALS (Collection 100, box 64, Special Collections, University of California at Los Angeles).

Amelia Stone Quinton (1833–1926) was a humanitarian reformer who worked in almshouses, infirmaries, prisons, and women's reformatories. She conducted weekend Bible classes for sailors and was an active member of the Women's Christian Temperance Union. In 1879 Mary Bonney enlisted her support to protect Indian land in Indian Territory from white encroachment. Together they established the Women's National Indian Association (WNIA). Quinton served as the association's president, 1887–1905, and continued as honorary president for the next twenty years.

1. A reference to the WNIA petition requesting that the president and Congress protect both Indian Territory from encroaching white settlers and Indian treaty rights. The petition was accompanied by "An Earnest Petition," written by Quinton, which detailed the forced removal of the Five Civilized Tribes from the Southeast. A 300-foot-long petition, signed by thirteen thousand citizens, was presented to President Rutherford B. Hayes on Feb. 14, 1880.

TO WILLIAM HAYES WARD

Brevoort
Tues. Am
Jan. 27 — [1880]

Dear Mr. Ward,

I hoped to have seen you this A.M. but the weather prevents my coming down. — I send you an article which I think of the greatest interest[1] & hope you will think so too; & I want very much to have it follow *up* the series you have already printed in the Ind[ependent] on the Ponca business: — but if you cannot print it either next week, or at latest the week after, I believe I must ask you to return it to me: — for it ought to come out soon. —

I wish I could see you, to tell you how the air is thickening with the smoke of this battle for the oppressed — to show a long letter I have had from that false souled man, Carl Schurz — & one from Gen. Crook — &c. &c. — I am almost appalled at the way things are pouring in! — & the way the people are *waking up* at last to this question — to our infamy — & the Indians' sufferings. — We are on the threshold of a great revolution — & the thieves who have been *fattening* on the seven millions a year spent in our Indian Policy, will do well to make all they can this year, for next year they will have small chance. —

I have been asked to write for Harpers Mag — The Chicago Tribune — & the Christian Advocate — on this subject — — but I think it wiser to stick to my *own* audiences for the present — with needle gun shots in the Tribune & Times. — I have however a long article coming out in the March Scribner — — & shall prepare one later, for Harpers — — Meantime I begin today, my solid work at the Astor Library — going back, *100 years* — to tell sharply & succinctly the history of our *"Century of Dishonor"*, — in a small book. —

Do come up & lunch with me some day — sending word the day beforehand — & then we can talk everything over —

Yrs ever—
H.J.

Do send me by bearer that second letter of Kembles — I want to see it. —

ALS (CSmH, HHJ MSS, HM 13980).
1. Probably a reference to "How the Indians Were Moved," *Independent*, Feb. 5, 1880, pp. 9–10.

TO THE EDITOR OF THE *TRIBUNE*

[January 30, 1880]

To the Editor of The Tribune.

SIR: A paragraph in the Washington dispatches of to-day's TRIBUNE, headed "The Ponca Indians,"[1] is so calculated to do harm to the Poncas, that I hope you will permit me to call attention to the fact that not one word is said in it about that tribe. All its statements are in reference to the Cheyennes: but the casual reader would get the impression that they referred to the Poncas.

H.H.

New York, Jan. 30, 1880.

Printed in the *Tribune*, Jan. 31, 1880, p. 5, as "Cheyennes Not Poncas."
1. This front-page article dealt almost exclusively with the five thousand Northern Cheyennes living in "utter idleness" in Indian Territory.

TO THE EDITOR OF THE *TRIBUNE*

[January 31, 1880]

To the Editor of The Tribune.

SIR: In your capital editorial note this morning, you say: "The two most serious hindrances to a satisfactory solution of the Indian question are Indians and white men."[1] Any problem is embarrassing when one of its factors is addicted to scalping men, torturing women, and braining children. The problem becomes still more embarrassing when "one" of the "factors" has no way of making known to the people what the other "factor" has done to him. In connection with the present attempt to rouse a sweeping sentiment of indignation and denunciation against the band of 4,000 well-nigh helpless Utes in Colorado, because twelve of their number have committed murder and rape, and some 300 or 400 of them undertook to prevent the marching of United States troops into their lands, I wish to tell to the American people a few of the atrocities which Colorado white men committed upon Indians only fifteen years ago.

In June, 1864, Governor Evans,[2] of Colorado, sent out a circular to the Indians of the Plains, inviting all friendly Indians to come into the neighborhood of the forts and be protected by the United States troops. Hostilities and depredations had been committed by some bands of Indians, and the Government was about to make war upon them. This circular says:

In some instances they (the Indians) have attacked and killed soldiers, and murdered peaceable citizens. For this the Great Father[3] is angry, and will certainly hunt them out and punish them; but he does not want to injure those who remain friendly to the whites. He desires to protect and take care of them. For this purpose I direct that all friendly Indians keep away from those who are at war, and go to places of safety. Friendly Arapahoes and Cheyennes belonging on the Arkansas River will go to Major Colby [Colley],[4] United States Agent at Fort Lyon, who will give them provisions and show them a place of safety.

In consequence of this proclamation of the governor, a band of Cheyennes, several hundred in number, came in and settled down near Fort Lyon. After a time they were requested to move to Sand Creek, about forty miles from Fort Lyon, where they were still guaranteed "perfect safety" and the protection of the Government. Rations of food were issued to them from time to time. On the 27th of November, Colonel J. M. Chivington,[5] a member of the Methodist Episcopal Church in Denver, and Colonel of the 1st Colorado Cavalry, led his regiment by a forced march to Fort Lyon, induced some of the United States troops to join him, and fell upon this camp of friendly Indians at daybreak. The chief, White Antelope,[6] always known as friendly to the whites, came running toward the soldiers, holding up his hands and crying "Stop stop!" in English. When he saw that there was no mistake, that it was a deliberate attack, he folded his arms and waited till he was shot down. The United States flag was floating over the lodge of Black Kettle,[7] the head chief of the tribe. Below it was tied also a small white flag as additional security, a precaution Black Kettle had been advised by United States officers to take if he met troops on the Plains. In Major Wynkoop's[8] testimony given before the committee appointed by Congress to investigate this massacre, is the following passage:

Women and children were killed and scalped, children shot at their mother's breasts, and all the bodies mutilated in the most horrible manner. * * * The dead bodies of females profaned in such a manner that the recital is sickening, Colonel J. M. Chivington all the time inciting his troops to their diabolical outrages.

Another man testified as to what he saw on the 30th of November, three days after the battle, as follows:

I saw a man dismount from his horse and cut the ear from the body of an Indian and the scalp from the head of another. I saw a number of children killed; they had bullet-holes in them; one child had been cut with some sharp instrument across its side. I saw another that both ears had been cut off. * * * I saw several of the 3d Regiment cut off fingers to get the rings off them. I saw Major Sayre[9] scalp a dead Indian. The scalp had a long tail of silver hanging to it.

Robert Bent[10] testified:

I saw one squaw lying on the bank, whose leg had been broken. A soldier came up to her with a drawn sabre. She raised her arm to protect herself; he struck, breaking her arm. She rolled over, and raised her other arm; he struck, breaking that, and then left her without killing her. I saw one squaw cut open, with an unborn child lying by her side.

Major Anthony[11] testified:

There was one little child probably three years old, just big enough to walk through the sand. The Indians had gone ahead, and this little child was behind following after them. The little fellow was perfectly naked, travelling in the sand. I saw one man get off his horse at a distance of about seventy-five yards and draw up his rifle and fire. He missed the child. Another man came up and said: "Let me try the son of a b——. I can hit him." He got down off his horse, kneeled down, and fired at the little child, but he missed him. A third man came up, and made a similar remark, and fired, and the little fellow dropped.

The Indians were not able to make much resistance, as only a part of them were armed, the United States officers having required them to give up their guns. Luckily they had kept a few.

When this Colorado regiment of demons returned to Denver they were greeted with an ovation. The *Denver News* said: "All acquitted themselves well. Colorado soldiers have again covered themselves with glory;" and at a theatrical performance given in the city, the scalps taken from three Indians were held up and exhibited to the audience, which applauded rapturously.

After listening, day after day, to such testimonies as these I have quoted, and others so much worse that I may not write and THE TRIBUNE could not print the words needful to tell them, the committee[12] reported: "It is difficult to believe that beings in the form of men, and disgracing the uniform of the United States soldiers, and officers could commit or countenance the commission of such acts of cruelty and barbarity"; and, of Colonel Chivington: "He deliberately planned and excecuted a foul and dastardly massacre, which would have disgraced the veriest savage among those who were the victims of his cruelty."

This was just fifteen years ago, no more. Shall we apply the same rule of judgment to the white men of Colorado that the Government is now applying to the Utes? There are 130,000 inhabitants of Colorado; hundreds of them had a hand in this massacre, and thousands in cool blood applauded it when it was done. There are 4,000 Utes in Colorado. Twelve of them, desperate, guilty men, have committed murder and rape, and three or four hundred of them did, in the convenient phrase of our diplomacy, "go to war against the

Government"; *i.e.*, they attempted, by force of arms, to restrain the entrance upon their own lands—lands bought, owned and paid for—of soldiers that the Government had sent there, to be ready to make war upon them, in case the agent thought it best to do so! This is the plain English of it. This is the plain, naked truth of it.

And now the Secretary of the Interior has stopped the issue of rations to 1,000 of these helpless creatures; rations, be it understood, which are not, and never were, a charity, but are the Utes' rightful dues, on account of lands by them sold; dues which the Government promised to pay "annually forever." Will the American people justify this? There is such a thing as the conscience of a nation—as a nation's sense of justice. Can it not be roused to speak now? Shall we sit still, warm and well fed, in our homes, while five hundred women and little children are being slowly starved in the bleak, barren wildernesses of Colorado? Starved, not because storm, or blight, or drouth has visited their country and cut off their crops; not because pestilence has laid its hand on them and slain the hunters who brought them meat, but because it lies within the promise of one man, by one word, to deprive them of one-half their necessary food for as long a term of years as he may please; and "the Secretary of the Interior cannot consistently feed a tribe that has gone to war against the Government."

We read in the statutes of the United States that certain things may be done by "executive order" of the President. Is it not [now] time for a President to interfere when hundreds of women and children are being starved in his Republic, by the order of one man? Colonel J. M. Chivington's method was less inhuman by far. To be shot dead is a mercy, and a grace for which we would all sue, if to be starved to death were our only other alternative.

H.H.

New-York, Jan. 31st. 1880.

Printed in the *Tribune*, Feb. 5, 1880, p. 5, as "The Starving Utes: More Questions for the People by 'H.H.': What White Men Have Done and Are Doing to Indians in Colorado." An editorial, p. 4, called attention to this letter.

Excluding the first paragraph, this letter is reprinted in *A Century of Dishonor*, pp. 343–46, and in the *Rocky Mountain News*, Feb. 29, 1880, p. 3, as "The Ute: When Greek Meets Greek Then Comes the Tug of War: Interesting Correspondence by Two Prominent Coloradans: Helen Hunt and W. N. Byers Take a Newspaper Tilt: The Ute as Seen from Two Stand Points." Byers's Feb. 6, 1880, rebuttal letter followed.

1. The Jan. 31 editorial, p. 4, entitled "Demoralizing the Indian Service," described the Indian Bureau as "a nest of rascality and corruption."

2. John Evans (1814–97), a midwestern-born physician, became the second governor of Colorado Territory in 1862. Although his role in the attack on Black

Kettle's village, better known as the Sand Creek Massacre, is a matter of debate, political enemies used it to discredit him. Forced to resign in 1865, Evans remained in Denver, became a prominent businessman, organized the Denver Pacific Railroad, and founded Colorado Seminary, later the University of Denver.

3. Reflecting the paternalistic attitude of the government toward the Indians, the term "Great Father" was used to denote the president of the United States.

4. On July 26, 1861, Major Samuel G. Colley (not Colby) was appointed agent for the Upper Arkansas Agency, which served the Indians along the upper Arkansas River in eastern Colorado and western Kansas. He remained as agent until August 1865.

5. An elder of the First Methodist Episcopal Church, John M. Chivington (1821–94) moved to Colorado in 1860. In 1862, as a major in the First Regiment of Colorado Cavalry (volunteer troops), he aided in the defeat of Confederate forces at Glorieta Pass in New Mexico. He resigned from the army in January 1865 but never could escape the stigma of the Sand Creek Massacre.

For more on Sand Creek see Hoig, *The Sand Creek Massacre*; Svaldi, *Sand Creek and the Rhetoric of Extermination*; Mendoza, *Song of Sorrow: Massacre at Sand Creek*; and Scott, *Blood at Sand Creek: The Massacre Revisited*.

6. White Antelope (1796–1864), a member of the Cheyenne Dog Soldiers, or warrior society, had helped bring peace in 1840 between his tribe and the Comanches and Kiowas. He was the spokesman for the Southern Cheyennes with Governor Evans and Chivington shortly before the massacre at Sand Creek.

7. Always eager for peace, Black Kettle (1803?–68) and White Antelope had met in council with Governor Evans and had agreed to move their village to Sand Creek, believing they were under the protection of the fort. Although Black Kettle survived the attack on his village at Sand Creek, during the battle of the Washita in 1868, he was killed by troops under the command of George Armstrong Custer.

8. Edward W. Wynkoop (1836–91), a founder of Denver, a sheriff of Arapahoe County, and a major in the First Regiment of Colorado Cavalry, was appointed commander of Fort Lyon in May 1864. He permitted Black Kettle and his people to camp near the fort, assuring them of their safety. In 1865 Wynkoop led a formal investigation of the Sand Creek massacre and in 1866 became the Southern Cheyenne and Arapaho agent at Fort Larned, Kansas.

9. Alfred Sayre (1834–1926), a lawyer by profession, moved to Colorado and joined the Third Regiment of Colorado Cavalry in 1864. He commanded one of the five battalions at Sand Creek. He later became adjutant general of Colorado and a mining operator and engineer.

10. Robert Bent (1840–89) was the eldest son of Owl Woman and Colonel William Bent, co-owner with his brother Charles of Bent's Fort in southeastern Colorado. Robert was forced by Chivington to guide the soldiers to Black Kettle's village, where two brothers, a sister, and his mother, Owl Woman, were living. Owl Woman died in the battle, and his brother George was wounded. Robert Bent later gave eyewitness testimony during a government investigation.

11. Scott J. Anthony (1830–1903) arrived in Colorado in 1860 and worked as a miner until commissioned captain and later major of the First Regiment of Colorado Cavalry. Initially in command at Fort Larned, he replaced Wynkoop at Fort Lyon in

Nov. 1864 and ordered Black Kettle and his people to move to Sand Creek, some forty miles away. Following the massacre, Anthony guided survey parties and construction crews for the Union Pacific and Northern Pacific. He eventually returned to Denver and went into business.

12. There were four investigations of Sand Creek in 1865. In Jan. Wynkoop took affidavits and testimony at Fort Lyon; in Mar. the Joint Committee on the Conduct of the War heard testimony in Washington; from Feb. through May a military fact-finding commission met in Denver; and from Mar. to June the Joint Special Committee of Congress took testimony in Washington, D.C., at Fort Riley, Kansas, at Fort Lyon, and at Denver.

On Jan. 4, 1865, Chivington had resigned his commission and thus could not be tried by a military court. At the conclusion of the lengthy hearings, the military commission, assigned only to gather facts, could draw no conclusions and had no power to make recommendations.

TO BISHOP HENRY B. WHIPPLE

Brevoort House
Feb. 5. 1880

Bishop Whipple,

Dear Sir —

I have just read the accounts of the Massacres in Minnesota in 1862,[1] — and the record has enabled me to do more justice [to] the feelings of the settlers there, than all I have ever read before. I do not wonder that the citizens of the western states, at that time, demanded that all Indians should be removed. — Now — the next thing is — what *led* to those massacres? Can you tell me of any authentic account of the events before the massacres? — anything other than I can learn from the Official Reports of the Int. Dept. all of which I have, and am studying carefully. —

I propose to write a short history of the dealings of our Govt. with the Indians for the past century: — I wish to give, in this, full narrations of the chief massacres of Indians by U. S. troops: will you kindly send me a list of all which in your opinion would be best worth describing? — together with the names of any books which you would advise me to consult?

I am sure that you are keeping a close watch over the fast gathering clouds of indignation on the part of the American people. Public sentiment is certainly coming round, as it rarely has been, in so short a time, and Hayt's[2] fall is a symptom of a better time coming soon. — I have great hopes of seeing the Indian race on its legal feet in a years time. —

Yours truly
Helen Jackson

Mrs. Wm S. Jackson
Brevoort House
New York.
P.S. The Sand Creek Massacre & the Massacre of the Cheyennes at Fort
Robinson, I have already written. —

ALS (Henry B. Whipple Papers, P823, Box 14, Minnesota Historical Society, St.
Paul, Minnesota; hereinafter cited as MnHi, Whipple Papers).

Henry Benjamin Whipple (1822–1901) became the first Episcopal bishop of Minnesota in 1859 and the following year established a mission among the Sioux. Actively
tending the wounded and comforting the bereaved following the 1862 Minnesota
Santee Sioux uprising, he also personally appealed to President Abraham Lincoln on
behalf of the Indians. As a result, only thirty-eight of the over three hundred Sioux
prisoners were executed.

1. The sedentary Santee Sioux lived on a small reservation along the upper
Minnesota River. Corrupt trading practices, the disruption of the Civil War, the con-
tinual encroachment of white settlers, the lateness of their annuity monies, and sheer
hunger resulted in the 1862 Indian uprising led by Little Crow. Hundreds of
Minnesota residents were killed, and the Sioux were removed to either Nebraska or
the Dakotas. The most recent studies of this uprising include Schultz, *Over the Earth I
Come: The Great Sioux Uprising of 1862*; and Anderson, *Little Crow: Spokesman for the
Sioux*.

2. See HHJ to the *Tribune*, Jan. 3, 1880, note 7, above.

TO WHITELAW REID

[February 12 — 13, 1880]

Dear Mr. Reid—

Would it be of any use for me to ask you as a personal favor to me, to
publish these letters of Sec. Schurz's & mine, in full? — Nothing that has
happened has made me feel so badly as the way the thing is presented in the
Tribune this morning.[1] I understand from Gen Fiske[2] that if the Tribune could
not print the *whole* as we had arranged it, he was to take it all away & give it to
me, to try some other paper — As it stands there & now, it hurts the Ponca
case *immeasureably*.

— Sec. Schurz has been much too clever for us. He dishonorably sent the
correspondence to the Daily Advertiser,[3] *after* having given it to Gen. Fiske,
with the distinct understanding that he (Gen. F[isk]) was to print it *if* I commented!—I believe that Sec. S[churz] divined our plan, which was to print it,
in the Tribune with comments showing the trickiness & feebleness of his letters

&c. — & then the Severalty Bill below — with my comments on that:[4] — and he whisked the correspondence into the Advertiser, uncommented on, & alone, trusting as he safely might to the carelessness & stupidity of the *average* reader to take his showing of plausibility for truth.

— Now can't you possibly print the letters, with a short Editorial *note* showing them up? — As a kindness to *me*, as well as to the Indians — & as a blow to Schurz? He is no doubt *chuckling* at this minute over the Tribunes *re*statement of the very things he wanted stated? — If you can't do this, — send the letters back to me today, please, & I will try somewhere else: — but no place will be half so good as the Tribune.

Yours truly

Helen Jackson

Brevoort House

Thurs. P.M.

Friday, AM. —

I open this, to thank you over & over for the splendid Editorial this Am.[5] — Please give my warm personal compliments to the man who wrote it: It is the best single stroke dealt yet.   H.J.

ALS (DLC, Reid Papers).

1. On Feb. 12, 1880, p. 2, the *Tribune*, in an article entitled "The Indian Problem: How Secretary Schurz Would Solve It," only mentioned the HHJ/Schurz correspondence and did not print the text of any of the letters.

2. Although HHJ clearly wrote Fiske in this letter, she is probably referring to Clinton Bowen Fisk, president of the Board of Indian Commissioners. There was, however, a New York merchant named Josiah M. Fiske who actively sponsored the Poncas, but newspaper accounts did not describe him as a general.

3. In a one-sentence introduction, noting the interior secretary's consent, the *Boston Advertiser* had printed the correspondence in full on Feb. 7, 1880, on the front page as "The Ponca Suits: The Letters between Mrs. Jackson (H.H.) and Mr. Schurz."

4. The Feb. 12 *Tribune* article that HHJ complained about did include the full text of Senator Alvin Saunders's Jan. 12 allotment bill as well as her lengthy comments on the bill. She noted that under Saunders's bill the Utes would lose over eleven million acres. "And will the American people read it carefully," she wrote, "and see whether they believe that this bill was drawn up for the purpose of benefiting the Indians, or for the purpose of opening millions of acres of land for white settlers?"

5. On Feb. 13, p. 4, in a lengthy editorial, the *Tribune*, informing its readers that the Indians were worse off than the former slaves, pointed out that the Indian Bureau had more control over the Indians and their property than the czar of Russia had over his subjects. The sole remedy included confirmation of Judge Dundy's decision and the granting of lands in fee simple.

From the beginning the *Tribune* had supported the Ponca cause. For example in a Feb. 5, 1880, editorial, p. 4, entitled "Congress and the Poncas," the editor had written: "On the very first issue of the order for the removal of the Poncas THE TRIBUNE warned the Department that it was not only a barbarous outrage but a robbery in which the law would not support them." The editor continued: "We have never ceased to protest against it."

TO WHITELAW REID

[February 14, 1880]

Dear Mr. Reid,

I have just received from Mr. Tibbles the enclosed paper written by the Rev. A. L. Riggs,[1] at his (Tibbles') request.

It seems to me a strikingly able paper — & it has great weight — coming from Mr. Riggs who has lived with the Indians all his life. He & his family & one other Missionary were the only persons spared by the Sioux in the great Massacre in Minnesota in 1862. He has the confidence and love of every tribe on the plains. —

I hope you will like to publish this: if not, will you kindly let me have it again, at once. The public ought to have it in some way, immediately.

I was very sorry about the letters: but I presume you are right. The Secretary outwitted Gen. Fiske that time. —

Yours truly

Helen Jackson

Brevoort House

Sat. Eve. Feb. 14.

If you print this paper, will you not mention these facts about Mr. Riggs's position and experience in an "Ed[itorial] Head[ing]."

ALS (DLC, Reid Papers).

Reid wrote the following on the letter: "Mr. Hassard = What do you say to this? WR." Hassard's reply was: "There are good things in it — enough of them to make it desirable — though it is verbose and on that account feebler than it ought to be. It could be packed a little closer. JH." This was probably in reference to the Riggs paper.

1. The Reverend Alfred Longley Riggs (1837–1916), a Congregational minister, was a missionary among the Santee Sioux for the American Board of Commissioners for Foreign Missions, 1870–83. He later continued his missionary work for the American Missionary Association and served as principal of the Santee Normal Training School. Between 1876 and 1915 he wrote various publications in the Siouan language and was a trustee of Yankton College.

TO WHITELAW REID

[February 22, 1880]

Dear Mr. Reid

I have just been down to the Trib. office — hoping against hope that you might be there — to carry my reply to Mr. Byers' most astounding letter.[1]

It seems to me of the greatest importance to me personally that this reply should come out tomorrow morning — that these misstatements should be met promptly & forcibly. —

I am sure you will approve the letter — There is not a word of personality in it — I do not even mention Byers by name.

The letter consists almost solely of quotations from the *sworn testimony* given before the Committees on the S[and] C[reek] Massacre: and of quotations from the Secretarys own Reports of the Dept. of the Interior. —

I am sure as Byers letter was so direct & gross an attack on me & my statements you will allow me the privilege of an immediate defense of both: —

Yours ever truly

Helen Jackson

Brevoort House—Sunday Eve. *22 Feb. 1880*, 9:30—

ALS (DLC, Reid Papers).

1. William N. Byers (1831–1903) worked in the West as a U.S. deputy surveyor until drawn to Colorado by the discovery of gold in 1859. He established the *Rocky Mountain News*, remaining its editor and publisher until 1878. Later he served as postmaster of Denver and president of the Chamber of Commerce and organized the Denver Tramway Company.

Byers's letter to the *Tribune*, published on Feb. 22 as "The Starving Utes: A Reply to Questions Asked by 'H.H.,'" p. 5, was in response to HHJ's Jan. 31 letter to the *Tribune*. For HHJ's rebuttal, see Feb. 22, 1880, below.

TO THE EDITOR OF THE *TRIBUNE*

[February 22, 1880]

To the Editor of The Tribune.

SIR: In reply to the letter in Sunday's TRIBUNE, headed "The Starving Utes," I would like to place before the readers of THE TRIBUNE some extracts from sworn testimony taken in Colorado on the subject of the Sand Creek massacre. The writer[1] of this letter says:

The Cheyenne and Arapaho Indians assembled at Sand Creek were not under the protection of a United States fort.

The following testimony is that of Lieutenant Craven,[2] Senate Document, vol. 2, 1866–67, p. 46:

I had some conversation with Major Downing,[3] Lieutenant Maynard,[4] and Colonel Chivington. I stated to them my feelings in regard to the matter; that I believed it to be murder: and stated the obligations that we of Major Wynkoop's command were under to those Indians.

To Colonel Chivington I know I stated that Major Wynkoop had pledged his word as an officer and man to those Indians, and that all officers under him were indirectly pledged in the same manner that he was, and that I felt that it was placing us in very embarrassing circumstances to fight the same Indians that had saved our lives, as we all felt that they had.

Colonel Chivington's reply was that he believed it to be right or honorable to use any means under God's Heaven to kill Indians that would kill women and children; and, "damn anyone that was in sympathy with Indians," and "such men as Major Wynkoop and myself had better get out of the United States service."

This conversation was testified to by other witnesses. Major Wynkoop, it will be remembered, was the officer in command at Fort Lyon when this band of Cheyennes and Arapahoes came in there to claim protection, in consequence of the Governor's proclamation saying that,

All friendly Arapahoes and Cheyennes belonging on the Arkansas River will go to Major Colby [Colley], United States Indian Agent at Fort Lyon, who will give them provisions and show them a place of safety.

Major Wynkoop was succeeded in the command of Fort Lyon by Major Anthony, who continued for a time to issue rations to these Indians, as Major Wynkoop had done; but after a time he called them together and told them he could not feed them any longer: they would better go where they could hunt. *He selected the place to which they were to move on Sandy Creek.* They obeyed, and he gave back to them some of the arms which had been taken away. They were moved to Sandy Creek, about forty miles from Fort Lyon, partly "for fear of some conflict between them and the soldiers or emigrants," Fort Lyon being on a thoroughfare of travel. One of the chiefs, "One Eye,"[5] was hired by Major Anthony at $125 a month "to obtain information for the use of the military authorities. Several times he brought news to the fort of proposed movements of hostile Indians." This chief was killed in the massacre.

This is the testimony of Captain Soule,[6] 1st Colored[7] Cavalry:

Did you protest against attacking those Indians?

I did.

Who was your commanding officer?

Major Anthony.

Did you inform Major Anthony of the relations existing with Black Kettle?

I did. He knew the relations. I frequently talked to him about it.

What answer did Major Anthony make to your protests?

He said that we were going to fight the hostile Indians at Smoky Hill. He also said that he was in for killing all Indians, and that he had only been acting friendly with them until he could get a force large enough to go out and kill all of them.

This is the testimony of S.E. Brown:[8]

Colonel Chivington in a public speech said his policy was to kill and scalp all, little and big; nits make lice.

Governor Hunt[9] testified as follows: (Governor Hunt was one of the earliest settlers in Colorado. He was United States Marshall, Delegate to Congress, and afterward Governor of the Territory.)

We have always regarded Black Kettle and White Antelope as the special friends of the white man ever since I have been in this country.

Do you know of any acts of hostility committed by them or with their consent?

No, sir, I do not.

Did you ever hear any acts of hostility attributed to them by any one?

No, sir.

The regiment when they marched into Denver exhibited Indian scalps.

This is from the official report of Major Wynkoop Major commanding Fort Lyon.

In conclusion allow me to say that from the time I held the consultation with the Indian chiefs on the head-waters of Smoky Hill, up to the date of this massacre by Colonel Chivington, not one single depredation had been committed by the Cheyenne and Arapahoe Indians. The settlers of the Arkansas Valley had returned to their ranches from which they had fled, had taken in their crops, and had been resting in perfect security under assurances from myself that they would be in no

danger for the present. Since this last horrible murder by Colonel Chivington the country presents a scene of desolation. All communication is cut off with the States, except by sending large bodies of troops, and already over a hundred whites have fallen victims to the fearful vengeance of these betrayed Indians.
January 15, 1865.

The writer of this letter says in regard to the investigation of the Sand Creek Massacre by the Congressional Committee that "evidence was taken upon one side only," and "there was no answer for the defence."

A large part of the testimony is sworn evidence given by the Governor of Colorado, by Colonel J. M. Chivington himself, who planned and executed the massacre, and by Major Anthony, who accompanied him with troops from Fort Lyon. The writer of this article says that "the investigation was made for a certain selfish purpose, * * * to break down and ruin certain men."

The names of Senator Foster,[10] Senator Doolittle,[11] and "honest Ben Wade"[12] are the best refutation of this statement. It will be hard to impeach the trustworthiness of reports signed by these names, and one of these reports says:

It is difficult to believe that beings in the form of men, and disgracing the uniform of United States soldiers and officers, could commit or countenance the commission of such acts of cruelty and barbarity.

Of Colonel Chivington, it says:

He deliberately planned and executed a foul and dastardly massacre which would have disgraced the veriest savage among those who were the victims of his cruelty.

And of Major Anthony:

The testimony of Major Anthony, who succeeded an officer disposed to treat these Indians with justice and humanity, is sufficient of itself to show how unprovoked and unwarranted was this massacre. He testifies that he found these Indians camped near Fort Lyon when he assumed command of that fort; that they professed their friendliness to the whites, and their willingness to do whatever he demanded of them; that they delivered their arms up to him; that they went to and encamped on the place designated by him; that they gave him information from time to time of acts of hostility which were meditated by other hostile bands, and in every way conducted themselves properly and peaceably; and yet he says it was fear and not principle which prevented his killing them while they were completely in his power; and, when Colonel Chivington appeared at Fort Lyon on his mission of murder and barbarity, Major Anthony made haste to accompany him with men and artillery.

The writer of this letter says that the evidence given in this "so-called investigation" was "largely false and infamously partial." If this were the case why did not all persons so "infamously" slandered see to it that before the year ended their own version of the affair should reach, if not the general public, at least the Department of the Interior? Why did they leave it possible for the Secretary of the Interior to incorporate in his Annual Report for 1865—to be read by all the American people—these paragraphs?

> No official account has ever reached this office from its own proper sources of the most disastrous and shameful occurrence, the massacre of a large number of men, women and children of the Indians of this agency (the Upper Arkansas) by the troops under the command of Colonel Chivington of the United States Volunteer Cavalry of Colorado. * * *
>
> When several hundred of them had come into a place designated by Governor Evans as a rendezvous for those who would separate themselves from the hostile parties, these Indians were set upon and butchered in cold blood by troops in the service of the United States. The few who escaped to the northward told a story which effectually prevented any more advances toward peace by such of the bands as were well disposed.

And why did the Government of the United States empower General Sanborn[13] in the Council held October 12th, 1865, with the Arapahoes and Cheyennes, including the remnants of bands that had escaped from the Sand Creek massacre, to formally and officially repudiate the action of the United States soldiers in that massacre? General Sanborn said in this council:

> We all feel disgraced and ashamed when we see our officers or soldiers oppressing the weak, or making war on those who are at peace with us. * * * We are willing, as representatives of the President, to restore all the property lost at Sand Creek or its value. * * * He has sent out his commissioners to make reparation, as far as we can. * * * So heartily do we repudiate the actions of our soldiers that we are willing to give to the chiefs in their own right 320 acres of land each to hold as his own forever, and to each of the children and squaws who lost husbands or parents we are also willing to give 160 acres of land as their own to keep as long as they live.[14]

The writer of this letter, quoting the statement from a previous article in THE TRIBUNE, that the White River Utes, in their attack on Major Thornburgh's[15] command, fought "to defend their own lands—lands bought, owned, and paid for," asks:

"Bought of whom, pray?"

"Paid for by whom?"

"To whom was payment made?"

"Bought" of the United States Government, thereby recognizing the United State Government's right to "the sovereignty of the soil" as superior to the Indians' "right of occupancy."

"Paid for," by the Uter [Ute] Indians by repeated "relinquishments" of said "right of occupancy" in large tracts of valuable lands; notably by the "relinquishment" according to the Brunot Treaty of 1873, of 4,000,000 acres of valuable lands, "unquestionably rich in mineral deposits."—(Annual Report of the Secretary of the Interior for 1873, p. 464.)

"To whom was payment made?"

To the United States Government, which has accepted and ratified such exchanges of "right of occupancy" for "right of sovereignty" and such sales of "right of occupancy" for large sums of money by repeated and reiterated treaties.

The Secretary of the Interior has incorporated in his Annual Report for 1879 (in the report on Indian Affairs, p. 36) the following paragraphs:

Let it be fully understood that the Ute Indians have a good and sufficient title to 12,000,000 acres of land in Colorado, and that these Indians did not thrust themselves in the way of the white people, but that they were originally and rightfully possessors of the soil, and that the land they occupy has been acknowledged to be theirs by solemn treaties made with them by the United States.

It will not do to say that a treaty with an Indian means nothing. It means even more than the pledge of the Government to pay a bond. It is the most solemn declaration that any government of any people ever enters into. Neither will it do to say that treaties never ought to have been made with Indians. That question is now not in order, as the treaties have been made and must be lived up to whether convenient or otherwise.

By beginning at the outset—with the full acknowledgment of the absolute and indefeasible right of these Indians to 12,000,000 acres in Colorado, we can properly consider what is the best method of extinguishing the Indian title thereto without injustice to the Indians, and without violating the plighted faith of the Government of the United States.

The writer of this letter says:

In withholding supplies from the White River Utes the Secretary of the Interior is simply obeying the law. He cannot, except upon his own personal responsibility, issue supplies to a hostile Indian tribe.

Secretary Schurz has published in the Annual Report of the Department of the Interior for 1879 the following paragraph in regard to this case of the White River Utes:

The atrocity of the crimes committed should not prevent those individuals who are innocent from being treated as such, according to Article 17 of the treaty, viz: *Provided,* that if any chief of either of the confederated bands make war against the United States, or in any manner violate this treaty in any essential part, said chief shall forfeit his position as chief and all rights to any of the benefits of this treaty; but, *provided further,* any Indian of either of these confederated bands who shall remain at peace and abide by the terms of this treaty in all its essentials shall be entitled to its benefits and provisions notwithstanding his particular chief and band have forfeited their rights thereto.

The writer of this letter says, in allusion to the murders and outrages committed by some of the White River Utes, that "H.H. is the champion of the friends [fiends] who wrought the ruin." Have the readers of THE TRIBUNE so understood my protests against the injustice of punishing the innocent for the crimes of the guilty?

H.H.

New-York, Feb. 22, 1880.

Printed in the *Tribune,* Feb. 24, 1880, p. 2, as "The Sand Creek Massacre: A Slaughter of Friendly Indians: Reply of 'H.H.' to the Letter of William N. Byers— Citations from Sworn Testimony and Official Reports." Reprinted in *A Century of Dishonor,* pp. 350–56.

1. A reference to William N. Byers.

2. Lieutenant Joseph A. Cramer (not Craven) (1838–70) came to Colorado in the 1859 gold rush. Commissioned a second lieutenant in the First Regiment of Colorado Cavalry, he was stationed at Fort Lyon and strongly disapproved of the attack on Sand Creek. He later settled in Solomon, Kansas.

3. Jacob Downing (1830–1907) moved to Colorado in 1859 and opened a law office. A major in the First Regiment of Colorado Cavalry, he served on Chivington's staff at Sand Creek and later acted as Chivington's attorney during the army investigation of the massacre.

4. Lieutenant Joseph S. Maynard, First Regiment of Colorado Cavalry, was Chivington's adjutant. He mustered out in April 1865.

5. In Sept. 1864 Southern Cheyenne subchief One Eye, under dangerous circumstances, had carried a letter from Black Kettle to Major Wynkoop at Fort Lyon. One Eye had offered himself and his wife, who accompanied him, as hostages if Wynkoop would meet with Black Kettle and the other chiefs.

6. An abolitionist, Silas S. Soule (1843–65), enlisted during the Civil War at Lawrence, Kansas, but transferred to Company D of the First Regiment of Colorado Cavalry, becoming a captain. Present at Sand Creek, he refused to order his men to attack and later testified against Chivington. In April 1865, while serving as provost marshal of Denver, he was shot dead by a member of the Second Colorado Cavalry.

7. Should read "Colorado" not "Colored."

8. A captain in the Third Regiment of Colorado Cavalry at Sand Creek, S. E. Browne (1822–1902) had practiced law in Ohio before accepting an April 1862 appointment as the United States attorney for Colorado. He resigned in 1865 and opened a law practice in Denver.

9. Alexander Cameron Hunt (1825–94) served as territorial governor for Colorado, 1867–69. He successfully negotiated a treaty with the Utes in 1868, acquiring all their lands in Colorado. From 1870 to 1883 he was active in developing Colorado Springs and building the Denver and Rio Grande Railroad.

10. Lafayette Sabine Foster (1806–80) served in the U.S. Senate, 1854–67, the last two years as president pro tempore. He was a member of the Joint Special Committee investigating Sand Creek.

11. James Rood Doolittle (1815–97) served in the U.S. Senate, 1857–69. A member of the Senate Committee on Indian Affairs, he chaired the congressional Joint Special Committee investigating conditions of western tribes, 1865–67. Part of this committee investigated Sand Creek, taking testimony in Washington, and at Fort Riley, Fort Lyon, and Denver.

12. Benjamin Franklin Wade (1800–1878) served in the U.S. Senate, 1851–69. He signed the final report of the Joint Committee on the Conduct of the War, which investigated Sand Creek. His committee met with witnesses in Washington and with Chivington in Denver.

13. General John B. Sanborn (1826–1904) commanded volunteers during the Civil War. In Oct. 1865 he negotiated a treaty with the Cheyennes and Arapahoes at the Little Arkansas River and served as a civilian member of the Peace Commission established in 1867 by Congress to determine the causes of Indian hostilities and to negotiate peace treaties.

14. In article six of the Oct. 14, 1865, treaty with the Cheyennes and Arapahoes, the government condemned the attack at Sand Creek upon peaceful Indians "whose protection . . . had by lawful authority been promised" and made reparations of 320 acres to various chiefs and 160 acres to widows or children who lost a parent. See Kappler, ed., *Indian Treaties, 1778–1883*, pp. 887–91 (quotation on p. 889).

15. A West Point graduate who served in the Civil War, Major Thomas T. Thornburgh (ca. 1843–79) became commander of Fort Fred Steele, Wyoming, in 1878. In Sept. 1879 he led a company of men from the fort to the White River Ute Agency at the request of agent Nathan C. Meeker. He and some of his soldiers were killed by the Utes as they entered the reservation.

TO WHITELAW REID

[February 26, 1880]

Dear Mr. Reid —

While you are eating your oatmeal just turn your eye over these pages of farther testimony on that Sand Creek Massacre! Think of my having found *228* pages of testimony I had not seen except by quotation before.[1] — It is far the most damning record of the three — & yet Col. Chivington had full opportunity to bring all the witnesses he could rake scrape & rustle. —

Will you be able to print this for me tomorrow?[2] Do if it be a possible thing. I want to get it in & "out" before Byers has had time to cook up another reply, which he no doubt will. — But after I have published this, there will be no reason for my taking any farther notice of him: — and you know my dread of being "drawn in to a newspaper controversy"!

I have written a note to Mrs. Davis[3] & enclosed it to you to forward — & leave it open that you may see I put the thing exactly as you wished me to, about your having told me.

Yours cordially

Helen Jackson

Thurs AM. Feb 26, 1880

P.S. Senator Foster told me the story of the squaw which concludes this paper.

ALS (DLC, Reid Papers).

Reid wrote the following on the letter: "Mr. Hassard = Haven't we printed enough of this stuff? WR." Hassard replied: "I think so. J. H."

1. This was testimony from the army-directed military commission that convened in Denver from Feb. through May 1865.

2. HHJ is referring to her Feb. 28, 1880, letter to the *Tribune*, below. Also see HHJ to Reid, Mar. 1, 1880, below.

3. Rebecca Harding Davis (1831–1910), who began her writing career in the *Atlantic Monthly*, joined the editorial staff of the *Tribune* in 1869, serving for several years. She also authored sketches, stories, and novels. On Feb. 29, 1880, her article "Bottom Facts in the Indian Matter" appeared in the *Tribune*.

TO THE EDITOR OF THE *TRIBUNE*

[February 28, 1880][1]

To the Editor of The Tribune.

SIR: In reply to the assertion that the perpetrators of the Sand Creek massacre were "denied a hearing in their defence," I wish to state to the readers of THE TRIBUNE that in addition to the Congressional Committees from whose reports I have already quoted, there was appointed a Military Commission to investigate that massacre. This Commission sat seventy-three days, in Denver and at Fort Lyon. Colonel J. M. Chivington called before it in his "defence," all the witnesses he chose, and gave notice on the seventy-third day of the Commission's sitting that he did not "wish to introduce any more witnesses for the defence." He also had (and used) the privilege of cross-examining every witness called by the Commission. The evidence given before this Commission occupies over two hundred pages of Volume 2, Senate Documents for 1866-'67.

In reply to the assertion that "a great majority of the savage atrocities of that period occurred before" the massacre at Sand Creek, and that "comparatively few occurred after," I will give to the readers of THE TRIBUNE one extract from the report of the Indian Peace Commission of 1868. Alluding to the Sand Creek massacre, the report says:

> It scarcely has its parallel in the records of Indian barbarity. Fleeing women holding up their hands and praying for mercy were shot down; infants were killed and scalped in derision; men were tortured and mutilated in a manner that would put to shame the savages of interior Africa. No one will be astonished that a war ensued, which cost the Government $30,000,000, and carried conflagration and death into the border settlements. During the Summer and Spring of 1865, no less than 8,000 troops were withdrawn from the effective forces engaged in the Rebellion to meet this Indian war.[2]

The Commissioners who made this report were: N. J. Taylor,[3] President; J. B. Henderson,[4] John B. Sanborn, William T. Sherman, Lieutenant-General; William S. Harvey [Harney],[5] Brevet Major-general; Alfred H. Terry,[6] Brevet Major-General; C.C. Augur,[7] Brevet Major-General; S. F. Tappan.[8]

In reply to the assertion that the Utes have not "either bought or paid for any land," I will ask such of THE TRIBUNE readers as are interested in the subject to read the "Brunot Treaty" made September 13th, 1873, "between Felix R. Brunot, Commissioner for the United States, and the chiefs, headmen and men" of the seven confederated bands of Utes. It is to be found in the report of the Department of the Interior for 1873, p. 454.

In conclusion of the discussion as to the Sand Creek massacre, I will relate one more incident of that terrible day. It has not been recorded in any of the reports. It was told in Colorado, to one of the members of the Senate Committee at the time of their investigation: One of the squaws had escaped from the village, and was crouching behind some low sage brush. A frightened horse came running toward her hiding-place, its owner in hot pursuit. Seeing that the horse was making directly for her shelter, and that she would inevitably be seen, and thinking that possibly if she caught the horse, and gave him back to the owner, she might thus save her life, she ran after the horse, caught it, and stood holding it till the soldier came up. Remembering that with her blanket rolled tight around her, she might possibly be taken for a man, as she put into the soldier's hand the horse's bridle, with the other she threw open her blanket enough to show her bosom that he might see that she was a woman. He put the muzzle of his pistol between her breasts and shot her dead; and afterward was "not ashamed" to boast of the act. It was by such deeds as this that "the Colorado soldiers acquited themselves well, and covered themselves with glory."

H.H.

New-York, Feb. 28th, 1880.

Printed in the *Tribune,* Mar. 3, 1880, p. 5, as "The Sand Creek Massacre: 'H.H.' Takes a Final Shot at Mr. William N. Byers and His Account of the Affair." Reprinted in *A Century of Dishonor,* pp. 357–58.

1. In a Mar. 1, 1880, letter to Reid, below, HHJ requested that he backdate this letter to Feb. 28. Since the only extant copy is printed in the *Tribune,* there is no way of knowing the original date.

2. Before the attack at Sand Creek, generally only young braves, eager for a reputation, engaged in raiding; afterward many Southern Cheyennes, aided by other Plains tribes, attacked wagon trains along the Platte and Smokey Hill trails.

"The Rebellion" is a reference to the Civil War. The Civil War years witnessed a marked increase in Indian warfare, primarily because most frontier troops were withdrawn to fight the Confederacy.

3. Nathaniel Green Taylor (1819–87) practiced law, was a Methodist Episcopal minister, and served in the House of Representatives before his appointment as Indian commissioner in 1867 by President Andrew Johnson. He was chairman of the Indian Peace Commission.

4. John Brooks Henderson (1826–1913) was appointed to the Senate in 1862 to fill a vacancy and was elected the following year. He chaired the Senate Committee on Indian Affairs and in 1867 was appointed to the Indian Peace Commission.

5. William Selby Harney (1800–1889) fought during the second Seminole war in Florida, served in the Mexican American War, led a punitive expedition against the Sioux in 1854, and served as commander of the Department of the West until 1861. He retired from the military in 1863 and served as a member of the Indian Peace Commission.

6. Civil War veteran Alfred Howe Terry (1827–90) assumed command of the Department of Dakota in 1866 and again in 1872. Because of his judicial training, he was chosen for membership on various army and Indian commissions, including the Indian Peace Commission.

7. A graduate of the U.S. Military Academy and a veteran of the Mexican American War and Civil War, Christopher Columbus Augur (1821–98) commanded various military departments from 1867 until his retirement in 1885. Although chosen to serve as a substitute member of the 1867 Indian Peace Commission, Augur eventually became a regular member.

8. Samuel F. Tappan (1830–1913) was an abolitionist who covered the antislavery movement in Kansas for the *Tribune* before becoming assistant editor of the *Daily Herald* in Denver in 1860. A lieutenant colonel with the First Regiment of Colorado Cavalry, he was not at Sand Creek; however, he chaired the military commission investigating the massacre. He also was a member of the Indian Peace Commission

and helped negotiate the 1867 Treaty at Medicine Lodge Creek in Kansas with the Cheyennes, Arapahoes, Comanches, Kiowas, and Kiowa Apaches.

TO WHITELAW REID

[February 29, 1880]

Dear Mr. Reid,

Mr. Tibbles telegraphed to me late last eve. asking me to get that manuscript of Rev. A. L. Riggs, and send it immediately to Mr. Cook[1] who would use it in Boston. —

Can you send it to me today? I should send to the office direct for it, but I fear it will have to be "looked up" in somebody's desk. —

I have only just seen Byers' little card of Friday.[2] I had over-looked it. How pitiful and at the same time audacious the man is. I am at a loss to understand his reiterating the lie that "they were never heard in defense": It is simply ludicrous, or would be if it were not so calculated to do harm. —

I do hope you will print my second batch of evidence, tomorrow morning? — and I will send a short preliminary sentence to be added to it. — Send me back word by the boy if you *think* it will go in tomorrow & if so I will send the paragraph down this PM to the office. —

I am sure I recognize Mrs. Davis's motherly touch again this A.M. — I really must *see* that woman to thank her; only I don't want her to put it to people's heads that it isn't worth while for them to read all the conflicting evidence & evidences on both sides — because that is just what keeps up the growth of public sentiment.

Yours ever truly
Helen Jackson

Brevoort House
Sunday, AM, Feb. 29, 1880.

ALS (DLC, Reid Papers).
 1. Possibly a reference to the Reverend Joseph Flavius Cook (1838–1901), a graduate of the Andover Theological Seminary who, beginning in 1874, led the Monday noon prayer-meetings in Tremont Temple in Boston for twenty years. For the 131st Monday lecture on the subject of the "wrongs of the Ponca Indians," see "The Monday Lectures: By the Rev. Joseph Cook—with Preludes," *Boston Advertiser*, Nov. 4, 1879, p. 4. He was a strong supporter of the Ponca cause.
 2. Byers's rebuttal was published on Feb. 27, 1880, p. 5, as "The Sand Creek Massacre: A Card from William N. Byers in Reply to 'H.H.'s' Letter to Tuesday Tribune."

TO ANN SCHOLFIELD (FISKE) BANFIELD

Brevoort House
Sunday Eve
Feb. 29 — [1880]

Dear Annie —

I havent the least idea whether I owe you a letter or not but for fear I do — I'll drop a line to you today. I am harder at work than I ever worked in my life — from 10 till 4. every day at the Astor Lib —

This with trying to return calls & now & then go out to dinner — keeps me in a whirl from one weeks end to another. — I have undertaken to write a short history of the U.S. dealings with the Indians for 100 years¹ — & it is an exceedingly tiresome task — but I hope to accomplish something by it — I cannot but think that I have already accomplished something in the way of rousing public attention to the outrageous injustice of our treatment of those poor creatures. —

I expect to work here till June 1*st* at least — Will will probably go back to Col[orado] next week — for a month or so — but will be here more than half the time. In June I am going to *Colorado* to write up the condition of the Indians there — for Harpers Mag[azine] — I think this will be a most interesting journey —

If you don't hear from me — assume that all is well —

Love to all —

Ever lovingly
Helen

ALS (CoCC, WSJ II, box 3, fd. 31).
Ann Scholfield (Fiske) Banfield (1834–1903) was HHJ's sister. Following their mother's death in 1844, the sisters were sent to live with different relatives and saw each other only during vacations. Ann married Everett Colby Banfield, who served as solicitor of the Treasury Department, 1869–77. HHJ married her second husband, WSJ, in a simple Quaker ceremony at the Banfield's home in Wolfeboro, New Hampshire.
1. A reference to *A Century of Dishonor.*

TO WHITELAW REID

Astor Lib.
Mon. Morn.
1st Mar. 1880

Dear Mr. Reid —

I won't reiterate those things which you told me, so facetiously the other morning. You had heard "five thousand times" — But I will try to move your compassion by asking you how *you* would feel, if such a card as that of Byers on Friday were lying day after day, unanswered: — His persistence in his lies, is something marvellous; — and I know very well, one word from an "old Settler" and a *man*, outweights volumes from me. —Please send me that MSS of Riggs today without fail. I think from Tibbles' telegram, they have some immediate use for it in Boston.

Excuse these torn sheets from my note book.

The Enclosed pages are to be *prefixed* to those now in the printers hands — If the opening sentences of the paper as I originally wrote it need altering in consequence of this addition, will you kindly have it done, and please have it *dated back to Saturday.*[1]

Yours truly

Helen Jackson

ALS (DLC, Reid Papers).
1. Reid backdated her letter.

TO WHITELAW REID

[March 2, 1880]

Dear Mr. Reid —

You are entirely right, on re reading that paper, I see that it was entirely too long. — Now commend me for candor unprecedented among the authors of Rejected addresses. — I have boiled it down as you suggested — & I don't believe Byers will *dare* to say another word. — Do get it in for me tonight if it is a possible thing: — I am really indebted to you for forcing me to put it into this much more telling shape:[1] — people that are already interested & on the right side, do not *need* any more extracts — & those who are on the wrong side would not bother themselves to read a column, but will read a paragraph of succinct rejoinder. (Simply from the Anglo Saxon love of a fight.)

The little incident of the Squaw & death, I think makes a fitting *close* to the matter. — It was only this last month that Senator Foster told me the story, & even now — fifteen years afterward, his voice trembled, telling it: —

I enclose for you to read, a note from Mrs. Davis: — that you may see what a pleasure you procured for me by telling me she wrote that Editorial. Such words as these from her give me renewed faith & courage to keep on working. —

I enclose another short paper which I hope you will think it worth while to print.[2] It certainly exposes more forcibly one of Sec. Schurz's *lies*. — It has been in your office once — was given to Mr. Shanks[3] by Gen. Fiske who happened to be here just as I was finishing it. — & I asked him to take it down. — Mr. Shanks returned it with the accompanying note, from which I inferred that he did not read the article or know that *I* wrote it. — as I think he could have no doubt of my being careful to say no single *word* which official Reports do not corroborate.

Yours ever—

H.J.

When you return Mrs. D[avis]'s note — please tell me the no. of your house. I am tired of writing "Lower East Corner" on envelopes — *and I propose* to send a great many envelopes to hit you at oatmeal time, before June 1st —!

Tues. morning.—

2 March, 1880

ALS (DLC, Reid Papers).

   1. A reference to her Feb. 28, 1880, letter to the editor, above.

   2. HHJ may be referring to her Mar. 21, 1880, letter to the *Tribune*, below.

   3. Probably William Franklin Gore Shanks (b. 1837), who once served as office manager of *Frank Leslie's Weekly* and wrote *Noble Treason*, a tragedy.

TO WHITELAW REID

Brevoort House

Wed. Morn.

3 March, 1880

Dear Mr. Reid —

   Mr. Jackson says "considered as a controversial weapon" this mornings paper of mine is "worth all I ever" did before, "put together."[1] — I think so too: and I shall run the risk of boring you, by thanking you over again; —

   Thank you too, for putting it in so quickly. —

   I suppose you do not want to take me as a "fencing pupil"? If I am in danger of being "drawn in" to any more controversies, I would like to carry them on under your instructions.

Yrs truly

H.J.

ALS (DLC, Reid Papers).

   1. A reference to her Feb. 28, 1880, *Tribune* letter, above.

Thomas Henry Tibbles,
newspaper editor and
reformer. (T552, 3,
Nebraska State
Historical Society)

TO THOMAS HENRY TIBBLES

Brevoort House
March 4, 1880

Dear Mr. Tibbles,

I wrote at once to the Tribune Office for Mr. Riggs's manuscript, as soon as I received your telegram, but I did not get it for two days: — it was in type & had been printed: So I sent the proof to Mr. Cook as you directed. I hope it was in time for the use you had proposed to make of it.

I have found the Report you sent me of the testimony in regard to the Northern Cheyennes: I shall add some of this testimony to my account of the

Cheyenne Massacre in my book.[1] When will the rest be out? Let me have it, as soon as it comes out.

I suppose you have followed the *Byers* letters in the Tribune. His lies have been more astounding even than Kembles & Schurz's. I think he will not reply to my last letter. If he does, I shall take no notice of him. I have covered all the ground.

I have written out the history of the Cheyennes — the Winnebagoes — & the Delawares — & am now at work on the Sioux. I shall not be able to give the full history of more than *eight* or possibly ten of the tribes. I think: — the rest must be condensed into paragraphs. —What tribes would you recommend me to take in addition to those I have named? —

I would like very much to get, if I could, — from some one having access to Washington Records — a summary of the chief & most glaring failures on the part of the Govt. to pay the annuity provisions — Do you think I could get that?

Please keep me advised of all of interest that happens — and send me a copy of the *new bill* as soon as possible.[2]

My regards to Standing Bear, Bright Eyes & the Wood Worker. — I hope you will bring all the other Indians on here for a grand meeting in the Academy of Music. It would draw well now. *I am* sure. —

Yours truly
Helen Jackson

ALS (Helen Hunt Jackson Collection [#7080-B], Special Collections Department, Clifton Waller Barrett Library in the Alderman Library, University of Virginia, Charlottesville, Virginia; hereinafter cited as ViU, HHJ).

1. A reference to *A Century of Dishonor*.

2. Possibly a reference to the Ute Bill, which had passed the Senate on Apr. 12, 1880. This bill would implement provisions of the current Ute agreement.

TO THE EDITOR OF THE *TRIBUNE*

[March 21, 1880]

To the Editor of The Tribune.

SIR: Allow me to call attention to eleven curious dead letter laws in the United States:

1. Any citizen or resident of the United States entering any territory secured by treaty to the Indians for the purpose of hunting or grazing therein— fine within $100 and imprisonment within six months.

2. Entering the territory secured to the Indians south of the Ohio River, for any purpose whatever, without a passport from the property authority—half the above penalty.

3. Entering the Indian Territory with a hostile intention and committing any offence against the person or property of any friendly Indian which would be punishable if committed upon a citizen within our jurisdiction—fine within $100 and imprisonment within one year; if property be taken or destroyed, renumeration in double value; and if murder be committed, death. (Suppose this law was carried out in regard to the murderers of the chief Big Snake last Autumn, at Fort Reno, in Indian Territory, how many men would be hung besides the soldier who fired the first shot?)

4. Surveying or settling upon any land belonging to Indians, or attempting to do so—fine within $1,000 and imprisonment within one year.

5. Attempting to trade among the Indians as a trader, without license from the Government—fine within $100; imprisonment within thirty days and forfeiture of merchandise.

6. Purchasing from Indians any utensil for hunting or cooking or any article of clothing, except skins or furs—fine within $50, and imprisonment within thirty days.

7. Purchasing a horse from an Indian without a license—fine within $100; imprisonment within thirty days and forfeiture of the horse.

8. An Indian agent being concerned in any trade with Indians on his own account—fine within $1,000, and imprisonment within one year.

9. Treating with Indians for the purchase of land without authority from the Government—same punishment.

10. A foreigner going into the Indian Territory without a passport—same punishment.

11. Any Indian or other person committing within the Indian Territory any offence which would be punishable if committed within places of exclusive Federal jurisdiction—the same punishment as—is there provided for.— (Section 202, p. 518, Walker's American Law.)

Here are illustrations of the result of the neglect to enforce these laws:

In the report of the Indian Bureau for 1877, the agent for the Sioux at Standing Rock, Dakota, says:[1]

"The cutting of cord-wood on this reservation by white men to fill Government contracts and supply steamboats has provoked a very bad feeling among our Indians. They have, in council, denounced the Indian Department for not issuing a preemptory order prohibiting all wood contractors or their employees from going into our already much depleted forests to cut down the timber at such places and in such quantities as suits their own convenience, without any compensation to the Indians. They insist that they could cut all of the cordwood that would be necessary to supply the requirements of both the Government and the steamboats, and the benefit arising therefrom should inure to them and not to white men who have no interest in their welfare. They further say that the quantity of wood annually being cut at and near the agency by white men has become so great that they (the Indians) have serious apprehensions that they will be compelled to go a great distance in a few years to procure fuel. I have heretofore called the attention of the Department to this subject in special communications, and trust that it will receive such consideration as its importance demands, before the chopping of wood commences this season.

"Much difficulty is encountered in protecting the persons and property of Indians in Nebraska, on account of their not being under the protection of the laws of the United States. The timber from their reservations is taken by evil-disposed persons with impunity. Leading chiefs of Indian bands have been shot down in cold blood by white ruffians, and the perpetrators of the murders have personally reported the details to the local newspapers, boasting of their deeds, and yet these murderers are not even arrested. Popular opinion and prejudice against the Indian render the State laws inoperative and a dead letter in such cases, and high authorities decide that the United States Courts have no juris-diction. If the United States would have justice done to its wards in this State, it must extend over them the protection of its laws, and mete out to them equal justice with the white man, if it is not prepared to give them equal rights." (Report, in 1874, of Barclay White, the Friend[2] who was in charge at that time of the Northern Superintendency.)

H.H.

New-York, March 21, 1880.

Printed in the *Tribune*, Mar. 27, 1880, p. 2, as "The Indian Problem: 'H.H.' Enumerates Eleven Laws Which She Says Are a Dead Letter—Results of Neglecting to Enforce Them."

1. In 1876 William T. Hughes was appointed agent at Standing Rock Agency, located on the west bank of the Missouri River near Fort Yates, Dakota Territory.

2. To improve the quality of agents and superintendents, the Grant administration chose agents and other employees nominated by various missionary boards. By 1872 thirteen Protestant denominations were selecting Indian Office field officers. The Hicksite Quakers took charge of the Northern Superintendency, which included six Nebraska reservations. Barclay White, a member of the Philadelphia Yearly Meeting's Indian committee, headed the Northern Superintendency from 1871 until it was abolished in 1876.

TO WHITELAW REID

Sunday Morning
April 4,— 1880

Dear Mr. Reid,

Unfortunately I have an engagement on Monday at one oclock — somebody *else*'s axe, — not mine — that wants grinding! — I will come on Tuesday: — and meantime will you not print this little *clincher* to that splendid letter in this morning's Tribune about the Cheyennes?[1]

I do not suppose you can form the least idea of how happy this mornings Tribune *could* make a person who had the Indian cause at heart.

I really begin to have great hope that before another year has passed great reforms will have been accomplished. I have received several letters from a Miss Bonney,[2] principal of the Chestnut Hill [Street] Female Seminary in Phila. She has been at work for six months back, getting signatures to a petition, to the President on the subject — & has sent one with *13000* signatures, representing *15* states. — She is now initiating movements in *all* the states for a monster petition to the next Congress — to have several hundred thousand names: Such a petition as that will tell, will it not? — hundreds of thousands of names, & from every state in the Union — Has such a thing ever been done before?

Yrs truly
Helen Jackson

Please give this a good place — or an Ed[itorial] Head[ing] if it has to go into that "genteel asylum," the Letters from the People.—

ALS (DLC, Reid Papers).

1. A reference to "The Northern Cheyenne Outbreak: The Senate Investigation into the Causes of the Trouble—A Terrible Record of Broken Treaties and Shameful Neglect by the Government," which appeared on Apr. 4, 1880, p. 1. The following day the *Tribune* printed "The Massacre of the Cheyennes: Vivid Descriptions of That Bloody Incident of the Winter of 1878 by Two of the Chiefs of the Band," along with a short editorial note on the Cheyennes, pp. 1 and 4, respectively. This article presented testimony by Wild Hog and Old Crow before the Senate investigating committee.

Jackson's "clincher" was her Apr. 4 letter to the *Tribune*, below.

2. Mary Lucinda Bonney (1816–1900), founder of the Chestnut Street Female Seminary in Philadelphia (later the Ogontz School for Young Ladies), was an active member of the Woman's Union Missionary Society of America for Heathen Lands, president of the Women's Home Mission Circle, which worked among the American Indians, and founder and first president of the WNIA. Under her direction the second WNIA petition included fifty thousand signatures, and the third petition had one hundred thousand.

TO THE EDITOR OF THE *TRIBUNE*

[April 4, 1880]

To the Editor of The Tribune.

SIR: I would like to add to your Washington correspondent's graphic account, this morning, of the sufferings which maddened the Cheyennes into running away from Indian Territory, a brief account of what befell them afterward.

They surrendered to Major Carleton[1] on the 23d of October near Camp Sheridan, Nebraska. They surrendered only on condition that they should not be taken back to the Indian Territory. This was promised them. They were then taken to Fort Robinson and confined. Here they reiterated their expressions of desire to live at peace with our people, but said "they would kill themselves sooner than be taken back to the Indian Territory. These statements were confirmed by Red Cloud[2] and other friendly Sioux chiefs, who assured us that the Cheyennes had left their reservation in the Indian Territory to avoid fever and starvation, and that they would die to the last man, woman and child before they would be taken from the quarters in which they were confined. All this information was promptly reported to higher authority and instructions urgently requested; but no action was taken until the very last days of December, when orders were received to move them South." This is taken from General Crook's official report.

The army officers remonstrated again and again; over and over they reiterated the statement that these Indians would not consent to go back to the Indian Territory. At last there came stern orders from the Interior Department, "use sufficient force to carry them back." Then the officer in command at Fort Robinson in despair tried to starve them into consenting to go. He stopped the issue of all supplies to them; of fuel, also; and at this time, says General Crook's official report, "the thermometer at Fort Robinson showed a range from zero down to nearly 40° below."

After two days this commanding officer begged the women and children to come out and be fed. They refused. On the night of the fourth day these starving, freezing men and women broke out of their prison, overpowered the guards, fled—escaped their pursuers day after day, till they had marched some sixty miles, carrying their children in their arms, killing one or two stray cattle and eating the flesh raw. At last they made a stand in a ravine, and sold their lives as dearly as possible, charging on the soldiers with knives after their last cartridge was gone. Not a man was left alive, and only forty-five of the women and children. The eight who were spoken of in the Washington letter as having survived the massacre, were confined in another part of the fort, and did not take part in the outbreak.

Immediately after this massacre, Red Cloud, a Sioux chief, came to Fort Robinson and entreated to be allowed to carry the widows and orphans to his tribe to be taken care of, and the United States Government kindly allowed him to do so.

H.H.

New York, April 4, 1880.

Printed in the *Tribune*, Apr. 11, 1880, p. 5, as "The Massacre of the Cheyennes: 'H.H.' Adds to the Painful History."

1. Probably Ohio native Caleb Henry Carlton (b. 1842), a major in the Third Cavalry, who fought in the Civil War and later served as an officer in the Tenth, Third, and Seventh Cavalry.

2. Red Cloud (1822–1909), an Oglala Sioux headman, led his warriors against the forts on the Bozeman Trail in 1865–66, forcing the government to abandon them. He signed the 1868 Sioux peace treaty, toured Washington, D.C., and New York in 1870, and settled down at the Red Cloud agency.

TO WILLIAM HAYES WARD

[mid-March–early April 1880]

Dear Mr. Ward,

I have been more than overworked — or I should have been to see you or written to you, before this — But I have been thinking each day I should hear from you or see you, and so have put it off. I have been working every day at the Astor Lib. from 9. till 4!! — and I have five Chapters of my Indian Book done, —

"*A Century of Dishonor*"

"A Sketch of the U. S. Governments dealings with some of the Indian tribes."

I call it a *Sketch*, that nobody may arraign me for not writing a history & telling everything. To do that would take *years*, & *volumes*. —

I give an outline of the experiences of a tribe — broken treaties — removals — &c. — telling the history of each tribe straight through, by *itself*. In this way, I am sure these will be much more intelligible & interesting & effective to rouse peoples attention. It is like getting interested in the personal history, for instance, of the Ward family — or the Jackson! —

My first chapter is simply a lawyers brief — on the original "right of occupancy" — how recognized, stated, enforced — the *Law of Nations* as to

treaties & their violations. I have been through all the law authorities in the
Astor Lib. on their points from Grotius[1] & Vattel[2] down to Wheaton[3] &
Woolsey[4] — & I have read this chapter to *two lawyers* who both say there is not
a waste word in it — & that it is a very strong "brief". —

Now what I am coming at, is this — Do you want to publish the first five or
six chapters of my book in a series of articles in the Ind[ependent]?[5] — I think
it could help much to get the thing before the people which is what I am after.
— Each chapter would make two articles of from 3000 to 5000 words each —
but they are largely citations & all those could be in small print: — the first two
numbers — my "brief" — then, the history of say — the Cheyennes — Winnebagoes — Sioux —Delawares — & some one other tribe. — I would like to
read you the first chapter — & say the Delawares to show you just what it is. —
I am sure it is of great interest & value: — I have put an enormous amount of
solid work in it — they are *exact* transcripts from *Official* Records — & all the
heart & soul I possess have gone in! —

I infer as you never replied to my note about that $25 the Ind[ependent]
owes me for the Holmes Poem, that the publishers declined to pay it. Is it not
strange they can do such things? — Let me hear from you soon, about this —
because I want to try some other papers — if the Ind[ependent] doesn't take it.
— Harpers Weekly wants it very much — Mr. Conant[6] has been to see me
twice about it — but they want it all boiled down into short articles, which I
simply cannot do: — Much as I would like to hit their audience. It would take
me another six months to do it & be harder than the first time. —

Yrs ever—

Helen Jackson

The Berkeley —

Corner 5*th* Av. & 9th St.—

P.S. Cant you come up to lunch tomorrow & talk this over & hear the 1st
chapter? —

ALS (CSmH, HHJ MSS, HM 13992).
    1. Hugo Grotius (1583–1645), a Dutch jurist and statesman who wrote, among
other things, *De Jure Belli et Pacis* (1625), establishing modern public international law,
and an *Introduction to Dutch Legal Science* (1631).
    2. Emmerich de Vattel (1714–67) was a Swiss jurist, whose *Le Droit des Gens*
modernized international law. For a brief summary of both Grotius and Vattel, see
Norgren, *The Cherokee Cases: The Confrontation of Law and Politics*, p. 29.
    3. Henry Wheaton (1785–1848) served on the commission to revise the laws of
New York State and held diplomatic posts in Denmark and Prussia. He was the author
of *Elements of International Law* and a *History of the Law of Nations*.

4. Theodore Dwight Woolsey (1801–89) was appointed president of Yale University in 1846, a position he held for the next twenty-five years. He specialized in political science and international law; his *Introduction to the Study of International Law,* published in 1860, went through several editions.

5. Ward printed the following in the *Independent* in 1880: "One of the Early Indian Removals," May 20, pp. 3–5 (in *A Century of Dishonor,* pp. 308–17); "The Conestoga Massacre," June 3, pp. 2–3 (in *A Century of Dishonor,* pp. 298–308); "The Gnadenhutten Massacre of 1782," June 24, pp. 4–5 (in *A Century of Dishonor,* pp. 317–24); and "The End of a Century of Dishonor," Jan. 13, 1881, pp. 4–5 (in *A Century of Dishonor,* pp. 286–97).

6. Samuel Stillman Conant (1831–85) was managing editor of *Harper's Weekly* from 1869 to 1885.

TO WILLIAM HAYES WARD

[April 22 (1880)]

Dear Mr. Ward,

The more I think it over — the more I feel that it could be a serious loss to my book — to begin the series of papers in the Independent without that first chapter: and the friends I consult, think as I do, about it. —

Would you be willing to print the *last*-half of it — and let me write a little opening paragraph something to this effect —

"The question of the right of occupancy having been already treated in this paper" — I *omit* that part of my first chapter — and proceed to the considerations of the standards binding on nations in their relations with each other &c? —

If you will do this, I will decide at once to print the series in the Independent.[1] —

As the book will not be published until the last of November — we shall not want to begin the series before August: that would give two papers a month for Aug. Sept. October — & one in Nov. —

In the mean time, there are three separate stories of massacres, which I would like to have you print at once, if you can: (that will half pay for my ticket abroad!)[2]

— And by the way, if I see anything especially suited to a short letter for the Independent —, in London or Norway, or Scotland, or Italy, or Prague, or Nuremburg, I suppose you'd like a letter now and then wouldn't you? — I shall only be away June, July, & August. —

Yours always truly
Helen Jackson

Berkeley
Thurs. Eve. April 22. —

ALS (CSmH, HHJ MSS, HM 13984).

1. Apparently Ward did not agree, because no such article appeared in the *Independent,* although some of HHJ's other articles did.

2. See note 5 in the preceding letter.

TO CHARLES DUDLEY WARNER

[May 2, 1880]

Dear Mr. Warner,

I want to use in the Appendix to my book, Walkers resumé of the Indian Tribes, which he has used as one of the chapters in his "Indian Question."[1]

Of course I am quite at liberty to take it without leave, for it is all in the Official Reports of the Ind. Dept. — but I think it more courteous to ask permission: — and have written to do so. — Will you kindly enclose the note to him? I take it for granted that you know his address.

Bertie went to the country on Friday. — She will be in, she says, as often as twice a week — and I have asked her to come and sleep here, whenever she comes in, but I do not expect to see her at all.—

My friend Mrs. Lloyd, (Jessie Bross)[2] of Chicago is staying with me now convalescing from a piece of Dr. Emmett's[3] butchery — She will set out for Chicago on the 8*th* or 9*th* — and I may go with her, and on to St. Louis to meet Mr. Jackson for a three days lark and Goodbye. — If I don't do this, he will try to come here — but not to see me off, that I could not bear at all. — I never want again, one human being I know, on the wharf, when that dreadful wheel begins to go round. —

I shall finish the story of the Cherokees tomorrow, and that finishes my book, — except a short "Conclusion." — Seven tribes written out — Delawares — Cheyennes, Sioux, Poncas, Nez Perces, Winnebagoes — & Cherokees —: that is as many as people will stand I think. In the Appendix, a lot of odds & ends, to be referred to by foot notes — — my letters & Byers' on the Sand Creek Massacre, — three other notable massacres — Schurz's letters & mine on the Ponca case — etc. —

I shall take the Mss. to Harpers to read this week, I think.

If I go to St. Louis I shall be away from the 8*th* to the 18th — Shall be here from the 18*th* to the 25th. — If I do not go to St. Louis shall be here till the 25th — on that day I go to Boston — and sail on the 29*th* — ie. unless I change my mind & conclude to stay at home & write plays all summer!

My! If we could make one third as much as Boucicault[4] made — say $200,000 — wouldn't we take our hundred thousand a piece & go up the Nile together with our respective families! I believe I do want to go. I thought I didn't. — My best love to Mrs. Warner.

We dine at Mrs. Botta's tonight — & I am going to Mrs. Youmans's[5] afterward. —

Yours ever
Helen Jackson
or "William"

Berkeley,
May 2, 1880

ALS (CtHT-W, Warner Collection).

1. Francis A. Walker (1840–97) was an economist and statistician who directed the Ninth Census and served as commissioner of Indian affairs, 1871–72. His annual report of 1872 along with two other essays was published as *The Indian Question* (1874). He believed in settling Indians on reservations and protecting their rights. Walker's report appeared in *A Century of Dishonor*, pp. 411–58.

2. Jessie was the daughter of William Bross (1813–90), elected lieutenant governor of Illinois in 1864. Her husband, Henry Demarest Lloyd (1847–1903), was a noted journalist and author.

3. Possibly Thomas Addis Emmet (1828–1919), an 1850 graduate of Jefferson Medical College in Philadelphia. He was visiting physician to the Emigrants' Refuge Hospital on Ward's Island, New York, before becoming assistant to J. Marion Sims, the pioneer gynecologist at the Woman's Hospital in New York in 1855. In 1861 Emmet became surgeon-in chief and in 1872 visiting surgeon at the Woman's Hospital. In 1879 he wrote *The Principles and Practise of Gynecology*.

4. Dion Boucicault (1820–90), a Dublin-born actor and dramatist, came to New York in 1853. Averaging more than two plays a year, he originated the system of casting in New York and then toured the country.

5. Possibly Eliza Ann Youmans (b. 1826), who applied scientific studies to children's education. During the 1870s and 1880s she published several books on botany and contributed to the *Popular Science Monthly* and other periodicals.

TO HENRY MILLS ALDEN

Berkeley,
Thursday Am.
May 6 1880

Dear Mr. Alden,

I wrote the last word of the last chapter of my book yesterday. It was an odd feeling: — not wholly a pleasant one. — I shall not be as wholly content in any other place I fancy, as I have been in these four months in the Astor Library. —

Now I want to have a talk with the Messrs. Harper about publishing it. — Can you make an appointment with them for me, — for either tomorrow morning — or Saturday morning, or this afternoon. — I go to St. Louis for a few days, and leave on Sat. afternoon and would like to see them before I go, and have the Mss. in their hands for reading while I am away.

We sail on the 29*th* and you will be glad to know that I have concluded an arrangement with the Scribners for two articles on the Passion Play,[1] and with the Atlantic for four articles on the journey, "Bits of Travel."[2] —

Would it be possible for me to get from the Harpers, a copy of the old account of the Passion Play which you published ten years ago? I recollect that there was a good deal of historical information in it which would be of use to me in writing mine.

Yours truly

Helen Jackson

ALS (Helen Maria Fiske Hunt Jackson Collection, [Banc MSS 71/139z], Bancroft Library, University of California, Berkeley, California; hereinafter cited as CU-B, HMFHJ Coll.).

Henry Mills Alden (1836–1919) first published in the *Atlantic* but spent over fifty years working with the Harpers, first as managing editor of *Harper's Weekly* and then as editor of *Harper's Magazine* from 1869 to his death.

1. HHJ's essay on the Passion Play at Oberammergau was published by Scribner's successor, *Century Magazine*, in Mar. and Apr. 1883 and reprinted in Helen Jackson (H.H.), *Glimpses of Three Coasts*, pp. 384–418.

2. The *Atlantic* essays included "Bergen Days," June 1881, pp. 770–84; "Four Days with Sanna," July 1881, pp. 39–59; "The Katrina Saga," Sept. and Oct. 1881, pp. 366–77 and 518–32; "Glints in Auld Reekie," Sept. 1883, 363–75; and "Chester Street," Jan. 1884, pp. 12–25; all reprinted respectively in *Glimpses of Three Coasts*, pp. 221–44, 245–76, 277–321, 175–95, 196–218. In addition *Century Magazine* in Sept. 1883 published "A Burns Pilgrimage," reprinted in *Glimpses of Three Coasts*, pp. 153–74.

TO BISHOP HENRY B. WHIPPLE

The Berkeley, New York

May 22 — 1880

Bishop Whipple

Dear Sir,

By the mistake of a clerk to whom I gave the envelope to weigh, a parcel of newspaper slips was sent to you yesterday without any accompanying word of explanation. — Pardon my assuming that they would be of interest to you.

The book at which I have been engaged all winter is done. I have written Sketches of the Poncas, — Sioux — Cheyennes — Winnebagoes — Nez Percé's, Delawares & Cherokees. — also some of the early Massacres, and Removals — and one chapter, the opening chapter, entirely on the Right of occupancy, the Laws of Nations as affecting the faith and obligation of Treaties. — In an Appendix there will be miscellaneous matter to be referred to by foot notes — all bearing on the subject.

I have asked President Seeyle[1] to write an introduction to the book — and I wish very much to have a brief preface, a sort of benediction from you. Would you be willing to write it?[2] I am sure it would be of great value in recommending the book to a large circle of readers.

The title of the book is to be "A Century of Dishonor — A Sketch of the United States Governments dealings with some of the Indian tribes" —

It is more than half quotations from the Official Records. — and I cannot but think will do good.

It cannot be published till Dec. 1st — on account of the Elections, which kill all interest in everything. —

I sail for Europe next week — for a three months rest after my work: but I shall return in Sept. to supervise the bringing out of the book. —

Anything sent to the care of Roberts Bros. Boston, will be forwarded to me wherever I am — or will reach me in Boston, up to *the* morning of the 29th —

Yours respectfully
Helen Jackson

ALS (MnHi, Whipple Papers).
  1. Seelye's introduction to *A Century of Dishonor* was completed on Dec. 10, 1880.
  2. Whipple accepted HHJ's invitation and completed his preface on Nov. 11, 1880.

TO WILLIAM SHARPLESS JACKSON

Berkeley.
Sat. Eve.
May 23rd [1880][1]

Dearest Will —

I have an idea that I have done today one of the best days works I ever did in my life — I have had a long talk with young Mr. Harper[2] — (Mr. Harry as he is called) and have agreed to have them publish the "Century of Dishonor".

— They are to fill out their contract, which is a most ponderous affair of three pages! & send it to me tonight to sign.³ They are to pay me *$250* down on the day of publication — being so much in advance on the royalty which is to be the usual one of ten per cent on retail price of all copies sold. — This payment down on day of publication *lets me out* with Niles, you see — and it is quite out of Harpers usual line — Mr. Phayre⁴ the man I saw yesterday, flatly refused to do anything of the kind — So my going down this morning was an inspiration & has given me a different feeling altogether about the whole thing. I like "Mr. Harry" very much — he is not more than thirty — fair — greenish gray eyes — hair as light as mine — prompt pleasant & brisk. — They *want* the book — that was plain, as I talked the matter over — & they anticipate a good sale. —

The question was raised of its being published simultaneously in London — & Mr. Harper advised me by all means as I was going there, to try through Mr. Conway⁵ to arrange for that — by doing so — & having it come out there one *week* in advance of publication here. I can have 10 per ct. on all copies sold there, also! — This was great news to me, Mr. Harper says that they are quite likely to reprint it, as it reflects so severely on the U. S. Govt !! & that I might as well have the *benefit* of the sales! — Now it is a question in my mind whether I as an American *ought* deliberately to sell to an English publisher such an attack on my nations good name. What do you think? I have never suspected myself of having any patriotism —but I feel a sort of unwillingness to be the voluntary instrument of exposing my country's shame to those Hinglish!⁶ — even if I did make a few hundred dollars by doing go. — Still — if the book were to have a wide sale, it might be of good advantage to me & prepare the way for reprinting other books — besides giving me more money on this one. —

I feel in great spirits over the prospects of the book — I am persuaded it is going to have a wide sale — & do good. —

One of the Harpers "Readers" sent in a written opinion of it, which says "It compels sympathy & attention even from minds which hate the subject & are weary of it— It contains much valuable information on our own countrys history & condition which is hard to find elsewhere. It is sure to find a large sale, & will be valued & referred to for a long time to come!" — This is from a lawyer, Mr. Harper said.—

In case it is to be published in England, I must get either Sally⁷ or Col. Higginson to read the proofs for me at *once,* so that the Harpers can send over advance sheets — I shall ask the Col. I think. I can trust him implicitly and I can't trust Sally in all matters. — Dear me, how I wish I had you here to read over this big contract before I sign it. — It is "as much as even" I understand it!

Your pictures have come from Chicago tonight—They made me feel like a
big baby — — the one in the hat is a scream — the other is a bad picture — as
I knew it would be when I saw the man let in the flood of light on the left — &
don't you remember how I kept urging you to put your chin down — & the
man kept letting you stick it up again — & you can see the result — how it is
thrown forward. Still the picture is a likeness & has a characteristic expression
— & I shall kiss them both hundreds of times before I see you again. —

AL (CoCC, WSJ I, box 1, fd. 5).
1. May 23 was a Sunday not a Saturday.
2. Joseph Henry ("Harry") Harper (1850–1938), author of *The House of Harper*
(1912) and *I Remember* (1934), became a partner in Harper & Brothers in 1877 and
was in charge of the literary and periodical department.
3. The contract, dated May 21, 1880, is in Harper & Brothers Papers, NNC.
4. J. F. Phayre, who worked at Harper's for over forty years, was Joseph Wesley
Harper's assistant.
5. After several years as a Methodist circuit rider, Moncure Daniel Conway
(1832–1907) attended Harvard Divinity School and became a Unitarian pastor in
Washington and later a Congregational minister. An abolitionist, he edited an antislavery paper and wrote several books on slavery before moving to England in 1864 to
become pastor at the South Place Chapel in London. He resigned in 1884 and
returned to America. Among his more than seventy books were a two-volume history
of Thomas Paine and biographies of George Washington, Thomas Carlyle, and
Nathaniel Hawthorne.
6. A corruption of the word "English."
7. Sally was HHJ's nickname for Sarah Chauncey Woolsey (1835–1905), who
wrote under the pen name "Susan Coolidge" and first met HHJ during the Civil War
years. Woolsey had an extensive literary career, which included writing children's
fiction, poetry, and travel articles and editing scholarly volumes of letters by prominent
women. She worked for Roberts Brothers and their successors, Little, Brown & Company, as an editor and manuscript reader. She and HHJ often vacationed together, and
in the summer of 1872 they traveled to northern California.

TO CHARLES SCRIBNER

[late May 1880]

Dear Mr. Scribner —

Thanks. I'll show you the Paris gown it buys, and you will command my
wisdom in the sale.

I will be at home at 2.30 P.M. tomorrow, to see Gen. Crook & yourself,
with great pleasure.

I think it is "hardly fair" in you to tantalize me now, by the implication that you might have thought of the publication of the Indian Book — when I especially threw out my little feeler on Saturday, (don't you remember I said "of course you don't want to buy that copyright"? —) and you dismissed it with a scornful smile! — The Harpers think the book will sell — I am going down there this P.M. to have my final talk with them and an explanation of the ponderous three page contract which I do not in the least understand —: and which seems to me "hardly fair" in some points. —

They sent me Saturday one of the "opinions" on the book, which gave me great pleasure and renewed my courage. It was from one of their readers — a lawyer of standing they say.

He says

"The book is too good to Con[gress]. It compels sympathy & attention even from minds which hate the subject and are weary of it. It contains much valuable information on our own countrys history & condition which it is hard to find elsewhere. It is sure to find a large sale & will be valued & referred to for a long time to come." —

The Harpers advise me to arrange through Mr. Conway, for simultaneous publication in London, & secure copyright there also — How does that strike you? I will ask you tomorrow. —

Yours very truly
Helen Jackson.

ALS (Charles Scribner's Sons Archives, Author Files I, box 82, Princeton University Library, Princeton, New Jersey).

Charles Scribner (1854–1930) became head of Charles Scribner's Sons at the death of his brother, John Blair Scribner. In addition to publishing major American writers, Scribner's published *St. Nicholas* and *Scribner's Magazine*.

TO WILLIAM SHARPLESS JACKSON

Parker House
Friday night.
May 28, 1880

Will dear — this is my last night on dry land! — not so dry as it might be either, for we have had a splendid shower — such a relief as it was — The whole city seemed to have a different expression after it. There has really been great suffering from the heat & drought.

— Today I have done all the last things — this afternoon Col. Higginson called & I talked the book all over with him, & explained as far as was possible all the parts where I saw a chance of mistake. He is very glad to read the proof for me — and it is an unspeakable load off my mind. He looked much better than when we saw him last fall, better dressed & in better health. —

Niles is pretty sorry about the book I think — & a good deal nonplussed by the Harpers giving me a royalty in advance — "I would have given you as much as they did" he said. (I did not tell him how much.) —

"But you didn't *offer* anything" I replied.

"No, I know I didn't" he said.

— I said "Well you lost your chance at it. I should have accepted an offer of $1000 for it, at once — & now I am mightily glad you didn't take it, for I expect to make two or three!" — which I really do. —

Mrs. Walter Cabot[1] was here last night — & the Goddards — — Mr. Goddard is going over to see me off — so is Mr. Fiske[2] — & Mr. Niles said he should — Mr. Houghton[3] also! — quite a galaxy of publishers: —

I called today at that Youth's Companion office — & saw one of the Editors Mr. Butterworth[4] — Mr. Mason[5] was away. — They would like some *half dozen* papers from me, about any specially interesting thing I see abroad — & will pay me *$30* a letter — So if I can only pick up material enough — there is $180 more —

Scribners —	$300
Atlantic	600
Advertiser	180
Youths Companion	180
	1260

— If only I can write all that worth, won't I be pleased, pretty nearly pay for the trip — perhaps *quite* pay for it. —

Tonight I have been out to the Horsfords[6] — they are all well, & in good spirits — Trudy the one you saw with her baby last fall, has another baby born today — a son — at this rate she will be the mother of a big family before she knows it. —

Your last letter to me came tonight — I have just a lingering hope of one more — but don't look for it much — I am wondering what you wrote to Prof. H[orsford]. He said tonight that he thought you would come out & join us, oh! My Will! What a joy that would be. — Then I'd let the Col. do all the bringing out of my book & we'd go to Gastein[7] & spend the whole of September. How you would enjoy climbing over those hills & watching all those Russians &

Austrians — & talking with old Dr. Proell.[8] — A month in Gastein with you, my darling — all to myself — it makes my cheeks grow hot to think of it. — Goodbye my precious husband —Write regularly twice a week — Monday & Thursday —

Your own Peggy,

Baring Bros. London will be our standing
address — we shall keep them advised of all our
movements. —

P.S. You didn't send the shoe bag — & I had to buy one today —I wonder if you know this little wild flower — the Arethusa — Dr. Nichols gave it to me today. It is most exquisite. Boys are selling great bunches of Solomons Seal on the street here. I think Ill take one to sea with me. —

P.S. I shall give to Mr. Fiske[9] tomorrow, my contract with Harpers to mail to you. I have no envelope big enough — —Also a copy of the form of the petition that Phila. woman[10] is sending out to be signed. — It is capitally wondrous — *just right* I think. — I enclose to you *one* of the four letters I found waiting for me here. The other three were all from publishers of leading books asking permission to include some of my articles in their collections! —

AL (CoCC,WSJ I, box 1, fd. 9).

1. Mrs. Walter Cabot was the former Elizabeth Rogers Mason (1834–1920).

2. Since HHJ includes this Mr. Fiske along with other publishers it may possibly be Amos Kidder Fiske (1842–1921), who was connected with the *Annual Cyclopaedia* for fifteen years before becoming editor of the *Boston Globe*, 1874–77. From 1878 to 1897 he was on the editorial staff of various New York newspapers, especially the *Times*. On the other hand, "Mr. Fiske" could be her lawyer, Charles H. Fiske of Weston, Massachusetts.

3. Henry Oscar Houghton (1823–95) established the publishing house of Bolles & Houghton in 1848. In 1852 Houghton and James Brown of Little, Brown & Company founded H. O. Houghton & Company, which created the Riverside Press. After buying out various publishing houses, Houghton eventually established Houghton Mifflin & Company, which published not only books but also the *Atlantic Monthly*.

4. Hezekiah Butterworth (1839–1905), associated with *Youth's Companion*, 1870–94, was known primarily as a juvenile and patriotic writer.

5. Mott, in volume 2 of his five-volume *A History of American Magazines, 1850–1865*, lists the various editors of the *Youth's Companion* but not a Mr. Mason. However, between 1867 and 1929 Perry Mason & Company published the magazine. Possibly HHJ is referring to this Mason.

6. HHJ's second son, Warren Horsford Hunt or "Rennie," was named after Professor Eben Norton Horsford (1818–93). HHJ accompanied the professor and his

daughters, Mary Catherine and Cornelia, to Europe while Higginson read proofs of *A Century of Dishonor*. Horsford, a graduate of Rensselaer Polytechnic Institute, was the Rumford professor of applied science at Harvard, 1847–63. He founded Rumford chemical works in Providence, Rhode Island, producing chemicals based on his inventions. He also was a prolific author on archaeological topics.

7. During the late summer of 1869 HHJ had visited Gastein, Austria.

8. Dr. Gustave Proell, a Gastein resident, had rented HHJ a room during her 1868–69 trip.

9. A reference to her lawyer, Charles H. Fiske.

10. A reference to Mary Lucinda Bonney.

TO WILLIAM HAYES WARD

Parthia.
Sunday, June 6. 1880

Dear Mr. Ward,

I quite forgot whether I wrote you just before leaving Boston. The heat puts every thing out of my head. If I did not, I will now — and, if I did, to re-remind you will not do harm, that the three Indian articles you have are to go with my book, and should therefore be printed as soon as may be — and *copies sent* to Mr. Phayre, Harpers. —

The Conestoga and Gnadenhutten massacres, first: and the "One of the Early Removals" last:[1] this last being placed in the Appendix. —

The voyage has been about unparallelled — smooth seas & uninterrupted sunshine — but I have been horribly ill all the way. We shall not reach Liverpool till Wednesday: — head winds all the way — and the Parthia is a slow tub.

Let me know if you want anything. — No! There is no use. I have promised now more than I can do. I hope that you will tell the publishers of the Ind[ependent] that the Advertiser & the Youths Companion both want all the letters I'll send them at $30 a letter!! (and prefer *short* ones at that!) —

Yrs ever
H.J.

ALS (CSmH, HHJ MSS, HM 13988).

1. See note 5, HHJ to Ward [mid-Mar.–early Apr. 1880], above. Ward had already published "One of the Early Indian Removals" on May 20, 1880. The article was published first, not last, and furthermore did not appear in the appendix but in the main part of *A Century of Dishonor*.

TO MONCURE DANIEL CONWAY

Liverpool.
Thursday, June 10 — 1880

Dear Monk —

Charge it to seasickness that I sent you such a stupid telegram yesterday — when I might just as well have written — will explain when I see you — 1stly however — here I am: & that needs explanation — not a very long one — Prof. Horsford was coming with two of his daughters — & they urged me to come — & I came — for four months only — go back in Sept: — couldn't possibly leave Mr. Jackson any longer, & he couldn't possibly come — we are going to Norway, Sweden — Vienna — Pesth [Budapest] —Gastein & the Passion Play! Do you wonder I could not resist? — Everybody hooted at me for hesitating: all the same I should have been a brute if I hadnt — & Im not sure Im not a brute to come — If I am, I am homesick enough for my husband, to pay me for it — It isn't the not seeing him, so much as the thought of that horrible ocean: — however never mind that — he *made* me come — 2dly — the business —

I've been hard at work all winter in N. York — seven & eight hours a day — (at Astor Lib. from 9. till 4 —) on a book.

      "A Century of Dishonor

       A Sketch

of the U.S. Govt's dealings with Some of the Indian Tribes."

The Harpers are to publish it — & they want me to try to arrange for its simultaneous publication here — — they told me to see you about it — You were their agent — & this is what I want to see you about — before we run off to Scotland — where we are to take a dash — before sailing for Bergen.

I hope you are quite well — we were much frightened by the first rumors of your illness — but soon saw the statements that you were well again. — Dear me how I wish you were going with us to OberAmmergau — I am to write two articles for Scribners about it — & I want to make them very good. — Goodbye —Were off for Chester in a few minutes. —

High Holborn Hotel — Sat. Eve. — Let me know when you will be there — Goodbye — Regards to Mrs. Conway.

Yrs ever
Helen Jackson

ALS (Moncure D. Conway Papers, Butler Library, Columbia University, New York, New York; hereinafter cited as NNC, Conway Papers).

TO MONCURE DANIEL CONWAY

[after June 10, 1880]

Dear Monk —

As usual the English mind does not do the unusual — After expressly saying on Tuesday, you recollect — that I should be notified yesterday of Mr. Chatto's[1] decision in regard to the book — they sent me no word whatever & made no appointment with me whatever — So I arrive today at noon to find that all has been sent to *you!* — So far as I can gather from this manager, they don't want to publish the book — only to buy 250 copies of it — — Now I *want* it published here — & with the distinct arrangement that it is to be published one week in advance — & I have 10 per ct. royalty on the retail price of all copies sold same as in America. —

Try hard for this for me won't you? How absurd; of course you will, mean time, I shall write to Harpers to send you out the first two *chaps*, as soon as *possible* — or if not possible before you leave — as soon as possible *afterward* to any publisher you find willing to undertake it, *contingently* on seeing the sheets. —

I hate to go off leaving this at loose ends so — but there is no help for it & I know you'll do all you can.

Your letter came this Am. Thanks for it — Love to Mrs. Conway — Goodbye —

Yrs ever
H.J.

ALS (NNC, Conway Papers).
1. Probably Andrew Chatto (1840–1913) of Messrs. Chatto and Windus, London book publishers. Andrew was the third son of William Andrew Chatto, author and editor.

TO MONCURE DANIEL CONWAY

Bergen, Norway
July 25, 1880.

Dear Monk,

I found nothing from you at Hull — & nothing has come here. — So I am still in the dark on many points on which I should like to be in the light.[1]

Mrs. Steen[2] turns out to be a species of angel. She has been of the greatest use to me —: and I heartily love her —, which is a good deal to say. — I have been off with her, on a journey up the Hardanger and Sogne Fjords — &

without her should have seen little of Norway — or to speak more properly — still *less* than the little I have seen! — A whole summer would be nothing for Norway. — I hope Mr. Jackson and I will come another year and spend the greater part of the summer here.

Will you & Mrs. Conway come with us?

You are just about off for America — so I send this line across to greet you on your arrival.— Take time to write me a word & tell me what the Harpers did about the book — & where you will be to be found when I come back in October. —

And if I never come back, remember that I have that Indian book, as my last charge to all who love me — to help *it*, & help the Indians all they can. — The thing I can't understand is that all you who so loved the Negro, & worked for him, should not have been ever since, just as hard at work for the Indian, who is on the whole much more cruelly oppressed; with the name of a certain sort of freedom, but prisoner in fact — left to starve, and forced into poisonous climates to die — he is far worse off than the average slave ever was — and is a higher nobler creature. Sometimes I despise myself for having come away — but there seemed nothing to do till the autumn. —

Don't expect me to say anything about Norway — It is too grand — the only simile I know for these fjords is one that will not mean anything to you — unless you go to the Yo Semite[3] — which you won't.— If the sea ran through the Yo Semite Valley & you could sail at the base of El Capitan, that would be like the sailing in and *on* these Fjords.

— I hope the terrible heat of which we read in N. York & elsewhere in America will be over before you arrive. It makes me shudder to think of it. — Here I am wearing winter clothing —and am just now, suffering from a severe cold because I incautiously went out with only a warm woolen fur trimmed cloak & *not* a thick jacket in addition: — My love to Mrs. Conway — and a grand good time to both of you — which you're sure to have, I fancy. —

Send me a line — to Barings Bros — & I'll get it in about a *month*: — ugh — this distance is something awful. — Goodbye—Yours as ever,

H.J.

ALS (NNC, Conway Papers).
    1. Conway was trying to located an English publisher for *A Century of Dishonor*.
    2. Conway had given HHJ a letter of introduction to Mrs. Susanna Steen, the wife of a Norwegian judge.
    3. In 1872 HHJ and Sarah Chauncey Woolsey had visited Yosemite Valley. HHJ subsequently wrote several articles for the *Independent*.

TO BISHOP HENRY B. WHIPPLE

Berkeley.

Oct. 29. 1880

My dear Bishop Whipple,

I cannot find words to thank you for your kind interest in my book, and your consenting to give me a Preface for it. I hope when you have leisure to look over the Proof you will be still more pleased with its character.

I am going however to take the liberty of asking you not to make the personal reference to *me* in your preface, which you kindly suggested. — As my connection with Gov. Hunt[1] was only by marriage, and I have since, married again, I am sure you will see, on second thoughts, the objection to any reference to that former connection. My sister-in-law has always been one of my dearest friends: She is a very sweet and lovable woman, and has borne her great trials with a rare fortitude: but she is not especially in sympathy with my work on this Indian Question, much as she loves me. She regards me as a variety of fanatic — only one degree less objectionable than the old Abolitionist with whom, as you know, Gov. Hunt had no sympathy whatever — and she still holds the conservative views, which the force of events would I think have, before this time, caused her husband to change, had he lived.

I have endeavored from the beginning to keep my own personality as much out of sight as possible in my writings on this subject. My own individual reputation, as a writer, is, so far as it goes, against me in this work. It has been the sum and substance of many a reply or retort that I took "*the poetical view*" of the Indian Question — and I have wished I had never written a line of verse in my life. —

Pardon all these words about myself. It is only to explain why I ask you to give your benediction in the Preface — *not* to *me*, in anyway shape or manner, — only to the book as a presentation of the wrongs of the Indians and the infamy of our Government. —

Yours truly

Helen Jackson

P.S. My address will be here till Nov. 18*th*.
Berkeley, corner 5*th* Av. & 9th St. after that, care Harpers Bros. will reach me wherever we may be.

ALS (MnHi, Whipple Papers, P823, Box 14).

1. Washington Hunt (1811–67) was the brother of HHJ's first husband, Edward Bissell Hunt, who died on Oct. 2, 1863, while experimenting with a prototype submarine. He served as New York governor, 1850–52.

TO WHITELAW REID

[November 22, 1880]

Dear Mr. Reid —

Here I am again. I haven't the courage to present myself face to face — Will you let me in? — Now that the election is over, has not the Tribune time and room for some further work on the Indian Question?

The Tribune editorial note[1] only showed how truly artful, how artistically artful Carl Schurz is. I know that this years Rep[ort] would be manipulated and worded all to one end: — in fact my own notion is that there will be little use, after this in going to the Ind. Bureau Rep[orts] for any true records: Agents are not going to send, and the Dept. is not going to publish any *more* such histories as they have unwillingly and carelessly left in their Official volumes up to date: — they have found them too formidable weapons in the hands of enemies.

This Ponca petition to be allowed to stay in Indian Territory *is* the climax of the Dept's infamous cunning.[2]

Just what hocus-pocus was at bottom of it, it will be hard to prove — but that it was a trick, there is no manner of doubt. *150* of those "happy & contented" Poncas have already run away, & are in Dakota today! and that the Chiefs should find it so "hard to control" their young men, is a very strange thing, if they are so pleased with Indian Territory. It was a blunder to have that phrase in.— I hope to be able in a few days to write a short article on that matter.

I hope very much you will print this for me at once,[3] before people have forgotten that editorial note. —

Yours truly —
Helen Jackson

Hanover House
Corner 15th St. & 5th Ave.
Monday AM.
Nov. 22, 1880

ALS (DLC, Reid Papers).

1. The Nov. 22, 1880, editorial note, p. 4, informed *Tribune* readers that the commissioner's annual report was in print and optimistically reflected the steady progress made during the year.

2. The Nov. 22 *Tribune*, p. 2, printed excerpts from the commissioner's annual report. The last item mentioned was the Ponca petition, signed on Oct. 25, 1880, in which the Indians relinquished all rights to their Dakota lands, requesting in return a title to their present lands in Indian Territory.

3. A reference to HHJ's Nov. 22 letter to the *Tribune*, below.

TO THE EDITOR OF THE *TRIBUNE*

[November 22, 1880]

To the Editor of The Tribune.

SIR: I observe in to-day's Tribune, in an editorial note commenting on the report of the Indian Bureau for 1880, three points to which I would like to call the attention of the American people.[1]

I. THE TRIBUNE has learned from this report that the Indians have made "such progress in agriculture that the Indian Commissioner believes that the day is coming when the tribes will be self-supporting." The report of the Indian Bureau for 1872 (Francis A. Walker, Commissioner), states that 130,000 of our Indians were even then self-supporting on their reservations, "receiving nothing from the Government except interest on their own moneys, or annuities granted them in consideration of the cession of their lands to the United States."

II. THE TRIBUNE finds proof that the condition of the Indians is "steadily improving" in the fact that, according to this last report of the Indian Bureau, "Reservation Indians are everywhere asking titles to their lands in severalty." The reports of the Indian Bureau for years have been full of the repeated and pathetic requests of Indians for "titles to their lands in severalty." As far back as the terrible Sioux massacre, in Minnesota in 1862, there were scores of "farmer Indians"—Sioux—who had had their farms "allotted" to them, and were begging for the patents promised. "The crops belonging to these Indians were valued (at the time of the massacre) at $125,000. They had large herds of stock of all kinds, fine farms and improvements. The United States troops engaged in suppressing the massacre, also the prisoners taken by them. In all some 3,500 men, lived for fifty days on this property," says one of the Indian Bureau reports. "These Indians were friendly." They had "acted as scouts for the Government." They had "never committed any acts of hostility," says the same report; and, what is still more wonderful, they remained friendly during four years, "while compelled to a vagabond life by the indiscriminate confiscation of all their land and property."

Bishop Whipple writing in 1866, in behalf of these Sioux, eloquently advocating their claims on the Government for compensation for these confiscated land, says:

> These farmer Indians had been pledged a patent for their lands. Unless we violated our solemn pledges these lands were theirs by a title as valid as any title could be. They had large crops, sufficient to support General Sibley's[2] army for weeks. They lost all they had; crops, stock, clothing, furniture. In addition to this they were

deprived of their share in the annuities, and for four years have lived in very great suffering. You can judge whether $5,000 (the sum appropriated to be divided among them) shall be deemed a just reward for the bravery and fidelity of men who, at the risk of their own lives, were instrumental in saving white captives, and maintained their friendship to the whites.

I submit to you, sir, and through you hope to reach all who fear God and love justice, whether the very least we can do for all these friendly Sioux is not to fulfill the pledges we made years ago, and give to each of them a patent of eighty acres of land, build them a home and provide them with seeds and implements of husbandry?

The Winnebagoes, in Nebraska, are reported by the Indian Bureau, as far back as 1868, as "exceedingly anxious for the allotment of their lands in severalty." In 1869: "Preparations are being made for allotting lands to heads of families." In 1870: "The allotment of land in severalty to the Indians has been nearly completed, each head of the family receiving eighty acres"; and, "the Indians anxiously look for the patents to these, as many have already commenced making improvements." In 1872 their agent[3] writes that "the Winnebagoes are disheartened by the non-arrival of these patents. They have waited three years since the first allotments were made. It is difficult to make them believe that it requires so long a time to prepare the patents, and they are beginning to fear that they are not coming." In 1876 the Indian Bureau reports that "each head of a family" in the Winnebago tribe "has his patent for eighty acres of land"; and all issue of patents has been "discontinued except to the Wisconsin branch of the tribe and the sick list."

Now, let us see how much allotments in severalty and "patents" are, in the estimation of the Department of the Interior, worth, when they are given to Indians.

In the same report (1876) the Secretary of the Interior says that "as a matter of economy the greatest saving could be made by uniting all the Indians on a few reservations, the fewer the better:" and the Indian Bureau seconds the Secretary's suggestion, and adds that all the Indians in Kansas, Nebraska and Dakota, a part at least of those in Wyoming and Montana, could be induced to remove to the Indian Territory.

In these sentences were foreshadowed the policy and the movement which took shape last winter in the infamous bill presented by Senator Saunders,[4] of Nebraska for the "removal" of all the Indians in Nebraska to the Indian Territory.

III. THE TRIBUNE says that the Indians' condition, being thus "steadily improving," is "far from hopeless." All this "steady improvement" is neither basis nor ground for hope, unless it can compel justice. Are the Winnebagoes any better off with their "patents for eighty acres of land" than without them, if neither the citizens of Nebraska nor the United States Government consider those patents worth the paper they are written on? Will the seven thousand Indian children who are now, according to the last report of the Indian Bureau, being taught to "read and think," be better off or worse, happier or less happy, when they are sufficiently educated to "read" for instance such documents as the speech of the Hon. G. M. Lambertson,[5] the United States Government Attorney, before Judge Dundy in Omaha, last year—a speech five hours long, said to be ingenuous and eloquent—to prove that Indians "not being citizens or persons, under the law, are not entitled to the protection of the writ of habeas corpus;" or, such reports as have been issued by the Department of the Interior annually, for the last four years, steadily recommending the breaking of treaties with Indians, on the grounds of "public policy," and "a very general and growing opinion that observance of the strict letter of treaties with Indians is, in many cases, at variance with their own best interests and with sound public policy." Will they be better off or worse, happier or less happy, after they have been taught to "think" logically and clearly of their own position as human beings outside the pale of the protection of the law, and of the position of their race to-day helpless in the hands of the United States Government?

Of the Cherokee Indians the Department of the Interior has published within the last three years such statements as these:

It has been but a few years since the Cherokees assembled in council under trees or in a rude log house with hewed logs for seats. Now the Legislature assembles in a spacious brick council-house, provided with suitable committee rooms, Senate chamber, Representative hall, library and executive offices, which cost $22,000. Their citizens occupy neat hewed double log cabins, frame, brick or stone houses, according to the means or taste of the individual, with ground adorned by ornamental trees, shrubbery, flowers and nearly every improvement, including orchards of the choicest fruits.

Their women are usually good housekeepers, and give great attention to spinning and weaving yarns, jeans and linsey, and make most of the pants and hunting jackets of the men and boys. The farmers raise most of their own wool and cotton, and it is not an uncommon sight in a well-do-do Cherokee farmer's house to see a sewing machine and a piano.

They have ample provision for education of all their children to a degree of advancement equal to that furnished by an ordinary college in the States. They have seventy-five day-schools kept open ten months in the year, in the different settlements. For the higher education of their young men and women they have two commodious and well-furnished seminaries, one for each sex, and in addition to those already mentioned they have a manual labor school and an orphan asylum.

They have (and this is true also of the Choctaws, Creeks, Chickasaws and Seminoles) a constitutional government, with legislative, judicial and executive departments, and conducted upon the same plan as our State Governments, the entire expenses of which are paid out of their own funds, which are derived from interest on various stocks and bonds—the invested proceeds of the sale of their lands, and held in trust by the Government of the United States—which interest is paid the treasurers of the different nations semi-annually, and by them disbursed on national warrants issued by the principal chief and secretary, and registered by the auditors.

They are an intelligent, temperate, industrious people, who live by the honest fruits of their labor, and seem ambitious to advance both as to the development of their lands and the conveniences of their homes. In their Council may be found men of learning and ability, and it is doubtful if their rapid progress from a state of wild barbarism to that of civilization and enlightenment has any parallel in the history of the world. What required 500 years for the Britons to accomplish in this direction they have accomplished in 100 years.

To this people, when they were removed by force from their homes in Georgia forty years ago, the United States Government gave seven million acres of land in the Indian Territory by one of the most solemn treaties words have ever framed. Of this treaty the Department of the Interior, only so far back as 1870, said: "The Cherokees and the other civilized Indian nations hold land in perpetuity by titles defined by the Supreme Court of the land. The United States agreed to 'possess the Cherokees, and to guarantee it to them forever.' . . . The inducement to the bargain set forth in the treaty was the 'anxious desire of the Government of the United States to secure to the Cherokee nation of Indians a permanent home, and which shall under the most solemn guarantee of the United States be and remain theirs forever—a home that shall never in all future time be embarrassed by having extended around it the lines or placed over it the jurisdiction of a territory or State, or be pressed upon by the extension in any way of the limits of any existing State.' To assure them of their title a patent for the territory was issued."

But in 1876 the Department of the Interior had already brought itself to say that affairs in the Indian Territory having become "complicated and embarrassing, the question is directly raised whether an extensive section of the country is to be allowed to remain for an indefinite period practically an uncultivated waste, or whether the Government shall determine to reduce the size of the reservation." Here, four years ago, were foreshadowed the policy and the movement which have taken shape to-day in the attempts of adventurers to found colonies on the Cherokee's lands, and in the attempts of railroad monopolists to secure by legislation the opening up of the Territory.

These are a few of the "facts of the Indian question;" they do not come under the head of "rhetoric." What avails "steady improvement," patient, heroic, though it be, against the "hopelessness" of the position of a race helpless against such combinations and precedents as these? It would be utterly "hopeless" except for the fact that at last the attention of the American people is being awakened to the true position of the matter and merits of the case. The American Nation does not care for "rhetoric" and is not given to sentimentalizing. But it does believe in "fair play," and means that every man on the continent shall have it.

H.H.

Nov. 22, 1880.

Printed in the *Tribune*, Dec. 5, 1880, p. 8, as "Broken Indian Treaties: A Letter From 'H.H.': A Review of Some Points in the Report of the Indian Bureau—Beneficial Effects of Granting Lands in Severalty—The Indians Disheartened and Their Case Made Nearly Hopeless by Governmental Disregard of Solemn Treaties."

1. A reference to a lengthy editorial, p. 4, probably written to call the reader's attention to the *Tribune* article, p. 2, same issue, entitled "Condition of the Indians: Acting Commissioner Marble's Report—Advancement toward Civilization—the Number of Indians—Their Desire for Education—A Petition from the Poncas," p. 2.

2. Henry Hastings Sibley (1811–91), an American Fur Company trader, was elected the first governor of Minnesota in 1857. During the Minnesota Sioux war, he commanded the militia and successfully defeated the Indians in September 1862.

3. A reference to Howard White.

4. Alvin Saunders (1817–99) left his native Kentucky and moved to Iowa, where he served in the state senate. He was also governor of Nebraska Territory, 1861–67, and a U.S. senator from Nebraska, 1877–83.

5. Part of Lambertson's cross-examination can be found in Tibbles, *The Ponca Chiefs*, pp. 66–90; see especially pp. 92–93 for a brief explanation of Lambertson's speech.

TO WHITELAW REID

[November 30, 1880]

Dear Mr. Reid —

Did you receive a communication from me, some time ago, ten days I think — in re Ind. Bureau Report?[1] — And are you going to print it? And if not, will you kindly send it back to me? And will you also tell me frankly whether it is going to be of any use for me to try [to] get a foot hold again in the Tribune columns, on this subject. — because if the policy of the paper is to be in favor of the new R. R. schemes in Ind. Territory, — of course I understand that you can't print my articles: which will be all as dead against any such schemes, as possible. — And if you will only give me a frank hint to this effect, I'll try for some other field for my "campaign documents" — Sorry as I should be to have to fight from behind any less formidable defences than the Tribune. You took such splendid ground in the summer on the Ponca question that I hoped you would be all ready for the fray this fall. — the Boston people are coming forward superbly — are just about sending a com[mission] of four to Indian Territory to expose the fraud of this published Ponca Petition — The President is to be asked for a *safe conduct* for this Commission — so that the Indian Agt. may not order them off the Reservation as he did Tibbles last summer.[2] If the President refuses this, his refusal will be sent all over this country. I think he will not dare. But neither will Carl Schurz dare to let the Commission go. It is the tightest place that Arch Hypocrite has got into yet. — Now he asks for an appropriation of *$55,000* to subsist those Poncas! — less than *400* of them all told. — And Dawes's bill for removing them all & establishing them in good homes in their old lands was but $50,000. — Does anybody think it can take $55,000 to subsist 400 men women & children, in Indian Territory, a year?

Yours truly
Helen Jackson

Berkeley
Corner 5th Av. & 9th St.
Tuesday, Nov. 30, 1880.

ALS (DLC, Reid Papers).

1. A reference to HHJ's Nov. 22, 1880, letter to the *Tribune*, above.

2. At the request of the Omaha Ponca Relief Committee, Tibbles, accompanied by Henry Fontenelle as interpreter, secretly visited the Ponca band in Indian Territory in June 1880. He conferred with various chiefs, explained they had been illegally removed, and offered the assistance of the Omaha Committee to return them to their original reservation. Tibbles's report of the incident, published by the committee, did not agree with that of Ponca agent William Whiting, whose letter to the Indian commissioner was published in the *Tribune*, June 29, 1880, p. 2. For Tibbles's account, see, *Buckskin and Blanket Days*, pp. 224–35.

TO WHITELAW REID

[December 1, 1880]

Dear Mr. Reid,

I see, — nevertheless I will not promise not to beg you to print a few words for me now and then.

Now let me bore you with a word of reply to two points in your letter.

You say the subject does not seem to arouse popular interest. — How you can think this I do not understand in face of the facts that in Phila. Boston — Worcester — Dorchester — Brookline there have been within the last ten days large and enthusiastic meetings for the sole purpose of discussing the Indian question: — and that the Episcopal Convention gave hours upon hours to its discussion, and finally appointed a Committee of three Bishops and several clergymen and laymen to "watch the action of Congress" in regard to it this winter: a thing unprecedented in the church history. — # [marginal note: # and the Gov. and both Senators of Massachusetts[1] are in the field active and strong, as defenders of the Ponca's rights.]

I hardly take up a newspaper that I do not see some paragraph bearing on it. — It appears to me that so general a waking up as there has been on this question within the last year has seldom been seen in so short a span of time: and I cannot but believe as I am often told by friends of the Cause, that my articles in the Tribune and the Tribune Editorials last winter have had very much to do with it. —

Some Quaker women in Philadelphia[2] have been at work for nine months with their agents in every state in the Union getting signatures to a mammoth petition to be presented to Congress this winter. They count on over *100,000* names representing every state and territory in the Union. Is not that a popular interest? —

But even supposing there were not a popular interest, — is it not the function of a great and powerful newspaper to create such an interest? — If the N. York Tribune *kept up* the tone it took in the Editorials last summer, at the time the Indian Agent on the Ponca Reserve arrested Tibbles and put him off the Reserve — it could kindle a blaze of public indignation in two months. —

Fancy how — caring for the cause as I do — I feel when I realize all this — and then get such a note from you, as this of today! I doubt if there is any such misery in this world as the misery of being helpless and powerless when you want to right wrongs, and put a stop to injustice.

One thing more; you say the Indians "*will not* settle" on lands "after the fashion of white people"! — They do. They have. They will, and the facts I cite in this letter you say you are going to print "soon" (!) prove it.[3] I doubt if the same number of white men, situated as the Indians have been for the last hundred years would have done *half* as much! I don't believe that in the bottom of your heart you mean what you say, of course that has *got* to be the plea on which their lands are to be taken from them. No other could make *even* Congressmen and railroad men seem decent in their own eyes!

Yours sorrowfully—

Helen Jackson

The Berkeley
Dec. 1*st* 1880.

ALS (DLC, Reid Papers).

1. The Massachusetts senators were Henry Laurens Dawes and George F. Hoar. Dawes (1816–1903), a lawyer, served in both houses of the Massachusetts legislature, was elected to the House of Representatives, 1857–75, and served in the Senate until 1892. His most important work was as chairman of the Committee on Indian Affairs and author of the 1887 Dawes Severalty Act, which alloted former reservation lands in severalty. In 1895 he chaired the Commission to the Five Civilized Tribes.

Hoar (1826–1904) also served in the state legislature and the House of Representatives, 1869–77. Elected to the Senate in 1877, he served until his death in 1904.

2. A reference to Mary Bonney and the WNIA. Bonney was not a Quaker but a Baptist. According to Amelia Stone Quinton, HHJ had visited WNIA officers in Philadelphia shortly before beginning her crusade. See Quinton, "Care of the Indian," in *Woman's Work in America*, p. 374.

3. A reference to HHJ's Nov. 22, 1880, letter to the *Tribune*, above, which was not printed until Dec. 5.

TO CHARLES DUDLEY WARNER

[December 3, 1880]

Dear Mr. Warner —

I don't know if newspapers ever copy each others Editorials—but if they do, can't you copy this one of Brooksie's?[1] — And won't you *go for* Sec. Schurz's Report? —

The Arch Hypocrite, publically to come forward as the *advocate* of Indian's "rights to their lands" — & "inspiring them with a sense of individual responsibility"— alloting to them lands in severalty &c — — When for *twenty* years the poor creatures have been *begging* for all these things!

In *1862* scores of friendly Sioux in Minnesota had had farms "allotted" them — & were not only "Self Supporting" on them, but well to do — — Their crops stock &c. were estimated at over $200,000 — the summer of the Massacre — & they were driven off their farms & bundled down to Dakota where they nearly starved for two years — & yet they had nothing whatever to do with the Massacre only to try to *save* whites which they did at the risk of their lives & rescued many! —

And in *1876 every* head of a family in the Winnebago tribe (in Nebraska) had had his farm "allotted", & a *patent* for it beside, & was "self supporting", & yet in the same Report which stated these facts the Secretary calmly recommended the removing of *all* Indians out of Nebraska to Ind. Terr[itory]! —

— And now he has the face to flaunt his philanthropic "policy", in his farewell. —

Sens. Dawes & Hoar see the Pres. tomorrow eve — to ask a safe conduct for a Committee to go to Ind. Terr[itory] & get at the *truth* about that last Ponca petition — the most infamous fraud ever perpetrated yet. — If the Pres. *refuses* the safe conduct, the country will know it.

When are you coming again? Love to Mrs. Warner

Yours ever
H.J.

Berkeley
Dec. 3. 1880. —

ALS (CtHT-W, Warner Collection).

1. Noah Brooks (1830–1903) was a frequent contributor to the *Overland Monthly* and personal friend of Abraham Lincoln. In 1866 he became managing editor of the *Alta California*, published in San Francisco. He joined the *NY Times* in 1871, serving as editor, 1876–84, before becoming editor of the *Newark Daily Advertiser*.

The editorial that HHJ wanted copied was in the Dec. 2, 1880, *NY Times*, p. 4. Brooks was more critical of the Indian system than of Secretary Schurz. "At first, we assume, the Secretary did not realize how deeply the Indians [Poncas] had been wronged by this order [of removal]," he wrote. Then Schurz did nothing because "things had gone too far for him to reverse the official drift of things." Describing the official Indian policy as "exceedingly variegated and ramshackle," Brooks concluded that the "Poncas were driven from their homes in order that the majesty of the law might be vindicated."

TO CHARLES DUDLEY WARNER

Berkeley.
Mon. Am.
Dec. 6. [1880]

Dear C. D. W.,

"Business end of a hornet" is the best thing I have heard for fifty years. It has lifted me up & strenthened me: — *Please send* me the Courant which has your Ed[itorial] on the subject of I[ndians][1] — I want all the Editorials I can muster. —

I hope you'll print the article I sent you yesterday[2] — —I've sent *ten* copies away to be reprinted — in the West, & here — I am determined people shan't believe in Carl Schurz's high & loftly ground tumbling if I can help it. — And here is the President endorsing him in the message — & saying that "*his* plan of educating the Indians is the only solution of the problem"!—

His plan! — I declare I think I shall burst a blood vessel some day in my indignation at the cheek of that man: —

Give Judge Dundy a rousing cheer, for this last decision won't you:[3] — now we'll see whether the Dept. will transport those Poncas home again to their *legally owned* homes! —

The world moves. —Whether we shall be in the Berkeley on the 16*th* The Lord only knows: —We are liable to leave on that day — as the three weeks for which the ancient McVickar maiden[4] [saidth?] she could rent her rooms are up on that date.—

— Mr. Jackson thinks he will go back to Col[orado] the last of this week. — I am enveloped in doubt as to what to do with myself for two months: — it may be Washington — At any rate, come here on the 16*th* & if we are not here, they'll know where we are. —

That Performing Bear the N. Y. Tribune — is out in a fiery Editorial this Am.[5] — the Ponca case — taking to *itself* the credit of all the change in public opinion in the past year — &c. &c. — & this after writing to me only a week ago that there really seemed to be too little popular interest in the subject to warrant their centering on the campaign again! —

Keeping my article 13 days — then publishing it in the *Sunday*[6] crime which no man reads — in short doing all they dared do short of suppressing it!

Yours till the end of the war, & after—
H.J.—

ALS (CtHT-W, Warner Collection).

1. Warner's editorial, "Mr. Secretary Schurz's Report on Indian Affairs," *Hartford Courant*, Dec. 6, 1880, p. 2, quoted several paragraphs from HHJ's Dec. 3, 1880, letter to him.

2. Possibly a reference to her Nov. 22 letter, above, which the *Tribune* printed on Dec. 5.

3. Judge Dundy had recently decided that the Ponca Indians were entitled legally to lands in both Nebraska and Dakota. See *Tribune*, Dec. 6, 1880, p. 4.

4. Possibly a reference to HHJ's landlady.

5. The editorial, "The Ponca Case," which appeared in the *Tribune* on Dec. 6, 1880, p. 4, noted: "In nothing has the power of the press, as representing an intelligent and firm decision of popular will, been more apparent than in the modification of policy which it has compelled from that department towards the red man in the last year." The paper claimed that it "was first to utter a protest against the illegality and dishonesty" of the Ponca removal, which it described as a "despotic measure."

6. A reference to HHJ's Nov. 22, 1880, letter, above, which was not published until Dec. 5.

TO HENRY LAURENS DAWES

[December 10, 1880]

My Dear Mr. Dawes —

Mrs. Goddard has just written to me, of the President's consenting to send a Committee &c.[1] — I take the liberty of enclosing to you her letter — as I know she is a friend of yours. —

For God's sake Mr. Dawes, don't let that Committee go, as it stands. — Carl Schurz has organized it — not a man in it can be absolutely trusted not to be either hoodwinked or influenced, except Gen. Crook. — & possibly Walter Allen.[2] — I don't know him. — Gen. Crook is an army officer — and must be silent, as he has been again & again or lose his commission. He loves the Indians & is their true friend — but he can't serve them now.—

Tibbles's instincts have always proved right, sooner or later. — He is right now about this Committee. — No Govt. Committee — met by Govt. Agents, and *their selected interpreters*, will ever know the truth. That is just the way these Poncas have been cheated before. — Oh Mr. Dawes, *insist* on *Alfred Riggs*, going, if you can get nothing else. I implore you.

Yours truly
Helen Jackson

Dec. 10. —

ALS (Henry Laurens Dawes Papers, Library of Congress, Washington, D.C.; hereinafter cited as DLC, Dawes Papers).

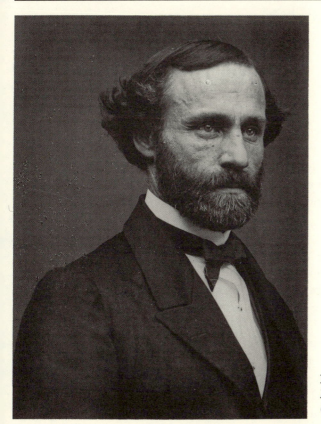

Henry L. Dawes,
Massachusetts senator.
(Library of Congress)

1. President Hayes's special commission was composed of Generals George Crook and Nelson A. Miles and two civilians, William Stickney of the Board of Indian Commissioners and Walter Allen of the Boston Committee.

2. Walter Allen (1840–1907) of Newton Highlands, Massachusetts, was a correspondent, writer, and editor on various newspapers including the *Boston Advertiser*, where he was the Washington correspondent.

The commission submitted its final report in Jan. 1881. Allen, convinced that the Poncas in Indian Territory had been prevented from joining Standing Bear's group, wrote a separate minority report. When accused in the Feb. 2, 1881, issue of the *Nation*, p. 65, of "improperly" making his report public, Allen wrote a stinging letter of rebuttal on Feb. 5, 1881. See "Mr. Walter Allen's Report," *Nation* 31 (Feb. 17, 1881): 110–11; see also *Nation* 31 (Mar. 3, 1881): 141.

The commissioners, with Riggs along, arrived at Niobrara on Jan. 11, 1881. For a report of their visit see the *Niobrara Pioneer*, Jan. 14, 1881, p. 4.

TO HENRY LAURENS DAWES

New York.
Berkeley.
Corner 5th Ave. & 9th St
Dec. 10. 1880

Dear Mr. Dawes,

Thank you very much for your letter.

I quite agree with you that even the shadow of a suspicion of what is technically known as "lobbying" should not rest on a woman: and in this feeling, — intensified in me by a great dislike of Washington life in every way — I said at first to the friends suggesting my going there, that nothing would induce me to do so.

But would it not be possible for me, in a quiet and unnoticeable way — (now at the Capital) — to make opportunities of reading a few statistics — a few facts, to men whom it is worth while to convert?

Mrs. Goddard suggested that I might find a perfectly quiet and inconspicuous boarding place with a colored woman, in whose house your family had at one time boarded.

If I could do some such thing as this, — I believe —judging from the effect I have several times been able to produce by reading a few pages out of my book to men who had never thought on the subject, and were astonished at the true facts. —I believe I might help a little: — but I should yield to your judgment entirely — and if you think I should lose more than as I shall gain, in my position as advocate of the Indians' rights, I will not come.

I am busy now making a series of extracts from Sec. Schurz's Reports for the 4 years of his "administrative period" in which he has the audacity to say that in the "*greater part of it,*" the policy of consolidating Indians has been "abandoned"! —He is a very stupid man to make false assertions so easily disproved by his own words. I hope to have this in the Times in a few days[1] —I will send you several copies. —

Yours truly
Helen Jackson

ALS (DLC, Dawes Papers).

1. This letter [mid-Dec. 1880], below, was ultimately published in the *New York Herald* on Feb. 1, 1881, p. 11.

TO LYMAN ABBOTT

[December 11, 1880]

Dear Mr. Abbott —

Mr. Jackson tells me that he saw in a copy of the C[hristian] U[nion] a capital Editorial on Schurz's Report.[1] — Can you send me a copy of it? I am so glad you saw through that audacious document. For pure cheek and lying I never saw its equal. I hope you saw my letter in the Tribune touching some points in it.[2] I have just finished a very careful collection of Extracts from his three previous Reports, which I hope to have printed in a few days —and perhaps you will think it worth while to copy it. I will send it to you. —

I note your kindly saying you will retain a "preemptive right" to my next work on Home Education. — You shall have it, certainly — perhaps before spring — but I am very busy at *present.*

Yours truly
Helen Jackson

Berkeley
Dec 11. 1880.

ALS (Chapin-Kiley Manuscripts, Special Collections and Archives, Amherst College Library, Amherst, Massachusetts).

Lyman Abbott (1835–1922) practiced law before becoming a Congregational minister. He started his literary career reviewing books for *Harper's Magazine,* was editor of the *Illustrated Christian Weekly,* and in 1876 began his association with Henry Ward Beecher and the *Christian Union,* which became the *Outlook* in 1893. Abbott became editor-in-chief when Beecher resigned in 1881. After Beecher's death in 1887, Abbott continued in his editorial capacity but also served as pastor of Beecher's Plymouth Congregational Church in Brooklyn until 1899.

1. The Dec. 8, 1880, issue of the *Christian Union,* p. 489, published a critical editorial, noting: "it must be confessed that the administration of the Indian Department for the past four years has not been such as to justify implicit confidence in the opinions of the Secretary of the Interior."

Previously, on the front page of the Nov. 24, 1880, issue, the *Christian Union* had printed an uncritical lengthy summary of the report of the Indian Bureau.

2. A reference to HHJ's Nov. 22, 1880, letter to the Tribune, above.

TO THE EDITOR OF THE *NEW YORK HERALD*

[mid-December 1880]

To the Editor of the Herald:—

In the report of the Interior Department for the current year, the Secretary says that in the beginning of his administration he accepted the opinion of those who had gone before him in the department, that it was best for "the Indians to be gathered together on a few large reservations," but that on "more extensive observation and study of the matter" he became convinced "that this was a mistaken policy," that it would be vastly better for the Indian and more in accordance with justice, as well as wise expediency, to respect their home attachments, and leave them on the lands they occupied. He says that "the policy of changing, shifting and consolidating reservations was therefore abandoned, except in cases where the lands held by the Indians were not capable of useful development," and that "during the larger part" of his "administrative period" the "policy, pursued as a fixed line of conduct," has been "to respect such rights as the Indians have in their lands they occupy."

A few extracts from the reports of the Indian Bureau during the four successive years of this "administrative period" are of interest in connection with the above statements.

In his report for 1877 the Secretary says:—"The Indian Territory has room for most of the Southwestern tribes, which should be gradually located there as they come under the control of the government. One or two reservations in the Northwest, this side of the mountains, and a similar consolidation of reservations on the Pacific slope, to be determined upon after more minute inquiry into local circumstances, will accommodate the Northern Indians. The interspersion of Indians and whites, which is so apt to lead to troublesome collisions, can in this way be considerably limited and greater facilities will be afforded for the promotion of civilization." He adds:—"The report of the Commissioner of Indian Affairs, which I herewith present, contains valuable suggestions as to the policy to be pursued."

The Commissioner's report opens thus:—"In considering any comprehensive scheme for the civilization of the Indian race it is indispensable at the outset to throw aside the sentimentality that is so fashionable in our day and to treat the subject in a practical and common sense way."

The Commissioner then goes on to enumerate seven features of this "practical and common sense way." The seventh is, "A steady concentration of the smaller bands of Indians on the larger reservations." He says:—"Experience has demonstrated the impolicy of sending Northern Indians to the Indian Territory. To go no further back than the date of the Pawnee removal it will be seen that the effect of a radical change of climate is disastrous, as this tribe alone in the first two years lost by death over eight hundred out of its number of 2,376. The Northern Cheyenne have suffered severely, and the Poncas who were recently removed from contact with the unfriendly Sioux, and arrived there in July last, have already lost thirty-six by death, which by an ordinary computation would be the death rate of the entire tribe for four years. In this connection I recommend the removal of all the Indians in Colorado and Arizona to the Indian Territory." * * * "The true remedy for these evils (the Indians' restlessness and the enormous expense of transporting annuities and supplies to them) is their immediate removal to the Indian Territory, where 58,000 square miles are set apart for the use of Indians, where they can be fed and clothed at a greatly diminished expense, and where, better than all, they can be kept in obedience and taught to become civilized and self supporting." It is a curious illustration of ignorance or thoughtlessness, or both, that the Indian Bureau should have been under the impression that there would be no "radical change of climate" for the Utes involved in moving them from Colorado to Indian Territory.

This is the "policy" of 1877, the policy which the Secretary now says he discovered was "mistaken," and that, therefore, for "the greater part of his administrative period," it was "abandoned." The reports of the department for the following year give no symptom of any such discovery or abandonment.

In 1878 the Secretary opens his report by stating that in his last annual report he sketched "a plan of an Indian policy" which he now "firmly believes would in the course of time, bring satisfactory results." The first point in this policy, he says, is "the permanent location of the Indians on a smaller number of reservations." He says:—"The consolidation of a number of agencies has been undertaken," and gives details of such consolidation. He says:—"The Northwestern tribes will in the course of time have to be concentrated in a similar manner on a few reservations east of the Rocky Mountains and on the Pacific slope."

In the report of the Commissioner of Indian Affairs for this year are still further details of this "policy." A bill has been drawn up by the Indian Bureau and sent to the House Committee, "providing for the removal and consolidation of certain Indians in the States of Oregon, Colorado, Iowa, Kansas, Nebraska, Wisconsin and Minnesota, and the Territories of Washington and Dakota." The Commissioner says:—"A reduction of twenty-five reservations and eleven agencies will thus be effected," and there will be "restored to the public domain 17,642,455 acres of land." He says that "since the presentation of this bill to the committee a more particular investigation of the subject has convinced" him that "further consolidation of like character are not only possible, but expedient and advisable. There is a vast area of land in the Indian Territory not yet occupied. Into this should and may be gathered the major portion of the Indians of New Mexico, Colorado and Arizona." He says that one of the most "forcible arguments which can be presented in connection with the subject is the fact that the expenses attending the removal and consolidation of the Indians as herein proposed will be more than met by the sale of the lands vacated." * * * That "much of the land is valuable only for its timber, and may be sold for an appraised value for an amount far in excess of the price fixed by law, and yet leave a large margin of profit to the purchaser into whose hands the lands will fall," and that he "can see no reason why the government should not avail itself of these facts." He says also, that "the lands belong to the Indians and that they are clearly entitled to receive the full value of them when sold."

In plain English, this is the position:—These 17,642,455 acres of land which are to be "restored to the public domain," "belong to the Indians." Nevertheless, the Indians are to be compelled to sell them and move away. These 17,642,455 acres of land belonging to the Indians, the Indians are "clearly entitled to receive the full value of the same when sold." Nevertheless, the lands are to be so sold as to "leave a large margin of profit to the purchaser into whose hands they will fall," and the Indians are to be compelled to expend a large portion of that remainder of the "value," which they do finally receive, in paying the cost of their own involuntary, coerced "removal and consolidation," and the Indian Bureau can "see no reason why the government should not avail itself of these facts."

The Commissioner adds that "every means that human ingenuity can devise, legal or illegal, have been resorted to for the purpose of obtaining possession of Indian lands." It would seem so.

And this is the Indian "policy" of 1878 as set forth in the reports of the Secretary and the Commissioner. Evidently it has not yet been made clear to the Secretary that the policy of 1877 is mistaken and he has no idea of abandoning it.

In his report for 1879 the Secretary makes no announcement of any change in the "policy" of the department. He complains that it has been "frequently said that we have no Indian policy," and says, "this is a mistake at least so far as this department is concerned." He then enumerates five features of this policy. The feature of removing or consolidating Indians he no longer mentions in that phraseology. In this report he calls it—"To dispose with their consent of those lands on their reservations which are not settled and used by them, the proceeds to form a fund for their benefit which will gradually relieve the government of the expenses at present provided for by annual appropriations." This sounds better to the ear. It is only necessary, however, to go on to the more detailed report of the Commissioner to see that the policy of the department is still unchanged and has been acted upon throughout the year.

The Commissioner says:—"In my last annual report the policy and economy of consolidating many of our Indian agencies were urged at length, with the recommendation that the surplus lands be sold and the proceeds thereof be used for the benefit of the Indians. During the current year the Omaha and Winnebago agencies have been consolidated, and the Red Lake and Leech Lake agencies have been consolidated with the White Earth Agency," &c. He reiterates the recommendations made in 1877, that "all the Indians in Colorado and Arizona" should be moved to Indian Territory, and the recommendation made in 1878, that "all the Utes should be removed at once to Indian Territory."

And this is the Indian policy of 1879, as set forth in the reports of the Secretary and the Commissioner. Evidently it has not yet been made clear to the Secretary that the policy of 1877 was "mistaken." Evidently it is not yet "abandoned."

There remains the fourth and last year of this administrative period above referred to. Do we find this "mistaken policy" abandoned in this fourth and last year?

Let those answer who are familiar with the terms of the "agreement," which the Colorado Utes were last winter compelled to make; a "consolidation" on a bigger scale than has been made with any tribe since 1795: a "consolidation" by which there were "restored to the public domain" over eleven millions of acres of land of priceless value, lands of which the Indian Bureau had said:— "let it be fully understood that the Ute Indians have a good and sufficient title to 12,000,000 acres of land in Colorado," and that these Indians were "originally and rightfully possessors of the soil, and that the land they occupy has been acknowledged to be theirs by solemn treaties made with them by the United States." The Utes, "owners" of these lands, were forced to sell them to the United States government for an annuity which will amount, "annually forever" (if paid), to about $12.50 a head all round. By this "consolidation" the Utes—those of them who are left in Colorado—are just as surely condemned to death by starvation as if they had been chained to rocks in Caucasus with this additional inhumanity, that their dying will take longer. And this "consolidation," the Secretary says, was "repeatedly and urgently recommended by the Department of the Interior."

And this is the "policy" of 1880.

H.H.

Printed in the *NY Herald*, Feb. 1, 1881, p. 11, as "Schurz versus Schurz: 'Phenomenal Inconsistency'—Citations from His Reports in Past Years Conflicting with the Latest Report—When Was the Policy of Consolidating Reservations Abandoned?—Some Testimony on This Point."

TO WHITELAW REID

[December 16, 1880]

Dear Mr. Reid —

I have just received a note from Mr. Taggart[1] saying that you will "print the substance of the extracts I sent you in a few days."[2] —

— Will you kindly let me know what that phrase "Substance of the extracts" means. — I wrote you that you might change my title, and leave off the motto, if you objected to them; and you might omit the commenting sentences which I put in as connecting links between the sets of extracts: — but this is all the change I am willing to have made. —

I wish the article printed as by me under my initials, with the opening paragraphs unaltered: — and with the *extracts in full*, and exactly as I arranged them. —

Nothing less or different will attain the end—the complete exposure from Schurz's own mouth of Schurz's dishonesty.—

If you cannot print the paper in this way, please return it to me by first mail — as I am very anxious to have it reach the public, before they have forgotten the scathing editorials which have been written on Schurz's reply to Gov. Long.[3]

Yours truly
Helen Jackson

Brevoort House
Dec. 16. 1880
over —
PS.
Will you kindly let me know, also, the outside limit of the "few days". — I would rather forego having it in the Tribune than wait as long as the last paper waited.[4]   —

ALS (DLC, Reid Papers).

1. Possibly William Marcus Taggart (b. 1852) or his brother Harry L. Taggart (b. 1845), whose father John Henry Taggart (b. 1821) established *Taggart's Times* in Philadelphia.

2. Probably a reference to her mid-Dec. 1880 letter, above, which was eventually published in the *NY Herald*.

3. Schurz's letter to Massachusetts governor John D. Long, prompted by the governor's sympathetic speech on behalf of the Ponca Indians at Tremont Temple in Boston, was written on Dec. 9. It is reprinted in Schurz, *Speeches, Correspondence and Political Papers*, 4:50–78. See also "The Poncas Defended: Governor Long Replies to Secretary Schurz," Dec. 21, p. 1, in the *Tribune*. See also "Mr. Schurz and the Poncas" and "Boston and the Poncas," Dec. 13 and Dec. 17, 1880, pp. 1 and 4, in the *NY Times*.

John Davis Long (1838–1915) was elected to the Massachusetts state legislature in 1875 and served as governor, 1880–82, during which time he was actively involved in defending the Poncas. He was a member of the House of Representatives, 1883–89, and in 1897 was appointed secretary of the navy by President William McKinley.

4. HHJ's Nov. 22, 1880, letter to the *Tribune*, which appeared on Dec. 5, took two weeks to be published.

TO THE EDITORS OF THE *NEW YORK EVENING POST*

[December 22, 1880]

To the Editors of the Evening Post:

It was a very natural mistake in the editor[1] of *St. Nicholas* to suppose Bright Eyes to be a "Ponca maiden" because she has been before the public for more than a year as interpreter for the Ponca chief Standing Bear. The fact is known that she is an Omaha, and has lived on the Omaha reservation all her life, with the exception of two years which she spent at Miss Reed's school in Elizabeth, New Jersey.

The Omaha and the Ponca languages are so similar that to know one is to know both, and the two tribes are in many ways closely allied to each other. One of the leading chiefs of the Ponca tribe is Bright Eye's uncle.[2] That an Indian girl with only two years' study in an English school can write such English as we see in this sketch in the St. Nicholas,[3] and as we saw in the preface (also written by Bright Eyes) to the "Story of the Ponca Chiefs," reviewed in the EVENING POST last winter, is a fact worthy of the attention of all people who believe that Indians "cannot be civilized."

H. H.

Brevoort House, New York, December 22, 1880.

Printed in the *NY Evening Post*, Dec. 29, 1880, p. 3, as "Bright Eyes and Her People." HHJ's letter immediately followed an article entitled "A Talk with the Poncas: Private Pow-wow with the Visiting Chiefs: What White Eagle and Standing Buffalo Have to Say for Themselves and Their People."

1. The editor of *St. Nicholas* was Mary Mapes Dodge (1831–1905), who began her editorial career in 1870 as associate editor of *Hearth and Home.* When *St. Nicholas* was established by the Scribner Company in 1873, she not only named the new magazine but became its editor, serving until 1905.

2. A reference to White Swan: see HHJ's Mar. 2, 1881, letter to Longfellow, note 1, below.

3. Susette La Flesche's letter, along with letters written by her sisters, Rosalia (1861–1900), Marguerite (1862–1945), and Susan (1865–1915), appeared in the Letter-Box section of *St. Nicolas*, Sept. 1880, p. 918. Monthly letters from children across the country were published in this section. See Street, "La Flesche Sisters Write to St. Nicholas Magazine," pp. 515–23.

TO HENRY LAURENS DAWES

[December 23, 1880]

My Dear Mr. Dawes —

It is asking a great deal — and asking what I have no right to ask — but I hope you will forgive the liberty I take, in asking you to send me one line in regard to these Ponca Chiefs now in Washington.[1]

Does one member of the party speak English? Are they allowed to be seen freely? — Do you believe their report to be a true one? — Would the Secretary allow Bright Eyes to come on & be interpreter for them. —

It is impossible for me to believe that there is not a trick somewhere at bottom of this thing. —

My husband has said all along, — that Sec. Schurz had but one thing to do; make the Poncas contented by any & all means, & so turn the tables on everybody.

It seems he was right, if these chiefs tell the truth, and fairly represent the tribe. — of course the fact that money has been spent liberally to surround them with such comfort that they choose now to stay in Indian Territory does not in the least alter the status of the case up to date — but it does alter it now — and puts the recent meetings & speakers in Boston in a vexatious & false position. I still believe these chiefs were "coached" before leaving home — and that an unbiased Commission, with an Interpreter of their own, would get a different verdict from the tribe as a whole.

Pardon this interruption on your time. My great interest in the question is my only apology.

Yours truly
Helen Jackson

Brevoort House
Dec. 23. 1880

ALS (DLC, Dawes Papers).

1. Several Ponca chiefs from Indian Territory arrived in Washington on Dec. 21 and the following day met with Schurz, along with Crook, Stickney, and Allen, three members of the Ponca Commission. The Indians stated that they desired to remain in Indian Territory and were willing to sell their Dakota land. Later they appeared before the Senate Ponca Investigating Committee chaired by Iowa senator Samuel Jordan Kirkwood. See "What the Poncas Wish," Dec. 23, 1880; "Justice to the Poncas," Dec. 25; and "The Wrongs of the Poncas," Dec. 29, all on the front page of the *Tribune*.

TO MR. PAYNE

Brevoort House
Dec. 28. 1880

My dear Mr. Payne

Thank you very much for promising to get signatures to the Petition.[1]

The best sources of information as to the U.S. Govt's treatment of the Indians are the Official Reports of the War Dept. & the Dept. of the Interior, "The Indian Question" by Francis A. Walker is also a good book — and a pamphlet by Gardiner G. Hubbard — called I think, but am not sure — The Indian Problem —[2]

"Our Indian Wards," by Manypenny,[3] formerly Indian Commissioner is a book full of information, crudely thrown together.

My own book is in no sense a history — It is as its name shows only a Sketch — & only of seven of the tribes—simply to show some of our causes for national shame. —

It will be published Jan. 25. by Harpers Bros. — and I hope very much it may do some good in arousing peoples attention to the Subject.

With many thanks for your kind interest in the matter. I am

Yours truly
Helen Jackson

ALS (ViU, HHJ, #7080-B).

Without a first name, it is impossible to know for certain the identify of "Mr. Payne." He could be William Morton Payne (1858–1919), a teacher, linguist, critic, and author who was associated with the Chicago *Dial*.

1. This is probably a reference to a WNIA petition.

2. Boston lawyer Gardiner Greene Hubbard (1822–97) was interested in public welfare as well as Indian issues. He later became a trustee of George Washington University, founder and first president of the National Geographic Society, and director of the Bell Telephone Company.

3. George W. Manypenny (1808–92) was commissioner of Indian Affairs, 1853–57, and negotiated numerous treaties to clear Indian claims from Kansas and Nebraska. His book *Our Indian Wards* (1880) presented his theories on civilian control, assimilation, and land allotment. He was especially critical of the army's handling of Indian affairs. He served on a commission to secure Ute ratification of an agreement negotiated after the Meeker massacre.

TO MONCURE DANIEL CONWAY

New York.
Dec. 28. 1880

Dear Monk,

Of all the muddles which I ever knew anything about, this muddle at Chatto & Windus's about my book is the queerest.

The London agent of Harper's has written them, that "C[hatto] & W[indus] did make to Mr. Conway a written offer, etc." but that "Mrs. Jackson called herself & *declined* this offer, & proposed to take the book to another publisher!" —This passes my disintanglement[?]. I not only did not decline the offer — I did not even know it was an offer till your letter overtook me at Hull! — & thus I understood distinctly that it rested with Harpers to decline or accept — & that the whole thing was in your hands anyhow. —

—There is certainly some hocus pocus about the thing somewhere — because when I passed through London in Sept. I went again to C[hatto] & W[indus] to see if anything had been decided, & they told me they had heard nothing from Harpers, but that some advance sheets of the book had just been sent over & had that very day been sent to their Reader. Nothing was then said to me about any impression that I had declined the offer etc. etc. — ! I suppose this explains your not telegraphing as soon as you arrived, about the title.[1] —

I'm sorry it has gone by the board — for the book is likely to have a large sale — here, & I think would have had a fair one in England. —

I have been hoping daily for a line from you — or a telegram: it seems but a few days however since you sailed; and a dream that you were here at all. — I have since have had already more winter than we had last year in the whole season. I should like to go to a sunny clime, if there is one anywhere. — Goodbye.

Yours always —
Helen J.

Brevoort House.
Address: *Roberts Bros.*

Boston — always, wherever I am that will find me. —

P.S. — Dec. 30

Mr. Joseph Harper[2] told me today that if they sent those 250 copies to C[hatto] & W[indus] — I would have only ten per cent on the price C[hatto] & W[indus] paid them, ie — 50 cts. a volume. — That was what I said to you, I thought it would be —do you remember? — So it is of no amount at all so far as the *money* is concerned — but I would have liked to have it published there, aside from money considerations.

ALS (NNC, Conway Papers).
HHJ enclosed a poem entitled "No Man's Land," which is not reproduced.

1. J. F. Phayre at Harper & Brothers wrote HHJ on Aug. 24, 1880 (CoCC, HHJ II, box 2, fd. 24), about the negotiations with Chatto & Windus. The London firm wanted to change the title to "The Red Man's Wrong," which Phayre thought would cause confusion. He also mentioned that Higginson had arranged the appendix with the aid of her memoranda.

2. Joseph Wesley Harper (1830–96) joined his father at Harper & Brothers in 1850. He became a partner in 1869, assuming control of the literary department.

TO ALEXANDER CATLIN TWINING

New York
Brevoort House
Dec. 28. 1880

My dear Prof. Twining,

I thank you very heartily for your kind note of the 26*th* inst[ant].

It is true that I have been at work for some time on a book relative to the treatment of the Indians by the U. S. Govt.— but it by no means purports to be a "history".

To write that would take volumes. I have merely given sketches of the history of seven of the most interesting tribes. The record is indeed a bleak one: and I hope that my book may be instrumental in drawing attention to the wrongs which we have inflicted on those helpless creatures. Bishop Whipple has written a preface to it, and President Seelye an introduction — and I think their names will add weight to what I have said. My material has been drawn almost entirely from the Official Records of the government. The book is more than half made up of literal quotations from them. —

I was very glad to meet your son[1] the other day — and hoped to have seen him again: but he has not found time yet to call on me. I cherish always the pleasantest remembrances of your kind friendship for Major Hunt and for myself² — and I hope to have the pleasure of seeing you again at some future time. —

Yours very truly
Helen Jackson

ALS (Alexander Catlin Twining Papers, MSS #2, box 13, item 138, Library of New Haven Colony Historical Society, New Haven, Connecticut).

A graduate of West Point, Alexander Catlin Twining (1801–84) was a professor of mathematics and natural philosophy at Middlebury College in Vermont, 1839–49. After retirement he returned to his engineering practice and worked on various inventions.

1. A reference to Kinsley Twining.

2. Following the death in 1863 of Maj. Edward Bissell Hunt, HHJ's first husband, Twining, assisted by Professor William P. Trowbridge of Washington, D.C., attempted to develop the major's "sea miner," a prototype submarine.

TO THE EDITORS OF THE *NEW YORK EVENING POST*

[December 29, 1880]

To the Editors of the Evening Post:

It is certainly very much to be regretted that the later phases of the "Ponca question" have developed such antagonism and mutual recrimination between parties all professing to be the Poncas' best friends.

Without entering at all into the merits of the question as a whole, or discussing the disputed point as to what is best to be done with the unfortunate tribe now, I would like to correct one missapprehension which has grown out of Secretary Schurz's letter in reply to Governor Long; I refer to the impression as conveyed in an editorial note in the Evening Post last evening, and still more strongly in an editorial in *Harper's Weekly*¹ of January 1, that the present administration of the Indian Bureau is not responsible for the removal of the Poncas to the Indian Territory. This is a mistake. It is true that the appropriation for their removal was made before Secretary Schurz took charge of the department, but the removal did not begin until two and a half months afterward. On May 16, previous to the 4th of March, nothing had been done. Efforts had been made to get a consent from the tribe, but they had failed. The order was then given to remove them without their consent, and troops were sent to enforce the order. This was in spite of protests from the missionaries at the Santee and Yankton agencies and from leading citizens of that neighborhood, all explaining the wrong and asking that proceedings be stayed. A Niobrara lawyer, Mr. Trehor,[2] went to Washington and presented the case to Mr. Schurz in person, and as late as the last week in April telegrams and letters were sent to him from Niobrara citizens asking only for delay and investigation. These facts, with the dispatches, letters, contracts, etc. proving them, are all set forth in the report of the Senate committee which investigated the Ponca case last winter.

It has also been said that Congress having made an appropriation for this removal, the removal was therefore obligatory on the department. This has not been the position taken by the department heretofore in similar cases; as is shown by its neglect to remove the Winnebagoes out of Wisconsin, when an appropriation was made by Congress for that purpose. In the report of the Indian Bureau for 1872—only eight years ago—the commissioner says that appropriations have been made to remove these Winnebagoes to their respective tribes west of the Mississippi, but "the removal has not been undertaken" and the commissioner doubts "whether it can be accomplished without additional and severe legislation on the part of Congress, as the Indians are attached to the country and express great repugnance to their contemplated removal from it."

In 1876 the agent of the Winnebago reservation in Nebraska[3] writes of these Wisconsin Winnebagoes: "Nearly all of them objected to removing from Wisconsin to their new reservation in Nebraska, and as a natural consequence soon returned after being compelled to do so.*

*For the past three years the sum to which the Wisconsin Winnebagoes would have been entitled had they remained on their reservation, amounting in all to $48,521 07, has been set apart awaiting such act of Congress as will give relief to the premises."

These facts dispose conclusively of the assertation that a Congressional bill appropriating money for the removal of a tribe of Indians is a law which must be immediately obeyed, or persistently enforced by the Indian Bureau. Not only were the Wisconsin Winnebagoes permitted to wander back at will to their old homes; but for three years all the annuity money which would have been due them on the Nebraska reservation was scrupulously set aside to accumulate for their benefit.

These discrepancies and many others like them, well known to all persons familiar with the official records and acts of the Indian Bureau, explain the strong desire on the part of "well-meaning persons in Massachusetts" and elsewhere, to make sure that the ten Ponca chiefs who have now expressed a desire to remain in Indian Territory, really represent the wishes of that part of their tribe now there. It seems tolerably certain that they do not represent the wishes of that fourth of the tribe who have already run away to Dakota.

H.H.

New York, December 29, 1880.

Printed in the *NY Evening Post*, Jan. 4, 1881, p. 4, as "The Poncas and the Winnebagoes."

In a lengthy editorial, "The Indians and the Sentimentalists," on Jan. 3, 1881, p. 2, the *NY Evening Post* called attention to this Dec. 29 letter, which obviously was to have appeared in the same issue as the editorial. Instead, HHJ's letter appeared the following day. The editorial described HHJ as "the best informed and the most practical of the representatives of Massachusetts sentiment" on the Ponca subject. However, the sentimentalists, instead of being practical and joining with politicians to reform Indian affairs, were hindering the work by refusing to accept the fact that the Indians in Indian Territory were content. HHJ included a copy of this editorial with her Jan. 6 [1881] letter, below, to Warner.

1. The editorial, "Secretary Schurz and the Poncas," *Harper's Weekly*, p. 2, placed part of the blame for the past Indian policy on "the languid indifference of the public mind to every aspect of the question," because Indians were perceived as uninteresting and remote. However, Schurz was praised for treating the subject "fully and candidly" in his annual reports. The editorial criticized the recent attacks upon Schurz, "whose character and course in public life are the earnest of upright conduct," and concluded that he defended himself "conclusively against all charges of remissness or injustice."

2. An undated clipping from the *Boston Advertiser*, found in CoCC, HHJ I, box 6, fd. 26, makes a brief reference to Trehor. No further information about him could be found.

3. This statement by agent Howard White was made in his 1877 report, not in 1876. See *Annual Report of the Commissioner of Indian Affairs, 1877*, p. 149.

TO HENRY LAURENS DAWES

Brevoort House.
Dec. 30. 1880

Dear Mr. Dawes.

I owe you an apology perhaps for sending you my second telegram: but I was afraid to put anything in the newspapers, simply on Bright Eyes's or Tibbles's authority: the result has proved that I was right in not doing so: as Bright Eyes it seems had already seen her uncle (in Mrs. Claflin's[1] company) when she telegraphed me, in the following words

"Dawes asks me to answer telegram to him. Secretary did prevent me seeing my uncle. Inspector Haworth[2] admitted it on witness stand this morning."

At a time when the enemies of the Indians cause, are so ready to make capital out of every possible and impossible thing, it is difficult to be cautious enough in what one says publicly: and I am very glad now that I did not put a paragraph in the papers about this matter. — I have called the attention of two newspaper men to the parts as stated in the special dispatch to the Tribune,[3] and hope it will be touched upon Editorially.

I ought to have explained to you in my second dispatch that I had no idea of using your name at all: all I wished to know was if the *facts* were as represented to me. —

Poor Bright Eyes and Tibbles are both over wrought and excitable — as it is only natural they should be: — and do not realize the impolicy of even the slightest exaggerations. —

I would be very glad to hear from you, if you have any real hope of the truth's being got at, by this Commission. Gen. Crook (whom I know slightly) wrote me that Riggs[4] was to meet them in Ind[ian] Terr[itory] — I enclose an editorial from the Tribune[5] which may have escaped you — part of which I think I had some hand in inspiring. It is next to impossible now to do anything in the papers. Either Schurz or Gould[6] is at bottom every where! — Our best friend in N.York. — Brooks of the Times — sails for Europe in a few days, and after that, the Times will be closed against us. —

Yours truly
Helen Jackson

ALS (DLC, Dawes Papers).

1. Mary Bucklin (Davenport) Claflin (1825–96) was the wife of Massachusetts congressman William Claflin (1818–1905).

2. A career Indian service employee, 1873–78, James M. Haworth was agent at the Kiowa Agency, which served the Kiowa, Kiowa-Apache, and Comanche Indians living along the upper Arkansas River area. He also was a special agent at the Quapaw Agency in Indian Territory (northeastern Oklahoma) during the spring of 1879 and a special agent-at-large at Fort Hall Agency in southeastern Idaho beginning on Oct. 9, 1879.

In Nov. 1880 he had spent ten days conferring with the principal chiefs of the Ponca group in Indian territory. He concluded that they wished to remain on their new reservation instead of returning to their former Dakota home. He presented this viewpoint before the Senate special committee chaired by Kirkwood. See "The Wrongs of the Poncas," *Tribune*, Dec. 29, 1880, p. 1.

3. Possibly a reference to "The Wrongs of the Poncas: Testimony before the Senate Special Committee—Mr. Tibbles and Bright Eyes Dissatisfied with the Investigation," *Tribune*, Dec. 29, 1880, p. 1.

4. Sponsored by eastern humanitarians, Alfred L. Riggs, longtime missionary among the Poncas and Omahas, accompanied Crook's commission as interpreter.

5. Probably a reference to "Secretary Schurz's Apology," *Tribune*, Dec. 24, 1880, p. 4, written by Rebecca Harding Davis. See HHJ to Davis, Dec. 30, 1880, below.

6. Jay Gould (1836–92) began his investment in railroads after the Civil War. Concentrating on struggling western railroads, he acquired the Union Pacific, Kansas Pacific, Denver Pacific, Central Pacific, and much of the Texas and Pacific.

TO REBECCA HARDING DAVIS

New York
Brevoort House.
Dec. 30. 1880

Dear Mrs. Davis,

I'm sorry you can't "do" the notice of my book. I counted on you bringing out the facts as I want them brought out. I don't care what is said about the book as a book, that is, I don't care, comparatively speaking: of course I care somewhat; but the thing I want most is that the notices of the book shall help to circulate the real *knowledge* on the Indian Question. Can you do anything about getting it well noticed in Phila.?[1] — I'll see that you have one of the advance copies.

I am sure you wrote that superb shot of an Editorial in the Tribune last Friday[2] — Is it the one you spoke of, which had been kept waiting? I thought so: — but I think you ended it with that Alligator sentence — did you? — And that Reid added the closing paragraph? I had had a talk with him the day before — and left him much encouraged: — Confidentially I'll tell you why — because I discovered that he despises Schurz — likes to make him uncomfortable — believes him a trickster & a liar —

— So all that can be done incidentally for the Indians, by showing up Schurz will get room in the Tribune. — If you are in the way of dealing another blow at him, before long, just let me give you a fact or two that may be of use —

He says, the hypocrite, in this last Report of his, — that when he entered on his Dept. he accepted the theory of his predecessors, that the true policy was to concentrate the I[ndians] on reservations — but that observation convinced him that this was "*mistaken*," & that the "policy of shifting, changing & consolidating reservations was therefore *abandoned*" — & that for "*the greater part* of his administrative period" the policy pursued as "a fixed line of conduct" has been "to respect the rights of the Indians to the lands they occupy"! — Did ever you know such *cheek*? — Not only has the course of this Dept. been diametrically opposite to this in point of *facts* — but its own Reports *each* year have *systematically* and persistantly *advocated* this same "shifting, changing,

& consolidating!" — Even in *1879* — the Ind. Com.³ says, "In the last annual Report the policy & economy of consolidation was urged at length . . ." he enumerates several which have been made, & says "These movements are in the right direction & there should be many more of like character. By the concentration of Indians the time needed to civilize them will be shortened, & the sale of their lands will contribute largely to their support in the future"! —

He *repeats* the recommendation he made in 1877, that "all the Indians in Colorado & Arizona should be removed to Indian Terr." — & that "all the Utes should be removed at once to Indian Terr."! —

Would you think a man would *dare* to lie like that? But he trusts to nobody's remembering the Annual Reports of the Depts —even from years back. — I wish you could continue to give him a sharp prod about this, & show up the lie. — I shall try to publish a set of extracts showing it. —

Bright Eyes is in Washington now — as you have no doubt seen — in this wretched Ponca business⁴ — Her address there is *Metropolitan* Hotel, — but how long she will stay, I don't know. —

I'm afraid I shall not be here when you come — for I am planning to go to Boston in a few days — but if I am here, it will be at the Brevoort — & how glad I shall be to see you I need not say. —

Yours ever
Helen Jackson

ALS (ViU, Richard Harding Davis Collection #6109-A, box 14).

1. Rebecca Harding Davis lived in Philadelphia with her husband, L. Clarke Davis, editor of the *Philadelphia Public Ledger*.

2. The editorial appeared as "Secretary Schurz's Apology," *Tribune*, Dec. 24, 1880, p. 4.

3. Ezra A. Hayt was Indian commissioner, 1877–80.

4. Both Susette La Flesche and Thomas Henry Tibbles were in Washington appearing before Kirkwood's special Senate committee.

TO THE EDITOR OF *HARPER'S WEEKLY*

[ca. January 1, 1881]

To the Editor:

In your remarks upon "Secretary Schurz and the Poncas" in your issue of January 1, 1881, are three serious misstatements of fact, which I would like to correct.¹

I. The writer says:

"Secretary Schurz inherited a very grave difficulty. The old policy of care-less wrong toward the Indians had ceded the Ponca Reserve to the Sioux in 1868. The Poncas had been removed."

The Poncas had *not* been removed when Secretary Schurz took charge of the Interior Department. They were not removed until two months and a half after that time. They were removed by and in consequence of Secretary Schurz's express and reiterated orders, and these orders were given by him in the face of and in spite of remonstrances from various sources—from eight of the Ponca chiefs; from the missionaries of the Yankton and Santee agencies; from a Mr. Trehor, a lawyer of good standing in Niobrara, who went to Washington, and presented the evidence in person; and from Mr. Westerman,[2] a Western merchant of high standing, who both wrote and telegraphed to Secretary Schurz setting forth the great wrong and cruelty of the proceeding.

The facts, letters, dispatches, statements, contracts, in regard to this removal of these Indians, are all to be read in the report of the Senate committee that investigated the case last winter. There is not a shadow of discrepancy between them. The Poncas were removed under Secretary Schurz's orders, and in spite of the protests both of the Indians themselves and of white men who were their friends.

II. The writer says that the removal took place "after an alleged consent on their part."

The testimony before the Senate committee proved not only that this "alleged consent" was known by the government authorities not to be genuine or complete, but that it was deemed necessary to send troops to enforce the order for the removal.

III. The writer says that one reason for not allowing the Poncas to return to their old reservation was that it would necessitate the "dispossession of the Sioux," and "open the possibility of a Sioux war."

The fact is that the Sioux utterly refused to occupy the reservation, saying that it belonged to the Poncas, and they would not have it. The Red Cloud and Spotted Tail bands did most reluctantly consent to go there for a few months in the first winter; but only after being told that their supplies had already been sent out, to be delivered to them there, and it was too late to change. On a written pledge that they should be returned to White Clay Creek in the spring, they consented to go; and the record of their return is entered in the official reports of the Indian Bureau as follows:

"The Indians were found to be quite determined to move westward, and the promise of the government in that respect was faithfully kept."

From that day to this the Sioux have not occupied the old Ponca Reserve, and say they never will. They are now friendly to the Poncas; and the Sioux chief Red Cloud most gladly consented to do all in his power to assist the attorneys for the Poncas in bringing suits for the recovery of their lands, which had been so unjustly ceded to his tribe.

H.H.

Printed in *Harper's Weekly*, Jan. 15, 1881, p. 35, as "A Letter from H.H." An unsympathetic editorial entitled "The Ponca Question," p. 34, called readers' attention to HHJ's letter. HHJ enclosed both a copy of her letter and the editorial in a Jan. 4, 1881, letter to Warner, below.

1. This *Harper's Weekly* editorial, p. 2, concluded that the country and Indians would be "exceeding fortunate if his [Schurz's] successor in the Interior Department unites so much ability, integrity, intelligence, and devotion to the public interests and to the welfare of the Indians as Secretary SCHURZ has shown."

2. German-born Herman Westermann (not Westerman) emigrated to the United States in 1852. In 1859 he arrived in Niobrara, Nebraska, where he opened and ran an Indian trading post until 1880. He then became owner of a mercantile store in Niobrara. At various times he served as justice of the peace, postmaster, and county treasurer.

TO CHARLES DUDLEY WARNER

Boston
Parker House
Jan 3. 1881

Dearest of Editors —

When you do such splendid things as this last slap at Schurz why don't you send them to me? Don't you know that every such blow on our side, saves me a solid bit of wear & tear? — And who do you think showed it to me? — *Joseph Harper* —& in the next Harpers Weekly you'll see a "letter from H.H." correcting 3 of Curtis's[1] vicarious lies about Schurz & the Poncas! I thought they wouldn't print it — but they will — accompanied however by "editorial comments from Mr. Curtis", Mr. Harper wrote me! — I quake a little — but I don't care — the 100,000 people who read the other will read what *I* say contradicting it — & it can't help doing some good. — The Eve. Post also promised on Friday, to print some day, this week, a short letter for me.[2] — Keep your eye out for it & copy it if it appears for it is telling. —

— I have seen Tibbles — Goddard & E[dward] E[verett] Hale. — Schurz hasn't [been] whipped yet ! — and I don't think he will. — If I can only get my collected extracts from his four Reports printed, it will be the worst blow he has had yet — Some friends of mine are now at work trying to get the Herald *either* to print them, or return them to me! —

—The history of that article's experience is a tale to make you weep.[3] —

. . . .

Yrs ever—

H. J.

Roberts Bros

Boston,

t[ill] f[urther] n[otice]

I trust the elegance of my envelope will atone for the sloppy look of these "bolt" sheets. — all the paper I possess at the present moment.

ALS (CtHT-W, Warner Collection). The final paragraph, in which HHJ complains bitterly about her Saturday trip on the railroad, has been deleted.

1. George William Curtis (1824–92), who joined the Brook Farm Association in 1842, was a friend of Henry David Thoreau, Nathaniel Hawthorne, George Ripley, and Ralph Waldo Emerson. In 1850 Curtis joined the editorial staff of the *Tribune* at the same time that Ripley was serving as literary editor. Curtis served on the editorial staff of *Putnam's Monthly Magazine* in 1853 and eventually became editor-in-chief of *Harper's Weekly*.

The "vicarious lies" appeared as "Secretary Schurz and the Poncas," in the Jan. 1, 1881, *Harper's Weekly*, p. 2. The "editorial comments" that accompanied her letter appeared as "The Ponca Question."

2. A reference to her Dec. 29, 1880, letter that appeared in the Jan. 4 *Evening Post*, above.

3. HHJ finally got this letter published in the *New York Herald* on Feb. 1, 1881, p. 11.

TO CHARLES DUDLEY WARNER

[January 4, 1881]

Dear Mr. Warner —

What do you think of an Editor who after a pleasant personal interview in which he agrees to publish your letter, accompanies it by such a slap in the face as this?[1] — And what do you think of an idiot, who after praising a contributor as a well "informed" person, goes on to write an Editorial based on the assumption that the said contributor's facts stated in said article, are not facts at all![2]

I hope you'll feel inclined to give this Sperry[3] a whack for this narrow ignorant low Editorial. I didn't think he was so poor a creature. —

The way in which all those New York men over look the significance of the fact that one quarter of the Poncas have *already* run away, is something inexplicable to me; — & the way they jeer at Massachusetts & sentimentalists is insufferable.—

If you do anything about these facts & slips send it to me. — Be sure. —

If I recover from my Saturday's journey here, I shall go to the Horsfords in Cambridge on Friday for a week. If I don't, I shan't! — At any rate, send to Roberts Bros. — I shall not go back to N. York till the 15*th* or 20*th* —

Carl Schurz[,] Mr. Tibbles has heard from Washington[,] has had *100,000* copies printed of his reply to Gov. Long — is having it pasted on to his Report for 1880 — & sending them all over the country! of course he hasn't had 100,000 printed — but even if he has had 10,000 — it will produce a great effect. He is badly scared — plainly — — but I fear he has power to persuade the country he is right. — My only hope is in the Commission. — Gen. Crook will get at the truth. —

Yrs ever —

H.J.

Parkers —
Tues, Ev.

Jan 4, —

ALS (CtHT-W, Warner Collection).

1. A reference to Curtis's comments on her *Harper's Weekly* letter; HHJ included copies of both the comments and her *Harper's* letter to Warner.

2. A reference to the Jan. 3, 1881, *NY Evening Post* editorial, p. 2, entitled "The Indians and the Sentimentalists."

3. Watson Robertson Sperry (b. 1842) joined the editorial staff at the *NY Evening Post* in 1871. He was managing editor, 1875–81.

TO WILLIAM HAYES WARD

Boston.
Jan. 6. 1881

Dear Mr. Ward —

What do you think of this for unfairness —? A letter by me correcting misstatements in an *Editorial* in Harpers Weekly — is called by Curtis "a letter traversing some statements recently made by Secretary Schurz." (Is Schurz an Editor of the Weekly?) — Curtis says my letter "disregards entirely the acknowledgement of the Secretary that he afterwards ascertained the consent of the Poncas to be only alleged"! —

1stly — I was not dealing with any document of the Sec.s. — All I said on that point was in reply to one assertion of the Editorial, which I quoted.

2dly — my facts proved that it was not "afterward but *before,*" that the Sec. knew that consent to have been only "alleged."

In regard to his own ludicrous (in view of all this years discussion on the Ponca case) — blunder in stating that the Poncas had been removed before the Sec. came in, Curtis says it was "*inexact!*" — I think that is a delicious word in the connection. — Wouldn't it make a capital heading for a short Editorial note? — and don't you want to give the Weekly a good *whack* for this piece of unfairness towards me? — I wish you would. —You see they did not *dare* not print my letter, because they knew I would print it in the Tribune if they refused. — But I think Curtis deserves to be shown up, for such unfairness, — of course I can't reply: but I trust several of the papers will — & I count on you among them. — It is a bad sign when an attacked man's friends have to resort in defending him, to such openly unfair means. — Before the next two months are over the truth will be known about this Ponca business — & then the Secretary will be shown up in a most unenviable light. I really think now, that he is an unprincipled *liar.* — I sent you the chapter on the Cherokees[1] a few days before I left N.York — hope it will go into two n[umbers]. — It will come in good time just now.—

Yours ever—
Helen Jackson

Parkers Boston
Jan 6.— 1880 [1881]. —
Address *Roberts Bros.* Boston

ALS (CSmH, HHJ MSS, HM 13993).
    1. Her Cherokee article appeared as "The End of a Century of Dishonor," *Independent,* Jan. 13, 1881, pp. 4–5.

TO CHARLES DUDLEY WARNER

Jan. 6. [1881]

Dear C. D.W —

I suppose you cant "whack" every body who whacks me — but if you haven't yet whacked the Post — perhaps you can "whack Curtis at the same time. — Just look at this![1] —

A letter I send to correct misstatements in an *Editorial* in the Harpers Weekly, Curtis calls a letter "traversing some statements recently made by Sec.

Schurz." — (Traversing is good — one meaning being to "go through"!) — But is Sec. Schurz an Editorial writer in this weekly?

— Then Curtis says "The letter of H.H. disregards entirely the acknowledgement of the Sec. that he afterwards ascertained the consenting of the Poncas to be only alleged" —

1st — I wasn't alluding to any statements of the Sec. pro or con.

2d. My facts proved that it was before & not afterward that he knew that consent to be only alleged & not real. —

It is a bad sign when an attacked man's friends, in defending him have to resort to openly unfair devices. —

I think it of the greatest importance that every possible means should be used to expose Sec. Schurz — no matter if he is going out so soon — He is trying to go out in a blaze of glory, which blinds peoples eyes, to all the enormities 1st of the System under which he has had his power — second, of the use he has made of that power. —

"Inexact" strikes me as a good word too — almost as good as "traversing." — Oh noble man with a newspaper — traverse this Curtis for me! — Mrs. Rebecca Harding Davis wrote me the other day —

"Oh for a week of the Tribune": — So say I. —

— I can't come & see you while it is snowy & blowing, & sloppy, & windy & bronchitis — & — and cold in the head & — If Shipton[2] is mistaken & we see another summer —or even Spring, I'll come — I long to, as you know — & there's that Play, which I'd much rather write then Letters to Harpers Weekly — but all that is in the future. —

The "wet copy" of the "Century of Dishonor" is here. I read & reread it fondly.— but with some terror. I don't know what they'll do to me:— However they can't help some people's believing me on the 20th. You shall have a copy — the 25th —the book is out.

Yours forever — & love to Mrs. Warner —

H.J.

Address — Roberts Bros. —

[marginal note: Send me every egg you lay — & I'll do the cackling! —]

ALS (CtHT-W, Warner Collection).

1. A reference to three newspaper clippings she had enclosed with this letter: her Dec. 29, 1880, NY Evening Post letter, the editorial by Sperry, "The Indians and the Sentimentalists," and an unidentified article, "The Escaped Poncas," which summarized the report of four clergymen who had visited Standing Bear's group living on the Niobrara River.

2. Mother Shipton, a British prophetess, possibly mythical, prophesied the end of the world in 1881. According to the *Colorado Springs Gazette*, Feb. 16, 1878, p. 1, Mother Shipton was a noble lady and a friend of Roger Bacon.

TO JOSEPH W. HARPER

[January 6, 1881]

My dear Mr. Harper,

If it is fair dealing to call a letter correcting "three serious misstatements of fact made in an Editorial in Harpers Weekly," a letter traversing some statements recently made by Secretary Schurz — I do not know what fair dealing is: — that is, unless Secretary Schurz is an Editorial writer in the weekly, which I do not suppose. —

To say that "The letter of H.H. disregards entirely the acknowledgement of the Secretary that he *afterward* ascertained the consent of the Poncas to be only alleged", is unfair dealing: whoever wrote the Editorial in question! For my facts showed that that it was *not* "afterward," but *before* that he knew the consent was only alleged. —

There have been a good many unfair things written on this Indian business, first and last — but I don't know one, which in its way, is as subtly unfair as this. And it is a bad sign for an attacked man, when his friends in defending him, are driven to measures openly and unqualifiedly unfair. —

I say this to Mr. Curtis, through you, asking your permission to do so — because Mr. Curtis did not reply to the personal note I sent him with my communication to the Weekly. —

Yours truly
Helen Jackson

Parker House
Boston, Jan. 6. 1881

ALS (CoCC, HHJ II, box 1, fd. 9).

TO CHARLES DUDLEY WARNER

[January 19 (1881)]

Dear Mr. Warner —

I have had sent to you today — no — tomorrow — the "Century of Dishonor,"— Do all you can for it, in way of getting in salient *facts* before the people — never mind about the book as a *book* — but *cram* the facts — such as the no. of self supporting I[ndians] — the breaking of our treaties — the utter impossibility of their having been thoroughly civilized & successful, when they have been moved so often — & above all — the clause in so many of those early treaties, giving them permission to "punish as they see fit," any white settlers going on their lands. —This last is most important in its bearing on the *prejudice* against the I[ndians] by reason of their massacring whites in those early days. —

They almost *never* massacred any who kept on their own grounds! except in the wars of the French & English when they were hired to. —

I go to Washington on Friday. Pray for me and write to.

2107 Penn. Av.

(Miss Risley Seward)[1]

Breathlessly yrs ever

H.J.

Brevoort House
Wed. Eve.
Jan. 19. — Mrs. Goddard & I nearly died over your Persian art —It even diverted us from the Poncas. —

ALS (CtHT-W, Warner Collection).

1. Olive Risley Seward (ca. 1844–1908), the daughter of the Jacksons' friend Hanson A. Risley, was adopted in 1870 by William H. Seward, the former senator and secretary of state. In 1873 she edited *William H. Seward's Travels around the World*.

TO GEORGE WILLIAM CURTIS

Washington.

Feb. 5. 1881

Dear Mr. Curtis —

Thanks for your note from Albany, last month.

Of course I perceived that your Editorial was simply "an abstract of Mr. Schurz's views": but it was not put forth as such. Had it been, I should have taken no notice of it. It was put forth as the opinion, the conviction of Mr. Curtis and as such carried great weight to 100,000 people. —

I enclose a series of extracts from Schurz's Reports, which I hope you will do me the favor to read. If they do not fairly convict him of having in this last Report attempted to set himself right before the newly aroused sentiment of this country by audacious denials of the true facts of his policy, — I am greatly mistaken.

If you had been present at the cross-examination of the Ponca Commissioners, on which he based his despatches to the Ass[ociated] Press, the next day, I am sure you would have seen thru these & forever abandoned all faith in his honesty and fairness.

Yours truly

Helen Jackson.

ALS (George William Curtis Papers, Staten Island Institute of Arts and Sciences, Staten Island, New York).

TO CAROLINE DALL

[February 8, 1881]

Dear Mrs. Dall —

The points I want brought out in the notices of my book — are

1*st* that the Indians "*right* of occupancy" was a right recognized by all the nations — a thing to be *bought* & *sold* — see 1st chapter

2*d* that the Indians massacres of whites in the early days were almost without exception, either *instigated* or *hired* by the English French, or Amer. commanders — or they were the result of the provision put in *all* our early treaties that if white intruders crossed the Indians lines "The Indians may punish him as they see fit!" — See for instance *P. 36.* — treaty with Delawares.

3*rd* that *132,000* of our Indians are self supporting in their reservations — receiving no dollar of aid from Govt. except the interest money due them on the price of their lands. # [marginal note: # proof that Indians will "*work*"!] See p. 336.

4*th* evidences of character & intelligence in the Indians testimonies to that effect.

See Laws of the Delawares p: 396 — App[endix] — speeches of ditto in 1793. — p. 41. —

— testimonies — in App[endix] p. 374.

5.— present condition of the Cherokees — as civilized as any *rural villages* in our land. — See p. 296. —

6 — cruelties of whites to Indians See Chapter ninth. —

I am very glad you are going to give a stroke on this question from your vigorous pen. — The book has had good notices so far as I have seen, except for the N. York Tribune[1] — notices just of the sort I want, holding up the *facts*: that is all people need. —

I hope I shall see your notice[2] — send it to *Roberts Bros.* if I have left W[ashington] — Anything sent there, will always find me, wherever I am. —

Yours very truly

Helen Jackson

Washington

Tues. Am. Feb. 8. 1881

ALS (Caroline H. Dall Papers, Massachusetts Historical Society, Boston, Massachusetts).

Caroline Wells Healey Dall (1822–1912), an advocate of women's rights, published collections of her lectures, as well as *The College, the Market, and the Court; or Woman's Relation to Education, Labor and Law* (1867).

1. Describing the Indian as "an ugly and vicious creature" in its Feb. 4, 1881, review, p. 6, the *Tribune* called *A Century of Dishonor* "one-sided," portraying the government as "invariably" dealing unjustly with the Indians when "in many instances" it had fed, clothed, and paid annuities to "thousands of lazy savages who will not work for a living." Furthermore the government had been forced to choose between breaking "unwise" treaties or "blocking the civilization of a continent."

2. Dall wrote her review on Feb. 13, 1881, and it was published several days later in the *Courier* as "The Story of Indian Wrongs: Mrs. Dall on Helen Hunt Jackson's 'Century of Dishonor'—A Record That Causes a Woman to Blush for Her Race." Dall's review followed HHJ's format exactly. In her concluding remarks, Dall wrote: "Politically speaking, I have not the smallest idea who is to blame for the story which makes me blush. But behind the democrat and the republican alike, stands human nature which ought indignantly to disclaim the responsibility."

TO JOSEPH BENSON GILDER

[February 11, 1881]

Dear Mr. Gilder,

Bright Eyes cannot write the notice of this Indian book[1] — I quite agree with her that she ought not to. It is written by a friend of hers — & by a man to whom the Indian cause owes a great deal. — She is going to write an introduction to it — & endorse its *spirit* &c., all she can — The publishers had written to her some time ago & asked this. —

Mr. Tibbles & she have gone together over the book & corrected some of the most glaring errors in it — & the publication of the book will probably be delayed until those corrections have been made. —

It is a great pity that the first man who has undertaken to make a novel on the Indian question, should have made such a bad one — — & have even got names wrong by the dozen. —

Send me word how much I owe you for those Heralds. —

Yours ever

H.J.

Washington

Feb. 11. 1881

ALS, Personal-Miscellaneous (Helen Hunt Jackson), New York Public Library, New York, New York (hereinafter NN, P-M [HHJ]).

Joseph B. Gilder (1858–1936) was a reporter and assistant city editor at the *NY Herald*, 1877–80. In Jan. 1881 Gilder and his sister, Jeannette Leonard Gilder (1849–1916), founded the weekly *Critic*. He served as co-editor for twenty-eight years. Eventually Jeannette assumed editorial control, a position she held until 1906, when the *Critic* merged with the revived *Putnam's*.

1. A reference to *Ploughed Under: The Story of an Indian Chief* (1881), attributed to William Justin Harsha, son of the Reverend W. J. Harsha, pastor of the Omaha First Presbyterian Church and member of the Omaha Ponca Committee. The younger Harsha also wrote *A Timid Brave: The Story of an Indian Uprising* (1886) and "How 'Ramona' Wrote Itself," *Southern Workman* 59 (Aug. 1930): 370–75. The first edition of Ploughed Under carried no author's name; Mark in *A Stranger in Her Native Land: Alice Fletcher and the American Indians*, p. 127, credits Tibbles with writing it, although the evidence is circumstantial.

TO CHARLES DUDLEY WARNER

[February 12 (1881)]

Dear C. D. W —

What has become of you? Have you struck any blows for us? & if so why haven't you sent them to me. —

I send you Dawes's crushing reply to this Arch Villain[1] — It is what Dawes *ought* to have said in the beginning. —

Think of Schurz *daring* to charge Dawes with lying! —

That day when Dawes went to Schurz & talked personally with him (which Schurz now denies) —he says he found Schurz full of a letter he had just written in *reply* to me,[2] & he made him listen to the whole of it! —

— Schurz is determined to push through this Bill which gives the Poncas *no choice*[3] — he has prepared this Bill in defiance of the Com[mission] & of the *President* & he means to *bully*, or intrigue, or bayonet it through.

Yrs ever—

H.J.

Sat. Feb. 12 —

Washington

ALS (CtHT-W, Warner Collection).

1. On Jan. 31, 1881, Dawes made a speech in the Senate criticizing the government's failure to punish the murderers of Chief Standing Bear's brother, Big Snake. Secretary Schurz took offense at the speech and on Feb. 7, 1881, wrote an open letter, which was placed on the desks of all the senators and later published in various newspapers. The *Boston Evening Transcript* reprinted it as "The Ponca Question: Reply of Secretary Schurz to Senator Dawes," in the Feb. 10, 1881, issue, p. 2.

2. HHJ wrote two letters directly to Schurz, one on Jan. 9, 1880, and a second on Jan. 22, 1880. Of course, she could also be referring to any of her critical letters to the editor.

3. Crook and his commission (Miles, Stickney, and Allen) had recommended that the Indians be given one year to select their permanent home. However, Schurz's bill allowed the Poncas in Indian Territory to select land allotments only within Indian Territory, while the Poncas in Dakota and Nebraska had the choice of returning to their old reservation. Ultimately, in Mar. 1881, the final Ponca bill allowed the Indians to select lands on the reservation of their choice.

In "The President and the Indians," the *NY Times*, Feb. 3, 1881, p. 4, described the Interior Department as "misrepresent[ing] the facts" and concluded that it was fortunate for President Rutherford B. Hayes "that the obstinacy of Secretary Schurz has given him [Hayes] the opportunity to show how honorable are his own motives in this matter."

TO LYMAN ABBOTT

[February 21, 1881]

Dear Mr. Abbott,

Of course you have noticed the paragraphs to the effect that "100 influential men" — in Boston are going to give Schurz a dinner. This is the cleverest trick he has played yet, & that is saying a great deal. —

But I think a great deal may be done beforehand to take the wind out of its sails, by judicious comment in the papers. They were being silly to crow before hand. — The day before I left W[ashington] — Senator Dawes received a letter from a Boston man of high position[1] saying that he had refused to join in the dinner. Considering it "an insult to the Gov. & to the Mass. Senators." # [marginal note: # I think it would be well to find out how many *more* "influential men" refused to join in that dinner!] — I think so too, & I hope to get some paragraphs started in half a dozen papers at once, on the subject. Can't you help? —

The day before Schurz laid that open letter arraigning Dawes on the Senators desks, he said in W[ashington] — that he was "going now to carry the war into Africa."[2] — & he will no doubt make at this Boston dinner his final grand effort at covering up the corruptions & outrages of his Indian policy. —

Senator Ransom[3] said at a dinner in W[ashington] last week, that his daring to arraign a Senator in that way, on the Senate floor, was an outrage which the Senate owed it to itself to resent & rebuke. —

I wish also to call your attention to Gen. Miles's endorsement of all that Allen said in that cross examination before the Senate Committee on the Ponca case. —

Yours truly

Helen Jackson

Brevoort House.

Feb. 21*st*, 1881

ALS (Abbott Memorial Collection: Lyman Abbott Autograph Collection, Bowdoin College Library, Brunswick, Maine).

1. Boston businessman William Henry Lincoln (1835–1925), active in the Ponca cause, was angered by the retirement dinner for Schurz. He informed Dawes that he and many others had decided to hold a public meeting "to show that the sense of Massachusetts is not on the side of Mr. Schurz. — but with you. —" See W. H. Lincoln to Dawes, Feb. 28, and Mar. 3, 5, and 22, 1881 (DLC, Dawes Papers).

2. The statement "to carry the war into Africa" first appeared in a special dispatch to the *Boston Advertiser* and was later reprinted in "A New Ponca Bill: Secretary Schurz's Ingenious Plan to Defeat the President's Recommendations," *Tribune*, Feb. 11, 1881, p. 1. The reporter explained that Schurz's statement has been misunderstood; he did not mean he was "going to assault the Ponca Commission, but to assail, overthrowing and humiliate the President himself by thwarting the enactment of his recommendations into laws."

3. Matthew Whitaker Ransom (1826–1904) was a North Carolina senator, 1872–95.

TO CHARLES DUDLEY WARNER

[ca. February 21, 1881]

Dear C. D. W. —

Of course you have seen the notices of the Boston dinner to be given to Schurz — "100 influential men," & "friends of Dawes's[.]"

The day before I left Washington, Dawes had a letter from one of the most influential men there, saying that he had refused to join in this dinner regarding it as "an insult to the Mass. Senators & the Gov." I think so too — it is one of the cleverest dodges Schurz has been up to yet! & that's saying a great deal. —

Now it seems to me a good deal to be done to take "the wind out of the sails" of it, by judicious *comment* beforehand. Don't you think so? & will you help? They were very foolish to *crow* in advance! — I hope to get some squibs started in half a dozen papers in a few days — —You do something *good* wont you?

Senator Ransom said at a dinner in W[ashington] last week, that Schurz's undertaking to arraign a Senator on the Senate floor in the way he did Dawes was an *outrage*, which the Senate owed it to itself to promptly rebuke — to rebuke it, as a body — I think so too. — but nobody did it. —

I have lost eight whole days — funny how I grudge it — with two Scribner articles promised at once! — besides all the skirmishing & scalping I want to do — I got a nasty attack of bronchitis in W[ashington] — & did not leave my room for six days — — came from my bed to the cars on Sat — to come here — am better today — but still very weak & good for nothing. —

Note how this talk of Miles corroborates *every word* Allen said at the cross examination by Schurz. — oh I would give a sum of money if you could have seen that whole thing. I never never shall forget the malignity & craft of Schurz's face — never. —It was a study. I could *paint it*, if I knew how to paint. —

Goodbye — we are at the Brevoort my mate & I — shall be here two weeks or three —

Yrs ever —
H.J. —

P.S. Have you noticed my book yet? If not when you do, make a point about the *Nez Perces* — & Chief Joseph — & the reasons given for taking away from him by Ex[ecutive] order in 1875, the reservation given him by Ex[ecutive] order in 1873. — & then pitch in for sending them back to Idaho now.[1] —

The notices have been better than my wildest hopes — & so far as I know Schurz hasn't lifted a hand to attack me —suspicious — he may have something brewing. —

ALS (CtHT-W, Warner Collection).

1. The *Hartford Courant* reviewed *A Century of Dishonor* on Mar. 1, 1881, p. 1. Respecting HHJ's wishes, Warner made sure that most of the review was devoted to the Nez Percés. He did make a pitch for returning the Indians.

TO WILLIAM HAYES WARD

[February 23, 1881]

Dear Mr. Ward —

Here is a little essay I have been led to write, for the necessity of making some such wine to keep myself patient, under a twelve days loss of time from a sharp attack of bronchitis. — which shut me up six days in my room in Washington, & has shut me up here, ever since my arrival on Sat. last. —

I was so sorry to miss seeing your sister in W[ashington] — I went to the house to see her, the day I heard of her being there but she had gone, the day before. —

I want to see Mrs. Clemmer's letter[1] — I was so glad she took an interest in Bright Eyes. I hope you have made some notes on the points I have sent you from time to time: — & have you yet noticed my book? If so please send me the papers, my Independent now goes to my sister in N. Hampshire. —

— Sec. Schurz has made a desperate fight in this last month — but spite of all his tricks lies, devices of all sorts, slandering innocent girls — & men above reproach — browbeating Commissions & Committees — — cheating Associated Reser[vation] Agents etc.— he is worse off today than ever before — but not nearly so badly off as he deserves to be. — I am very glad to have had this month in Washington — it has been a great experience of the melancholy state of things —

Can't you come up some day & see me? — I shall be a prisoner in my room I fear, for two or three days yet —

Please send me everything you have printed on the Indian question —. The Christian Union[2] has been splendidly outspoken — which I did not expect.

Yours ever

Helen Jackson

Brevoort House
Feb. 23, 1881

ALS (CSmH, HHJ MSS, HM 13994).

1. After originally writing for the *Springfield Republican*, Mary Ames Clemmer (1839–84) moved to Washington, D.C., in 1866 and began her column "A Woman's Letters from Washington" for the *Independent*. These informal descriptions of prominent people and political and social happenings established her literary career. She also was a novelist.

Clemmer's letter appeared in the Feb. 17, 1881, *Independent*, pp. 2–5. It summarized the Ponca story, quoted Standing Bear, and included personal impressions of Susette La Flesche.

2. On Jan. 5. 1881, p. 1, the *Christian Union* praised the president for appointing a commission to visit the Poncas; the Jan. 26 issue, p. 78, defended "Bright Eyes" when the *Springfield Republican* called her a "phenomenal liar"; the Feb. 2 issue, p. 101, described the Ponca commission's recommendations; the Feb. 9 issue, p. 125, described President Hayes's message to Congress on the Ponca issue; and the Feb. 16 issue, p. 150, criticized the Interior Department bill, which did not give the Ponca Indians the choice of homeland.

TO WHITELAW REID

[February 26, 1881]

Dear Mr. Reid —

Thank you and bless you. —

— If anything is ever accomplished in the way of justice to those Poncas, it will be due to the N. Y. Tribune more than to any other newspaper in the country — (more than to all others!) —

I hope you will think it worth while to print this short article I enclose. —

It is a small item in the testimony before that Ponca Committee which has escaped even *my* attention till today. I wish I had had it two weeks ago. — But the ill Schurz can do by no means comes to end on the 4th of March.[1]

He has circulated his open letter to Dawes, all over the country, in *pamphlet* shape; also his letter to Gov. Long. —

The "Ladies Treaty Making Society of Phila."[2] have just printed 2000 of Dawes's reply. — & they will [follow next week into every editor's & minister's hands?] —

Yrs truly

Helen Jackson

Brevoort House

Feb. 26. 1881.

P.S. I'm not quite sure that you will think I know you well enough, either to be glad — or to say I am glad, of the news I hear of your engagement to Miss Mills.[3] — But I am heartily glad, — all the same. — And I hope you won't wonder at my saying so. — You know I met Miss Mills at Mrs. Botta's one night, and you were there too — and I recollect her sweet bright face very well; and I recollect thinking of this very thing, then: though I had heard no word spoken by any one of it. —

It gives me hearty pleasure to think of the happiness you are both entering on — So please add mine to the mountain of good wishes which are piling up for you.

H.J.

ALS (DLC, Reid Papers).

1. Schurz resigned as interior secretary on Mar. 4, 1881, to take an editorial position with the *NY Evening Post*.

2. Reference to what later became the WNIA.

3. Reid married Elizabeth Mills (1858–1931) on Apr. 26, 1881. Mrs. Reid, a philanthropist, was active in supporting hospitals; during the Spanish American War she served as head of the nursing division of the Red Cross. Their son, Ogden Mills Reid, took over the editorship of the *Tribune*.

TO HENRY WADSWORTH LONGFELLOW

[March 2, 1881]

Dear Mr. Longfellow,

Will you give me half an hour? And will you allow me to refer to your past cordial kindness to me, as my only apology for this intrusion on your time?

I want to say a few words to you in regard to Sec. Schurz's position on the Indian question. And I want to preface my words by telling you that a year and a half ago when I began to look into the history of our Govt.s dealings with the Indians, I was so enthusiastic an admirer of Carl Schurz, that I would not permit one of the Ponca agitators as they are called to say a word in my presence against him. At that time, no evidence that could have been laid before me by any man would have made me think ill of him: and it was with very great pain that I came slowly, — solely in consequence of my study of the Records of his own Bureau, to change my opinion. I mention this fact, that you may see how very different my position in regard to the matter is from that of those persons who have become antagonistic towards him simply in regard to the matter of the Poncas. That is only one case out of scores.

Of course it has been impossible for you, and for Dr. Holmes, and many of the gentlemen who have signed the invitation to this dinner to Schurz, to even follow the newspaper controversy on the Ponca business, much less to get at the numberless points and facts not brought to surface in it, and I do not at all wonder that there has been in many minds a reaction in favor of Schurz, produced by some of the methods of his assailants. I have greatly regretted some of the phases and shapes the thing took, and until recently have felt that it was neither wise nor worth while to make direct attacks on the Secretary. — he being no worse than his predecessors — and the root of the trouble being in the system. But he has developed within the last few months such malignity towards innocent people, and such astounding and wholesale lying, that I feel now that every true friend of the Indians ought to help in denouncing both him and his methods.

When it was said by the correspondent of the Springfield Republican that Bright Eyes was a "phenomenal liar" for having said that she was not permitted to see her uncle,[1] it was Schurz who told what he knew to be a dastardly cruel lie: which is proved —

1*st*. by the sworn testimony of the Rev. Mr. Dorsey[2] before the Senate Committee. He testified that he heard Haworth say to Schurz "I have arranged that she shall not see her uncle till after the papers are signed."

2*d* By the written statement of the Editor of the Republican, when compelled to give his authority, that it was "Carl Schurz himself."

I know of no more striking illustration of the helpless position of the Indian outside the protection of law, than that a respectable paper like the Republican, unthinkingly printed in regard to that helpless Indian girl, a slander it would never have dared to print in regard to any woman who had father brother husband or friend legally able to hold the Editor responsible for it.

I enclose to you an article of my own,[3] which by simple citations from Schurz's own Reports proves him to have egregiously lied in his last one — attempting to take credit to himself for having long advocated the policy which he *now* sees that the people demand; but which he never has either advocated or practiced.

I enclose also an Editorial from the Worcester Spy which better than anything which has been written in concise shape, shows the enormity of his crime in regard to the Poncas, also the repeated misrepresentations he has made in regard to his not being responsible for their removal.

It is a curious point bearing on the law of heredity that this Editorial is written by a grandson of the Jeremiah Evarts,[4] who, fifty years ago wrote a series of eloquent letters in the National Intelligencer, signed Wm. Penn, in behalf of the Cherokees.

I assure you that every statement in this Editorial is strictly true, and can be proved by sworn testimony and official Reports.

I enclose also an Editorial written by Chas Dudley Warner[5] on the subject. There are only two papers so far as I know of any standing, that endorse Schurz's course in this matter: the N. Y. Eve. Post and the Nation. The Ed. of the Eve. Post[6] is a personal friend of Schurz's, and stands by him heart and hand, as is right. We all must trust to that: there is probably no man so bad that he will not have a following of friends who judging his acts by him, and not him by his acts, will believe in him to the end. — The Nation, would of course, be a priori against "Sentimentalists"; and I concur I heartily sympathize with it, in that: but it has in this matter been so antagonistic from the start that it has not taken the trouble to inform itself accurately, even on points where both sides agree, and has therefore made some ludicrous misstatements claiming for Schurz what he never dared to claim for himself.[7]

I wish also to tell you of a recent order of Mr. Schurz's which came to light in the Report of the Ponca Commission. It is in the testimony of the Rev. Alfred Riggs, missionary to the Santee Sioux, whose reservation joins the old Ponca reservation in Dakota. Standing Bear and his party, now on that reservation, are free men — (freedmen): — so pronounced by a U. S. Court. They are working hard for a living: but having been forced to leave all their possessions behind them in Ind. Territory, are very poor and need help. The Hicksite Friends in Pa. knowing the Agent on the Santee Reservation wished to send aid to these Poncas through him, Mr. Schurz forbade him to deliver it!

"The Santee Agent has received orders not to have anything whatever to do with the relief which his religious Society wished to distribute through him," is Mr. Riggs's testimony. —

Is not this malignity? Is not this tyranny? Has the Interior Dept. any right to forbid its employees to give charity to *any* suffering human beings? —

I wish also to call your attention to the fact that Sec. Schurz ordered the Govt. Atty. in Nebraska,[8] to oppose the habeas corpus suit for the release of the Poncas, on the ground that Indians were not "persons"!

Do you think a man who ordered such an argument as that is entitled to be called the friend of the Indian?

He has (since the excitement on the subject) claimed great credit to himself for not having appealed from Judge Dundy's decision in that case. But he knew perfectly well that there was nothing which the friends of the Indians so much desired as that he *should* appeal from that decision. He knew very well that such an appeal would carry the case right into the Supreme Court — the only course which would test the thing once for all — the only *chance* the Indians have, for getting the protection of the law assured to them all: — a decision of the Supreme Court to that effect then, would have given the protection of the law to every Indian in the country, and taken the ground from under the feet of the Indian ring at one stroke: — and *this*, Carl Schurz hindered, and Carl Schurz alone!

I wish also to tell you, that the famous Severalty Bill which he framed, and introduced, and has so boasted of, was, as he framed it, an infamous Bill; and would have, as White Eagle said of it "plucked the Indian like a bird." And, the minute that Bill was, thanks to the Mass. Senators and Senator Morgan,[9] so amended that it could have passed without so much danger to the Indian, and without the profit to land speculators orginally provided for in it, — that minute the men in charge of it, Schurz being back of them, — *ceased to push it* — refused to bring it up for farther discussion, for fear it might pass! This I know, for I was in Washington, and watched it all.

I wish to tell you also that he has framed and introduced a Bill now in regard to the Poncas, *denying* them the freedom of choice between the two reservations, as recommended by the Pres. and by the majority of the Ponca Com[mission]. Why does he do this? Because he knows that, if they once indicated that they really have that choice, in less than one year they will nearly all be back in Dakota again. On this point, I myself had great doubts till I talked with Gen. Crook and Gen. Miles. They both say this. Gen. Miles in the strongest terms.

I mail to you today a copy of my book, the "Century of Dishonor." I hope you will find leisure to glance at it sufficiently to see that I have not contented myself with a superficial study of this subject: — and that my convictions are not based on my partizan showings of facts. I have carefully read every Official Report of the Govt. on Indian affairs for the last hundred years; and I do most honestly believe that no one can do that, and not be led to feel as I feel on this question.

Yours most truly

Helen Jackson

New York
Brevoort House
March 2, — 1881

ALS (Henry Wadsworth Longfellow Papers, bMS Am 1340.2 [2971], Houghton Library, Harvard University, Cambridge, Massachusetts; hereinafter cited as MH, Longfellow Papers).

This letter is almost an exact duplicate of a letter to Oliver Wendell Holmes (MH, Holmes Papers, bMS Am 1241.1), reprinted with annotations in Mathes, "Helen Hunt Jackson and the Campaign for Ponca Restitution, 1880–1881." To conserve space, only one has been reproduced here.

Henry Wadsworth Longfellow (1807–82), who published his first poem in 1820, taught at Harvard until 1854. Due to his popularity, by 1900 his poetry had been translated into a dozen languages. Among his best known works are "The Village Blacksmith," *Evangeline*, *Hiawatha*, and *The Courtship of Miles Standish*, which sold more than fifteen thousand copies on the first day it was published.

According to Tibbles in *Buckskin and Blanket Days*, p. 218, when Longfellow first met Susette La Flesche he earnestly said, "*This is* Minnehaha" (referring to the wife of his famous character Hiawatha).

1. Bright Eye's (Susette's) uncle, White Swan, had accompanied other Ponca chiefs east to meet with the government commission chaired by Senator Samuel Jordan Kirkwood that was investigating the Ponca removal. She claimed that she was denied access to her uncle until after he had spoken to the commission and agreed to remain in Indian Territory. However, in "Our Washington Letter," *Springfield Republican*, Jan. 6, 1881, p. 4, the special correspondent called her a "phenomenal liar" while describing Secretary Schurz as "the best friend the Indians ever had in the interior department." In an editorial, the *NY Evening Post*, Jan. 7, 1881, p. 2, picked up the story. The women in Boston came to Susette's defense; see the *Springfield Republican*, Jan. 11, 1881, p. 4.

2. Episcopal minister Owen Dorsey was at the Omaha Agency on the day Standing Bear and the other Poncas were arrested. He spent two years among the Omahas working on a philological study of their language. He also was the interpreter engaged for the chiefs by the Interior Department.

3. Probably a reference to HHJ's mid-Dec. 1880 letter to the editor of the *NY Herald*, above.

4. Jeremiah Evarts (1781–1831) practiced law before devoting the remainder of his life to Christian missionary work. A founder of the American Board of Commissioners for Foreign Missions, he became its secretary in 1821. He personally investigated the conditions of southern Indians, particularly the Cherokees, and in 1829 wrote twenty-four articles in the *National Intelligencer*, under the pseudonym William Penn, opposing removal and supporting Cherokee land claims. For further information see Perdue and Green, *The Cherokee Removal: A Brief History with Documents*, pp. 94–105.

5. Possibly a reference to an item on the Senate Ponca Committee that appeared in the *Hartford Courant*, Mar. 1, 1881, p. 2.

6. The editor of the *NY Evening Post* was Parke Godwin (1816–1904), who practiced law for a short time before accepting an offer by William Cullen Bryant to work for the *Evening Post*, an association that lasted intermittently for forty-five years. When Bryant died in 1878, Godwin assumed the position of editor-in-chief, leaving his post only when the paper was sold.

7. The *Nation* strongly defended Schurz in "The Schurz Mystery," Feb. 24, 1881, pp. 125–26.

8. The government attorney who prosecuted Standing Bear in *Standing Bear v. Crook* was Genio M. Lambertson.

9. John Tyler Morgan (1824–1907), a lawyer and a Confederate brigadier general, was elected to the Senate from Alabama in 1876, serving until his death.

TO CHARLES DUDLEY WARNER

[March 3, 1881]

Dear C. D. W. —

You said as I felt, ten days ago — I wonder if there is anybody who hasn't had a "bronchial affair"! — I'm not out of my room yet but have recovered my wits, what there were of them — so am not as lonesome as I was! —

— The notice was not "poor"[1] — & if you hadn't looked at it through your bronchial tube you wouldn't have thought so. It is just the sort I wanted — gives the *facts* — I believe the notices of the book are going to do more good than the book. They have been simply *marvellous*: — Harpers sent me 75 the other day, all long — all complimentary & earnest & sympathetic. The N. Y. Tribune is the only paper that has failed me! —

I'm desperately sorry about the "Indian Feast" — had just telegraphed *again* for them — have ten envelopes with two others already in waiting for

them to go off to different people to create public opinion — *Everything tells,* —
& we haven't heard the last of Carl Schurz yet. If Kirkwood[2] goes in in his place
—it will be still Schurz! I quake & tremble.— & shall lose faith in the Lord, if
Kirkwood gets it. —

Yours forever—

H.J.

We are going to *Southern* California in two weeks: — for a two months trip —
Don't you envy us the sun & flowers? I am going to write four articles for
Harpers Mag. about it — to pay for the luxuries of the trip! & W*m* Jackson is
going to treat himself to the rest — my bronchial tubes smack their mouths at
the thought of the soft air — Really this climate is only fit for bears & tigers to
"growl & fight" in. —
We move over to the *Berkeley* on Sat. —
Brevoort.
March 3. — 1881.

ALS (CtHT-W, Warner Collection).
    1. A reference to the review of *A Century of Dishonor* in the Mar. 1, 1881, issue of
the *Hartford Courant*, p. 1.
    2. Iowa's Senator Samuel J. Kirkwood (1813-\94) chaired the Special Committee
investigating the Ponca removal. On Mar. 5, 1881, he was appointed by President
James A. Garfield to succeed Carl Schurz as secretary of the interior but resigned his
position upon the death of Garfield.

TO THE EDITOR OF THE *SPRINGFIELD REPUBLICAN*

[March 5, 1881]

To the Editor of The Republican:—
    In the year 1877 the following tribes were reported to the interior depart-
ment as anxiously entreating for individual titles to their lands: The S'Ko-
Komish Indians and other tribes in Washington territory; 13 different tribes at
the Siletz agency in Oregon; six tribes at the Grande Ronde agency, Oregon;
the Otoes in Nebraska; the Ottawas and Chippewas in Michigan; the Potta-
wottomies and Kickapoos in Kansas; the Sisseton and Wappeton Sioux and the
Sioux at Devil's Lake agency in Dakota; and seven small bands on Round
Valley reservation, Mendocino county, California. The reports from the
Washington territory Indians, and from those on the Round Valley reservation,
are fair illustrations of the manner in which the Indians' entreaties for titles to
their farms have been received by the government. An agent from Washington
territory writes: [1] —

Soon after coming to this territory as superintendent of Indian affairs, I discovered that the bane of our Indian system and the prime cause of its failure was the fact of communing tribes upon reservations like herds of cattle in fenced pastures without any individual property in the soil. So I set to work and succeeded in getting 12 of the 15 Indian reservations in this territory, including all in this agency, surveyed into 40-acre lots for the purpose of having the Indians take homesteads and obtain individual titles to the same like white men. As soon as surveys were completed I encouraged Indians to take claims on their reservations in accordance with the surveyed lines, build houses on and improve them, and I would see that every one who would do so would get a title or paper from the government for his claim. From the fact that the 6th article of the Medicine Creek treaty[2] provides (see revision of Indian treaties, pp. 562 and 563) that the Indians of said treaty should have the privilege of taking separate permanent homes on their respective reservations "on the same terms and subject to the same regulations as are required in the 6th article of the treaty with the Omahas, so far as the same may be applicable," and from the fact that said 6th article of the treaty with the Omahas[3] provides (see revision of Indian treaties, p. 639) "that the president may issue a patent to such persons or families as have made a location of land for a permanent home," I suppose that the faith of the government thus plighted would cause the Indians to receive the deeds thus promised as fast as the names of the Indians with the numbers and descriptions of their selection were reported. But I have been sadly disappointed so far; either the 6th or 7th article in each of the other five treaties with the Indians of this territory contains the same provision as that quoted from the 6th article of the Medicine Creek treaty; but I believe that none of the agents of said treaties have yet succeeded in obtaining any titles from the government for their Indians. Most of the Indians at this agency, especially those of the Puyallup reservation, took claims soon after the survey, and built dwellings, made "permament homes" on and improved their claims, and have procured their subsistence by the cultivation of their farms like white men. Many complied with the requirements of making "permanent homes" and improvements four years ago, and have been looking to me for the fulfillment of my promise to get the papers for their claims. Some few of them have lost faith and abandoned their claims, but the mass of them have great faith in my promise to them, and are still working away on their claims, believing that "Washington" will not let them lose their homes and labor.

The agent of the Round Valley reservation in Oregon[4] writes in this same year:[5]—

This reservation was established in 1856, and by an act of Congress March 3, 1873, was established in its present form. The Indians were encouraged to believe that they would have this as their permanent home and have land given to them for their individual homes. Four years have passed away. Messrs. Thomson, Browne and Eberly (trespassers on the reservation) hold their former homes under a claim of swamps and overflowed land, and the stockmen hold the range as they did in

1872. . . . . The Indians failing to get the land and range promised them, and Congress cutting down the appropriations annually, they are fast losing confidence in promises, and as a result a fearful reaction has taken place. . . . A failure on the part of the government to keep faith with the Indians is the cause of most of our troubles with them.

In 1878, the agent of one of these same Washington territory tribes writes:[6] —

Early last fall they had reason to believe that patents would soon be given them, and for a time were greatly elated, but soon after their hopes were again cast down by the news that a different policy had been recommended by the department. Some at that time abandoned their lands, the improvements on which were worth hundreds of dollars, and went out into the public domain and took up new lands away from their relatives and friends, and commenced anew to hew out homes for themselves which will not be subject to the changes incident to reservation life. . . . Among the freaks[?] which some of them have taken the past year, has been their effort to become citizens under the naturalization laws, quite a number having taken out their first papers under the impression that by so doing they would be secured against removal to some other reservation.

Could anything be more touching than the picture of these men, born on American soil, striving in their helplessness and despair to get freemen's foothold on that soil by the processes provided for the naturalization of foreigners? "Work for a living or get out of the way."

H.H.

New York, March 5, 1881.

Printed in the *Springfield Republican*, Mar. 9, 1881, p. 4, as "Faithlessness with the Red Man: 'H.H.' on a Phase of the Indian Question: The Indian's Demand for Lands in Severalty at the Opening of Secretary Schurz's Administration."

1. Gordon A. Henry was appointed a special agent on July 15, 1874. This quote from his report dated Aug. 20, 1877, for the Puyallup, Nisqually, and other Indian tribes can be found in *Annual Report of the Commissioner of Indian Affairs, 1877*, p. 190.

2. There were two treaties signed at Medicine Lodge Creek, Kansas, that included this sixth article: Oct. 21, 1876, with the Kiowas and Comanches, and Oct. 28, 1876, with the Cheyennes and Arapahoes.

3. This Omaha treaty was negotiated on Mar. 16, 1854, by Commissioner George Manypenny in Washington, D.C.

4. This should be California instead of Oregon.

5. A reference to Agent J. L. Burchard, *Annual Report of the Commissioner, 1877*, p. 41.

6. This quote from Edwin Eells, agent at S'Kokomish Agency, Aug. 20, 1878, can be found in *Annual Report of the Commissioner, 1878*, pp. 137–38. Eells had been appointed on Apr. 17, 1871.

TO HENRY WADSWORTH LONGFELLOW

[March 10, 1881]

My dear Mr. Longfellow

Many thanks for your kind note. I do not wonder that you were "amazed and confounded." — Were it possible for you to look into the Official Records at length, you would be still more so. I enclose a little article of mine just printed in the Springfield Republican:[1] by which you will see how many of the comparatively unknown tribes were beseeching for "severalty", at the time Sec. Schurz took charge of the Dept. Did he issue to many of these tribes, certificates of their farms? No!

— He has contented himself with framing a bill, which as it stood, as it came from his hands, was an infamous steal of Indian lands. — But in his last Rept. he laid great stress on the "encouraging symptom" that Indians were now — (in 1880!—) "asking for their lands in severalty." —

This is a fair specimen of his hypocrisies.

Yours truly
Helen Jackson

New York.
The Berkeley.
March 10. —

ALS (MH, Longfellow Papers).
  1. A reference to HHJ's Mar. 5, 1881, letter, above.

TO OLIVER WENDELL HOLMES

[March 19, 1881]

My Dear Dr. Holmes.

I take the liberty of troubling you once more with a document, which I hope you will find time to read.

It is Senator Dawes's reply to Schurz: — now published as a Tract by the Ladies Treaty Keeping Association of Phila.[1] — This is the speech which the Nation not being informed as to the real points of the case, called "irrelevant" — It is in fact most crushingly relevant — a complete rejoinder — and an unanswerable one.[2] —

It is of no sort of consequence to the Poncas who did or did not move them: — but it is of consequence, that the man who has systematically thwarted & hindered every movement for them pertaining to their lands — and every movement to secure legal protection for the Indians as a *race*, should be thoroughly understood by the people — and not be allowed to divert the public mind from the main issues and immediate practical measures. — His present attitude as Chief Speaker at meetings on the Indian Question, seems to me a good deal like Pharaoh masquerading in Moses' clothing; and deceiving everybody even Aaron![3] (Armstrong.)

Yours truly
Helen Jackson

New York
The Berkeley.
March 19. 1881
P.S.—

I have marked one point in this speech, the Sec. has repeatedly asserted this, ie. that he was compelled to carry out that "law."

There was no *"law"* in that sense, at all. And the Dept. has never before taken that ground in regard to Acts of Congress providing for the Removal of Indians. See pp. 244, & 250 of the Century of Dishonor. The Winnebagoes there spoken of were not removed till *long* after the Act providing for their Removal: and when they ran away from the new reservation back to the old, *nothing* was done about it!

ALS (Oliver Wendell Holmes Papers, Library of Congress, Washington, D.C.).

Oliver Wendell Holmes (1809–94), a Harvard graduate, practiced medicine in Boston before returning to his alma mater for a distinguished thirty-five-year teaching career. A gifted lecturer and a popular writer, he wrote both verse and prose. He is probably best known for *The Autocrat of the Breakfast-Table*, which originally appeared in the *Atlantic Monthly*.

1. A reference to what would become the WNIA. Sending along a copy of this pamphlet, on Mar. 12, 1881, Amelia Stone Quinton wrote Dawes that she was so sure that he would approve of it that it did not occur to her to ask permission. See Quinton to Dawes, Mar. 12, 1881; see also Quinton to Dawes, Apr. 2, 1881, both in DLC, Dawes Papers.

2. The *Nation*, which was sympathetic to Secretary Schurz, on Feb. 17, 1881, p. 104, in an editorial noted: "Mr. Dawes made his reply on Friday, and a more irrelevant one could hardly be imagined."

3. Aaron was the older brother of Moses. Thus HHJ suggests that Schurz was so convincing as a friend of the Indian that he could fool even the most ardent defenders, including Samuel Chapman Armstrong.

TO WILLIAM HAYES WARD

The Berkeley. —
Mar. 23. [1881]

Dear Mr. Ward —

I have been hoping to get down to see you — but am still much under the weather. — have only been out three times, for a short drive.

I am preparing however to set off for California on April 1*st* or 2d — I forget whether I told you that I was going to write a series of articles for Harpers Mag. on South California.[1] I have received today a check for $25 from you — You still have one poem, "Harvest"[2] — & I enclose two others — & would be very glad if Mr. Bowen would pay me the $50 for them, now, before I go — I find the Christian Union pays on acceptance when desired — they have just paid me $100 for four prose articles, which they had requested me to write.[3] —

I was sorry Mr. Twining[4] dismissed my book with only that short paragraph. I suppose there must have been some special reason for doing so. — "without honor in his own country", I thought to myself when I read it! — The subject as a whole has never had a hearing yet, in the Ind[ependent] — but I see you are on Schurz's side of the controversy — If I had *time* & opportunity, I could convince you how wicked, insincere, & hypocritical he has been — however — as Edward Everett Hale wrote me yesterday "give Schurz rope enough & he'll hang himself." — But he is the most adroit liar I ever knew. — & it is trying to human nature to see him posing now before the country as the chief friend & champion of the Indians!

— The man who murdered the Cheyennes — the Nez Perces — robbed the Poncas — & cheated the Utes! — all in one four years! — It is like *Pharoah* masquerading around in Moses robes! —

I shall set off — April 1*st* I think — — Perhaps you'll find a half hour to run up & see me — if not — goodbye for a few months —

Yrs ever—
Helen Jackson

ALS (CSmH, HHJ MSS, HM 13996).

1. Although commissioned to write four articles for *Harper's Magazine*, HHJ was forced to turn down the offer because she could find no one to accompany her to California.

2. Her poem "Harvest" appeared in the June 30, 1881, *Independent*.

3. The *Christian Union* printed five of her essays: "Seeds of Fear," June 8; "Ringeriget," July 6, 13, and 20; "Burnt Children," Sept. 28; "A Victory of Love," Nov. 2; and "A Stone Mason's Garden of Eden," Nov. 23.

4. Kinsley Twining served as one of several literary editors during the 1870s and 1880s at the *Independent*.

TO HENRY LAURENS DAWES

[May 8, 1881]

Dear Mr. Dawes,

I presume you know that Gen. Miles presented a paper to Pres. Hayes, asking for the return of the Nez Percé's & Chief Joseph to the Idaho Reservation by Executive Order.

Pres. Hayes assured him that it should be "arranged all right." —

Of course, that was the last heard of it. —

Can you find out if that paper was turned over to the Int. Dept. or in any way acted upon?

I would be very glad to know about this.

If Gen. Garfield[1] has come into possession of the paper — or if it is in the War Dept. — or the Int. Dept. —

I am watching with great interest the fine snarl of things in Washington at present.

I suppose it is a bad time to ask anybody to do anything outside the routine fight over Robertson[2] but I am sure nothing crowds out the Indians from your mind. —

Yours truly
Helen Jackson

P.S. Address
 The Berkeley
 Corner 5th Av. & 9th St.
 New York.
My regards to your wife & daughter.

May. 8. 1881

Gen. Miles himself cannot learn any thing about that paper, he tells me. — —It is his intention to follow up the subject. I told him I would write & ask you to inquire of the Depts — & the Pres. —They will attend to *you*.

ALS (DLC, Dawes Papers).
 1. James Abram Garfield (1831–81), the twentieth president of the United States, served in the Ohio Senate and commanded troops during the Civil War, becoming a major general. He was a member of the House of Representatives, 1863–80; although elected to the Senate in 1880, he never served because he became the Republican candidate for the presidency and won.

2. William Henry Robertson (1823–98), a state politician, helped secure the presidential nomination for Garfield, who appointed him collector of the port of New York.

TO HENRY LAURENS DAWES

[May 15, 1881]

My dear Mr. Dawes —

Many thanks for your kindness in seeing the Pres. for me.

The "Permit" reached me yesterday morning. — I do not know how much it will give me beyond the certainty of not being put off the Reservations! — "Such courtesies as may be *properly*" extended, may be very slender. — If you are on familar and pleasant terms with Sec. Kirkwood, could you ask him some day whether I would be permitted to spend any *time* on the Reservations — and to go freely into the houses of the Indians and talk with them, as much as I like? —

My going has been a *fifth* time deferred.[1] The fates seem to be against me. Miss Horsford (who is to go with me) was thrown from their carriage in Boston, on Wed. and her arm so badly injured, that the doctor says she cannot travel for ten days yet. — This will make it too late for us to stop in Omaha: and I shall therefore postpone my visit to the Reservations till September — when I trust Mr. Jackson can go with me, and we can take time to do it thoroughly.

With warm regards to Mrs. Dawes & Miss Anna,[2] & many thanks to yourself.

I am —
Yours very truly
Helen Jackson

Mrs. W*m* S. Jackson
The Berkeley
Corner 5th Av. & 9th St.
New York —
May 15, 1881

ALS (DLC, Dawes Papers).

1. HHJ is referring to her trip to California to write articles for *Harper's Magazine*.

2. Anna L. (1851–1938) Dawes, his daughter, worked closely with her father in defending the Indians.

TO THE EDITOR OF THE *TRIBUNE*

[May 24, 1881]

To the Editor of The Tribune.

SIR: The readers of THE TRIBUNE will remember that there were printed in THE TRIBUNE of May 15 some speeches of Sioux chiefs.[1] These speeches were made at a meeting of the leading men of the Indian bands now living near Fort Keogh, in Montana, and were forwarded to the War Department (at the chiefs' request) by Colonel Whistler, the officer in command at that post.[2] It is impossible to read these speeches without be[i]ng profoundly moved by them. They express only one sentiment. They are simply prayers to the United States Government that these Indian bands may be allowed to stay in their own country and earn their own living.

There is much to be regretted that the speeches were not accompanied by a short statement of the present and past condition of the bands represented by these chiefs. The first two, "Hump"[3] and "Horse Road,"[4] with their bands, surrendered to General Miles in the spring of 1877. There were about 350 of them all told, Sioux and Cheyennes. To this band were added in 1878 150 more Cheyennes, a part of the band that fought its way up from Indian Territory and was finally massacred, men, women and children, at Fort Robinson.[5] From that day until now these Indians have been self-supporting. The United States Government has not spent a dollar on them. They are tilling little farms; are industrious, peaceable and orderly; they live by selling the produce of their farms and by hunting. General Miles says he has known an Indian woman to sell $12 worth of vegetables in a day. If any one of them misbehave, he is dealt with by the legal authorities of the nearest town, just as any white man would be. When they wish to go off on hunting excursions they have a pass from the commanding officer at the post, to show that they are friendly Indians. In every other respect they have been for nearly four years living as free and independent lives as any farmers in New-York or Massachusetts.

Listen once more to their words: "I want to raise my children the same as whites," says the chief Big Road;[6] "I want to be quiet and friendly with everybody. What I say I want you to send off quick. I want to go to work. These Indians all think the same. Secretary Schurz was here and saw all this land. I want him to help us and tell the Great Father." Says Spotted Eagle:[7] "I have done all I could and did what General Miles said. I want you to hold me strong all you can. I am a friend of all the whites. I like farming. I want you to help me. I don't want to go down to an Agency."

Last summer 1,500 of Sitting Bull's Indians,[8] hearing of the contented and prosperous condition of these Indians, came down from Canada of their own accord, surrendered to General Miles, and asked to be allowed to settle down and live as the others were doing. So eager were they to show their good faith that they went to work at once, and in less than three months ploughed up 400 acres of land. As soon as their first crops shall have been harvested, these Indians also will become self-supporting like the others. One of the chiefs of these last bands says: "Hump and the Cheyennes have been here a long time with the soldiers. I saw this and would like to stay here." Another says: "We all came back here and want to raise our children here; and we don't want to go away from this country. General Miles told us a few words last fall. He said we had done right in coming back to our own country; he said he liked that. He told us we were going to raise our children and be rich in the future, and said he would help us all he could. I hope General Miles will succeed in whatever he tries to do for us. We will all be glad to hear from the Great Father and from General Miles."

These Sioux Indians love their country with a passion akin to that of the Swiss mountaineers. They have lived in it for hundreds of years; and it is a glorious country. The stranger who has once seen and tasted its crystal waters finds other waters dull and lifeless in comparison. Even in midwinter a Sioux Indian will break the ice on the Yellowstone River, jump in and bathe with delight; and General Miles says he has often seen them going barefooted in the snow to save wearing out the gay moccasins of which they are proud. They are the hardiest, strongest race on the globe; and their qualities of mind and soul are the qualities of which heroes have been moulded ever since the world began.

What does the United States Government now propose to do with these hundreds of free, industrious, orderly, law-abiding, self-supporting men, who ask nothing but to be left unmolested, to continue to be self-supporting, law-abiding, orderly, industrious and free! It proposes to remove them from their homes; to herd them; to imprison them on the reservations, whose bounds they may not cross without the permission of whatever Agent the chances and changes of politics may put over them, with the arbitrary power of a dictator in his hands! Can the Interior Department show any good and sufficient reason why men who have supported themselves for nearly four years, and molested nobody, should be treated in this fashion?

H.H.

New-York, May 24, 1881.

Printed in the *Tribune*, May 28, 1881, p. 5, as "What the Sioux Chiefs Want: A Letter from 'H.H.': The Reasonable Request of the Sioux to Be Left in Their Present Free and Self-Supporting Condition."

1. A reference to "What the Sioux Chiefs Want: A Conference at Fort Keogh—Speeches by Six of the Leading Men," *Tribune*, May 15, 1881, p. 1. The Sioux were divided into three regional groupings (Santee, Yankton, and Teton), each further divided into smaller subgroups.

2. Joseph Nelson Garland Whistler (1822–99) graduated from West Point in 1846 and fought in the Mexican American War, the Civil War, and the Sioux wars of the 1870s.

3. Hump (d. 1908) was a young Miniconjou (Teton) Sioux warrior who fought in Red Cloud's war against the forts along the Bozeman Trail, 1866–68. He also participated in the 1870s Sioux wars, was at Little Bighorn, and temporarily joined Sitting Bull in Canada. Hump was a member of a delegation of Sioux chiefs in Washington, D.C., to lobby for better conditions.

4. Horse Road was a lesser-known Miniconjou whose short speech was included in the *Tribune* article.

5. This band of Northern Cheyennes, led by Dull Knife, had surrendered and were imprisoned at Fort Robinson. When informed they were to be returned to Indian Territory, they escaped and were hunted down.

6. Big Road was an Oglala (Teton) Sioux whose short speech was included in the *Tribune* article.

7. Spotted Eagle was a member of the Sans-Arc, a subdivision of the Teton Sioux.

8. Sitting Bull (ca. 1831–90), a Hunkpapa (Teton) holy man, was elected in 1869 as war chief of the Sioux Nation. He led his warriors into battle during the 1860s and 1870s and was present at the Battle of the Little Bighorn, after which he led his followers to Canada. Upon his return to the United States, he spent two years imprisoned at Fort Randall, South Dakota, before moving to Standing Rock Agency in 1883. For a short time he traveled with Buffalo Bill's Wild West show. Caught up in the Ghost Dance movement of 1890, Sitting Bull was killed by Sioux Indian police under orders to arrest him.

PART TWO

The Cause of the California Mission Indians and the Writing of *Ramona*

Introduction

Ramona

IF I COULD WRITE A STORY THAT WOULD DO FOR THE INDIAN A THOUSANDTH PART WHAT UNCLE TOM'S CABIN DID FOR THE NEGRO, I WOULD BE THANKFUL THE REST OF MY LIFE.

HELEN HUNT JACKSON TO THOMAS BAILEY ALDRICH, MAY 4, 1883

IN THE FALL OF 1881 JACKSON AGAIN RECEIVED AN ASSIGNMENT TO WRITE articles on California, this time from Richard Watson Gilder for *Century Magazine*. On December 10 she boarded the train; arriving in Los Angeles on the eighteenth, she settled into the elegant, three-storied Pico House.

Jackson took up the cause of the California Mission Indians even more tenaciously than she had that of the Poncas. She repeatedly visited the Luiseño villages of Pala, Temecula, Pauma, Rincon, Pachanga, Potrero, and La Jolla; the Cahuilla villages; the Cupeño village of Agua Caliente (Cupa) on Warner's Ranch; the Ipai villages of Mesa Grande and Santa Ysabel; and the Serrano village of Saboba. Moved by their valiant effort to eke out a meager existence, Jackson described the Mission Indians as helpless against the white onslaught but intelligent, industrious, and peaceful when given a chance. By the late nineteenth century, their condition was worse than that of the Poncas. Former mission lands had been secularized by the Mexican government, but since original Mexican land grants had protective clauses for Indian occupants, some continued to farm ancestral lands; the less fortunate scattered to inaccessible valleys and mountains or lived "like gypsies in brush huts" on the outskirts of various white settlements. Jackson summarized the history of the area between secularization and the Mexican American War as "a record of shameful fraud and pillage, of which the Indians were the most hapless victims."[1]

Her most important contact was Antonio Coronel, a lifelong friend of the Indians whom she had met through Francis Mora, bishop of Monterey and Los Angeles. Sitting in Coronel's comfortable adobe home in the western suburbs of Los Angeles, surrounded by orchards, vineyards, and orange groves,

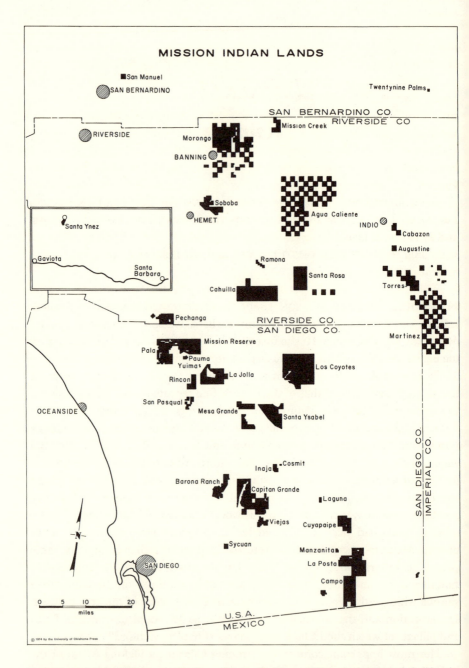

Reproduced from Warren A. Beck and Ynez D. Haase, *Historical Atlas of California* (Norman: University of Oklahoma Press, 1974), map 58. Copyright © 1974 by University of Oklahoma Press.

Jackson listened to the old gentleman strum his guitar and sing or relate vivid stories of early California and the Indians, translated by his wife, Mariana.[2]

Provided with an itinerary by Coronel, Jackson left in late January 1882 for Santa Barbara. She visited San Fernando Mission, was received cordially by the custodian, and stopped at the del Valle family rancho, Camulos, near Piru, some sixty miles northwest of Los Angeles.[3] Retaining much of the old California rancho charm, Camulos provided Jackson with background that she later used for the Moreno home in *Ramona*. She arrived at Santa Barbara on January 23 and remained a month,[4] taking short daily excursions, which included visiting the mission and borrowing books from the Franciscans. During the first week of March 1882, she boarded a steamer for San Diego and settled in at the Horton House. She was introduced to prominent citizens, including businessman Ephraim Morse and his wife, who provided useful information for her articles.

The vicinity of San Diego offered abundant research potential.[5] The first Franciscan mission in upper California, San Diego de Alcalá, had been established in 1769. Neighboring San Luis Rey, founded three decades later, had eventually extended its influence to the Pala Valley, where a granary and later a chapel or *asistencia*, San Antonio de Pala,[6] were established in the summer of 1816. In addition, San Juan Capistrano, founded in 1776, was farther north on the coast. Finally, the hills and valleys surrounding San Diego were still home to remnants of the Mission Indians.

Accompanied by the local parish priest, Father Anthony D. Ubach, Jackson visited the villages of San Pasqual, Temecula, and Pachanga. The San Pasqual Valley, set aside by the U.S. government as an executive order reservation in 1870, had been preempted by white settlers following the recent revocation of the order. Father Ubach remembered when the village had three hundred residents who farmed over six hundred acres of land. However, in the winter of 1882 a small white settlement had crowded the Indians out; only a small adobe chapel, a cemetery, and a dozen adobe houses remained of the once prosperous Indian village. The lone Indian resident labored for the farmers who had dispossessed his people; the rest of his people had "fled into secret lairs like hunted wild beasts."[7] Whenever Ubach came to say Mass, however, several hundred Indians came out of the hills to attend.

The Temecula Valley, home of descendants of the San Luis Rey Mission Indians, had been protected by a clause in an old Mexican land grant; but settlers had brought suit in a San Francisco district court, and a writ of ejectment had been issued against the Indians in August 1873. They were evicted two years later; some moved three miles away to hot, barren, and

Pachanga Canyon—home of the Temecula Indians, ca. 1895. (California Historical Society, Title Insurance and Trust Photo Collection, Department of Special Collections, University of Southern California Library)

almost waterless Pachanga Canyon.[8] On June 27, 1882, Pachanga was set aside as an executive order reservation by President Chester A. Arthur. When Jackson returned in May 1883, she found a tremendous change. Orchards had been started, stock corrals and a government school had been built, and four times as much grain had been planted.[9]

On the last day of March Jackson arrived in the San Jacinto Valley to visit the village of Saboba at the foot of the mountains. Mary Sheriff, the government schoolteacher, introduced her to some of the 157 residents. Members of the Serrano and Cahuilla tribe, they industriously tilled wheat fields, maintained irrigation ditches, worked in peach and apricot orchards, and lived in substantial adobe houses. Sadly, Sheriff informed Jackson that part of the land, which had been granted in 1842 to José Antonio Estudillo by the Mexican government, had been sold to M. R. Byrnes, a San Bernardino merchant, who wanted the Indians removed. The original grant had included most of the valley below the village; however, in an 1878 survey, the village, streams, and nearby farms had been incorporated.[10]

After a visit to Riverside and San Bernardino, Jackson returned to Los Angeles to await the arrival of Henry Sandham, hired to illustrate her articles. At the end of April Jackson and Sandham took a ten-day jaunt to Mission San Juan Capistrano and the villages of Pala, Potrero, Temecula, Rincon, and Pauma. Located about twenty miles from Mission San Luis Rey on the San Luis Rey River, the Pala Valley had been a mission outpost. During the 1830s, as many as a thousand Indians gathered for weekly Mass; now the dilapidated old chapel was only half full during services. Farther up the river and along the foot of Palomar Mountain were the settlements of Pauma, Apeche, Rincon, and La Jolla, which they did not visit. By executive order in 1875 Pala, La Jolla, and Rincon had all been set aside as reservations.[11]

The wagon trip to Pala, which Jackson portrayed in an *Independent* article, required a full day's travel from San Juan Capistrano. Jackson, the *Century* artist Henry Sandham, and the driver did not arrive until late, taking shelter in the home of the widow of an Austrian colonel and her son, probably members of the Golsh family.[12] During her stay, Jackson witnessed a memorial service for an old Indian woman and later accepted the daughter's invitation to visit Potrero, some ten miles away. She spent a comfortable night in a neatly made bed with lace-trimmed sheets and pillowcases, unaware until morning that most of her host family had spent the night on the earthen floor in the kitchen.[13]

The villages of Rincon and Pauma lie near Potrero and Pala. At Rincon, with its two hundred residents, Jackson and Sandham found fields of barley, wheat, hay, and peas as well as flocks of sheep and a herd of cattle. The Pauma village on the San Luis Rey River was located at the Pauma Ranch, owned by Bishop Francis Mora. The right to the free use of arable lands as well as pasturage for livestock was tenuously guaranteed to the Indians by a clause in the original 1844 land grant.[14]

The weary travelers returned to Los Angeles at the end of April, and Jackson settled into the comfortable Kimball Mansion boarding house. One evening Abbot Kinney was seated next to her.[15] Born in New Jersey, Kinney was wealthy, well read, European educated, and more importantly spoke Spanish and was acquainted with California land laws. Much to Jackson's delight, he showed a sincere interest in the Indians. She invited him to accompany her on the next village tour, and soon a strong bond was forged between the wealthy young man and the matronly author.

Jackson, now joined by her husband, made preparations in early May for a twenty-day journey to Monterey with Kinney and Sandham. Concerned about the fate of Saboba, before departing, she wrote fellow Coloradoan Henry

Teller, newly appointed secretary of the interior, that without government protection the Indians would be driven from their lands.[16]

The party boarded the steamer *Los Angeles* for Santa Barbara, the first leg of the trip to Monterey. Delighted with Sandham's sketches, Jackson found the young artist as "enthusiastic about the romance & picturesqueness of the region" as she was.[17] In mid-May they climbed into a carriage heading for San Luis Obispo; two days later they arrived at the village of Jolon, which Jackson immortalized in an article for the *Independent*.[18] They finally arrived at Mission San Carlos Borromeo on the Carmel River.

The tour completed, the Jacksons made plans to sail from San Francisco to Oregon in mid-June. With the fate of Saboba weighing heavily on her mind, Jackson wrote Secretary Teller offering to join an investigative commission and write an official report. "I believe I am capable of writing judiciously and with exactness, even when I feel intensely," she added.[19] Teller directed Indian commissioner Hiram Price to authorize her to visit the Mission Indians, locate suitable lands within the public domain as permanent reservations, and furnish detailed descriptions of all lands. In turn, the Interior Department would draft executive orders setting the lands aside.[20]

At the end of their Oregon tour, the Jacksons returned to San Francisco. Will left for Colorado, while his wife remained behind to do additional research for her *Century* articles at the Bancroft Library,[21] a large private collection owned by Hubert Howe Bancroft, businessman, historian, and collector of Western Americana. In a July 7 letter from Price, Jackson learned of her formal appointment; she accepted with great pleasure.[22] Reluctant to undertake this task alone, she had written Teller requesting that Abbot Kinney be appointed to serve on the commission; he agreed.

Back in Colorado during the fall of 1882, Jackson reflected on her appointment. She outlined what she understood to be the "scope and intent" of the investigation in an October 31 letter to Price, who concurred and assured her that she was not obligated to visit every village but could use the services of the Indian agent and others. He agreed to pay the additional expense of the interpreter she had requested, but suggested that they use the agency interpreter, if Mission Indian agent S. S. Lawson could spare him.[23]

Chronic bronchitis, exacerbated by the altitude in Colorado Springs, caused Jackson to head east in mid-November. Although she customarily moved between New York and Boston during the winter months, she had hoped to leave for California in early February 1883. However, a severe case of influenza kept her shut up in her rooms. Finally, she headed west in mid-February. The journey did wonders for her health problems. Immediately upon arriving in Los Angeles, she began work on behalf of the Cahuilla Indians at San Ysidro, who for generations had lived above the Agua Caliente village in San Ysidro Canyon. She soon learned that Armin Cloos and Chatham Helm had homesteaded both ends of the canyon, cutting off available water to the Indians. Already one child had died of starvation. The Indians' desperate appeal to agent S. S. Lawson went unanswered.[24]

Following a visit to the government land office to locate lands patented to homesteaders, Jackson conferred with United States court commissioner Henry T. Lee, who recommended a formal survey. Writing to Commissioner Price in mid-March, she learned that the San Ysidro land had already been surveyed. No funds were available for future surveys.[25] Undaunted, Jackson continued to search through land-office files in Los Angeles, worked closely with Lee, and wrote letters to various officials. On April 2 she and Kinney met with Pablo, the captain of the San Ysidro village, who had walked over a hundred miles from the village with two companions to confer with Commissioner Lee. Pablo's face reminded Jackson of Abraham Lincoln's "grief-stamped face."[26]

Jackson's diligent work paid off. In mid-April she learned that Cloos's homestead entry would be canceled by the General Land Office in Los Angeles and the Department of Justice would set aside Helm's patent on the grounds that his land had not been available for homesteading. Agent Lawson, who had initially informed the Indian Office about the San Ysidro case in December 1881, was jubilant. "Just what I told them in my last letter on the subject, might, and should be done," he wrote Jackson. He would take special pleasure in watching the old reprobate Helm "take up his bed and walk" out of the Indian village.[27]

Other Mission villages still remained threatened, especially Saboba, which had recently been ordered to move. Jackson corresponded regularly with schoolteacher Mary Sheriff and asked Ephraim W. Morse to search the land office records in San Diego for a clause in the original Mexican grant protecting these Indians in their possession of cultivated lands. Having done everything possible from Los Angeles, in mid-March Jackson and Kinney journeyed to Saboba to confer with Sheriff about the pending removal. From Saboba they headed for San Jacinto and to San Bernardino to meet with Agent Lawson on March 17,[28] before returning to Los Angeles.

On March 24 Juan Diego, a Cahuilla Indian, was murdered by Sam Temple, who turned himself in, claiming self-defense. The justice of the peace and the six-man coroner's jury ruled the shooting justifiable homicide. It was "easy to see that killing of Indians is not a very dangerous thing to do in San

Diego County,"[29] Jackson later noted in an article for the *Independent*. Three years earlier she had written about the death of Henry Harris, a Winnebago Indian, whose murderer was also freed because "it was only an Indian that was killed."[30] Thus Jackson was already sensitized; the murder of Juan Diego remained so firmly etched in her mind that when writing *Ramona* she used the incident to create the fate of Alessandro, Ramona's husband.

In early April Jackson, Kinney, Henry Sandham, and their driver set out for a month-long carriage tour of Indian villages. Sometimes the terrain dictated leaving the carriage behind and proceeding by horseback. Conditions were often less than comfortable for the fifty-three-year-old commissioner, who one night was forced to sleep outdoors in her fur cloak. They arrived at San Bernardino on April 4 and traveled to San Jacinto and Saboba to meet with Captain Rogas, Saboba headman, and others.

On April 10 Jackson's party arrived at the Cahuilla village on the slopes of the San Jacinto Mountains. They spent the morning conferring with Mrs. Mary J. Ticknor, teacher of the forty to fifty village children. Ticknor, a widow with a ten-year-old daughter, lived in a room adjoining the schoolhouse. Jackson was impressed with the woman's fortitude, which enabled her to live on the desolate reservation. The nearest white person was ten miles away.[31]

Jackson approved of the women teachers; already Mary Sheriff had become a confidante. She liked Flora Golsh, who taught at the village of Agua Caliente on Warner's Ranch, but disapproved of her brother, Arthur Golsh, who taught at the Temecula Day School at Pachanga. She questioned his morals when she learned he had gotten an Indian girl pregnant. Later, when writing her report, Jackson recommended that only female teachers be employed in government Indian schools.

From Cahuilla the commissioners headed south to the Warner Ranch Indians, who lived in five separate villages, the largest being Agua Caliente. This land had been granted in 1844 by Governor Manuel Micheltorena to Jonathan Trumbull Warner (Juan José Warner), a naturalized Mexican citizen. However, former governor John Gately Downey of Los Angeles had recently purchased it. Although Downey had been tolerant of the Indians, employing them at sheep-shearing time, the Indians rightly feared they would be ejected from their lands.[32]

Leaving Warner's Ranch, Jackson and her companions headed for nearby San Ysidro, where they learned that Cloos had recently sold his homestead to a poor old widow who was unaware that her claim was questionable. They also visited the home of Chatham Helm; his wife, whom Jackson described as coarse and shrewish, answered their knock and bragged about helping the Indians through the winter. Jackson was appalled at this woman's "boasts of kindness . . . to the poor creatures they themselves had robbed of the means of livelihood."[33]

Five miles from the head of San Ysidro Canyon, the commissioners found a small valley accessible only by a steep and narrow trail—home of the Los Coyotes Indians. Only eighty-two in number, they were an active, robust, and finely made people, who had substantial homes, raised cattle and horses, and planted beans, corn, wheat, barley, and pumpkins.

The Indians' peaceful existence, however, was disturbed by the presence of William B. Fain, an acquaintance of Helm, who only recently had offered to buy their land. When the Indians refused, Fain informed them he had already filed and was prepared to remain. Jackson later learned at the land office that his papers, filled out incorrectly, had been returned. When the commissioners arrived, Kinney found Fain cutting down Indian timber and building a corral. Informed of the Interior Department's action against Cloos, Fain agreed to take seventy-five dollars for his improvements, but later recanted, vowing to stay. In the report, Jackson noted that "nothing . . . but authorized and authoritative action on the part of the agent . . . will stop his [Fain's] proceedings on the ground."[34]

The well-wooded and well-watered Santa Ysabel Ranch, adjoining Warner's Ranch, was the next stop. This ranch, owned by a Captain Wilcox, contained several small villages; the largest was Santa Ysabel with a population of 171. The village had no school, and residents did not even own a wagon with which to carry surplus wheat to market.[35]

Above the Santa Ysabel village, the commissioners found the village of Mesa Grande, which in 1875 had been set off as a reservation. Jackson discovered that the village was outside the survey lines; and although the best agricultural land had already been preempted by white settlers, the Indians still managed to eke out a meager existance, raising grain and maintaining a few fruit trees. Her travel notes recounted incidents when settlers, armed with certificates of homestead from the local land office, had thrown Indian residents off their land. The situation was so complex that Jackson and Kinney were unable to make any recommendations; instead, they merely informed government officials of the conditions.[36]

To the south, Capitán Grande also had a complicated history of white intrusion. In 1853 a large band of Diegueño Indians were moved there from San Diego by Colonel J. B. Magruder, commanding officer at the military post at the San Diego Mission. When a reservation was set aside in 1875, the village site was outside the boundaries, and lands reserved for the Indians were mostly barren canyon walls. Settlers who moved onto the arable lands included Dr. D. W. Strong and Charles Hensley. Strong had initially rented land for bee raising and then filed on the land, while Hensley had actually purchased a small adobe house before filing. Several others, including Captain Amos P. Knowles, homesteaded immediately after obtaining Indian signatures on rental agreements.

To strengthen her case for Indian rights to Capitán Grande, Jackson sent Commissioner Price a copy of Magruder's orders and affidavits by the village captain and Father Ubach, attesting to longtime Indian occupancy. Unknown to Jackson, in July 1881 Agent Lawson had also written to Price requesting that these same lands be set aside as an executive order reservation.[37] (Not until the fall of 1886 were orders issued by the secretary of the interior for the removal of Charles Hensley, James Mead, and Amos P. Knowles from Capitán Grande Reservation.)[38]

After a short return to San Diego, on April 22, the Jackson/Kinney party traveled thirty miles to visit the Sequan Indians. Wretchedly poor, these Indians numbered less than fifty. Their cultivated lands had diminished with the encroachment of settlers, and they could no longer even pasture any cattle. Jackson suggested they be moved to Capitán Grande, once it had been cleared of illegal settlers.[39]

In early May the commissioners made a quick tour of Pala, Rincon, and Temecula. Although the eighty hard-working Diegueños who lived in the Conejo village adjacent to the Capitán Grande Reservation were not visited, Jackson conferred with their captain in San Diego and learned much from a Mrs. Mariette Gregory, who was well respected by the Indians.[40] For information on the 560 Desert Indians, mostly Cahuilla, who lived in the Cabezon Valley, Jackson and Kinney turned to Captain John Quincy Adams Stanley, whom they had met in Los Angeles. Sending out runners with an invitation to attend a council, Stanley explained to the audience of over one hundred, representing eight local villages, that ill health had prevented Jackson from visiting them personally. A former special agent in southern California, Stanley was cordially received by the Indians, who expressed their displeasure with Lawson because he had never visited them.

In late May Stanley sent his report and a letter to Jackson. He had made no promises but hoped something could be accomplished.[41] He also wrote Secretary Teller and Lawson, who complained about government-sponsored commissions that made "promises" they were "without authority & without the power to fulfill."[42] Stanley mailed Lawson's letter to Jackson, who was displeased that the agent was annoyed at her failure to meet the Indians personally.[43]

Irritated with Lawson's attitude, Jackson again became embroiled in a controversy. However, unlike Schurz, who, by allowing the Ponca removal to proceed, deserved criticism, Lawson had repeatedly alerted officials to the worsening condition of the Indians. Sounding much like Jackson, Lawson, in a December 1878 letter to Commissioner Ezra Hayt, described the wrongs inflicted upon the Indians as representing "the blackest page in our Indian history."[44] Regrettably, most of his requests were in vain, although he did succeed in getting a few executive order reservations established.

A spirited correspondence between Jackson and Lawson had begun in the spring of 1883. Unfortunately, most of Jackson's letters are incomplete drafts. In his March 2 letter, Lawson had acknowledged receipt of her February 26 letter and expressed surprise at her appointment; no one in the Indian Office had informed him. He agreed to the use of his interpreter and suggested a conference either in Los Angeles or at his San Bernardino agency. Informing Jackson that he had just been ordered to remove the Saboba villagers, he noted that "in the name of justice and humanity they ought not to be removed from their present homes."[45]

On June 1 Lawson complained to Commissioner Price that although Jackson had come "ostensibly" to inquire into the Indians' condition, "she assumed the prerogative of the Agent." Driven by "mere sentiment" and having no knowledge of Indian character, she had stirred up discontent and bad feelings. Furthermore, she had ordered him to request the resignation of Arthur Golsh or she would report the teacher to the Indian Department. Jackson had done more harm than good; he hoped in the future to be delivered from female commissioners.[46]

Unafraid of confronting Jackson personally, after writing a vigorous defense of Golsh, Lawson informed her that "a better knowledge of the Indian character before starting on your mission would have been of incalculable value."[47] Two weeks later he complained to her about the credibility of the witnesses against Golsh and debated whether or not she had authority to become involved in the conduct of his agency.[48]

Lawson modified his criticism of Jackson upon learning that his interpreter, Jesús López, who had accompanied Jackson, had assured the Indians without her knowledge that he was speaking for her. It seems that López, who had a grudge against Lawson for prosecuting some of his "countrymen" for selling liquor to the Indians, was more than likely responsible for the discontent.[49] Although recanting on that one issue, Lawson refused to back down on Golsh's removal despite Jackson's evidence that five years earlier he had driven four families off their lands in Pala then patented it himself. New evidence revealed that Golsh had fathered a child at Pala and seduced an Indian girl at Pauma. Out of respect for his sister, Flora, who taught at Agua Caliente, Jackson and Kinney had not alerted the Indian Office but had written to Lawson instead.[50]

Five years as an agent had made Lawson skeptical about unsubstantiated rumors; therefore, he requested that Jackson reveal her sources.[51] She replied that the information about Pauma came from the ranchería captain and at Pala from the Indian woman bringing up the child. Without waiting for Lawson's answer, Jackson and Kinney forwarded to Commissioner Price an affidavit relative to Golsh and the Indian families he had driven off their lands.[52]

Lawson dismissed the teacher, reminding Jackson that Golsh's Pala land dealings had occurred before he had become agent. Learning from Golsh that he had been unable to drive away the Indian girls when they came to his classroom after hours, Lawson became more sympathetic. Furthermore, Golsh accused Jackson of listening only to his enemies and threatened to sue both commissioners. Apparently no suit was filed; Jackson never referred to the matter again.

Returning from a month-long tour of eighteen villages in May, Jackson not only continued her correspondence with Lawson but engaged in a furious exchange of letters on behalf of the California Indians. During her Ponca reform period, because she had no official status, she had been forced to rely for support upon influential acquaintances like Whitelaw Reid, William Hayes Ward, and Charles Dudley Warner. During her California period, however, instead of writing to editorial and publishing friends, she turned to government officials, all initially strangers except Henry Teller. The requests she made of these officials were no less demanding than those made of her editorial friends earlier.

Jackson was essentially a one-woman show during her Ponca phase but was part of a partnership during the latter half of her California period. While she wrote the official government report and letters to officials and friends, Kinney headed for Washington, D.C., to speak to government officials about various matters they preferred not to send through the mail.

Instead of publishing her findings in letters to the editor, during her California period she mainly published articles in the *Independent* and *Century Magazine*. During her Ponca phase she had written *A Century of Dishonor*, a nonfiction study based largely on public documents. She ended her California phase with her novel *Ramona*, based on true incidents. Finally, instead of sitting in the Astor Library, researching past events, Jackson returned to a technique that she used in writing travel articles, some of which were later published in *Bits of Travel* and *Bits of Travel at Home*.

Jackson was no longer aimlessly wandering and reporting on interesting or strange and exotic sights; now she had a focus, a passionate crusade, which had begun with her introduction to Standing Bear and Susette La Flesche. An emotional connection had been formed and would be reinforced and strengthened after her first visit to Saboba and other Mission villages. She had met face to face with the human side of the Indian issue and had come to realize that they, too, wanted and deserved recognition of their rights. Armed with an official commission, much like an investigative reporter on assignment, she engaged in field research and participated in arduous, long trips in uncomfortable wagons or on horseback to otherwise inaccessible locations, gaining evidence to present to government officials. She was now part of the drama, an eyewitness to the threat against the Indians' land, and took matters into her own hands. She urged the cancellation of settlers' homestead claims, requested executive order reservations, enclosed affidavits, complained about imperfect Indian land surveys, and hired the Los Angeles law firm of Brunson & Wells to defend the Indians,[53] guaranteeing legal fees for services rendered in case the government did not authorize the firm.

Home in Colorado by June 1883, Jackson began work on the final draft of her 56-page report. Primarily dealing with the Mission Indians in the three southernmost counties of California, her report recommended resurveying and patenting reservations to Indian residents with a 25-year trust period (allotment in severalty at government discretion); removing white trespassers; purchasing the Pauma Ranch located between Rincon and Pala, owned by the Catholic Church,[54] and the Santa Ysabel Ranch; and ordering two inspections annually for all villages and settlements. A law firm was to be hired; a more judicious distribution of farm equipment implemented; a fund established for food and clothing for the aged and sick; and more schools, especially at Rincon and Santa Ysabel, constructed.

Although she submitted her report the first week in July, Jackson did not receive reimbursement until November 4, 1883. Two months later, on January 10, 1884, the draft of a bill and a printed copy of the Jackson/Kinney report were submitted by Commissioner Price to Secretary Teller, who sent them to President Arthur. On January 14 the bill went to Congress;[55] on July 3, 1884, it passed the Senate but failed in the House. The bill was resubmitted in November 1885 by Indian commissioner John D. C. Atkins but again failed. With strong support from the Women's National Indian Association and the Indian Rights Association, the Indian Office presented the bill yearly until

January 12, 1891, when the "Act for the Relief of the Mission Indians in the State of California" finally passed, six years after Jackson's death.[56]

By November 1883 Jackson could reflect on a job well done. She and Kinney had helped save several tracts of land, the report and her *Independent* articles were completed, and the aggrieved Agent Lawson had resigned. His replacement, J. G. McCallum, had taken office on October 1, 1883; two months later he made a three-hundred-mile tour of various Indian villages and undertook the building of schools at Rincon and Santa Ysabel as recommended by the Jackson/Kinney report.[57]

Now with time on her hands, Jackson again could think about writing a novel. In October the plot had flashed through her mind in less than five minutes; frightened by its power, she had rushed into her husband's room to recount it. But not until the following month did she write to her California friends, Ephraim W. Morse, Antonio and Mariana Coronel, and Mary Sheriff, requesting more information. Her annual bout of bronchitis forced her in late November to move to New York, where she settled in at the Berkeley Hotel. Shortly thereafter, she informed Thomas Bailey Aldrich, editor of the *Atlantic*, that she was going to write a long story, which would take three to four months. It was all planned in her mind—so well thought out that it was practically half done.[58]

The first word of *Ramona* was written on December 1, 1883, and Jackson found it impossible to write fast enough, scribbling two to three thousand words a morning. Twice she was stricken by a persistent cold and once by a case of "nervous prostration."[59] Charles Dudley Warner, a frequent visitor, observed that she seemed completely possessed and that "chapter after chapter flowed from her pen as easily as one would write a letter to a friend."[60] On the night of March 9, 1884, only a few pages remained to be written. And although she never wrote anything more than a letter in the evening, she continued until eleven.[61] Upon finishing the last sentence, she put her head down on her desk and cried. "My life-blood went into it—all I had thought, felt, and suffered for five years on the Indian Question," she noted in a letter to Thomas Niles at Roberts Brothers.[62]

Beginning in May 1884,[63] *Ramona* was serialized in the *Christian Union*. It was published in book form by Roberts Brothers in Boston in November. The story was fiction based on actual events that Jackson moved around to suit her purpose. Kinney noted that they had met with many of the characters "whose pictures were afterwards drawn with fidelity" in the novel.[64] Jackson herself wrote Aldrich: "A Cahuilla Indian was shot two years ago exactly as Alessandro is—and his wife's name was Ramona and I never knew this last fact until Ramona was half written."[65]

Ramona Lubo, the widow of Juan Diego, was assumed by many to be the Ramona of Jackson's novel. She is shown here at the Cahuilla Reservation, ca. 1895. (Seaver Center for Western History Research, Los Angeles County Museum of Natural History)

As reviews appeared, Jackson realized that for some readers she had failed to create a sympathetic feeling for the Indians. Perhaps her novel had been too interesting. Distressed that Aldrich missed her reform message, she only wished that he had felt the "Indian side of the story" more deeply. "I care more for making one soul burn with indignation and protest against our wrongs to the Indians," she exclaimed, "than I do even for having you praise the quality of my work."[66]

Not all reviewers missed her message. H. E. Scudder in *Atlantic Monthly* noted that the reader, although indignant about the mistreatment of the Indian, never lost interest, and "the wrongs sink deeper into the mind than if they had been the subject of the most eloquent diatribe."[67] Albion W. Tourgée in the *North American Review* noted that "a strain of angry, tender, hopeless protest against wrong pervades" the book; Jackson presented "the cry of the poor and the weak borne down by the rich and the strong—the cry of the half-converted Indian ground beneath the feet of civilized saints!"[68]

Ramona's impact has been stronger in the literary world as a romantic love story than in the Indian reform arena as a condemnation of avaricious white settlers. A contemporary reviewer in the *Critic* called it "one of the most tender and touching [love stories] we have read for a considerable period";[69] another called it "a prose Evangeline, . . . a sweet and mournful poetic story";[70] and yet a third described it as a successful love story, "a little overweighted with misery," but totally inadequate in presenting the Indian problem.[71]

Jackson's disappointment over the reception of her book was reflected in a letter to Amelia Stone Quinton, longtime president of the Women's National Indian Association. "I do not dare to think I have written a second Uncle Tom's Cabin — but I do think I have written a story which will be a good stroke for the Indian cause."[72] Ironically, a year later a reviewer in the March 1885 issue of the *Overland Monthly* called *Ramona* the best California novel yet written, with more poet than reformer emerging. However, it possessed "no burning appeal, no crushing arraignment, no such book as 'Uncle Tom's Cabin.'" It was "an idyl—sorrowful, yet never harsh."[73]

Ramona's failure to become the *Uncle Tom's Cabin* of Indian reform in no way detracted from its success, particularly as a strong boost to tourism in southern California. In the ten months before Jackson's death, *Ramona* sold fifteen thousand copies, seven thousand of those during the first three months.[74] Since then it has gone through hundreds of reprintings and inspired numerous screen and stage versions, including the Ramona Pageant in Hemet, California, which has been performed for almost three-quarters of a century, as well as a score of books written by authors claiming to have discovered the "real" Ramona, the "real" Alessandro, or the "real" rancho where the story took place. Many of these claims, however, are apocryphal.[75]

Having done everything she could to promote her book, Jackson returned home to Colorado Springs; three weeks later, on June 28, 1884, she fell down the stairs and broke her left leg. Her confinement did not prevent her from writing letters on behalf of the Indians, however. When her leg failed to heal, to escape Colorado's winter, she moved in November to Los Angeles.[76] Once settled, she renewed her letter writing. But as her health worsened, believing she had contracted malaria, she fled to San Francisco in mid-March.[77] Less than two weeks later she wrote her husband that she was dying and only hoped that *Ramona* and *A Century of Dishonor* had helped the Indian cause. "They *will* tell in the long run," she wrote. "The thought of this is my only consolation as I look back over the last ten years."[78]

Unable to eat, Jackson shed forty pounds; yet her concern for the Indians continued to consume her diminishing energy.[79] She wrote a friend that she was honestly and cheerfully ready to die. "My 'Century of Dishonor' and 'Ramona' are the only things I have done of which I am glad. . . . They will live, and . . . bear fruit."[80] She regretted that she had not accomplished more. Four days before her death, she asked President Grover Cleveland to read *A Century of Dishonor* in the belief that he was "destined to strike the first steady blow towards lifting this burden of infamy from our country, and righting the wrongs of the Indian race."[81]

At four in the afternoon on August 12, 1885, with her husband by her side, Helen Hunt Jackson died, apparently of cancer. She was buried on her beloved Cheyenne Mountain near Colorado Springs. While her death inspired numerous poems and eulogies from the literary community, it spurred members of the Women's National Indian Association and Indian Rights Association and Lake Mohonk Conference participants "to continue and complete the work inspired by her pen, and labored for to the end of her life."[82]

1. "Report of the Condition and Needs of the Mission Indians of California, Made by Special Agents Helen Hunt Jackson and Abbot Kinney, to the Commissioner of Indian Affairs" (hereinafter referred to as "Report"), pp. 2, 5, respectively, for the quotations. "Report" has been reprinted in *A Century of Dishonor*, pp. 458–514 (quotation on p. 462); see also Mathes, *Helen Hunt Jackson and Her Indian Reform Legacy*, p. 190, notes 82–83.

2. HHJ wrote about Coronel in "Echoes in the City of the Angels," published in the Dec. 1883 *Century Magazine*, the last of four articles. "Father Junipero and His Work" appeared in the May/June issue, "The Present Condition of the Mission Indians in Southern California" in Aug., and "Outdoor Industries in Southern California" in Oct.; all reprinted in Helen Jackson (H.H.), *Glimpses of Three Coasts*, pp. 3–128. For more on Coronel, see Woolsey, *Migrants West: Toward the Southern California Frontier*, pp. 138–59.

3. See Smith, *This Land Was Ours: The Del Valles and Camulos*, pp. 177–98, for an interesting chapter on HHJ.

4. See HHJ to Aldrich, Feb. 21, 1882, MH, Aldrich Papers; *Santa Barbara Daily Press*, Feb. 14, 1882; and Marriott, "Helen Hunt Jackson in Santa Barbara," pp. 85–92.

5. See Carrico, "San Diego Indians and the Federal Government: Years of Neglect, 1850–1865"; and Banning, "Helen Hunt Jackson in San Diego."

6. For Pala, see Carter, *Some By-ways of California*, pp. 1–23; and Carillo, *The Story of Mission San Antonio de Pala*, pp. 6–39.

For San Luis Rey, see Engelhardt, *San Luis Rey Mission*; and Weber, ed., *King of the Missions: A Documentary History of San Luis Rey de Francia*.

7. Helen Jackson (H.H.), "The Present Condition of the Mission Indians in Southern California" (hereinafter referred as "The Present Condition"), in *Glimpses of Three Coasts*, p. 89; see also "Report," pp. 460–61; and Father A. D. Ubach to A. F. Coronel, Jan. 8, 1883, CoCC, HHJ I, box 2, fd. 7.

8. "The Present Condition," pp. 82–86; for Pachanga, see "Report," pp. 504–6.

9. "Report," p. 505; see also H.H., "The Temecula Exiles," *Independent* (Nov. 29, 1883): 3–4.

10. Price to Teller, June 23, 1882, CoCC, HHJ I, box 2, fd. 7; and "Report," p. 479; see also pp. 480–81. For more on Saboba, see Garner, *The Broken Ring: The Destruction of the California Indians*, pp. 75–96.

For the first HHJ/Sheriff meeting, see Odell, *Helen Hunt Jackson*, pp. 188–91; for the Estudillo grant, see pp. 192–93. See also HHJ to Henry Teller, June 11, 1882, below.

11. The 1875 executive order by mistake included Rincon, Potrero, La Jolla, and Ya Piche as one reservation called Potrero: see Shipek, *Pushed into the Rocks: Southern California Indian Land Tenure*, 1769–1986, p. 100. The 1891 Mission Indian Commission established Rincon as a separate reservation, but deliberately combined the three mountain villages into one reservation called La Jolla.

12. H.H., "A Night at Pala," pp. 2–3; see also "The Present Condition," pp. 97–98; and "Report," pp. 502–3. HHJ visited Pala on Apr. 24, 1882; see Diary, CoCC, HHJ I, box 5, fd. 3.

13. "The Present Condition," pp. 98–100.

14. For Pauma and Rincon, see "The Present Condition," p. 100; and "Report," pp. 502–3.

15. A founder of the Pasadena Public Library and Sierra Madre College, Kinney also served as chairman of the California State Board of Forestry and as presiding officer of the Yosemite Commission. He founded Venice, California. See Odell, *Helen Hunt Jackson*, pp. 193–95; Alexander, *Abbot Kinney's Venice-of-America*; and Starr, *Inventing the Dream: California through the Progressive Era*, pp. 78–81.

16. HHJ mentions writing to Teller in HHJ to Mary Elizabeth Sheriff (later Fowler), May 4, 1882, below. Her letter to Teller has not been located.

17. HHJ to Aldrich, May 13, 1882, MH, Aldrich Papers.

18. H.H., "A Chance Afternoon in California," pp. 1–2. "Jolou" should be spelled "Jolon," possibly a typesetting error due to HHJ's poor penmanship.

19. HHJ to Teller, June 11, 1882, below.

20. Teller to Hiram Price, Commissioner of Indian Affairs, June 30, 1882, Letters Received, LR #11819 [11429-1170l]—1882, Special Case 31, Office of Indian Affairs, Record Group 75, National Archives, Washington, D.C. (hereinafter cited as LR, SC 31, OIA, RG 75, NA). See also Price to Teller, June 23, 1882, CoCC, HHJ I, box 2, fd. 7.

21. HHJ to Henry Oscar Houghton, July 3, 1882, MH, Houghton Papers. See also Jackson to Warner, Oct. 19, 1882, CtHT-W, Warner Collection; and Jackson to Henry Oak, Oct. 3, 1882, CU-B, Oak Papers. Oak served as librarian for Hubert Howe Bancroft's collection of Western Americana, which eventually became the nucleus of the Bancroft Library at the University of California. See also HHJ to William Alvord, July 12, 1882, CU-B, Alvord Papers.

22. Price to HHJ, July 7, 1882, Letters Sent: Land Division, vol. 49, LB 98, 434–439, OIA, RG 75, NA; and HHJ to Price, July 19, 1882, below.

23. HHJ to Price, Oct. 31, 1882, below. See Price to HHJ, Nov. 28, 1882, CoCC, HHJ I, box 2, fd. 5; and the answer, HHJ to Price, Dec. 14, 1882, LR #23457—1882, OIA, RG 75, NA.

24. "Report," pp. 488–90. See also Henry T. Lee to HHJ, Mar. 6, 1883, CoCC, HHJ I, box 2, fd. 6; HHJ to Price, May 5, 1883, below; W. B. Fain to Commissioner William A. J. Sparks, Mar. 25, 1886, LR #9237—1886, SC 31, OIA, RG 75, NA; and Mathes, *Helen Hunt Jackson and Her Indian Reform Legacy*, pp. 55–57.

25. HHJ to Teller, Mar. 2, 1883; see also N. C. McFarland to Teller, Mar. 15, 1883, LR #5189—1883, SC 31, OIA, RG 75, NA, and Price to HHJ, Mar. 15, 1883, CoCC, HHJ I, box 2, fd. 5.

26. H.H., "Captain Pablo's Story," p. 1. See also HHJ to Teller, Apr. 2, 1883, below.

27. S. S. Lawson to HHJ, Apr. 16, 1883, CoCC, HHJ I, box 2, fd. 4. For Cloos and Helm, see Price to HHJ, Apr. 2, 1883, and Apr. 21, 1883, ibid., fd. 5; HHJ to Price, Mar. 10, 1883, below; HHJ to Teller, Apr. 2, 1883, below; and N. C. McFarland, Land Office Commissioner to Teller, Mar. 15, 1883, LR #5189—1883, SC 31, OIA, RG 75, NA.

28. HHJ Diary, CoCC, HHJ I, box 5, fd. 3. HHJ had met Lawson on Mar. 15 and would meet with him on Mar. 18 and Apr. 4.

29. H.H., "Justifiable Homicide in Southern California," pp. 1–2. See Brigandi and Robinson, "The Killing of Juan Diego: From Murder to Mythology."

30. HHJ to the editor of the *Tribune*, Jan. 18, 1880, above.

31. For the Cahuillas, see "Report," pp. 481–85; "Present Condition," pp. 91–93; and H.H., "A Day with the Cahuillas," *Independent* (Oct. 11, 1883): 1–3.

32. "Report," pp. 485–88; see also Hill, *The History of Warner's Ranch and Its Environs*, pp. 158–65. The California Supreme Court heard the case of the Warner's Ranch Indians in Apr. 1899 and in Oct. decided against them, a decision upheld in May 1901 by the U.S. Supreme Court. In May 1903 the first group of Indians moved to Pala, which had been selected by a special commission as their new home.

33. H.H., "Captain Pablo's Story," p. 2.

34. For Los Coyotes, see "Report," pp. 490–92 (quotation on p. 491). Although HHJ mentions Jim Fane [Fain] as Helm's friend, according to Phil Brigandi, Ramona Pageant historian, it was actually William Berry Fain (1858–1929), Jim's nephew, who took over the Indian land. He was finally evicted after the Los Coyotes Indian Reservation was established in 1889. The uncle, James C. Fain, lived between Aguanga and Temecula at what is now Radec.

35. "Report," pp. 492–94.

36. Ibid., pp. 494–96.

37. Ibid., pp. 496–500. The affidavits of Apr. 24, 1883, by Anthony D. Ubach, Apr. 25 by Ignacio Curo, and Apr. 26 by J. S. Manasse that appear in "Report" are in CoCC, HHJ I, box 3, fd. 3. The complete set is also included in HHJ to Price, May 5, 1883, below.

For Price's answer, see Price to HHJ, May 16, 1883, CoCC, HHJ I, box 2, fd. 5. See also D. M. Strong to Ubach, Sept. 9, 1886; Ubach to Atkins, Oct. 8, 1886, LR #27553 [14110]—1886; and Lawson to Price, July 12, 1881, LR #12362—1881, all in SC 31, OIA, RG 75, NA.

38. Interior Secretary Lucius Q. C. Lamar to Commissioner John D. C. Atkins, Nov. 3, 1886, LR #14110—1886, SC 31, OIA, RG 75, NA.

39. "Report," p. 500.

40. Ibid., pp. 501–2.

41. Stanley to HHJ, May 28, 1882, CoCC, HHJ I, box 2, fd. 6, reprinted in "Report," pp. 507–8.

42. Lawson to Stanley (copy in HHJ's handwriting), May 23, 1883, CoCC, HHJ I, box 2, fd. 7. See also Stanley to Teller, June 23, 1883, LR #11939—1883, OIA, RG 75, NA.

43. Undated draft [early June 1883] from HHJ to Stanley, below; see also draft of HHJ to Lawson [May 31, 1883], below.

44. Lawson to Hayt, Dec. 27, 1878, LR #15-1879, SC 31, OIA, RG 75, NA; see also Lawson to Hayt, Dec. 17, 1878, LR #863—1878, ibid. For an example of a reply, see Acting Commissioner to Lawson, Mar. 8, 1881, Letters Sent–Land Division, vol. 39, LB 78, 105–6, OIA, RG 75, NA.

45. Lawson to HHJ, Mar. 2, 1883, CoCC, HHJ I, box 2, fd. 4.

46. Lawson to Price, June 1, 1883, LR #10808-1883 (included in #10049-1883), SC 31, OIA, RG 75, NA. See also Lawson to HHJ, June 7, 1883, CoCC, HHJ I, box 2, fd. 4.

47. Lawson to HHJ, May 21; see also May 13, 1883, CoCC, HHJ I, box 2, fd. 4.

48. Lawson to HHJ, June 6, 1883 (copy in HHJ's handwriting), CoCC, HHJ I, box 2, fd. 4.

49. Lawson to Price, June 22, 1883, LR #11732—1883, SC 31, OIA, RG 75, NA.

50. Draft of HHJ to Lawson, May 8 [1883], below.

51. Lawson to HHJ, May 9, 1883, CoCC, HHJ I, box 2, fd. 4.

52. HHJ to Lawson, May 12, 1883, below. See also HHJ to Price, May 5, 1883, and HHJ to Price, May 5, 1883 [Personal], both below.
Golsh rented land in Pala from Louis Ardillo, claimed it and the land of three others, and ordered them to leave. He filed on the land, which included four homes, enclosed fields, and an irrigation ditch, evicting twenty-nine people. Reluctantly, in Dec. 1882 Lawson informed the Indians that the sheriff would remove them if they did not leave voluntarily.

53. Draft of HHJ to Teller [early May 1883?], and HHJ to Teller, May 16, 1883, both below. The U.S. attorney general in a June 26, 1883, letter to Teller, LR #11698-1883, SC 31, OIA, RG 75, NA, informed the secretary of the appointment of Brunson & Wells as special assistants to the U.S. attorney on behalf of the Mission Indians.

54. Bishop Mora was willing to sell to the government for $31,000; "Report," pp. 512–13; and Mora to HHJ, May 14 and 21, 1883, CoCC, HHJ I, box 2, fd. 6.

55. U.S. Congress, Senate, "Message from the President of the United States," S. Ex. Doc. 49, 48th Cong., 1st Sess., 1884, pp. 1–7; the Jackson/Kinney report followed, pp. 7–37.

56. For the commission's work, see Mathes, "The California Mission Indian Commission of 1891: The Legacy of Helen Hunt Jackson."

57. For McCallum, see Mathes, *Helen Hunt Jackson and Her Indian Reform Legacy*, pp. 76–77, 80, 86, 100, 107.

58. HHJ to Aldrich, Nov. 24, 1883, below.
While Jackson was writing *Ramona*, Brunson & Wells informed Commissioner Price that the homestead entries of Mead, Hensley, and Strong at Capitán Grande were valid and that of Knowles was fraudulent. They recommended that the improve-

ments and interests of the three legal entries be purchased and suggested that Knowles be prosecuted. See Brunson & Wells to Price, Jan. 8, 1884, LR #848—1884, SC 31, OIA, RG 75, NA.

In Price to Brunson & Wells, Jan. 29, 1884, LS, Land Division, vol. 61, LB 121, 247–50, OIA, RG 75, NA, Price wrote that the entries of Mead and Hensley had been canceled on Jan. 8. Although Magruder had not legally created a reservation, he had proved the legitimacy of Indian occupancy, thereby removing the tract from the jurisdiction of land laws. Knowles's entry was canceled, while that of Strong had already passed to the patent stage, and no action could be taken.

59. The Contributors' Club, "How Ramona Was Written," p. 713.

60. Warner, "H.H. in Southern California," p. 321. See also "[Charles Dudley] Warner in Southern California made 'an estimate' of Ramona," *San Diego Union*, Mar. 18, 1887; "Ramona: How the Book Was Written in a Burst of Inspiration," *San Francisco Call*, Mar. 20, 1887, p. 9; James, *Through Ramona's Country*, p. 335; and Eastman, "Spinner in the Sun: The Story of Helen Hunt Jackson." Eastman also wrote a short sketch on HHJ entitled "The Author of Ramona."

61. HHJ to Aldrich, Mar. 10, 1884, below.

62. "Helen Hunt Jackson's Life and Writings," *Literary News* (April 1887): 100.

63. A month before, Byrnes brought action in the Superior Court of San Diego County against the Saboba Indians. The case came to trial in the summer of 1886, a year after Jackson's death. On July 3 the judge found in favor of Byrnes. Shirley C. Ward, Brunson & Wells's replacement, appealed, with the aid of the Indian Rights Association. On Jan. 31, 1888, the California Supreme Court decided in favor of the Indians because the original Mexican land grant had included their right of occupancy.

See Mathes, *Helen Hunt Jackson and Her Indian Reform Legacy*, pp. 80, 87–88, 93–94, 96–97 (see footnotes); see also Garner, *The Broken Ring*, pp. 75–95; Brunson & Wells to E. S. Stevens, Acting Commissioner, May 24, 1884, LR #10477—1884, SC 31, OIA, RG 75, NA. "*M. Byrnes v. A. Alas*—Copy Findings," "*M. Byrnes v. A. Alas et als.*—Copy Judgment," included with J. M. Dodge to Leland Stanford, Aug. 7, 1886, LR #6885—1886, Box 24, SC 31, OIA, RG 75, NA. The case text is in *Painter, The Condition of Affairs in Indian Territory and California*, pp. 92–102.

64. Quoted in James, *Through Ramona's Country*, p. 318.

65. HHJ to Aldrich, Dec. 1, 1884, below.

66. HHJ to Aldrich, Jan. 10, 1885, MH, Aldrich Papers. For an interesting review, see Powell, "California Classics Reread: Ramona."

67. "Recent American Fiction," p. 130.

68. Tourgée, "Study in Civilization," pp. 246, 251.

69. "Current Criticism: Something Very Rare," p. 22. Starr in *Inventing the Dream*, p. 60, describes *Ramona* as translating fact into romantic myth; see also pp. 55–63.

70. Shinn, "The Verse and Prose of 'H.H.,'" p. 323.

71. Elaine Goodale Eastman, "An Indian Love Story," *Southern Workman* (Feb. 1885).

72. HHJ to Quinton, Apr. 2, 1884, below.

73. "Book Reviews," *Overland Monthly* 2d s. 5 (Mar. 1885): 330–31.

74. HHJ to Charles Scribner, Feb. 21, 1885, NjP, Archives of Charles Scribner's Sons.

75. A selected bibliography of *Ramona* includes Mathes, *Helen Hunt Jackson and Her Indian Reform Policy,* pp. 76–94; James, *Through Ramona's Country;* Davis and Alderson, *The True Story of "Ramona";* Vroman and Barnes, *The Genesis of the Story of Ramona;* Stellman, "The Man Who Inspired 'Ramona'"; Hufford, *The Real Ramona of Helen Hunt Jackson's Famous Novel;* Allen, *Ramona's Homeland;* and Carter, "The Home of Ramona," in *Some By-ways of California,* pp. 57–76.

See also Nevins, "Helen Hunt Jackson, Sentimentalist vs. Realist"; Dobie, "Helen Hunt Jackson and Ramona"; for an interesting comparison of *Ramona* and the Jackson/Kinney report, see Byers, "The Indian Matter of Helen Hunt Jackson's *Ramona:* From Fact to Fiction."

76. HHJ to Kinney [Sept. 28, 1884], below.

77. HHJ to Aldrich, Mar. 8–21, 1885, MH, Aldrich Papers. This letter, begun in Los Angeles, was completed in San Francisco. See also HHJ to Kinney, Apr. 1, 1885, in James, *Through Ramona's Country,* p. 343; and HHJ to Edward Abbott, June 22, 1885, MeB, Abbott Memorial Collection: Edward Abbott *Literary World,* Lowell Tribute Scrapbook.

78. HHJ to WSJ, Mar. 29 [1885], below.

79. For example, she wrote Brunson & Wells about the Saboba case; although her letter has never surfaced, G. Wiley Wells's answer of Mar. 31, 1885, is reprinted in James, *Through Ramona's Country,* pp. 331–34. Wells explained that Byrnes had filed a suit to eject the Indians and the government had authorized Brunson and him to defend the Indians. Believing that legal right to the land was vested in the resident Indians, he concluded: "it is a burning shame and disgrace that there is no more interest taken in the welfare of these Indians than is shown on the part of the Government" (quotation on p. 334).

80. HHJ probably to Higginson [July 27, 1885], below.

81. HHJ to Grover Cleveland, Aug. 8, 1885, below.

82. "Third Annual Meeting of the Lake Mohonk Conference," in *Seventeenth Annual Report of the Board of Indian Commissioners for the Year, 1885,* p. 104.

TO THOMAS BAILEY ALDRICH

Los Angeles
Jan 17. 1882

Dear Mr. Aldrich —

I hear the San Juan paper is out[1] — but my Atlantic has not arrived — & if you will believe it, I can't buy one in this place. — If it will not bore you, to remember it, I wish you would ask the people down stairs, if they send my Atlantic, still to Col. Springs. I asked to have the address changed to *Roberts Bros*, the only address which is sure to reach me always. — When you have any proofs for me, send to them — — for I keep them notified always by telegraph of all moves. —

I have had an enchanting month here, and am shrinking from the change to Santa Barbara, which I make next week. I have been revelling in the society of delightful old Mexicans who recollect all the old Mission times; and "survivors" of the Mission Indians, 102, 117 years old: Two old women, Laura, and Benjaminia. — You see the Fathers were so short of names they had to make each one do double duty. —

— 117. repeated the Lords Prayer — Hail Mary, & Creed, & sang a psalm in Indian.

102 was popping corn in an iron pot over a few embers.

Today, I had them photographed, squatting in front of their straw hut. A most delightful group. Their brown skinny flesh hangs loose on their bones like soaked mummy!

I have found a Marianina, about as good as Katrina[2] — only unluckily she is a well born Mexican, with a home, and estate, & a husband 34 years older than herself — so I can't hire her to go all over California with me, & translate Spanish, as she does here. —

She is alive to her finger tips — full of fire, and curiosity, & sentiment — & adventure: — so young that she still thinks she wishes she was a man that she might go to the earth's ends: "When I die & get to see God", she said today, "I'm going to talk to him about that. It isn't fair: we can't do any of the things men do."—

Whoever will come & live a year on this coast, can make a book of romance which will live: It is a tropic of color and song. It is real pain to have to skim over it flying, as I do.—

My love to Mrs. Aldrich. — if I may.

Yours always
Helen Jackson
over

Thomas Bailey Aldrich, editor of the *Atlantic Monthly*. (By permission of the Houghton Library, Harvard University)

P.S. Do not forget that three weeks will be the necessary allowance of time, for proofs to come & go now: — fourteen days, the shortest: — some of my letters have been ten days on the road. —

ALS (Thomas Bailey Aldrich Papers, Houghton Library, Harvard University, Cambridge, Massachusetts; hereinafter cited as MH, Aldrich Papers).

In 1881 Thomas Bailey Aldrich (1836–1907) succeeded to the editorship of the *Atlantic Monthly*, serving until 1890. Although engaged in editorial work for thirty-five years, he was also a noted poet and novelist; his most well-known work was *The Story of a Bad Boy* (1870).

1. "A Mid-Summer's Fete in the Pueblo of San Juan," *Atlantic Monthly* 49 (Jan. 1882): 101–8.

2. A reference to Mariana (Mary Williamson) Coronel, wife of Antonio Franco Coronel. During her tour of Bergen, Norway, HHJ had hired Katrina as her interpreter. In "The Katrina Saga," *Atlantic Monthly* 48 (Sept. and Oct. 1881): 366–77 and 518–32, respectively, HHJ wrote of her travels with the young woman.

TO WILLIAM HAYES WARD

Los Angeles
Monday
April 10 — 1882

Dear Mr. Ward,

I received yesterday your note.— (*No* — the envelope!) —containing the cheques for $95 — for the three prose articles and poem.

— I was very sorry I did not have an opportunity to see you after my talk with Mr. Bowen[1] last fall: but I presume Mr. Twining gave you an account of all I told him. I hope I did you and Mr. Twining a good service by some things I said to the young man. —I have not seen any n[umbers] of the Independent this winter. I think perhaps my subscription has run out. I do not recollect about it. — If you could without too much trouble send me the three copies containing my prose articles — also the poem, I would be very glad of them. —

I enclose to you two little poems born of an enforced seclusion in the house this week, by a bad cold, & consequent intermission of my regular work here. — I have had a most interesting winter — a month here — one in Santa Barbara — then San Diego — Riverside, San Bernardino, & back here, where I am awaiting the arrival of the artist[2] who is to illustrate my articles. The subject of the old Missions has proved one of inexhaustible interest. I only wish I could give several years to it and make a book instead of two magazine articles. As for California of the present day, I think one should live here at least two years, to even see it! — We have grown too much accustomed to the idea of its size, to realize what is involved in that one mere fact. — It is an empire in itself.

Mr. Jackson will join me about May 1*st* & then we hope to journey into Oregon before returning home. — My Oregon papers (if we go there), will appear in the Atlantic:[3] — the California series in the Century.[4] — I hope you are well—& your sisters also.— Remember me to them — to Mr. Twining also — & believe me,

Always cordially yours —
Helen Jackson

ALS (CSmH, HHJ MSS, HM 13998).

1. Henry Chandler Bowen (1813–96) was the founder of several New York Congregational churches. In 1848 he helped establish the *Independent,* a weekly journal of Congregationalism and antislavery beliefs. Eventually the paper became nondenominational, and Bowen became sole proprietor as well as editor.

2. Canadian-born Henry Sandham (1842–1910), a resident of Boston, illustrated HHJ's *Century* articles, an edition of *Ramona,* and *Glimpses of California and the Missions.*

3. "Chance Days in Oregon," *Atlantic Monthly* 51 (Jan. 1883): 115–27; reprinted in Jackson, *Glimpses of Three Coasts*, pp. 129–49.

4. These articles in Century Magazine included "Father Junipero and His Work," May and June 1883, pp. 199–215; "The Present Condition of the Mission Indians in Southern California," Aug., pp. 511–29; "Outdoor Industries in Southern California," Oct., pp. 803–20; and "Echoes in the City of Angels," Dec., pp. 194–210; all reprinted in Glimpses of Three Coasts, pp. 30–77, 78–102, 3–29, and 103–28, respectively.

TO MARY ELIZABETH (SHERIFF) FOWLER

Los Angeles
Thursday
May 4. 1882

Dear Miss Sheriff,

I found on visiting Temecula[1] last week, that the work I had ordered there from the Indian women was none of it finished; so I would be very glad to buy that *sheet* off the bed of Jesus's mother![2] (Doesn't that sound strange?) — I think it was $5, she asked for it — and I enclose *$6* which will pay her for the sheet also — (I want it just as it is —) & I suppose leave a quarter over to pay Jesus, or some other boy for riding down to bring it to you. —

Please send it by *registered parcel* by mail, if your post office facilities admit of that: if not, send it by Express.

Address

Kimball Mansion

Los Angeles —

and send as soon as possible, for we shall be here only ten days more.

Since I saw you I have visited Pala, Pauma, The Potrero and the Rincon — and have bought many beautiful baskets: and at San Juan Capistrano some remarkable lace made by an old woman 85 years old, without glasses.

I shall have specimens of these baskets & the lace photographed for illustrations in my article in the Century: — the artist Mr. Sandham who arrived two weeks ago has also made some interesting sketches of the Indian houses & Indians themselves.

I have written a long letter to the Secretary of the Interior, Mr. Teller, whom I know personally, I have told him all about the position of these Indians here in S. Cal. and the certainty that they will be driven off every one of their homesteads in a few years, if the Govt. does not protect them. I hope something will come of the letter. —

Remember me warmly to Mrs. Jordan[3] — and believe me my dear Miss Sheriff,

always cordially yours

Helen Jackson.

I have received a very interesting letter from Mrs. Ticknor[4] —giving items of information — I heartily regret that I could not visit her village of Indians. —

ALS (CSmH, HHJ MSS, HM 14204).

Mary Elizabeth Sheriff (1841–1921) taught black freedmen in Pennsylvania before becoming the first government schoolteacher at Saboba in the San Jacinto Valley. After marrying Captain William Fowler, she was forced to resign on the pretext that only single women could be employed as government teachers. The couple settled in San Jacinto, and Mary wrote articles and spoke before various groups on the history of San Jacinto and the local Indians.

1. For an interesting history of this village, see Van Horn, "Tempting Temecula: The Making and Unmaking of a Southern California Community."

2. José Jesús Castillo lived with his mother, Rosaria, and his grandfather Victoriano at Corove, in a small canyon three miles from Saboba where Mary Elizabeth Sheriff was the government teacher.

3. Emmaline McCleary, later Mrs. J. C. Jordan (1833–1909), came to the San Jacinto Valley in 1878 and ran the local hotel where HHJ stayed during her first visit to the valley.

4. Mary Ticknor was the government schoolteacher at Cahuilla for seven years. Her death on May 7, 1888, so strongly affected the Indians that Mission agent Joseph W. Preston did not reopen the school until the following term.

TO JEANNE CAROLINE (SMITH) CARR

[ca. May 9 or 10, 1882]

Dear Mrs. Carr,

This is maddening — to have driven seven miles in this dust, & find you away was bad enough; but to have you gone to Los Angeles adds insult to injury — We got back Sunday night — after a most repaying ten days — San Luis Rey — Capistrano — & three Indian villages —

— on Monday we came out to Mr. Kinney's[1] to stay — — on Thursday I go back to town — & on that day I will call & see you on my way into town — on Sunday night we go to Santa Barbara by boat —

— I am sorry I have seen Pasadena again — poor dust draggled — sand smitten cypress — I can hardly believe my eyes — & I had been boasting to Mr. Sandham that it was a green bower from beginning to end: —

I don't know how you endure this dry heat & dust — it would drive me insane in a month: every nerve I possess is on edge yesterday & today — a shower of rain would set me all right in an hour. To think that there will be no drop of rain more sets me wild! — I look forward to our three weeks drive from Santa Barbara to Monterey with absolute terror. —

— Goodbye — I shall always feel defrauded to think of this lost afternoon I had planned to spend with you —

Yrs ever —
H.H.

ALS (Jeanne C. [Smith] Carr Collection, CA 111, Huntington Library, San Marino, California; hereinafter cited as CSmH, Carr Collection).

Vermont native Jeanne Caroline (Smith) Carr (1823/25–1903) was married to Ezra Slocum Carr (1819–94), a physician and professor who taught at the University of California at Berkeley, 1869–75. She became assistant superintendent of public instruction when her husband was elected state superintendent in 1875. In 1880 they moved to Pasadena, where Jeanne Carr developed her home, Carmelita, into a garden showplace. It is now the site of the Norton Simon museum.

1. New Jersey-born Abbot Kinney (1850–1920) was educated abroad before joining the family tobacco company as a buyer. But ill-health brought him to southern California in 1880, where he established his ranch Kinneloa, near Sierra Madre. He later founded the cities of Ocean Park and Venice.

TO HENRY TELLER

San Francisco,
Sunday June 11, 1882.

Dear Mr. Teller:

Here is a simple letter from the Indian boy, of whom I wrote you, the boy who had in eight months learned to read intelligently in the Fourth Reader, who is Captain of the Shewing Band,[1] and who had this last spring put in twenty acres of wheat, besides going to school. He is a splendid fellow, only twenty, with a fine cut, clear eyed & earnest sad face.

The teacher wrote and asked me if I thought a short plain statement from Jesus would do any good, and I told her that there was no telling what would or would not do good. It was worth while to try everything. She writes that it was hard to get him to write this; he was so afraid of seeming to beg for himself personally.[2]

A colony is going into this San Jacinto Valley this summer, and nothing but some sudden intervention can save these poor people. Jesus lives with his grand-father, Old Victoriano, a grand old chief, probably nearly 100 years old. They have a good adobe house, a vineyard, two orchards, and some stock. They have lived on this place over a hundred years. Victoriano's father planted the orchard and vineyard.

Such men as these want a title given to them individually. They dont want a land title in common with their tribe, any more than you would want a title in common with the Central City people, or Mr. Jackson with those of Colorado Springs.

I cannot tell you with what hope I look forward to your doing something sharp and decisive for the protection of all these old Mission Indians. If only there were something I could do too, to help, it would give me a greater happiness than I can express. I suppose it would be entirely out of the question, and preposterous on the face of it, for the Interior Department to send a woman along with a commission of investigation, and let the woman write the report! That is what I would like above all things, and I believe I am capable of writing judiciously and with exactness, even when I feel intensely.

Yours always cordially,
Helen Jackson.

Address always
Care Roberts Bros., Boston.

Typescript (Letters Received #11429-[11701]—1882, Special Case 31, Office of Indian Affairs, Record Group 75, National Archives, Washington, D.C.; hereinafter cited as LR #, SC 31, OIA, RG 75, NA).

1. More than likely a clerk in the Indian Office typed this letter and had difficulty reading HHJ's handwriting, for there is a question mark above "Shewing." HHJ probably meant shearing as in sheep-shearing band.

2. On May 19 HHJ wrote to Mary Sheriff, agreed that a letter written by Jesús Castillo was a good idea, and promised to forward it to Teller. See HHJ to Sheriff, May 19, 1882 (CSmH, HHJ MSS, HM 14205).

TO ANTONIO F. CORONEL

San Francisco
July 11, 1882

Dear Mr. Coronel,

Can you get for me a copy — or if the deed is very long and cumbersome — a memorandum of the salient points affecting the Indians, of that old deed of the Temecula Valley, where is recorded the marking off of the Indians lands?

Antonio and Mariana Coronel (shown here ca. 1888) were prominent southern California residents. (Courtesy Ramona Pageant Association, Hemet, Calif.)

I am going to give in my article on the Present Condition of the Mission Indians,[1] a special description of that Temecula settlement, and I would very much like to be able to quote from the legal documents in which their right to the land was defined. —

Mr. Jackson left for Colorado yesterday. We have had a delightful journey in Oregon. I shall stay here about two weeks longer to look over material in Mr. Bancrofts Library.[2] — Mr. Sandham and Mr. Kinney are still here. Mr. Sandham is making some illustrations of the placer mining regions — they will keep him here two weeks at least — and then he and Mr. Kinney will return to Los Angeles.

I shall return home by the Northern Route so I shall not see Los Angeles again this year.

With warm regards to Mrs. Coronel — and yourself.

I am always truly yours
Helen Jackson

Address
    Palace Hotel. —

ALS (Antonio F. Coronel Collection, Seaver Center for Western History Research, Los Angeles County Museum of Natural History, Los Angeles, California; hereinafter cited as Seaver Center, Coronel Collection).

Mexican-born Antonio Franco Coronel (1817–94) moved to Los Angeles with his family, where he taught school and served as territorial deputy, street commissioner, justice of the peace, and an inspector for the secularized missions under the Mexican government. Under American control, Coronel served as school superintendent, mayor of Los Angeles, and state treasurer.

1. "The Present Condition of the Mission Indians in Southern California" appeared in the Aug. 1883 *Century Magazine*.

2. Hubert Howe Bancroft's collection of Western Americana, housed at H. H. Bancroft & Company, his San Francisco mercantile and publishing firm, was sold in 1905 to the University of California, becoming the nucleus of the Bancroft Library.

Bancroft (1832–1918), a historian and publisher, came to California in 1852 to sell books for his brother-in-law. In 1856 he opened his own firm and began collecting books, initially on California history but soon on Mexico and the western states as well. From 1875 to 1890 Bancroft, aided by a dozen writers, completed a thirty-volume history of western North America.

TO HIRAM PRICE

San Francisco
July 19. 1882

H. Price
Commissioner of Ind. Affairs
Dear Sir,

Your letter of July 7th enclosing copies of letters of the Int. Dept. of dates June 23rd and 26th — is at hand.

Nothing would give me greater pleasure than to aid in any way in my power in securing homes for the Mission Indians in Southern California.

I have written a private letter to Secretary Teller in regard to the propositions of your letter, and if the matter can be so arranged that I can assist in carrying out the wishes of the Department I shall be very glad.

Yours respectfully
Helen Jackson

ALS (LR #13619—1882, OIA, RG 75, NA).

Initially elected to Congress in 1863, where he supported Indian reform, Hiram Price (1814–1901) returned to Congress, 1877–81, and was selected by fellow Iowan Samuel J. Kirkwood, newly appointed interior secretary, to become his commissioner of Indian affairs. Serving until 1885, Price promoted land allotment in severalty and established policies severely curtailing Indian religious customs. Near the end of his term he became critical of the Indian Office.

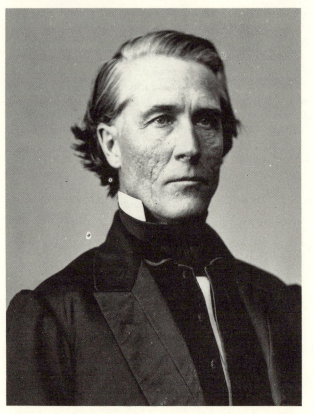

Hiram Price, commis-
sioner of Indian affairs,
1881–85. (Library of
Congress)

TO HENRY TELLER

Colo. Springs, Sept. 16, 1882.

Dear Mr. Teller:

I have heard from Mr. Kinney, and he says he will be very glad to serve with me on the proposed Commission in regard to the Mission building.[1]

I write to you at once, thinking that there might, perhaps, be some delay in arranging details of the plan, so that it would be well for me to have all papers, documents, etc., in hand, in case I shall decide to set about the work earlier than I had at first thought would be possible. I would like to have a clear understanding and definite figures as to the expenses of the trip.

Henry Teller, secretary
of the interior, 1882–85.
(Denver Public Library,
Western History
Collection)

My own notion would be, that I could not look the land over thoroughly,
visit the villages, examine the land titles, etc., in less than three—possibly
four—months. My own living there last winter cost me about $200 a month.
This included some driving; but not so much as we would have to do to visit
the remote Indian villages. I think there are some that could not be reached by
wagon. Though the roads to some are so bad that the Indian Agent Lawson[2]
has never yet visited them. But I shall see every one. I could get a good team
and driver for about twelve dollars a day; they bearing all their own expenses.
As near as I can reckon beforehand, I think that the ground could be covered
by $1200 for me; and then Kinney to keep an accurate account of his living
expenses, and have that paid in addition. Also we might have to hire an

interpreter. You understand, of course, that we don't either of us, want to make any money out of the "job." But on the other hand, neither is there any reason for one giving the Department anything more than one's time. My own time is worth to me, on an average, $200 a month, in easy literary work; but all that I am entirely willing and glad to forego, if I can be of any real service in getting permanent provisions made for these poor creatures.

I would like to have [a] letter from you, which would entitle us to full access to all land office records, titles, etc., bearing on our work.

I feel much more courage to undertake it, since Mr. Kinney's consenting to assist me, for I know him to be clear-headed, well-informed, and indefatigable in going to the bottom of everything he undertakes. He is also exceedingly keen witted; and being a land-owner and a resident in California, understands all about many matters which a stranger would be ignorant of; and therefore at the mercy of anybody and everybody who had an interest in deceiving him. Mr. Kinney is also interested in these Indians. Since seeing the two or three villages he visited with me, his feeling in regard to them has entirely changed. Before that, he was unaware how industrious and deserving many of them were; and how cruel the injustice had been of driving them off lands which they had cultivated for a hundred years. I believe, that with the facts well in hand, I could write a report which would be listened to, even in the American Congress; and might be the means of passing a bill, which you could so frame so to cover the ground once for all,[3] and leave that fragment of the Indian race safe for all time from the avarice of white men. At any rate, I should like to try.

Yours cordially,
Helen Jackson.

Mr. Kinney's name is,
    Abbot Kinney, of Kinneloa,
    San Gabriel, Cal.

Typescript (LR #18905—1882, OIA, RG 75, NA).
1. This sentence makes no sense. HHJ was not appointed to deal with any Mission buildings. Apparently the typist misread her writing, but because there is no original, it is impossible to ascertain her meaning.
2. Samuel S. Lawson, a native of Ohio, was appointed agent for the Mission Indians on July 1, 1878.
3. On Jan. 12, 1891, Congress passed the "Act for the Relief of the Mission Indians in the State of California," which essentially implemented many of the provisions of the final Jackson/Kinney "Report on the Condition and Needs of the Mission Indians of California."

TO ANTONIO F. AND MARIANA CORONEL

Col. Springs
Oct, 16. 1882

Dear Mr. & Mrs. Coronel,

I have heard often of you since we parted, — through Mr. Sandham, and later, through Mr. Kinney — and am very glad to know that you are both well. — I did not reach home until the 1st of August and since then I have been very hard at work on my papers for the Century. There are to be five in the series — Two on "The Franciscan Missions in California", one, on "The Present Condition of the Mission Indians", one on "Outdoor Industries in So. California" and the last one will be called "Echoes in the City of the Angels." — In this last one I shall give the curious old reminiscences I gathered from you — and describe the old Mexican lady with her little shrine, in the adobe hut at San Gabriel. Mr. Sandham writes me that he thinks the sketches he made while at your house, were the very best he took in California.

There is a possibility of my coming to So. California again next winter — on business in connection with the Indians — but it is not yet settled. — I want very much to come, if I can. Six inches of snow fell here last night, and the mercury went below freezing point; so I shall very soon be driven out of my home as usual. I shall probably go to New York before the middle of November. —

I am going to have the two silver balls you gave me, put at the ends of a narrow silver bar, for a breast pin — and if you will send me two more, I would like very much to get a pin made for you, Mrs. Coronel, just like my own. — I think it will make a very pretty pin: — You can send them in a little box, by mail — *Registered* letter.

I never have heard from Judge Sepulveda[1] whether the Bishop[2] gave his consent to my having those things from San Diego, & Capistrano. — Perhaps I have lost a letter from him, I have been so much on the move. —

With warm remembrances from Mr. Jackson and myself, to you both. I am
Always cordially yours
Helen Jackson

ALS (Seaver Center, Coronel Collection).

1. Ygnacio Sepúlveda (1842–1916) grew up on the family land grant in present-day Orange County. He became the U.S. chargé d'affaires in Mexico and was an assemblyman and superior court judge in Los Angeles.

2. Bishop Francis Mora (1827–1905) came to California from Spain in 1855. Ordained in Santa Barbara, he became rector at Monterey, San Juan Bautista, and in 1863 at Our Lady of Angels in Los Angeles. In 1878 he became the third Catholic

bishop of Monterey and Los Angeles, but poor health forced him to resign, and he returned home to Spain.

TO ROBERT UNDERWOOD JOHNSON

Col. Springs
Oct. 28 — 1882

Dear Mr. Johnson —

Your note of the 24th is at hand — and has made me tolerably unhappy. I can only hope that when you yourself read the articles you will find them more satisfactory than you seem to fear. Mr. Gilder[1] has often told me that he had never known any articles which read so much better in print than in Mss. as mine do. —

But there is one thing that I think you forget — or rather, do not understand — when you say that you want the "readers' hair to stand on end" — and compare my Mission Papers with James's Venice picture[2] and Daudet's sketch of Victor Hugo.[3] The Mission papers are historical: — they give in the very short space of two Mag. articles a sketch of a period of time nearly three quarters of a century — of a great religious work & its results. — They are lightened by some pictures of the present State of the ruined buildings — but they are not & from the nature of the case could not be, in the least sensational — nor in any way calculated to raise "hair on end." — To any but thoughtful & serious readers — perhaps to any not specially interested in that class of religious movements, they must of necessity seem dull. — They do not belong under the head of "descriptive writing" at all. —

The curious old reminiscences — relics memories etc. of which I spoke to you in my Los Angeles letter, all come into the last paper — "The Echoes in the City of the Angels:" The old Mexican & his young wife[4] — his personal reminiscences — the old woman & her shrine — etc. — all belong there: — I presume it is partly your recollection of these allusions, that has given you a preconceived theory of the Mission Papers. — The third paper on the Mission Indians had in it much more of what you appear to want —: is largely "descriptive". —

I do not know of anything I can add to the two first papers. It is like asking one to add to an *arch*: the whole plan & movement of the history — for that is what it is — were so carefully calculated & carried out.

— My plan may have been a faulty one — but such as it is, I believe it well executed: and I know that the articles have far more real value & substance than anything merely "descriptive" I have ever done. —

I shall continue to hope that when you see them in print you will be agreeably surprised *at their* quality.

Yours truly

Helen Jackson

ALS (Robert Underwood Johnson Papers, Butler Library, Columbia University, New York, New York; hereinafter cited as NNC, Johnson Papers).

Beginning his editorial career in 1873 at Charles Scribner's, Robert Underwood Johnson (1853–1937) became associate editor of the *Century Magazine* (then *Scribner's Monthly*) in 1881. When *Century* editor Richard Watson Gilder died in 1909, Johnson succeeded him as editor-in-chief.

1. Richard Watson Gilder (1844–1909) is known both as a writer and for his editorial work, first at *Scribner's Monthly* and later at its successor, *Century Magazine*. He was also involved in various civic and social movements, including civil-service reform, the kindergarten movement, and tenement improvement.

2. Henry James wrote at least two essays on Venice: "From Venice to Strassburg," published originally in the *Nation* 16 (Mar. 1873): 163–64; and "Venice," originally published in *Century Magazine* 30 (Nov. 1882): 3–23.

3. Alphonse Daudet (1840–97) was a French short-story writer and novelist who also contributed articles to various newspapers.

4. A reference to Antonio F. Coronel and his wife, Mariana.

TO CHARLES DUDLEY WARNER

Col. Springs

Oct 31. 1882

Dear Mr. Warner —

. . . .

It is odd that you & I like each other so much, & yet like such different things — I adored Vancouver — & Oregon — & all the old rubbishy places on the Pacific coast — I have just been down to Santa Fe & to Paso Del Norte, the Mexican boundary — & adored them. — I'm four fifths barbarian, I suppose. Nothing else can account for it. I have never loved Colorado so much as in this past two months — It has been the most beautiful autumn I ever saw, anywhere — not excepting Bethlehem. Mr. Jackson & I spent six successive Sundays in a spot of our own, on a brook rim, at bottom of a canyon — if that weather could have lasted, I could never have gone away. Yet it is clearer & clearer that I can't live at this altitude. It is hurting Mr. Jackson too. — Our doctor has told him he must get away — He doesn't see how he can: so I suppose he will stay till he must. Do you really have malaria in Hartford? — What a shame. — And are you really going to live all winter out of your own lovely house? — I wish I had a house for you to come to — Take an apartment in N. York — with one more *sunny open-fired* room than you want — & I'll go thirds with you on expenses for two months — (& half during the month William is there —) This is our budget at present — I must fly as soon as I can: — Shall go to N. York first. — He will come in December — Stay a month perhaps longer. — When he leaves for Col. I set out for So. Cal. again — where I am going as an authorized agent for the Int. Dept. to report on the Mission Indians & possible homes for them. — A Mr. Kinney who was with us during most of our Cal. journey — a wonderfully clever fellow — living in the San Gabriel Valley, is to be associated with me.— to prevent my being imposed on — & to do the parts I don't know enough to do. I am greatly rejoiced of the chance to do this work. Three times before, the Govt. has sent Agents to report on the condition of these Indians — & that is all that has come of it — But I have faith to believe that I can write a report which will reach Congressmen's hearts.

— There is not in all the Century of Dishonor, so black a chapter, as the history of these Mission Indians — peaceable farmers for a hundred years — driven off their lands like foxes & wolves — driven *out* of good adobe houses & the white men who had driven them out, settling down calm & comfortable in the houses! — What do you think of that? I'm no saner on the Indian question then I was — My book did not sell[1] — but somehow it stirred things — for you see books, pamphlets & mag. articles are steadily pouring out on the subject — and — the Northern Cheyennes have been allowed to leave Indian Territory![2]

The world moves. — I am heartily rejoiced that Mrs. Warner is so much better — Give her my love — & keep some yourself —

Yours ever —

H.J.

Mr. Jackson always sends regards to you both.

ALS (CtHT-W, Warner Collection). A lengthy paragraph not related to Indians has been omitted from this letter.

1. A reference to *A Century of Dishonor*.

2. By congressional authorization, in 1883 the Northern Cheyennes remaining in Indian Territory were allowed to move to Pine Ridge on the Sioux reservation in the Dakotas.

TO HIRAM PRICE

Col. Springs
Oct 31 — 1882

H. Price Esq.
Com. Ind. Affairs
Dear Sir,

I thank you for the expressions of confidence in your letter of the 16*th*. I hope that the results of my work will not disappoint you. I do not undertake the Mission without misgivings but I trust that my earnest interest in the matter may stand me instead of knowledge and experience; and I am sure that Mr. Kinney's clear headedness, and familiarity with the country will be an invaluable assistance.

Since the arrival of your letter I have given the subject much thought and I will now outline to you what I understand to be the scope and intent of our investigations.

1st   To ascertain how many there are of the Mission Indians — where living, and how.

2d   What, if any, Govt. lands remain in So. Cal. which would be available for reservations for them.

3*rd*   If there is no longer left Govt. land fit for the purpose, — which I strongly suspect, — what land or lands could be bought — and at what price.

4*th*   What the Indians' own feelings are about going on reservations.

So far as I can judge from what I saw and heard last winter, I believe that those Indians now living in villages there would almost rather die than be removed.

Yet, in many instances, the land where their villages stand, has been already patented to white men, and I am told, that in such cases there is no redress possible for the Indians.

Again, — I am entirely sure that to propose to those self supporting farmers, to submit themselves to the usual reservation laws and restrictions would be futile. It would be also, insulting. There is no more right or reason in an Indian Agent with the usual Indian Agent's authority, being set over them, than there would be in attempting to bring the white farmers of Anaheim or Riverside under such an authoritative control.

This complicates the question.

If this statement of what we are to do, meets your views, will you kindly have it put into shape in form of a letter of specific instructions; such as will give me full authorization under all circumstances, both with the Indians, and with all the Land Offices in the several counties.

There should be a separate letter authorizing Mr. Kinney and guaranteeing his expenses to act with me.

One item of expense has occurred to me since my letter to Mr. Teller; and that is, an Interpreter. In our visits to the Indian villages, we should need an Interpreter: and this should be provided for.

My own expenses I will rate, as I said to Mr. Teller, at $1200. This will cover my journey out and back, and I think, three months journeying and living there. If it takes longer, and costs more, I will defray the remainder myself.

I would like these letters in duplicate, to guard against accident.

My plan at present is to go out in January.

Yours respectfully
Helen Jackson

ALS (LR #19910—1882, OIA, RG 75, NA). Printed with some deletions in Lindley and Widney, *California of the South*, pp. 199–200; and in James, *Through Ramona's Country*, pp. 13–15.

TO HENRY CHANDLER BOWEN

Col. Springs
Nov. 6. 1882

Dear Mr. Bowen,

You recollect I told you that if I ever had any new propositions to make to the Independent in the matter of pieces, contributions etc. I should make them direct to you. —

I am going out to So. Cal. this winter, as official agent of the Int. Dept. to report on the condition of the Mission Indians, and the best method of providing homes for them. I shall visit every Indian village in the Southern counties — and make an exhaustive examination of their condition.

I propose to write a series of half a dozen papers giving minute accounts of all I see. I have not offered this series to any one — but thought, as I have done so little work for the Independent of late, I would offer it to you first.

Do you wish to engage the six papers, at $250 for the series — to be paid on the completion of it? — (that is, providing Mr. Ward would like it —)

— This is the price the Century pays me for a single paper — My series just completed for them, and to begin in the mid winter number, being of five papers — $1250 for the five. The Harpers were to pay me the same, if I had written the series for them. —You see therefore I should give you six papers for what they pay for one;[1] — and I suppose no one of my articles in the Mag. is longer than two of the newspaper articles would be. —The material would be worth more than that to me, in magazinable shape — but I would prefer to put it into familiar newspaper letters, to get the subject before the people, as preparatory to my Report to the Int. Dept. — Public sentiment will tell on the action of Congress in the matter. —

Please let me know by return mail if you would like to make this arrangement, as if you do not, I will make other arrangements at once. —

Yours very truly
Helen Jackson

Mrs. W*m* S. Jackson
Colorado Springs. —
P.S. I will not write a separate note to Mr. Ward, as this will answer every purpose, if you wish to consider the proposition.

ALS (CSmH, HHJ MSS, HM 13999).
    1. In 1883 the *Independent* published the following: "A Chance Afternoon in California," Apr. 5, pp. 1–2; "A Night at Pala," Apr. 19, pp. 2–3; "Justifiable Homicide in Southern California," Sept. 27, pp. 1–2; "A Day with the Cahuillas," Oct. 11, pp. 1–3; "Captain Pablo's Story," Oct. 25, pp. 1–2; and "The Temecula Exiles," Nov. 29, pp. 3–4.

TO HIRAM PRICE

Boston.
Dec. 14 — 1882

Mr. Price
Dear Sir,
    Your letter of Nov. 28*th* in regard to my going out to So. Cal. has only just reached me.
    I have written to Mr. Teller personally in reply to it: there being some points involved which I could not discuss in an official letter.

Yours with great respect —
Helen Jackson

Address
Care Roberts Bros. Boston Mass.

ALS (LR #23457—1882, OIA, RG 75, NA).

TO HIRAM PRICE

New York.
Jan. 15. 1883

H. Price Esq.
Com. Ind. Affairs.
Dear Sir,

Your letter of the 12*th* inst. enclosing my Commission to go to So. Cal. as Special Agent to report on the Mission Indians is received.

The present arrangement is satisfactory — and I shall set out next month, unless something now unforeseen detains me.

Should anything further occur to you, in the nature of suggestions or instructions, I would be most happy to receive them.

My permanent address is always Care Roberts Bros.

Boston
Mass.
Yours respectfully
Helen Jackson

Union Square Hotel
New York.

ALS (LR #1120—1883, OIA, RG 75, NA).

TO HENRY CHANDLER BOWEN

Union Square Hotel
Feb 13. 1883

Dear Mr. Bowen,

You said last year you hoped you could do something for me some day — You can do me a little favor today — I would very much like the payment on acceptance of some papers I have sent down to Mr. Ward: — I believe the whole will be $125, — & if you can let me have it today or tomorrow, it will be an accommodation as I set off for California on Friday, & have a good many affairs to settle up before going. —

I shall take very minute notes during my journeyings there & write up my papers for the Independent with the greatest care, in the summer after I return home.

You can make an announcement if you care to, that I have gone out, to make a Special Report to the Int. Dept. on the Mission Indians, & am to furnish the Ind[ependent] with a series of sketches of the Indian villages. —

My series in the Century begins in the May No.¹ —

Yours very truly
Helen Jackson.

ALS (CSmH, HHJ MSS, HM 14191).
1. The article in the May issue of the *Century* was the first installment of "Father Junipero and His Work."

TO HENRY TELLER

[March 2, 1883]

Dear Mr. Teller,

I have today had a long talk with Mr. Lee,¹ U.S. Court Commissioner here in regard to the Indian village of Agua Caliente² included in the tract filed on under Homestead Act³ by Armin Cloos,⁴ a mem[orandum] of which I sent you yesterday. —

Mr. Lee says that the first step necessary to protect these Indians rights is to have their tract surveyed. — It is not only covered by Cloos's application but the Indians say that Helm⁵ who owns the sections adjoining has twice moved his fences, taking in each time good fields of theirs.

Mr. Lee thinks the tract could be surveyed for from $200 to $250. — He knows a surveyor he would trust.

Many of the surveyors here are in league with the squatters to defraud the Indians.

Mr. Lee is a man of unassailable integrity — of high standing here — is warmly in sympathy with the Indians — and eager to give me all the assistance he can. —

Am I, or can I be empowered to order this survey? at the expense of the Department? —

Yours truly
Helen Jackson

Los Angeles
March 2 — 1883.

ALS (LR #4638—1883, SC 31, OIA, RG 75, NA).
1. Henry Thomas Lee (b. 1840) was admitted to the California bar in 1877 and established a practice in Los Angeles. He also served as a commissioner of the United States Circuit Court in the Ninth Circuit District of California.
2. What HHJ calls "Agua Caliente" in this letter is really the San Ysidro village that is now part of the Los Coyotes Indian Reservation in San Diego County.

3. The 1862 Homestead Act entitled American citizens and foreigners who had filed their first citizenship papers to select 160 acres of unclaimed but surveyed lands within the public domain.

4. Probably in the area as early as 1877, Armin Cloos had filed on land that included the village at the lower end of San Ysidro Canyon on Jan. 18, 1883. HHJ succeeded in having his entry canceled.

5. In the mid-1870s Chatham Helm (1824–1905) had taken over the land adjoining the village at the upper end of the canyon, effectively cutting off the Indians and allowing only a small amount of water into their village.

TO WILLIAM HAYES WARD

[March 3, 1883]

Dear Mr. Ward,

I was so influenced anew by the interest, & marvel of the cut "across lots" between New York & Los Angeles, that I could not resist jotting down a part of the impression; and I am quite sure you will like the letter.

I'm afraid it is too long — but I left out hosts of things I had put down in my note book. —

I find myself confronted in the outset of my investigating work, here, by heart sickening things. The little village of Saboba[1] of which I think I spoke to you, — is already *ordered* to "move"! — And even I myself, cannot see what the Int. Dept. can do under the circumstances — except move them. — The 700 acres on which this village stands — are worth $30,000 to $35,000 —

— It would not be of much use to ask Congress to pay $30,000 for a village of say *250* Indians![2]

And yet — those Indians have been farming that land — they & their fathers & grandfathers for a hundred years. — They have good adobe houses — fenced fields, irrigating ditches etc. —

They have never had a title. In the days of Mexican proprietorship, they did not need any. — The land is now "patented" to white men: — A San Bernardino shopkeeper owns this village.[3] —

My address will be *Roberts Bros. Boston* — till I return to Colorado. — I shall keep them advised of my movements. —

Yours truly
Helen Jackson

Los Angeles.
March 3*rd* 1883

ALS (NN, P-M [HHJ]).

1. HHJ had initially visited Saboba, in the San Jacinto valley at the foot of the San Jacinto Mountains, in Apr. 1882.

2. In "Report," p. 479, HHJ stated there were 157 residents in the village.

3. A reference to Irish-born Matthew R. Byrne (1833–92), who immigrated to the United States in 1841. Drawn to California by the gold rush, he eventually settled in San Bernardino, becoming a successful mercantilist, sheep raiser, and real estate investor.

TO HIRAM PRICE

Los Angeles
March 10 — 1883

Hon. H. Price
Dear Sir,

I have just discovered on file in the Land Office here, a letter from the Land Office in Washington on May 16, 1877 directing that the tract of land known as the San Ysidro Rancheria, five miles east of Warners Ranch,[1] be withdrawn from public sale or entry, until an Executive Order shall be issued setting it aside as a reservation for these Indians. —

This letter has not been in any way cancelled or revoked. —

It will be found in the volume marked with the initial C. — (May 16. 1877.)

It was preceded by a letter from Galpin[2] of the Indian Bureau, describing said Rancheria and saying that it would be set aside by Executive Order, for the Indians.

This is the rancheria which Armin Cloos's homestead entry, filed Jan. 15, 1883, takes in.

I sent to Secretary Teller last week a memorandum of this entry, which I presume has been referred to you. — I trust that there is yet time to save this village from a fate similar to that which has overtaken the village of Saboba in the San Jacinto Valley — in regard to which I understand that the order has been issued by the Department to move the Indians. — It is a terrible outrage on humanity — but I suppose the Department is powerless to interfere, — the land having been patented. —

The most hopeless thing in the situation here is the heartless indifference on the part of the whites to the fate of the Indians. The men who have patented this San Jacinto Valley know that this Indian village of Saboba has been there for nearly a hundred years: — its lands not only cultivated, but fenced and irrigated. — They do not recognize this as "occupation".

Yours truly
Helen Jackson

ALS (LR #5272—1883, SC 31, OIA, RG 75, NA).

1. This ranch, owned by former California governor John Gately Downey, was originally granted in 1844 to Jonathan Trumbull Warner (Juan José Warner). Warner (1807–95), a Connecticut native, engaged in the fur trade in California before opening a store in Los Angeles in 1836. He moved to Los Angeles in 1851, published a weekly newspaper, served in both houses of the California legislature, and was provost marshal of Los Angeles.

2. Samuel A. Galpin, chief clerk of the Indian Office, 1873–77, served under Commissioners Edward Parmelee Smith and John Quincy Smith. Early in his tenure Schurz appointed a committee to investigate John Quincy Smith's administration. As a result, both Smith and Galpin were removed from office in 1877.

TO JOSEPH BENSON GILDER

Los Angeles
March 12 — 1883

Dear Mr. Gilder,

I have the general feeling that it is not worth while to correct any misstatements in newspapers; but I really feel as if your wording of your paragraph about my errand to So. California conveyed so false an impression, that it should be followed by some sort of *re*-statement. —

You say that I have gone out, "empowered to act in behalf of certain ill treated Indians in the southern part of etc. —" —

Now all that I am commissioned to do, is to make a *Special Report* to the Interior Dept. on the general subject of the Mission Indians — their present condition, and the best way of providing them with lands in such a way that they can never be dispossessed. — This is of course in one sense, "acting for" them — ie. — in their behalf. — But I think your paragraph conveys the idea of something far more than acting *on paper* — simply by a report to the Int. Dept. —

What I hope is, that I shall be able to make so strong a report, that if the Secretary submits it to Congress, in connection with a Bill, based upon it, & asking for an appropriation for buying lands for these Indians, the Bill will pass. — In no other way can anything be effected. —

Mr. Abbot Kinney of San Gabriel, a young friend of ours, is associated with me in the Commission. Except for his assistance I should never have dared to undertake it. —

The third paper of my Century Series will be on the Present Condition of the Mission Indians.

Perhaps you will think this is all hypercritical. — If so, never mind. But as these little personal paragraphs always go journeying about from paper to paper for months, it seemed to me better for many reasons to have it set right.

The Secretary of the Interior might very well be annoyed at being suffered to have sent out a woman to do the impossible! — He himself cannot do anything to help these Indians except on an appropriation from Congress. —

A whole village — 150 or 200 — all just about to be "ejected" — from a tract they have cultivated for nearly 100 years — It is a horrible outrage — Yet I myself, cannot see what the Int. Dept. can do to help it. — The Indians had no title — never have had, in any sense which our Land Laws recognize.— The whole valley in which their village[1] lies has been *patented* to a Colony. — The 700 acres on which this little handful of Indians live, are worth $50 an acre! — What can you do? — It is heartrending: — but I see no help. — Yours ever truly

Helen Jackson

ALS (Joseph Benson Gilder Papers, Rare Books & Manuscript Division, New York Public Library, Astor, Lenox and Tilden Foundation; hereinafter cited as NN, JB Gilder Papers).

1. A reference to the village of Saboba.

TO MARY ELIZABETH (SHERIFF) FOWLER

Los Angeles
March 12 — 1883

Dear Miss Sheriff —

You will be surprised to learn that I am in So. California again; and still more to learn that I have come out to make a Special Report to the Int. Dept. on the subject of the Mission Indians. — I do not know that much can be done for them — their position is strangely helpless — the law being against them, it is disheartening to try to better their condition. — In the case for instance of these poor Saboba Indians I do not see what the Govt. can do now that the land is patented.— There is no going back on a patent. — I find that Mr. Byrne asks $30,000 for the 700 acres on which the village stands. It would be manifestly absurd for the Govt. to pay $30,000 for 150 Indians!— & I suppose there are no more than that in Saboba.

I hope however that I may be able to make such a Report, that no more patents will be granted — or entries allowed, without first ascertaining if there are Indian villages on the ground. —

One thing I would very much like to find out — perhaps you can ascertain from some of the Estudillos,[1] who I understand had the original Mexican Grant — was there in that original grant, a clause protecting these Indians in the lands they had cultivated? Such a clause was injected in many of the old Mexican Grants, where they covered tracts on which Indians were living. —

How old is the village of Saboba? — To what Mission did the Indians belong? —

— I shall visit as many of the Indian villages as possible, — Mr. Abbot Kinney a young friend of ours, from San Gabriel is assocated with me in this investigation and we propose to go to San Bernardino the last of this week, to see Mr. Lawson, and examine matters with him.

I think you wrote me, that you had changed your boarding place. Is your present house one in which Mr. Kinney & I could be accommodated? — would it be possible for us to go up to the Cahuilla[2] village as early as this? — Is there a house there where we could sleep? —

— Please answer these questions, if they are not too troublesome — and send the letter to care of Mr. Lawson in San Bernardino. —

Truly your friend
Helen Jackson

ALS (CSmH, HHJ MSS, HM 14206).

1. On Dec. 21, 1842, the Mexican government granted the 35,000-acre Rancho San Jacinto Viejo to José Antonio Estudillo. This grant was confirmed to his heirs by the U.S. District Court. The intitial survey did not include Saboba, but the 1878 survey, patented on Jan. 17, 1880, included not only the village but all the farms and nearby streams.

In Mexican California, Estudillo (1805–52) held numerous political positions, including revenue collector and treasurer at San Diego, assembly member, *alcalde* (mayor) and *juez* (judge) of San Diego, and administrator and majordomo at the mission of San Luis Rey from 1835 to 1840.

2. HHJ described Cahuilla as one of the most interesting that she and Kinney had visited. Ten miles from any white settlement, this village of one hundred fifty to two hundred residents was surrounded by cultivated fields. On the edge of the town was a continually running hot spring. See "Report," pp. 481–85. Today it is part of the Cahuilla Indian Reservation near the town of Anza in Riverside County.

TO EPHRAIM W. MORSE

Los Angeles —
March 12 — 1883

Dear Mr. Morse,

Will you kindly look, for me, in the Land Office Records of San Diego, for the patent of the San Jacinto Nuevo Colony[1] — I wish to know whether there were in the original grant, any clause protecting or recognizing the existence of the Indian village of Saboba which is within the tract patented — and from which the Indians are now notified to remove. —

The 700 acres on which this village stands, are the property of a Mr. Byrne in San Bernardino; and he calls on the Government to remove the Indians.

As they have been living there ever since the days of the San Luis Rey Mission, I think there must have been in the original grant, a clause, such as I find to have been in most of the old Mexican grants, protecting the Indians in the possession of all lands cultivated by them.

Thanks for your letter of the 9th. — I think we will not be in San Diego till next month.

With regards to Mrs. Morse —

Yours truly
Helen Jackson

ALS (James D. Phelan California Authors Collection, Book Arts and Special Collections Center, San Francisco Public Library, San Francisco, California; hereinafter cited as CSf, Phelan Collection).

Ephraim W. Morse (1823–1906) came to California in search of gold but instead opened up a general store in San Diego in 1851. A prosperous merchant and agent for Wells Fargo, Morse was also a prominent civil leader. He was secretary of the Board of Trade, city and county treasurer, city trustee, and a leading organizer of the first bank in San Diego County and the San Diego and Gila Railroad Company.

1. José Antonio Estudillo's grant was partitioned in 1882, and a group of investors organized the San Jacinto Land Association, which in 1883 laid out the present city of San Jacinto.

TO JEANNE C. (SMITH) CARR

Los Angeles.
Wed. Eve.
March 14 — 1883

Dear Mrs. Carr,

Mr. Kinney and I have decided that it is best to go to San Bernardino tomorrow — We may be back on Saturday, but I think probably not till next week. At any rate, do not look for me on Sunday: — And will you be kind enough to say to Mr. Rust,[1] that as soon as I get back, I shall drive out & see that collection about which I have been talking with him. — If I knew Mr. Rust's P.O. address, I would write to him, to explain about my delay in examining it. —

I was just now thinking what strange threads weave into our lives — Here am I depending for my chief help in this Indian business, — — in fact, I could not have undertaken it at all without his help — on the very man about whom, only twelve months ago, I said to you — "dont say anything to me about that man. I dont want to know a man who would put a great staring white house on a hill like that"![2] — Was not that silly? —

And if Mr. Kinney had not happened to come in to Mrs. Kimballs[3] to supper that night, — and had not happened to have been placed by my side — I should never have known him. — Such things make fatalists of us. —

As soon as I can after we get back I will come out & see you.

Yours ever —
Helen Jackson

ALS (CSmH, Carr Collection, CA 193).

1. In 1881 Horatio Nelson Rust (1828–1906) moved his family to Pasadena, California, where he served with Kinney on the library board and was a member of the Los Angeles branch of the Indian Rights Association. Both HHJ and Kinney recommended him to Commissioner Price as S. S. Lawson's replacement; however, Rust was not appointed until 1889. Upon completion of his four-year term, he continued his interest in Indians: for example, bringing thirty Navajos from Arizona to participate in the 1903 Rose Parade in Pasadena. His extensive collection of Indian artifacts was later sold to Yale and the University of Pennsylvania.

2. In 1880 Kinney bought 550 acres across Eaton's Canyon from Altadena and built a two-story house with a tower on the highest point.

3. The Kimball Mansion on New High Street in Los Angeles was run as a genteel boarding house, and HHJ preferred its comfort and good food to any of the local hotels.

TO MARY ELIZABETH (SHERIFF) FOWLER

San Bernardino
Monday, March 19, 1883

Dear Miss Sheriff —

I confess to having shed some tears over the children's letters. — I shall send them to Mr. Teller today.[1] I think he will put them in his pocket & go over & see the President. — I am not without hope that something can be done yet, to prevent their being moved — but I do not think it wise to hold out any such hope to them. —

If I were in your place, this is the way I should try to put it to them. —

1*st* The President is not like a King. He himself has to obey the *law*, just as much as any other man. —

The *law* is made by the Great Council, (Congress) To the Great Council go men from *every* state: — & they *all together*, make the law. — When it is made, *every*body must obey it. —

No white man can own any piece of land unless he has got the *papers* to prove he owns it. — not even the President can own any piece of land unless he has the papers to prove it.

The reason the Saboba people are in such trouble now, is because their *fathers* did not have any *papers* from the Mexican Government to prove the land was theirs. —

The Great Council have left a good deal of land *free*, to all people to go and live on, when they will select it, and then pay for their papers: — And of this *free* land, "Government Land", the President can give places to the Indians to live on: — and if the Saboba Indians have to be moved, he will give them, the very best there is left. —

I should think Jesus[2] could be made to understand this: — and Jesus himself ought to *file* under the Indian Homestead Act,[3] *at once*, for their place up in the Canyon; other wise, the first thing they know, that will be gone too. — I shall bring a copy of the Act with me, and explain it to him. —

— Don't, if you can help it, let any of them think I can "*help*" them. It breaks my heart. Do try to make them understand that all I can do, is to *tell* about them. — You might perhaps make them understand that, the story I shall write about them & about all the other Indians here will be read to the Great Council next winter. — They mustn't blame Lawson either. He has written *letter after letter* about them to the Dept. —

Please let me know when the Indians will get back from their sheep shearing — I had intended to set out as early in April, as it would be safe, to go into the mountains — —Probably about the 3*rd* or 4th. —

I do not know that there is any great advantage in my seeing the Indians to talk with them — I can say very little — I will not hold any hopes to the poor creatures —though I *have* a little myself — as I will explain to you when I see you. —

Mr. Kinney, who is associated with me, has gone today with Lawson to look at the San Gorgonio Reservation.[4] I go back to Los Angeles today. — Write to me there — *Kimball Mansion*. —Goodbye —.

With warm sympathy,   always your friend

Helen Jackson

ALS (Document Files, Research Archives, San Diego Historical Society, San Diego, California; hereinafter CSdHi).

1. HHJ had suggested that Mary Sheriff have some of her Indian students write to Interior Secretary Teller.

2. A reference to José Jesús Castillo. See HHJ to Mary Elizabeth (Sheriff) Fowler, May 4, 1882, above.

3. Congressional legislation passed on Mar. 3, 1875, granted Indians all the benefits of the 1862 Homestead Law without loss of their share of tribal funds. In addition, homesteaded lands were inalienable for five years after the granting of the final patent.

4. This was never a formal reservation. However, early in 1879 Lawson had proposed this desert tract adjacent to Southern Pacific Railroad lands near Banning to Indian commissioner Ezra Ayers Hayt as large enough to accommodate all the Mission Indians in the southern part of the state. Over one thousand Indians from Temecula, La Jolla, Saboba, Pauma, Pala, Potrero, Rincon, and San Luis Rey signed a petition protesting this sterile, unfit site; to his credit, Lawson forwarded the petition to the commissioner on March 26, 1879. See Lawson to Hayt, Jan. 8, 1879, and Mar. 26, 1879, LR #66-1879, SC 31, OIA, RG 75, NA.

TO MARY ELIZABETH (SHERIFF) FOWLER

Los Angeles —
March 20. 1883

Dear Miss Sheriff —

Please ask Mr. Estudillo[1] what "*promise*" it is, to which you refer, when you say "Mr. Estudillo's promise that the Indians should not be disturbed is recorded at Washington." — I have written to the Surveyors office in San Francisco, & the Surveyor General replies to me, that there was not, in the original Mexican grant to Estudillo any clause protecting the Indians. —

I think we will set off on our tour among the Indian villages in about two weeks — Say on the 2d or 3rd of April. —

— Will the sheep shearing band have returned by that time? — I would like to see Capt. Rogas[2] — & I want to see Jesus. — He must file on that canyon immediately if he wants to save it. - Let me know what Mrs. Ticknor writes about the weather — also if there is any sort of a place there where Mr. Kinney & I can be accommodated for a day or two. —

Yours cordially
Helen Jackson

ALS (CSmH, HHJ MSS, HM 14207).
1. This could be either José or Francisco, sons of José Antonio Estudillo. They were both in the San Jacinto Valley in 1883.
2. Juaro Rogas was the captain at Saboba.

TO MARY ELIZABETH (SHERIFF) FOWLER

Los Angeles
March 26 1883

Dear Miss Sheriff —

We shall go to San Bernardino on the 2d or 3rd of April — & reach your place the following day. — I have written to Mrs. Ticknor also — but if you have a chance to send her a message, it might be well to do so, as she may not get the letter. —

I hope the Saboba Capt. will be at home when we come — I want to have a talk with him, about the best course for them to pursue in regard to their village. — It is not impossible that they may establish a legal right to it yet! but don't say so to anyone.

Yours ever —
Helen Jackson

I hope the Websters[1] will be able to accommodate both Mr. Kinney & me — I think I told you that Mr. Kinney is associated with me in the Commission. —

P.S.—

Tues. Am.

Please send me word by return mail if possible what that "promise of Mr. Estudillo's that those Indians should not be disturbed," which you say is "recorded in Washington," really *was*: what shape — how recorded — Is there any copy of it in Estudillos possession or can he write the substance of it from memory. — There may be something in this of importance. — Do not give Estudillo to understand however that there is any project of a legal content — merely that I want to know every feature of the *equity* of the case. —

ALS (CSmH, HHJ MSS, HM 14208).

1. The Webster family owned a large ranch four miles north of San Jacinto, where they raised grain and livestock.

TO THOMAS BAILEY ALDRICH

Los Angeles.
April 1*st* 1883

Dear Mr. Aldrich,

Here is the Chester paper.[1] I hope you will like it. I think it is two years since I spoke to you of writing it. I see now that it was a kindly fate which kept me all this time from taking it up, — and saved it for the oasis of my salvation in the last six weeks.

When I have been unable to endure thinking and plotting and planning about Indians another minute, I have deliberately gone to Chester for a half day! and nothing any nearer home would have answered the purpose.

If you do not want the paper, please send it back to me here —C.O.D. — by Express. I do not like to risk it in these mails. — If you do take it, I would like the cheque sent here — I want a great deal more money just now than I can possibly have. —

Next week I set off with my Co-Commissioner Mr. Kinney on a tour among the Indian villages, which will take two or three weeks. I expect we shall return wrung dry of sympathy, by the sight of so much patient suffering. The gentleness and meekness of these people are enough to break your heart.

Fancy a village of 150 souls — living in houses they have built, on lands they & their ancestors have tilled for a hundred years — — peach orchards, apricot orchards, wheat fields irrigating ditches — fancy such a community as that, actually being obliged to "remove", — on account of never having had a title to the land —: the tract in which their village lies having been patented without their knowing it; — I believe they really will have to go — & the U. S. Govt. has little better than desert left to offer them.

My regards to Mrs. Aldrich. I shall bring her an Indian basket. —

Yours ever truly
Helen Jackson

P.S.
I was very sorry the Spring verses were too late. —

ALS (MH, Aldrich Papers).
1. "Chester Streets," *Atlantic Monthly* 53 (Jan. 1884): 12–25, was HHJ's reminiscence of her visit to Chester, England, during the summer of 1880. It was reprinted in *Glimpses of Three Coasts*, pp. 196–218.

TO HENRY TELLER

Los Angeles
April 2, 1883

Dear Mr. Teller,

Today the Captain of the San Ysidro Rancheria with two of his men arrived here in great trouble.[1] This is the rancheria I wrote you about; the one filed on, by homestead entry by one Armin Cloos last January; the one in regard to which the Indian Office sent [a] letter to Lawson, saying the Indians could contest Cloos' entry. The last move of Cloos is bringing more white men on to the ground, and offering to sell them land; filled the Indians with new terror, and there these poor fellows, one of them so lame, he walks with great pain, walked all the way here ninety miles, to see if Mr. Lee could help them. We have spent the greater part of the day talking with them by interpreter; explained to them, the process by which they could contest Cloos' entry, and we hoped to succeed then in getting the land as white men own theirs. To this Pablo replied, "If I own the land as the white men have theirs, then I must pay white men's tax; and we are too poor: the white men would tax it all away from us, and then my people would say I had deceived them. I dare not do it." I was astonished to see how clear this was in his mind. Mr. Lee then decided to take the enclosed affidavits,[2] and endeavor by means of them to stop Cloos' further proceeding. They will be forwarded to the Washington Land Office through the land office here, but I thought it wise to send you a copy privately, as I feared the matter might never be brought to your personal attention, and I have strong reason to believe that influences are brought to bear there in such matters, hostile to such rights as these. I am not without hope that this may be a case where you may have the power to interpose a "decision" yourself, which will at least block Cloos' game. The manner in which the Helms and he have deliberately robbed these peaceful industrious Indians, is the most rascally thing I have encountered yet. Nothing was ever done to Helm for shooting that Indian and nothing has ever been done to hinder their ursurpations of the Indian's fields. The Indians say he has moved his fence three times, each time taking in more of their til[l]able land. He has probably over-stepped his patent. I was disappointed at their refusal to make the effort to get the land, as white men hold it. But Col. Warner[3] says they are right, that the San Diego thieves would tax them out of it in two years. Since they have lost so much land by Helm and Cloos, they have grown wretchedly poor, pitifully so.

Yours truly,
Helen Jackson

Typescript (LR #7200—1883, SC 31, OIA, RG 75, NA).
1. A reference to Pablo, captain of the San Ysidro band of Cahuilla Indians, and José Moro and Gervazio, who walked from Warner's Ranch. HHJ, whom they had specifically requested to see, wrote of their situation in "Captain Pablo's Story," *Independent* (Oct. 25, 1883): 1–2.
2. Two statements sworn in early Apr. before Commissioner Henry T. Lee were enclosed. The first, signed by Pablo, Moro, and Gervazio, detailed Cloos's encroachment upon their land; the second, by Warner, attested to Pablo's reliability.
3. Warner acquired this title after serving as provost marshal of Los Angeles.

TO THOMAS BAILEY ALDRICH

Los Angeles
May 4 — 1883
Dear Mr. Aldrich —

. . . .

I am glad you like the Chester. I wish I had another such piece of work on hand to alternate with my Indian Report. — We have just got back from our tour through the Indian villages: (18 in all —) My opinion of human nature has gone down 100 per ct. in the last thirty days. Such heart sickening fraud, violence, cruelty as we have unearthed here — I did not believe could exist in civilized communities — and "In the Name of the Law."

If I were to write a story with that title, — all Indian —would you print it? I have never before felt that I could write an Indian story. I had not got the background, now I have, and sooner or later, I shall write the story. Has anybody used that title? — Is it not a good one? It seems to me so. — If I could write a story that would do for the Indian a thousandth part what Uncle Tom's Cabin did for the Negro, I would be thankful the rest of my life.[1] — I shall not get back to Colorado before the 1*st* of June — nor to the East, before October's last days. Then, I shall see you: and Mrs. Aldrich, whose face I never forget. It is in a gallery I have of portraits — not by Mrs. Whitman![2]

Yours truly
Helen Jackson

ALS, (MH, Aldrich Papers). The first part of this letter, which does not relate to Jackson's Indian work, has been omitted.
1. *Uncle Tom's Cabin*, written by Harriet Beecher Stowe (1811–96), was serialized in the antislavery periodical *National Era* before being published in book form. See Mathes, "Parallel Calls to Conscience: Reformers Helen Hunt Jackson and Harriet Beecher Stowe," *Californians* (July–Aug. 1983).

2. Sarah de St. Prix (née Wyman) Whitman (1842/43–1904) was a Boston artist who studied with William H. Hunt.

DRAFT TO HENRY TELLER

[early May 1883?]

Dear Mr. Teller,

I believe the Saboba village can yet be saved.

I have tonight had a long talk with a lawyer, a Mr. Wilson,[1] who is ready freely for love of the Indians, to undertake their cause in the State Courts here.

He believes that under the old California law of which I enclose a copy, these Indians right to their farms can be established. —

Mr. Wilson is the man who twelve years ago compelled the registration of two Indians here as voters — Simply to establish the fact that they are citizens 1*st* under the 14*th* amendment — next — 2*d* under the treaty of Guadalupe Hidalgo.[2] —

He has been the friend & councillor of the Indians in many difficulties — was with Whiting[3] at Pala, at the time of the insurrection there in 1871 —

He is clear-headed — determined — & full of sympathy. — I believe he would win the case. At any rate — it throws the burden of proof on Byrne — (the man who assumes to own the Saboba tract, under the patent of the San Jacinto Colony. —)

Byrne cannot drive the Indians off without bringing a suit of ejectment. — This suit Mr. Wilson says he will be glad to have the opportunity to contest. —

— If it is won, it will cut the Gordian Knot in other cases. — For instance, on one tract owned by Gov. Downey[4] of this town, there are four Indian villages. He has been for some time demanding their removal. — If the Saboba Indians can be proved to have a right to their lands, — all these other villages have the same. — Land owners will not be ready to bring suits of ejectment. —

— If you will withdraw the order sent to Lawson to move the Saboba Indians, — leaving the matter to await Byrne's bringing the ejectment suit, — one of three results will follow —

1*st* the Indians win — which will be a glorious triumph —

2d or they may lose — in which case they are no worse off than now — & time has been gained —

3*rd* Byrne rather than have a lawsuit hanging over his head, may offer to sell the little tract at a low price. —

I most earnestly trust that it will seem to you well to revoke this order & let the matter came to a legal test.

Yours truly

H.J. —

ALS (CoCC, HHJ I, box 2, fd. 8). No attempt has been made to show HHJ's draft corrections.

1. Possibly Christopher N. Wilson (b. 1830), a Ohio native, who practiced law in Washington, D.C., before moving to Los Angeles in the 1870s. Considered a friend of the Indians, he defended them in court.

2. The 1848 Treaty of Guadalupe Hidalgo ended the Mexican American War, resulted in the transfer of former Mexican lands in the Southwest to the United States, and recognized the Rio Grande as the boundary between Texas and Mexico.

3. Billington C. Whiting was appointed superintendent of the California Superintency on Oct. 12, 1866, and served until the summer of 1869. He was reinstated on June 20, 1870. He met with three hundred Indians at Pala in Sept. 1871 and effectively defused the situation. The so-called insurrection was really more rumor than substance, and, according to Whiting, local white settlers had never been in any danger.

4. A reference to Warner's Ranch. The four villages in 1883 were Agua Caliente/ Cupa (Warner's Hot Springs), Puerta La Cruz, Mataguay, and San Jose.

John Gately Downey (1826–94), the seventh governor of California, 1860–62, had immigrated to California from Ireland. He opened a drugstore in Los Angeles, engaged in ranching and real estate, established the town of Downey, and later went into banking.

TO HIRAM PRICE

Los Angeles.
May 5, 1883

Hon. H. Price
Com. of Ind. Affairs,
Dear Sir,

I forward herewith, affidavits in regard to Indians lands in Capitan Grande, and Pala.[1]

Both of these cases are as glaring instances of fraud and cruelty as the one of the San Ysidro Canyon, in which the Land Office has recently taken such prompt action. I earnestly trust that these men will be as decisively dealt with as were Cloos and Helm.

If the patents of Strong[2] and Knowles[3] can be vacated it will be no more than simple justice. Both Strong and Knowles went into the Canyon, recognizing the Indians' right of ownership, by asking their permission to put bee ranches there, and agreeing to pay rent for the privilege.

At the end of the first year when the Indians asked if they wished to rent the bee-pasture again, they replied that they intended to stay, and had filed, or would file on the land.

The Capitan Grande Reservation appears to have been surveyed with a careful eye to the interests of these squatters or any others who might follow them.

It is only explainable, — like several other reservations we have visited, — by deliberate fraud, unpardonable carelessness or colossal stupidity.

Its lines were never pointed out to the Indians, and appear to be very imperfectly understood by the squatters: but it did not take in the chief settlement or the cultivated fields of the Indians; and the greater part of it is on the steep stony mountain walls of the Canyon.

I enclose a copy of the order of Col. Magruder,[4] establishing the Indians in the Capitan Grande.

In the matter of Arthur S. Golsh,[5] I would say, that the Indians showed to us a letter written to them by Agent Lawson, saying that it was "a mean trick on Golsh's part"; but he knew no way to help them, and advised them to accept $10 each, and move off quietly, rather than be put off by the Sheriff.

This money was paid to them by a trader in the neighborhood, on a written order from Lawson: but the Indians signed no paper whatsoever.

I would suggest that in case the Land Office decision vacates these Patents, or cancels these entries, Agent Lawson be instructed and empowered to compel the squatters to move out, and to see to it that the Indians are reinstated in their old homes.

Respectfully,

Helen Jackson

Mem.

There are now left in the Capitan Grande Canyon about fifty Indians. The village is broken up. The Captain thinking they could keep a better hold on the remaining lands, by scattering. (The man Hensley[6] has his store in the adobe house in which the Capt. formerly lived). over

For this house, the Indian — being informed that he had to leave it, in any event — accepted from Hensley a hundred dollars: but no papers passed, in the transaction: and Hensley himself does not claim that the Captain sold to him, anything more than the house. —

ALS (LR #8650 [10347] [11342]—1883, SC 31, OIA, RG 75, NA).

HHJ recopied Magruder's orders (which have been omitted here) and enclosed them with this letter to Price along with the following comment: "This paper is in tatters—but is carefully preserved by the Captain of the Capitan Grande Indians. Some years ago, he gave it to a Mexican who promised to mend it for him, if he would pay him a horse, for so doing, the Capt. paid the required price, and the Mexican pasted the tattered fragments together by strips of paper. It is however illegible in several places."

1. These affidavits, later reprinted in "Report," pp. 496–500, included a "Copy of Col. Magruder's order, assigning the Capitán Grande Canyon to the Indians" (Feb. 1, 1853); a copy of an affidavit by Ignacio Curo, captain of the Capitán Grande Indians, and Marcellino; a copy of Anthony D. Ubach's affidavit testifying to Indian occupancy; a deposition of J. S. Manasse in the matter of the Capitán Grande Indians; the application of Daniel Isham, James Meade, Mary A. Taylor, and Charles Hensley; and an affidavit "In the matter of the claims of Arthur Golsh, Gaetano Golsh and others to a certain piece of land in said township a detailed description of which is filed herewith."

2. Vermont native D. W. Strong, a physician and beekeeper, had rented land from Curo for the purpose of raising bees. A year later he informed Curo that he would not renew the lease but instead intended to file on the land. Strong received his land patent on Sept. 15, 1882.

3. Captain Amos P. Knowles's homestead entry was declared fraudulent, and the Interior Department authorized his removal; however, as late as 1886 he was still living at Capitán Grande.

4. John B. Magruder (1810–71), a West Point graduate, was stationed in San Diego, 1850–53. During the Civil War he fought on the Confederate side.

5. Arthur S. Golsh was a son of Victor Emil Golsh, the supposed cousin of Emperors Franz Josef and Maximilian. Ordered out of Austria in 1866, the senior Golsh and his family ultimately moved to the Pala Valley of California, where some family members married local Indian women.

6. Charles Hensley, who homesteaded part of Capitán Grande on June 1, 1881, had originally purchased a small adobe house and a crop of barley from Curo, then filed on the land, moved into the village, and occupied Curo's home. Hensley claimed that when he purchased the house and the crop he had also purchased the land. Because of HHJ's diligent work, Hensley's homestead entry was canceled by the General Land Office on Jan. 8, 1884. However, as late as 1887 he still remained at Capitán Grande.

TO HIRAM PRICE

Personal   Los Angeles
                                                                                    May 5, 1883

Hon. H. Price
Com. of Ind. Affairs,
Dear Sir,

I send you by this mail a batch of affidavits of importance, and I take the liberty of writing a private letter to you, calling your attention to them, lest in the routine of the office, they may be long in coming under your eye. —

I have also to acknowledge the receipt of your letter of April 21*st*, in regard to Pablo's fears of taxation, and informing me of the Act. of Cong[ress] Jan. 18, 1881, making Indians taking lands under the Homestead Act, free of taxation for twenty years. —

I am exceeding glad to know of this: I am inclined to think however, that in case the Dept. is able to drive out Helm, and Cloos, and the whole — San Ysidro Canyon thus reverts to the public domain, it would be better to make it a reservation for the San Ysidro Indians, for the present, rather than to urge their taking up the land individually. They are too poor, and broken spirited. They have suffered terribly for the past few years, since Helm took their best lands, and cut off the water. Last winter a child died of starvation in the village: after that, they begged for bread at the Helms' hands. It will take some little time for them to recover tone and to believe in any possibility of any good in store for them. This is the case, in a greater or less degree, with all these Indians: but in all the eighteen villages we have visited, we have found only one band so destitute and so hopeless, as the San Ysidros. — The Agent[1] had never visited them: and their requests to him for protection in the matter of their lands, had brought no result. Had the policy of the Interior Dept. been, five years ago, what it is today, a great proportion of the present suffering, wrong, and perplexing confusion everywhere would have been saved.

I cannot express to you how grateful I feel for the prompt and energetic response which the Secretary and yourself have made in the matters already laid before you, by us. We did not feel that it would do, to defer them, till our final Report: but we had not dared to hope to see such immediate results.

If the Dept. can succeed in turning out the robbers in the Capitan Grande Canyon, # [marginal note: (# See affidavits forwarded by same mail with this)] and reclaiming that whole Canyon, as originally set off by Magruder, for the Indians; — and if those cruel Austrians, the Golshes can be routed in Pala; — and the San Ysidro Indians reinstated in their possessions, —not only will several great wrongs be righted but a most salutary impression will be made on the Californian mind.

At present, it is no exaggeration to say, that to the average new settler here, the presence of an Indian family, or an Indian community on lands he desires to own, is no more obstacle, than the presence of so many foxes or coyotes.

There is this, however, to be said, in excuse for the squatter, that the Land Office has taken the same position that he has, — ie — that Indian occupancy is not occupancy. — "Why did the Govt. put these lands in market, if it were not right for us to file on them"? has been said more than once, by resentful settlers. And the question was a logical one.

I hope that by the end of the month, we shall have our Report finished; and that we shall be able to recommend measures which will meet your approbation and assist materially in the preparation of a bill to meet the exigencies of the situation; so far, as, at this late day, it is possible, to meet them.

Yours very truly
Helen Jackson

ALS (LR #9103—1883, SC 31, OIA, RG 75, NA).
1. A reference to Mission agent S. S. Lawson.

DRAFT TO S. S. LAWSON

May 8th [1883]

Dear Sir —

In the course of our investigations at Pala & the neighborhood we heard some facts in regard to Arthur Golsh, which we think will be a very painful suprise to you. —

He is known to have had relations with an Indian girl at Pauma & is the father of a child now being brought up by its mothers brother at Pala. — We also heard that he drove off four families of Indians from their lands in Pala & patented the lands himself.

Except for our great respect for his sister[1] who is teaching at Agua Caliente, we should report these things to the Dept. — but out of consideration for her, we have decided to first make the suggestion to you, that he be requested if you think it advisable to do this — to resign. You are at liberty to send him a copy of this letter, as your reason for making the request. If he will immediately resign, we will make no farther allusion to him. We do this solely out of regard for his sister.

It is far better that the Pachanga children should be for a time without teaching than that the young girls be exposed to the dangers of this man's association with them. There are already rumors of the frequent presence in the school building of an Indian woman of notoriously bad character.

In view of the well known laxity of the morals of these Indian communities, it appears clear that young men should never be appointed as teachers, certainly in such isolated Indian villages as these. Women should be employed.

Please let us know — at once what course you will take in this matter, as we wish to send a letter to Miss Golsh informing her ourselves of the action we so much regret being obliged to take in regard to her brother. —

AL (CoCC, HHJ I, box 2, fd. 8).
1. Flora Golsh first taught at Agua Caliente (Warner's Hot Springs) and in 1890 transferred to La Jolla Indian School at the foot of Palomar Mountain.

TO HIRAM PRICE

Los Angeles
May 9. 1883

Com. Price
Dear Sir,
We earnestly recommend the setting off immediately by Executive Order as a reservation for Indians, the following tracts.

T. 4. S. R. 1. E. (S. B. M. Sects. 28. 32. N 1/2 of 33 & fract Sect. 31).

T. 5. S. R. 1. E. (S. B. M. S. 1/2 Sect. 3. S 1/2 Sect. 4. N 1/2 Sect 10. Fract. NE 1/4 Sect 9. & Sect 2).

This tract will include Indian Canyon, and other tracts adjacent to the Indian village of Saboba, in the San Jacinto Valley. We think that in case the Saboba Indians are finally ejected from their village, they might —, or at any rate a part of them might — be accommodated on these lands.

The Indian Canyon has a good stream of water in it. Several Indians are living there now, and have good wheat fields. It is strange that the elastic survey of the San Jacinto Ranch was not stretched so as to take in this Canyon when it took in the Saboba village.

Yours respectfully
Helen Jackson.

ALS (LR #8994 [9541, 11342]—1883, SC 31, OIA, RG 75, NA).

DRAFT TO S. S. LAWSON

Los Angeles.
May 12. 1883

S.S. Lawson Esq.
Indian Agent.
Dear Sir,

Your letter of May 9th has been received, and its contents duly noted.

The facts as to Arthur Golsh's conduct at Pauma, we heard from the Capt. of the Pauma Rancheria: those at Pala, from the Indian who is now bringing up Arthur Golsh's child.

Some of the most respectable whites at Pala also informed us of the same facts.

The only "rumor" connected with the matter was that about what is now taking place at Pachanga.

The accumulation of evidence seemed to us very strong.

The facts in regard to the land from which he drove off four Indians families, were substantiated by affidavits, which have been forwarded to Washington.[1]

We are sorry indeed to learn that there should be "other good and sufficient reasons" for Mr. Golsh's removal.

You will of course act in the matter according to your own judgment. # [marginal note: # We think it just that you should yourself investigate the character of Mr. Golsh, especially as you consider our information unreliable.] We have no authority in it, except to report upon it to the Dept. which as we have already stated we should be very sorry to do.

We are glad that you think there is no need of Miss Golsh's being made acquainted with this painful affair. —

AL (CoCC, HHJ I, box 2, fd 4).
1. These affidavits were sent to Commissioner Price on May 5, 1883, by HHJ.

TO MARY ELIZABETH (SHERIFF) FOWLER

Los Angeles.
May 13. 1883

Dear Miss Sheriff,

We have obtained from one of the best law firms in Los Angeles, a written opinion on the point of the Indians' right to stay on their lands, which they were cultivating and occupying at the time the grants including those lands were made.

It is the opinion of these lawyers, that the Indians can stay: that they have a *legal* right to do so; and can make a good case in the courts; that it was the Mexican law that no grant could convey away the land occupied by Indians: and that therefore whether there were in the grant, a special clause protecting the Indians, or not, the Indians claim can be supported.

I hope very much that this is so.

It seems too good to be true: and the results of law suits are always so uncertain, one dares not hope beforehand; but still we can never tell till we try. —

I did not think it best to say anything to the Indians, until we had investigated as thoroughly as possible and had found lawyers ready to undertake the case. —

I hope most earnestly that the Dept. will appoint this firm that we have selected, to be U. S. Attys in Los Angeles, for the taking up of all cases affecting Indians' interests.

— However that may be, — we have got them to promise to look after the case, if it comes up, before this is done. —

Now, this is what we think best for you to do.

1st. — Tell the Captain — & if he thinks best one or two of his best men — that they are to keep perfectly quiet — go on with their work, as if they were to stay there forever.

If any papers, of any sort whatever are served on them — or any one in the village, they must bring them immediately to *Bronson [Brunson] and Wells*[1] — lawyers in Los Angeles. — And they will tell them what to do.

2d. — Impress it on them as earnestly as you can, that they must not *say one word to any one* about this. It will be greatly to their disadvantage if it should get noised about, or even hinted or suspected, that there is any intention of defending their rights by law. There is no knowing what underhand or even violent steps Mr. Byrne might take if he had any suspicion that the Indians would resist by law. —

3rd. — For this reason it will be of great importance that *you* do not by word or *look*, show to any of the white people that you have any hope of such a result.

Let it continue to be supposed that the matter is still in abeyance, as it has been for so long, and that there is no knowing *what* the Govt. will do: — that Mr. Byrne has set his price on the land, and it remains to be seen whether the Govt. will buy it or not. —

I enclose the name of this firm on a paper, for the Indians to keep, in case you go away from Saboba.

Impress it on them that this is their *one* chance, & that I & Mr. Kinney advise them to try it.

It is a pity you can not speak Spanish. I suppose you will have to talk with them through Jesus. —

I cannot too strongly impress on you the necessity for their keeping all this *secret.*

— If no inkling of this gets out, I do not believe Byrne will take any steps towards driving them off, because he hopes to sell to the Govt. — And if all goes as I expect & hope, the first thing he will know, will be that he does not own that 700 acres at all! —

I set off for home on the 21st so there is not time for you to write me again here. — Write to Colorado Springs. Keep up good courage, & cheer the people up. I believe they will not have to go. —

Yours ever
Helen Jackson

ALS (CSmH, HHJ MSS, HM 14209).

1. Anson Brunson (1834–95) was admitted to the bar in Michigan in 1858 and moved to California in 1864, eventually settling in Los Angeles, where he served as judge of the superior court, 1885–87.

G. Wiley Wells (b. 1840), a graduate of Columbia Law School, became the U.S. attorney for Northern Mississippi in 1870. Elected to Congress in 1876, he resigned the following year to accept an appointment as consul-general to Shanghai, China. In 1879 he settled in Los Angeles and with Anson Brunson formed the partnership of Brunson & Wells, which dissolved when Brunson was appointed to the bench. Wells formed another partnership, which included his nephew Bradner Wells Lee.

DRAFT TO JOHN CHAUNCEY HAYES

[after May 14, 1883]

Chauncey Hayes

Dear Sir

Yours of the 14th is received & the contents duly noted.

We have obtained legal opinion & some evidence on the points you bring up. — & find these points not well taken.

We are sure therefore that you will be glad to learn the Int. Dept. has already begun action against some of those who have illegally seized upon I[ndian] lands, — & that we are confident that the Govt. will henceforth deal vigorously with all parties who are found practicing the dishonest devices which have been so prevalent in this century, in regard to I[ndian] rights.

There is one point on which we would be glad of any information you can give us ie — in regard to the P[achanga] I[ndians] —

Do you know of any attempt having been made or any steps having been taken by those I[ndians], looking toward the getting of their lands in severalty — before the P[achanga] Canyon was set aside for them by Executive Order? —

Yrs &c—

AL, (CoCC, HHJ I, box 2, fd. 6).

John Chauncey Hayes (1853–1934), a native of California and the son of Judge Benjamin Hayes, settled in San Luis Rey and went into real estate, notably purchasing land near Oceanside for the proposed railroad. He also was a mail contractor, 1878–82, and postmaster at San Luis Rey in 1884 before relocating to Oceanside, where he published a newspaper, served as deputy county assessor and deputy country clerk, and later practiced law.

TO HENRY TELLER

Los Angeles,

May 16, 1883.

Dear Mr. Teller:

We have decided to forward to you, in advance of our report, one of the recommendations we made in it. We hope it can be acted on immediately. From the promptness with which the Department of Justice acted in the Helm patent case, we trust this also will be done. See enclosed copy of recommendation. If these attorneys can be immediately empowered to act, I have great confidence that the Saboba village can be saved without a lawsuit and that the cases of the other Indian villages on grant lands, will be favorably determined. We have come to the conclusion on farther inquiry, that it would be unwise to leave the Saboba case in the hands of the Mr. Wilson, of whom I first wrote to you. He is a warm friend of the Indians, as goes without saying, from his having offered to defend their case without fees. But he is an eccentric man, with little or no standing at the bar, and frequently away for long intervals in the country at his bee ranches. The Saboba case might very easily go by default, before he could be found, when he is off on these trips. It is certain that it would in any event, be impossible for him to do the best that could be done for the case. It seems clear that the government ought to defend these Indians' rights. It would be inhuman to expect the poor creatures to do it themselves. They are too ignorant to do it. They are too poverty stricken to pay for it. And for that matter so far as expense is concerned, it will be far cheaper for the government to do this, than to move the village, and establish it elsewhere. But it is not a question of cost. It is a question of right and obligation. As I wrote you once before, there must be something terribly wrong in our land, and our Republic, if the government cannot protect a whole village of industrious peaceable farming people, like these Saboba Indians from being driven off lands they have tilled for over one hundred years. I know if you could see the village, you would say, "it shall be protected." I know if Attorney General Brewster[1] could see it, he would say the same thing. And if he could see and hear one half we have seen and heard in the last five weeks, he would not lose a day in appointing legal counsel here on the spot, for all those helpless, persecuted people. Los Angeles is the place to have it. San Francisco is too far off, and the U. S. Attorneys there are far too busy. It would be simply impossible for them to attend to cases in this southern country. (Los Angeles would really be in our judgment the proper place for the Mission Agency headquarters. It is but little farther from the Indian village than San Bernardino is. The land office is here. All the liquor cases are brought here to the U. S. Commissioner for first trial.)

Mr. Wells' plan for getting the Saboba case settled without a suit is as follows: If he is authorized by the department to bring the San Jacinto ranch patent up before the U. S. courts to be reopened on the grounds that the Indians residing on the grant were not secured in their tenure as the Mexican law required, and for other reasons, he will inform the various parties now interested in the ranch of this proposed action. He is confident that the owners would prefer to make an arrangement among themselves, surrendering to the Indians the small tract their village is on. Rather than stand the contest in court. There are reasons for their not wishing to have their patent opened. The first survey never took in this village at all, etc. If no such compromise is offered, he is ready to undertake the defense of the Indians against any suit of ejectment, which the owner of their tract shall bring against them.

If the Attorney General will appoint Messrs. Brunson and Wells in this manner, and if you can authorize their taking the Saboba case as indicated, will you have them duly notified? And will you kindly inform me by letter sent to Colorado Springs?

I shall leave for home on the 22nd. The body of our report is done, but the exhibits of the detailed facts and circumstances on which we have based it, I shall write out at leisure there. We shall make a very strong showing, I assure you, of a state of things, disgraceful to the administration by the Interior Department, under Carl Schurz, and before his day. It is harrowing to see how comparatively easy it would have been a few years ago, to do the fair thing by these people, and how next to impossible it is now.

Yours always cordially,

Helen Jackson.

P.S.— In the matter of compensation for the work done by this firm for the government in this case and in all others, they say they will leave it entirely to the Department, or to the Attorney General to determine. The firm will make no charges, Lest you think I am mistaken about this. I have [asked?] Mr. Wells to put it into writing.

Dear Mr. Teller, I would give worlds if I could talk with you about this matter. I am going away heart sick, in the realization of the helplessness of these Indians in the net work of villainies and cruelties surrounding them. I feel sure if these attorneys have this authority to act, all will be done that can be done for their protection.

They say a woman puts the whole of her letter in the post-script.

. . . .

Typescript (LR #10049 [10808, 10231, 10062,]—1883, SC 31, OIA, RG 75, NA). A rough draft of this letter can be found in CoCC, HHJ I, box 2, fd. 8. The 8th recommendation that HHJ included in her letter has been omitted. With a few changes it appeared in "Report," pp. 470–71, as recommendation 7.

1. Benjamin Harris Brewster (1816–88), a commissioner who in 1846 adjudicated the Cherokee Indians' claims against the United States, also served as attorney general of Pennsylvania, 1867–68. He was a special counsel for the government and, during the administration of Chester A. Arthur, was attorney general, 1882–85.

TO HIRAM PRICE

Los Angeles.
May 17. 1883

Hon. H. Price
Com. of Ind. Affairs
Dear Sir,

In our visit to the Indian village of Mesa Grande, we found a very old Indian, named Stephano Douro [Duro], whose case we are disposed to recommend for a Special Executive Order.

He has lived on his little place twenty three years: has a corn & wheat field, a vineyard etc. —

He is very old and very poor: lives alone with only a grandson to help him. He is pressed by white settlers. The whole tract of Mesa Grande has been pretty much taken away by the whites, in the last half dozen years, and the Indians driven off: though it was plainly the intention of the Govt. to have included it all in the Santa Ysabel Reservation. —

This old man has induced some white friend to survey his little place for him — and these are the figures:

E 2 of S E 4 of Sect. 8. T. 12. S. R. 2 E.

S. W. 4 of S. W. 4 of Sect. 9. T. 12. S. R. 2 E. (S. B. M.)

We promised to ask to have it reserved for him by Executive Order.

It is a small thing: but it will make one poor old creature very happy: I think there is a disposition on the part of some of the white settlers to stand by this old man: and he will probably be left unmolested, if the land is reserved.

Yours truly

Helen Jackson.

P.S. If this is done, Agent Lawson should be instructed to see to it that the information is communicated to Stefano and to the white settlers also. Agent Lawson himself, has never been at Mesa Grande.

ALS (LR #9440 [11342]—1883, SC 31, OIA, RG 75, NA).

TO MARY ELIZABETH (SHERIFF) FOWLER

Los Angeles
Sunday
May 20. 1883

Dear Miss Sheriff —

I write you one line more, just before setting off, to say that I have at this last moment made a positive arrangement with that law firm, Bronson [Brunson] & Wells, — to defend the case of the Saboba Indians — *even if the Government* does not authorize them to do it! — I could not bear to go away, & leave the matter in such shape that there could be the *least* chance of their not getting a chance at whatever hope there may lie for them in the law. — So I have myself guaranteed to the lawyers a certain sum for which they undertake to *see the case through,* if a suit of ejectment is brought against the village. —

All is now done that human agency can do — and I must say I feel very confident that those Indians will never be moved. — Mr. Wells is *greatly interested* in the case — is a very warm hearted humane man — & a very clever lawyer. — & he thinks they will win the case. —

You must write directly to him yourself if anything happens you think he ought to know — but above all make the Captain understand the importance of his being on the *watch* — and if any papers of any kind are served on any of the Indians, to bring them *here* immediately to Mr. Wells — & *tell nobody.*

The only loophole that I can see for an accident, is in the Indians' themselves being either *careless* — or suspicious about going to a lawyer. — But you must labor with them, till you get it clear in their minds — & make them understand that they will not have to pay the lawyers anything. If the Government does not assume the case, *I will!* — I can beg enough money to make up what I cannot pay myself, I know — & at any rate I have guaranteed it — & Mr. Wells has promised to do all that can be done. —

Yours ever—

H.J.

I am off tonight. —

ALS (CSmH, HHJ MSS, HM 14210).

DRAFT TO S. S. LAWSON

[May 31, 1883]

On returning home last night I found your letter of the 21st. —

Of course I need not say that its contents were a surprise to me — & that I exceedingly regret that the affair has taken such shape. —

I was very glad when in your letter of the 9*th* (in reply to my suggestion that in case Miss Golsh had to know our action in the matter I would prefer writing to her myself about it)[.]

You said "As to informing his sister of your action I think this quite unnecessary. It would only result in ill will toward the Commission. You have the same right to bring such information to the notice of an agent as any one else interested in the good of the Indian & it will be no detriment to our service if she remains ignorant of the cause why her brother is not continued in the service. So far as I am concerned it shall not appear that his removal if this result from faultless investigation, is on account of any action taken by you. In such case I assume the responsibilities myself." —

"You also said, that it had been your purpose to relieve Mr. Golsh at the close of the present quarter for other good & sufficient reasons[.]"

In this letter of the 21*st* you say you requested him to resign "for the reason set forth in our complaint." —

I do not doubt that you must have some strong reasons for thus changing your plan of proceeding — & you were of course at perfect liberty to give him all your reasons & the sources through which your information came. —

I am sorry that the young man thinks that we had any hostile animus toward him in the matter. — So far from that being the case, our sole motive in treating it in the way we did, by private letter to you, & the suggestion of his resigning, were kindly. In his annoyance & resentment it is probably only natural that he should think this — but our correspondence with you which you have of course preserved shows the contrary.

We would have been exceedingly glad both for his sake & his sister to have found any testimony which could have cleared him. As the charge that we only sought the testimony from his enemies is absurd in the face of it, but we did not know beforehand anyone's position in regard to him.

I am very sorry to hear what you have heard of Jesus Lopez's character[1] — You recollect at the time we left Sa[n] B[ernardino] you said we could not have a better man to go with us — & he certainly appeared so far as we could judge first to last to act honestly & sympathetically as Interpreter — I should be much disappointed in him, if it were to turn out that he had in any way been unfaithful in that capacity —

As to the suit which you say Mr. Golsh proposes to bring against Mr. Kinney & myself for defamation — of course I have nothing to say until I am called into court.

We did what we thought was right — & in the line of our official duty — We tried to do it in the kindest way to Golsh & what we thought would be the most satisfactory way to you — our information was sent in a private letter to you, in your official capacity — moreover, the matters of which we spoke were matters of public & general mention — & therefore formed upon all knowledge.

I hardly think that the "best legal talent" — would be found ready to undertake any such suit if the facts are *fairly* truthfully laid before them — Mr. Golsh's sole basis for action will be our letters to you.

I was very sorry not to be able to visit the Desert Indians, but I was exceedingly unwell the last week of my stay in L.A. — & dared not undertake the trip.[2]

Chief Cabezon sent two delegations begging me to come out, — & expressing so much chagrin at not seeing me, that I was really grieved not to be able to go — but I asked an old agent & friend of theirs whom I met in L.A. — Capt Stanley[3] to go out & see them, & convey to them my good wishes & regrets, & make a report which I could append to ours.

AL (CoCC, HHJ I, box 2, fd. 4). A copy of Lawson's May 21 letter to Jackson is in CoCC, HHJ I, box 2, fd. 4.

1. Jesús López was the agency interpreter assigned to HHJ and Kinney.
2. Lawson had criticized her for not visiting these Indians.
3. From the village of Temecula, acting as a special agent for the Mission Agency during the spring of 1865, John Quincy Adams Stanley had distributed seed corn and beans as well as wood for ploughs to the surrounding Indians. See his letters of Mar. 28, 1865, and May 19, 1865, to Austin Wiley, superintendent of Indian Affairs for California, in *Report of the Commissioner of Indian Affairs, 1865*, pp. 119–27.

DRAFT TO CAPTAIN J. Q. A. STANLEY

[early June 1883]

H.H.

Capt. Stanley

Dear Sir,

Your Report and letter reached me Sat. Evening.[1] I have not had time yet to thoroughly examine the Report but have no doubt — it will be of material value, and I am greatly obliged to you for undertaking the trip.

I also received your note enclosing Mr. Lawson's letter. I do not see that the letter calls for any reply from me, and I am surprised that he should have been annoyed at my asking you to report to me on the condition of the Desert Indians. No doubt some misrepresentations were made to him, by some one, or he would not have felt as he did. — My delegating to another any part of my investigation, which I was unable to make myself, was wholly legitimate, in fact it was not the expectation of the Dept. that I would be able to visit in person so many of the I[ndians] as I did.

I would have been glad to hear a little more in detail. I am sorry you did not mention what renumeration you would yourself think fair for your time. I have assumed however that $5. a day would perhaps cover it & accordingly enclose a cheque for $65. If this is satisfactory please let me know &c.

AL (CoCC, HHJ I, box 2, fd. 6). Jackson reprinted Stanley's report in "Report," pp. 507–8.

1. Stanley's letter, which was written on Monday, May 28, 1883, reached Jackson on Saturday, June 2.

TO HIRAM PRICE

Colorado Springs

June 1*st* 1883

H. Price Esq—

Com. of Ind. Affairs

Dear Sir,

In reply to your letter of May 16th, — yesterday received, — in which you say,

"With reference to the Pala reservation I have to state that the N. W. 1/4 of N. E. 1/4 and N. E. 1/4 of N. W. 1/4 Sec. 34 T 9. S. R. 2 W. was formerly included in the Reservation, but Agent Lawson having represented that the order setting it apart for Indians, should in justice to Mrs. Josephine Golsh,[1] whose husband had made a homestead entry covering these tracts on the 8th of November, 1875 be rescinded, these tracts were restored to the public domain by Executive Order of July 24, 1882. Under these circumstances and the fact that the lands covered by cash entry of March 7, 1876, has been so long patented I do not see that anything can be done for the relief of these Indians," —

— I have to say, that the land above alluded to is not the land referred to in the affidavits of Patricio Soberano, and Felipe Jogua, which we forward to you in our letter of May 5th.

There may have been some error in the description.

We were aware of the return of a part of the Pala Reservation to the public domain, and its patent to Mrs. Josephine Golsh, before Agent Lawson's representation of the justice of her claim.

There are Indians still living on that land, but in view of the Department's action in the matter, we did not deem it advisable to raise any question in regard to it.

But this other land is patented to Arthur Golsh. He drove the Indians from it by force and violence!

— See Affidavits of Patricio and Felipe, forwarded in our letter of the 5th inst. It is claimed that the land is now owned by his brother Gactano Golsh.[2]

It is a clear case in which the Indians should get their land back if possible.

Yours respectfully
Helen Jackson

ALS (LR #10231 [10049]—1883, SC 31, OIA, RG 75, NA). The partial draft in CoCC, HHJ I, box 2, fd. 5 is clearly dated June 2.

1. Josephine Golsh was the wife of Alfred Golsh (d. 1882), who had become a naturalized citizen in New York. His connection to the Golsh family referred to elsewhere is unknown.

2. Gactano Golsh might be Kayetan Golsh, a bachelor rancher and the first of the family to become a citizen of the United States. He acquired a quarter section homestead located northwest of the Pala Mission in 1883.

TO HENRY TELLER

Colorado Springs,
Private.   Wednesday, June 6, 1883.

Dear Mr. Teller:

Thanks for your note of May 21st. It followed me back from California, and I had it awaiting me here, on my return last Friday. I did not need any assurance of your determination to find some way of protecting those Indians if possible. I only wish you had eighteen years more, instead of eighteen months, to do it in. Mr. Kinney came east with us, and has gone on to New York. He will come to Washington immediately, and lay before you some matters about which we did not think it safe to write. I am sure that you will be impressed by his clear headedness, and grasp of things. I have never seen a man, without special professional training, and so young, (he is only thirty-one) whose intellectual processes on all matters, were as clean cut as his. He has just the type of mind, and just the sort of executive ability, that you will recognize and sympathize with, I know. And I am greatly hoping that you will wish to appoint him as Indian Commissioner for California, in place of Stoneman[1] who has resigned, (and who never amounted to anything while he was in; knows less really about Indian affairs there, than any man I talked with). Mr. Kinney is now thoroughly interested in the thing, conversant with it, enlisted on the right side, and I do not hesitate to say, that there is not in the whole state a man, who could or would do half as much for the Indians, and for the carrying out of the provisions of the bill which I hope next year will be passed for the relief of these Indians, as Mr. Kinney can, if he will only make up his mind to undertake it. It is a farce to speak of him as my "assistant" in the work we have done. It makes me feel guilty whenever I use the word. Except for his knowledge of land matters, insight into tricks, and discreet slowness in dealing with people, I should not have accomplished anything beyond a mere surface showing. As it is, I feel sure that you will say we have gone to the bottom of things, and put the situation clearly and concisely; and if nothing more were ever to result from our mission, than the saving the San Ysidro Indians, and the Los Coyotes, their lands, I should feel rewarded. But I hope for much more.

The body of our report is already written. I think it will take about three weeks more to prepare the appended exhibits, in which I propose to give the detailed accounts of the villages we visited, and the different situations and circumstances on which our report and recommendations are based. I suppose there is no special haste about sending in the report, as nothing would be done in way of a bill till next winter. I am glad to say that I shall only send you in a bill for about the original sum I reckoned my expenses at, with no extra charge for interpreters, etc. My driver acted as my interpreter all the way; and the other incidentals such as legal opinions, etc., will all be covered by $1,250. How shall I put this? Or will it be necessary for me to send any formal statement? The last letter of instructions said I was to be paid at rate of $500 a month, that sum to cover all expenses of interpreters, etc. The time can be rated, two months and a half (though it will really be four, by the time I have the report finished). But I want only just what I have spent, and that is between $1200 and $1300.

I hope very much you will be in Colorado this summer. There are scores of points I would be exceedingly glad to talk over with you, which cannot be discussed in writing. My third paper in the Century, on the "Recent condition of the Mission Indians," will appear in the August number. I suppose all persons unfamiliar with the time it takes to prepare illustrations, will be likely to think I wrote the article after undertaking our present investigations; but it was written last summer, after our first journey; the whole series of five papers, being in the Century people's hands last autumn. I am greatly relieved on reading the proof now, to find that I had so nearly grasped the truth of the situation. There are some respects in which I would now have stated it a little differently; but in the main, the article is right, and in good shape to make popular sentiment on the subject, and get some of the Congressmen I hope, ready for the bill next winter.

Pardon this long letter.

Yours always cordially,
and now gratefully,
Helen Jackson

Typescript (LR #10823—1883, OIA, RG 75, NA).
1. George Stoneman (1822–94), a veteran of the Mexican American and Civil Wars, moved to Southern California in 1871. He was appointed a California commissioner of transportation, an Indian commissioner in 1878, and a railroad commissioner in 1879. From 1883 to 1887 he served as state governor.

DRAFT TO S. S. LAWSON

[early June 1883]

Dear Sir —

Your letter of June 6th — & 7th — are both at hand today & contents noted. —

In letter of the 6th there are several facts that seems to show a misunderstanding on your part.

You speak of the "threat of reporting the matter to the Dept. being held over you to induce you to cause immediate resignation on Mr. Golsh's part[."] —

I cannot see in my letter to you in regard to A[rthur] G[olsh] any expression which supports the idea of a threat. Certainly nothing was farther from our intention. As I have already stated in my letter of the 31st our sole motive in treating the matter as we did was to have it arranged in the way kindest & most satisfactory — to you. —

You also say "it was clearly not the duty of the Commission to assume authority in the Govt. or conduct of the Agency." —

You will see on looking back at our 2d letter that we expressly disclaimed having any authority whatever in the matter except to report to the Dept. — which we very much wished to avoid doing —

You say "Capt. Matteo[1] informed me that when you inquired of him, he said Golsh was a good man so far as he knew — but that you seemed to doubt whether he was telling the truth & that you insisted that he *must* tell everything applying that he was keeping back something." —

I have no recollection of any Capt. by that name. If it is the Pachanga Capt. — I have only to say that I never saw him at all. He was ill in bed.

I have also to say that I did not hear any Indian say that A[rthur] G[olsh] was "a good man — so far as he knew" nor have any conversation whatever of the sort you quote[.]

This is probably an illustration of the misrepresentations which it has apparently been somebody's interest to make.

You say that "Mrs. Veal[2] and Mrs. Wolfe[3] took a conspicious interest in giving information about Mr. G[olsh].["]

This is not true. Both of those women were comparatively reluctant & cautious in their speech in regard to his character.

— You say "I requested him in my letter of the 21st to resign because I believed your authority to be trustworthy. Learning subsequently the source of your information I gave it no credance." —

But in your letter of the — when we told you our authority —You said "the statement &c — ["]

In regard to Jesus Lopez' character, I can only say that if I had known he's a notorious liar I should never for one moment thought of employing him as an Interpreter: —

If he be as bad a man as you now say, it is not at all certain that he reported truthfully to us what the I[ndians] said or truthfully to them either what we said to the I[ndians] or what they said to us. —

Referring to what you now state of J[ésus] L[ópez'] character, I can only repeat what I said before that we accepted him as an Interpreter on your recommendation —

I believe these are all the points in letter of the 6th needing reply. —

In regard to the letter of the 7*th* I have only to say that it fills me with surprise — So far from ever having said to any of the I[ndians] that their Agent was not working for their interests I, in several instances, explained to them that I had *myself* read *three* years reports of his in which he had told the Govt. about their troubles. I explained to them over & again that all depended on the Great Council[4] — & that all the Agent —or we could do, was to *tell* the Secretary & the Secretary could ask the Great Council. I spent much time in these parts & the Indians in several places expressed themselves greatly pleased & satisfied — & said it had never been so well explained to them before —

— There was however no conversation of this sort, so far as I recollect at Pachanga.

— We saw very few of the P[achanga] I[ndians] — The Capt. was ill in bed — Mr. Kinney went in & spoke to him for a few minutes — — I am totally at a loss to imagine how the confusion & ill feeling you describe as existing there has come about. —

As to my having given "Jose Pachito[5] a Commission as a General," — I am still now at a loss to know what that means —

All of the Captains & I believe two or three Generals begged us for "papers" to show to the white men — to keep the white men off their lands. To the best of my recollection they all had already papers signed by you, or by some one else, saying that they were Capts — or Genl, as it might be —

In view of the constant trespassing by whites on their lands filing on their villages &c — & of the new & decided stand now taken by the Int. Dept in protecting their interests ordering the Land Office to receive no such filings — & we thought this might be some protection for the poor creatures in a paper, signed by us. Stating these facts — we accordingly gave to every Capt. that asked for it, the following paper — which is as you will see, simply & solely for the whites — in no way purporting to control the I[ndians] —

— If you had seen one of the papers you would have understood it at once — & have been saved this annoyance — which I need not say that I greatly regret. —

Most certainly we should never have thought of giving such a paper to any Indian not already commissioned & recognized as Capt. or General — You were quite right in feeling as you say, that neither Mr. Kinney nor I would "so far disregard the claims of official courtesy." —

In fact so anxious were we to avoid even the appearance of any such thing, that, when the young General at Santa Ysabel — (who by the way, seemed very right minded & earnest in his care for his people) — asked us to have a copy of his paper posted up in San Diego, for his Indians there to see, we refused, telling him that the paper was not for the Indians at all, only for him to show to the whites. In every instance, we had the paper carefully read & explained to the Indians — & I can truly say that the possibility of its being misunderstood never occurred to me.

In conclusion I can only add that it is even yet inexplicable to me how all this confusion and misrepresentation have arisen & that I sincerely am very sorry for the trouble & annoyance they have caused you.—

AL (CoCC, HHJ I, box 2, fd. 8).
1. One of the Indian village captains.
2. Isabell (Ysabella) Place Veal, born in 1850 in Santa Barbara, was the daughter of a Chumash Indian woman and William (Guillermo) Place, who had jumped ship and settled in California. In 1873 Father Anthony D. Ubach officiated at the marriage of Isabell and William Veal (1837–1903), a German emigrant who had settled at Pala in 1868.
3. "Mrs. Wolfe" refers to Ramona Place Wolf (1846–94), who was Mrs. Veal's sister. Ramona married Louis Wolf (1833–87), a noted Temecula pioneer who had begun acquiring land as early as 1868. He also ran a general store at the Willows Station. For more details on Wolf, see Van Horn, "Tempting Temecula: The Making and Unmaking of a Southern California Community," pp. 30–32.
4. A reference to the U.S. Congress.
5. One of the village captains.

TO MARY ELIZABETH (SHERIFF) FOWLER

Sat. June 9*th* 1883
Col. Springs—

Dear Miss Sheriff —

Your letter of June 1*st* is only just here. It ought not to take eight days for a letter to come here —

I am exceedingly sorry to hear about the renting of the Saboba tract to Foster. — But you must tell the people not to be discouraged. I have great hopes that they will come out all right. —

They can pasture their stock up in Indian Canyon, if Foster drives it off the village tract. Indian Canyon is Govt. land & we have asked to have it set apart as reservation for the Indians. — It seems almost inhumane to suggest your staying in San Jacinto all summer: but I do honestly feel that it would be safer if you stay: — unless you can trust the Captain to go *straight* to Bronson [Brunson] & Wells if any paper is served on him, or on any one in the village.

— I am afraid you will be ill, if you do not have a change.

— I hardly knew what to say about the tables. Mr. Kinney was to have mine boxed for me and sent from San Gabriel by freight: — (they both going together from San Jacinto to his place) but Mr. Kinney has gone East & will not be in California again before the autumn.

However if Will Webster will see to having them drawn down the M[ountain] and keep them till autumn, I am sure Mr. Kinney would like one, and I should like the other. But I do not think the logs about which we spoke to Mr. Saunders[1] was manzanita wood, I think they were pine.

In great haste —

Yours always affly —

Helen Jackson

ALS (CSmH, HHJ MSS, HM 14211).

1. Amasa Saunders (1830–1902) operated a sawmill in Strawberry Valley on Mount San Jacinto, 1880–86.

TO EPHRAIM W. MORSE

Col. Springs

June 13. 1883

Dear Mr. Morse,

I received yesterday a copy of the San Diego Union, of June 1st containing a scurrilous paragraph in regard to my work as Indian Commissioner in So. Cal.[1]

From what I had seen of the San Diego community, I should not have supposed that any decent paper there, would have been willing to put before its readers such an indecent paragraph.

And I should also have supposed that a woman of my age, and reputation, would have been sheltered from just that kind of attack.

However, any one undertaking such service as I did, must be prepared for any & all expressions of hostility & antagonism: and no one whose opinion is worth caring for, would ever be influenced by statements made in such vulgar and indecent language as that of the paragraph in question. —

But, for my own personal satisfaction, I would be very glad if you could find out, in a quiet way, without mentioning my name, or intimating that I knew anything about it, who wrote the letter. It is dated San Luis Rey: but we were not in San Luis Rey at all:

— It also showed an acquaintance with some small points, such as my having had a room full of Indian baskets, at the Kimball Mansion — & Mr. Kinneys having collected botanical speciments on the route, which I cannot understand anyone's having known who was not on friendly & familiar terms with us. I am therefore very naturally anxious to know who it is, that was capable of such a malicious & low bred action, as the writing of that letter. — Not that I should for a moment dream of noticing it — in any way, public or private. — But if I am ever in So. California again I do not want to feel suspicious of everybody, who might by any possibility have written that letter.

With warm regards to Mrs Morse & to Mrs. Whipple.[2]

Yours ever truly
Helen Jackson

Mrs. W*m* S. Jackson
Colorado Springs
Colorado.

ALS (CSf, Phelan Collection).

1. This May 16, 1883, letter signed "Q." appeared as "An Indian Commission," *San Diego Union*, June 1, 1883, p. 3. The author noted that "the more expensive part of this junketing commission was a month's stay at the Kimball Mansion at Los Angeles, labeling and forwarding to Boston friends, the accumulated trumpery which had been shipped thither until an extra room at that aristocratic and expensive hostelry had been filled." The author suggested that "instead of commissioning a married woman and an old bachelor, two old maids be selected next time."

2. See HHJ to Abbot Kinney [Sept. 28, 1884], below, n. 1.

TO HIRAM PRICE

Private

Col. Springs
June 25 1883

Hon. H. Price,
Dear Sir,

I have just received a letter from San Diego, from Father Ubach,[1] the Catholic priest there, which fills me with uneasiness, and which I think I ought to report to you.

Father Ubach has been in charge of that district for seventeen years: is a humane good man, and a warm friend of the Indians, over whom he has great influence.

He writes

"Since I saw you, I went to Capitan Grande. Mr. Hensley is trembling for fear that Minister Teller will force him to clear out, which I sincerely hope will be the case, and thus remove another source of scandal from the midst of those poor Indians. I have lately learned that Dr. Strong and Co. are daily waiting the arrival from Washington of a Special Indian Commissioner. I fear through false and malicious information he and others may mislead this expected commissioner and thus leave things in status quo, and thus jeopradize your efforts to ameliorate the condition of my poor Indians. I have seen so much roquery and thievery in these matters."

You will pardon my trespassing on your time with a private letter in this matter, when I tell you that it is certain that any movement emanating from, or influenced by Dr. Strong, will be against the interests of the Capitan Grande Indians.

Any Special Commissioner appointed at his request — or arriving in San Diego to be under his influence will work mischief to those Indians.

Dr. Strong is the man (as you will see by the affidavits we forwarded relative to Capitan Grande matters) — who first robbed those Indians of their lands: he went in there, hiring the lands from the Indians — as bee pasture — and then refused to move out, filed on the lands & patented them. —

He was malicious in his whole bearing — antagonistic to the Indians from first to last. —

The Capitan Grande Canyon is a valuable tract: — and in its whole length and breadth, not only belongs to the Indians in the outset, but was formally assigned to them by Col. Magruder in 1853. —

Of all the "steals" that we unearted in San Diego Co. this of the Capitan Grande lands was one of the very worst: and this man Strong led the way in it, has assisted in the continuance of it, and I make no manner of doubt, has been plotting ever since we were there to prevent the Departments driving out any of the white settlers in the Canyon.

It is a great pity that his patent cannot be treated in the same way as was that of Chatham Helm, in the San Ysidro Canyon. —

He is just as wicked a thief and robber as Helm. —

I owe you an apology perhaps, for writing thus. But it is impossible for me to speak in moderate terms of this class of men. I hope very much to be able to forward our Report, next week. —

When you have read the "Exhibits" I have written out, in regard to band after band of Indians robbed in precisely this way, you will feel as deep indignation as I do.

It is not to be wondered at that many of the San Diego Co. men are uneasy and antagonistic, at the least symptom of the Departments intention to do justice to the Indians in matter of lands: for if complete justice were done, there would be a revolution in the County.

Yours truly

Helen Jackson

ALS (LR #11782—1883, SC 31, OIA, RG 75, NA).

1. Born in Catalonia, Spain, Father Anthony D. Ubach (1836–1907) came to San Diego in 1866 and took charge of the Catholic parish. During the spring of 1882 he took HHJ on a tour through various Mission Indian villages including Temecula and San Pasqual. According to many *Ramona* scholars, Ubach served as the model for Father Gaspara, although HHJ never expressly said so.

TO LEONICIO LUGO

[July 1, 1883]

My dear Leonicio:

I thank you for your note of the 24th of June. I received it today. It is written in good handwriting and very plain.

I would be glad to come to Cahuilla Valley again and see all of the people, but I do not know that I shall ever come to Cahuilla again. You must tell your father and all the people that I think of them very often. I have just finished writing the report which is to be sent to Washington to tell the government all I saw in South California about the Indians. It has taken me two months to write it all. It is 200 large pages long.

I hope you will keep on studying very well and learn to do sums in arithmetic and to do business like the Americans. I want all the Indians to work and save money and show that they can do all things as well as the Americans do.

Your friend,

Helen Jackson

Printed in the *Hemet News*, Apr. 15, 1932, p. 9, as "Indian Has Letter Penned in 1883 by Author of Ramona." This lengthy article also included Leonicio Lugo's recollections of the murder of Juan Diego at the hands of Sam Temple.

Leonicio Lugo (d. 1937) was born and raised at the Cahuilla Reservation, where his father, Fernando, was village captain during HHJ's visit. While attending Mary Ticknor's school, Leonicio met HHJ and, at his teacher's suggestion, wrote her a letter. This is HHJ's response.

TO HIRAM PRICE

Col. Springs
July 27 — 1883

Hon H. Price,

Dear Sir,

The enclosed slip[1] has just been sent to me from California.

It was either written or instigated by Lawson.

The Editor of the San Bernardino Times could of course know nothing of the matters referred to, except from Lawson.

You will note the lies in it.

1*st* That I "peremptorily demanded the removal of a teacher" when, as is shown by the correspondence placed in your hands by Mr. Kinney, we not only did not "demand" it: expressly said we had no authority to do anything except report to the Dept. which we should be sorry to do, and therefore suggested that Lawson should ask the young man to resign.

2*d* That I "gave an Indian a Commission as chief": where, as is shown in same correspondence, we gave no papers to any Indians not already commissioned, by Lawson or other agents —: and the papers we did give were in no way shape or manner, commissions: being merely giving information to whites in regard to trespassing on Indians lands etc.

3rd. — That the Agent had succeeded in abolishing chieftaincy.

The greater number of these Captains Generals etc. had Commissions signed by Lawson himself! —

4th. That I was "properly informed by Agent Lawson to confine myself to my proper business."

See same correspondence.

5*th* That "the Indian office proper does not take any stock in this female policy of the secretary."

I myself informed Lawson in my first interview with him, that it was you who first suggested to Mr. Teller to send me out as Agent to report on the Mission Indians! —

I earnestly hope it is true, as herein stated, that Lawson has resigned. If so, it would be idle to take up your valuable time, with this contemptible newspaper rubbish. But, if not, it is only proper that you should see this article, as still further proof of the man's animus and flame.

I shall hope soon to hear that our Report meets with your and Sec. Teller's approval.

Yours truly
Helen Jackson

ALS (LR #14177—1883, OIA, RG 75, NA).

1. The enclosed clipping, entitled "Trouble in the Indian Service," which appeared in the *San Bernardino Times,* also described HHJ as Secretary Teller's "pet appointee." The *San Luis Rey Star* of Aug. 4, 1883, p. 1, in "The Indian Agency," noted Lawson's resignation and described HHJ as a "busy body." The *Star* concluded, "in our opinion no woman should occupy the position of Indian Commissioner; it is no place for any member of the femine [*sic*] gender."

TO MARY ELIZABETH (SHERIFF) FOWLER

Col. Springs
Thursday
August 2 — 1883

Dear Miss Sheriff —

Your note of July 23*rd* gives me great surprise & pain.[1] I will do all I can: You may rest assured: — I hope I can get it righted. — If Lawson did it, it is because he thinks you a friend of mine. — Now that he has resigned I will say frankly that I believed him unfit for his place — and I am exceedingly glad that things have so come about that he has been forced to resign. —

Do not think of leaving your post. If the Govt. does not restore your salary to its old sum, I myself will send you $50 to spend for the people — so that you will not feel obliged to deprive yourself of the pleasure of helping them. But I am confident I can get it restored. There is no reason why it should have been reduced, except ignorance or caprice.

I am glad you are in San Diego resting. — I think all will go well with the Indians. The Attorney General has appointed that firm in Los Angeles, Brunson & Wells *Asst. U. S. Attys* — for the purpose of protecting the Indians rights — So I am greatly encouraged to hope. I will enclose a reply to Ramon.[2]

In great haste.

Always affly yours
H.J.

ALS (CSmH, HHJ MSS, HM 14213).

1. In Mary Sheriff to HHJ, July 23, 1883, included in HHJ to Teller, Aug. 5, 1883, below, the schoolteacher informed HHJ that her salary had been reduced by one hundred dollars while that of the Cahuilla and Warner's Ranch teachers had not changed. Lawson was not to blame. The reduction occurred because Sheriff's daily student attendance was less than that of the others, a point HHJ made in her Oct. 11, 1883, letter to Price. The salary was restored.

2. Ramon Cababi, one of Sheriff's students at Saboba, had written HHJ on June 28, 1883. HHJ sent the letter on to Teller.

TO HENRY TELLER

Col. Springs

Aug. 5, 1883

Dear Mr. Teller —

The despatch you sent me on Friday read —

"I will go to Manitou[1] in the morning."— So I went to the train yesterday noon hoping to persuade you & Mrs. Teller to come home with me and spend Sunday. There I met Mr. Wolfe[2] who told me that you had gone to Central.[3]

Tomorrow I go with Mr. Jackson for a few days trip into the Gunnison County.[4] We expect to be at home by the 11*th* or 12*th*.

I hope very much that soon after that date, it will suit your convenience to come and make us a visit, bringing Mrs. Teller with you. —

I am exceedingly anxious to see you; and talk over all the Indian matters in So. Cal. — I have not yet heard of the arrival of my Report in Washington: but I sent it over three weeks ago, by Express. — Rumors that Lawson has resigned have reached me, through the Cal. papers. I most earnestly hope it is true and that Rust will have the place.

The thing I especially wanted to see you about however, was in regard to Miss Sheriff the teacher at Saboba. — She writes me that she has just been notified that her salary is to be reduced $100, & asks me if I can possibly do anything to help her in the matter. — If it is Lawson who has recommended this, he has done it simply because Miss Sheriff is a friend of mine: — It is a great cruelty: — the girl has worked there like a missionary: —She spends a great part of her salary on these people — and as she says "those demands must be met, no matter how small the salary is." — She has to board in a ranch house five miles from the Indian village — and hire a horse & buggy every day to drive to it. — The place where she boards is the only house in the valley of even a pretence at decent comfort, yet it is a place where I could hardly imagine her being able to live:[5] — for even these wretched accommodations, she has to pay, I think it was $8 a week! —You see the $700 was barely a living salary. — Why she should be singled out for this reduction, and the other teachers of the Indian Schools left undisturbed, I do not understand. She is the best educated woman of the three, by far — and has the most exquisite gentleness and refinement of character. Her personal relation with her scholars was far closer and more affectionate, than either of the other teachers had. — I am sure if you were to see her, and her school, you would have Com. Price put that $100 back again on her salary. If it is necessary for the Ind. Bureau to save a hundred dollars somewhere, there must be places where it can be cut down with less injustice than in the Indian schools in San Diego Co! — Not one woman out of a thousand, would be fit to teach them —and I should say not one out of ten thousand could be hired, for any sum, to lead such a dreary disolate life, and endure such deprivations. —

If you cannot come to Col. Springs now, I will come to Denver to see you, at any time, you will appoint, after our return from Gunnison. — But I hope very much you will come here. It will give Mr. Jackson & me great pleasure to have you with us.

Yours always cordially
Helen Jackson

ALS (LR #17750—1883, OIA, RG 75, NA).
1. Manitou Springs is located near Colorado Springs.
2. J. S. Wolfe was a director of the El Paso County Bank along with WSJ. In 1877 he served as president of the Woman Suffrage Club of Colorado Springs. He also had been the U.S. collector of Internal Revenue Service for Colorado and the El Paso County delegate to the Republican state convention. His wife and Nebraska senator Alvin Saunders's wife were sisters.
3. Central City is a small city west of Denver.
4. Gunnison is west of Colorado Springs.
5. Sheriff boarded with the Websters.

TO ANTONIO F. AND MARIANA CORONEL

Col. Springs
Aug. 19. 1883

My dear friends,

Your letter of the 13th fills me with surprise. I also had been wondering why I did not hear from you, and if the Indian woman ever had finished the lace. — I think it was not more than a week after I reached home, that I sent you a line, to let you know I was safe in my own home, and very glad to be there. — I have had several letters go astray in this way within the last few months. I do not know where the trouble is. —

I have not been quite well, since returning. This high altitude — 6000 feet — gives me trouble, more and more each year I return to it. I envy you who live at sea level. —

I suppose you have seen that Indian Agent Lawson has resigned. Some very amusing paragraphs in the California papers in regard to it have been sent to me. — I think it will be a gain to the Indians to have him removed: though of course, there is always a danger of having a worse one. I do not know who is appointed in his place.[1]

My Report to the Interior Dept. went in a month ago; but I have not yet heard anything from it. The movements at Washington are very slow. — I shall see Secretary Teller here before long, and shall then learn what his plans are. I trust something will be done by Congress next winter, for the Mission Indians. —

Mr. Jackson has been suddenly called to the East — and will be away two or three weeks. This is almost intolerable to me. I do not like being alone in my house — and when he is away, there seems to be no reason why I should remain at this altitude which does me so much harm. — Mr. Kinney is having a good time, at the different watering places at the East. We hear from him occasionally, each time at a new place. He staid three days with us on his way through Colorado. —

I have been looking at the only photographs I have of myself — and really they are so bad, I cannot make up my mind to send you one. — I do not think you would want it. — If I ever get a good one, I will send you one. —

With warm regards to you both and my remembrances to Miss Merced.

I am always

truly yours —

Helen Jackson

P.S.— Father Ubach sent the things directly *here* by mistake: — so if you do not find those you have in the array I will let them wait — till I come again — or you get some big bowls from Mr. Bliss[2] to add to them. I enclose $5 for the lace. It is lovely.

H.J.

ALS (Seaver Center, Coronel Collection).

1. John Guthrie McCallum (1826–97), S. S. Lawson's replacement, took office on Oct. 1, 1883, and served until 1885. He originally arrived in San Francisco in 1854, became editor of the *Georgetown Weekly News*, and was elected to the state senate in 1856. As Indian agent he quickly became familiar with southern California real estate and later was a prominent founder of Palm Springs.

2. Possibly O. H. Bliss, a Los Angeles councilman and orange grower.

TO WILLIAM HAYES WARD

Col. Springs

Sept 30, 1883

Dear Mr. Ward —

Here is the South California series of papers at last. — I did not finish my Report to the Interior Dept. until the first week in July — & since then I have been much interrupted: — I hope you will like the papers — & that they will help to pave the way towards work in Congress next winter.

Please publish them in the order they are numbered. — & if you can publish them on six successive weeks, it will *double* their effectiveness in attracting the kind of attention I want to rouse.[1]

I do not want the money for them till the whole series is printed. It was agreed upon with Mr. Bowen you recollect that the price was to be $250 for the six. — (For this sum, the Independent is getting more than *twice* the amount of matter, that the Century paid me the same sum for.) —

Now do you want another series of six at the same price? — I offer them *first* to you, and would like to hear from you in reply as soon as possible. — I am going down next month, by Gen. Crooks invitation to visit him at his head quarters in Arizona[2] — I shall see all I can of Arizona — learn all I can from Crook & his officers about the Apaches — shall visit the Navajo tribe —& perhaps the Cliff dwellers & Moquis [Hopis]. — It will be a most interesting journey & full of novel incident & scene. — & I will put it all into six papers for you at $250 the series, if you want it. —

At last I have the copies of "Pot of Gold."[3] — I was sorry to be so troublesome — but I wanted the papers exceedingly. It is strange what became of the others. —

I think the proof reader ought to be just a little bit ashamed — bad as my writing is, — of the enclosed errors, — because they make nonsense! —

Yours always
Helen Jackson

ALS (ViU, HHJ [#7080-B]).
1. A reference to articles published after Sept. 30, 1883, in the *Independent*, which included "A Day with the Cahuillas," Oct. 11, pp. 1–3; "Captain Pablo's Story," Oct. 25, pp. 1–2; "The Temecula Exiles," Nov. 29, pp. 3–4; and "The Fate of Saboba," Dec. 13, pp. 1–2.
2. No further mention was ever made of this trip to Arizona.
3. Her "Pot of Gold" story appeared in the *Independent* (July 26, 1883): 1–2.

TO HIRAM PRICE

Col. Springs
Oct 11, 1883

Hon. H. Price —
Dear Sir,

I received some little time ago, a letter from Miss Sheriff the teacher of the Indian school at Saboba, San Jacinto, telling me that her salary had been cut down $100. She is much distressed, and embarrassed by this reduction. I mentioned the matter to Sec. Teller, when he was here, and gave him Miss Sheriff's letter; and he requested me to lay the thing before you in full.

I think if you could see the situation in the San Jacinto valley, you would feel that the teacher there, really earns as much salary as those at Agua Caliente and Cahuilla. I suppose the average attendance at her school is somewhat smaller: but her labors are no less; nor her needs. In fact, if there be any difference in the latter respect, between her situation and theirs, it is in favor of them. They live in rooms built on to their schoolhouses, do their own work, find their own food, etc. So it is in their power to economize as much as they choose, — or dare — (and I am quite sure they do, more than they should.)

But Miss Sheriff is obliged to board, at a rather dear rate. She is also obliged to hire a horse and buggy each day, to drive to her school, a distance of five miles.

There is no white man's house nearer than three miles to the Indian village, and none where she can board with any tolerable comfort. It was astonishing to me that she could endure life in the place where I found her.

She told me she would have built a little room herself, out of her small savings, in the Indian village, so as to be among the people; but in the uncertainty as to their remaining in San Jacinto it seemed foolish. She is as devoted as a missionary, & her life is one of real hardship. She is absolutely obliged to spend a considerable portion of her salary, in keeping the Indians. They are desperately poor: often ill: She nurses them, buys food for them etc. The loss of this $100 will cripple her sorely.

Cannot it be restored? I am sure that I am not exaggerating, when I say, that $700 is barely a living salary for any teacher in the So. Cal. Indian schools. No one who has not been on the spot can have the least idea of the hardships and deprivations of the work. I looked upon those women with veneration.

I hope most earnestly that it will be possible to give Miss Sheriff her old salary: — I greatly fear she cannot afford to remain for less: and her loss would be simply irreparable to the Indians.

She is, in some respects, the best teacher of all who are there: has a more thorough education, has had experience in teaching at the east, & has a wonderful gentleness and sweetness, and affectionateness of manner which give her a great hold on the people.

I have received from your office, the notification that the Vouchers I sent with our Report had been forwarded to the Second Auditor. There was no mention however of the Report. I suppose it must have accompanied the Vouchers — and I would be exceedingly glad to know if you have received it, and if it meets your approbation. I would suggest that a copy of it, with the Exhibits, should be sent to the new Agent for the Mission Indians. He will find in the Exhibits, an account of most of the Indian villages under his charge, and a careful showing of the present status of the land troubles in each one. He cannot get this information from Mr. Lawson, for many of these villages Mr. Lawson has never visited. Neither can he get it himself without spending a great deal of time and trouble. And I think he would not in some instances, be so likely, as we, to get at the exact truth. He will be surrounded in the outset by hordes of interested parties who wish to get him to ignore the Indian rights, as Lawson has done.

It has been suggested to me, that it might be of interest to the General Public, now that so much attention is being given to Indian matters, if our Report were printed in some newspaper, or periodical. — How would that idea strike you, as advantageous to the general Indian cause, or not?

I suppose the Report will be printed in pamphlet form, by the Dept. as was the case with the other Special Reports on the Mission Indians. In that case I would be glad of twenty or thirty copies, and I can so place them as to secure their being reviewed in the leading papers. —

Yours truly
Helen Jackson

ALS (LR #19173—1883, OIA, RG 75, NA).

TO EPHRAIM W. MORSE

Colorado Springs
Nov. 3. 1883

Dear Mr. Morse,

I am going to ask some help from you. — I want an accurate account of two things that have happened in San Diego County — 1*st* the ejection of the Temecula Indians from their homes in Temecula.[1] 2*d* the taking of a lot of sheep from some of the Pala or San Luis Rey Indians by Maj. Coutts.[2] — I think the legal records of both cases are in San Diego and if I am not mistaken Sheriff Hunsacker[3] was engaged in both matters. I recollect some talk with him about them but not definitely. —

I do not want these incidents to use, with real names, or in any way to make unpleasant feeling: but I want them carefully written out in detail. — I am

Colorado Springs
Nov. 3 1883

Dear Mr. Morse. I am
going to ask some help
from you. - I want an
accurate account of various
things that have happened
in San Diego county - 1st
the ejection of the Temecula
Indians from their homes
in Temecula. get the
taking of a lot of sheep
from some of the Pala
or San Luis Rey Indians I think
[illegible] (?) —
the legal records of both
cases are in San Diego.
and if I am not mis-
taken Sheriff Hunsacker
was engaged in both
matters. I recollect him
often talking with him about

P.S. Of course you have observed that Agent
Lawson has been removed. I think he was
a bad man: and I hope the new agent
will be a better one. I have received several
copies of the San Luis Rey Star, containing
slurring and contemptuous references to me in
connection with this change. It is plain that
the Indians have some bitter enemies in
San Luis Rey. —

Jackson's November 3, 1883, letter to Ephraim W. Morse. (Courtesy of Museums of San Diego History; Richard W. Crawford, Editor, *The Journal of San Diego History*)

there but not carefully.— I do not want these incidents to use, with real names, or in any way to make an unpleasant feeling; but I would retain them carefully written but in detail.— I am going to write an Indian novel, the scene laid in So. California. I would rather you did not speak of this, as I shall keep it a secret, until the book is done, from all except my own intimate literary friends. I hope that I can write a story which will do something to influence public sentiment on the Indian Question; more feelings perhaps than — Any rate I am going to try.— and the Temecula ejection will be a most valuable

piece of material: the main facts I have, as you have seen in my article on the Mission Indians:— but what I want in addition, is, the legal narrative — who did it — what preliminary steps — what time & year they were driven out — any & all details will help.— Of the (Couts) sheep case I know little — only enough to know that it would be a strong incident in my story.—

Any other facts or incidents which you can write out for me, I would be very glad of — and I need not say, warmly grateful to you for the time and trouble it will cost. If I did not know that you genuinely sympathize with the Indians, I should not venture to make such a request.

With regards to Mrs. Morse — & Miss Whipple—
Yours always cordially — Helen Jackson

going to write an Indian novel, the scene laid in So. California. I would rather you did not speak of this, as I shall keep it a secret, until the book is done, from all except my more intimate literary friends. I hope that I can write a story which will do something to influence public sentiment on the Indian question: more perhaps than my "Century of Dishonor." At any rate I am going to try: and the Temecula ejection will be a most valuable piece of material: the main facts I have, as you have seen in my article on the Mission Indians: — but what I want in addition, is the legal narrative — who did it — what preliminary steps — what time of year — they were driven out — any & all details will help.— — of the Coutt's sheep case I know little — only enough to know that it would be a strong incident in my story. —

Any other facts or incidents which you can write out for me, I would be very glad of — and I need not say, warmly grateful to you for the time and trouble it will cost. If I did not know that you genuinely sympathize with the Indians, I should not venture to make such a request.

With regards to Mrs. Morse — and Mrs. Whipple —

Yours always cordially —

Helen Jackson

P.S. Of course you have observed that Agent Lawson has been removed. I think he was a bad man: and I hope the new Agent will be a better one. I have received several copies of the San Luis Rey Star, containing slurring and contemptuous references to me, in connection with this charge.[4] It is plain that the Indians have some bitter enemies in San Luis Rey.

ALS (CSdHi, Document Files, Research Archives). Reprinted as "I Am Going to Write an Indian Novel, the Scene Laid in So. California . . . ," ed. Valerie Sherer Mathes, pp. 108–13.

1. The Temecula removal took place in 1875.

2. "Maj. Coutts" refers to Major Cave Johnson Couts (1821–74), a West Point graduate who served in the Mexican American War before arriving in San Diego in 1848. He was appointed an Indian subagent for San Diego County in 1853 and later served as a county judge in San Diego. In 1854 he moved to Rancho Guajome, where he lived for the rest of his life. In 1855 he was rumored to have caused the death of two Indians; see Carrico, "San Diego Indians and the Federal Government: Years of Neglect, 1850–1865," pp. 172–77.

3. Nicholas Hunsacker (1825–1913) moved to northern California in 1847 and settled in Contra Costa County, where he served two terms as sheriff. He moved to San Diego in 1869, established a freight line between southern California and Arizona, was sheriff of San Diego County, 1874–76, and served the court order that ejected the Indians from Temecula. He later turned to farming and stock raising and in 1882 moved to Arizona.

4. A front-page article, "The Indian Agency," in the *San Luis Rey Star*, Aug. 4, 1883, described Jackson as a "busy body" and "a meddlesome feminine pet" of Secretary Teller.

TO HIRAM PRICE

Colorado Springs
Nov. 6. 1883

Hon. H. Price

Dear Sir,

I received two days since a U.S. Treasury Draft for $1250, in payment, for my voucher forwarded with my Report last July. As there was no communication accompanying the cheque, I do not know how to acknowledge its receipt except through your office.

I was exceedingly glad to hear from you in regard to my Report. I had begun to feel that it was destined never to be read by any one.

It is a deep satisfaction to me, that you find the recommendations we made, wise ones — and that you will incorporate them in the Bill to be prepared for the Mission Indians relief.

Can you give me any idea how soon the Report will be printed in pamphlet form? Thanks for the offer of as many copies as I wish. I can place two hundred copies so that every copy will tell — and at least fifty will receive especial notice in the press.

If this could be done before the Bill comes up in Congress, it would tell, I think on the fate of the Bill.

I am coming to New York next week, and shall probably be there the greater part of the winter. My address will be — The Berkeley

Corner 5th Av. & 9th St.

I hope very much that I may have the pleasure of seeing you in the course of the winter.

Yours very truly
Helen Jackson

ALS (LR #20695—1883, OIA, RG 75, NA).

TO ANTONIO F. AND MARIANA CORONEL

Colorado Springs, Nov. 8, 1883.

My Dear Friends, Mr. and Mrs. Coronel:

I send you herewith the very bad picture of myself, which I think you will wish you had never seen. If you do, you are quite at liberty to burn it up.

I had forgotten that I paid you the five dollars for the work done by the Indian woman. Keep it, if you please; there may be something to come from Father Ubach to pay expressage on, or there may be a box to be made to hold all my stone mortars, etc., which Mr. Bliss is going to get for me one of these years. It may be well for you to have a little money of mine on hand to meet these possible charges. I have asked Father Ubach to send to me to your care the old looking-glass frame which I forgot to put into the box he sent here; it was really one of the things I cared most for of all the relics promised me, and I was exceeding sorry to forget it. He, however, did much to atone for this by putting into a box a piece of one of the old olive trees from the San Diego Mission. I shall present part of it to Archbishop Corrigan.[1] I think he will value a piece of one of the fruit trees planted by Father Junipero.[2] I am sure you will have rejoiced at the removal of Lawson from the agency of the Mission Indians. I hope the new man will prove better; he hardly can prove worse. I wish we could have selected the new agent ourselves; but it was a political appointment, of which we knew nothing until it was all settled. Our report has been favorably received, and its recommendations will be incorporated in a bill before Congress this winter. I hope the bill will pass. But I know too much of Washington to be sanguine. However, if we had accomplished nothing more than securing the appointment of Brunson & Wells, Los Angeles, as United States attorneys, to protect the Indians' rights to lands, that would be matter of gratitude. I suppose you have heard of that appointment. I hope through their means to save the Saboba village, San Jacinto, from being turned out of their home. Now, I am as usual asking help. I will tell you what my next work for the Indians is to be.

I am going to write a novel, in which will be set forth some Indian experiences in a way to move people's hearts. People will read a novel when they will not read serious books. The scenes of the novel will be in Southern California, and I shall introduce enough of Mexicans and Americans to give it variety. The thing I want most, in the way of help, from you, is this: I would like an account, written in as much detail as you remember of the time when you, dear Mr. Coronel, went to Temecula and marked off the boundaries of the Indians' land there. How many Indians were living there then? What crops had they? Had they a chapel? etc. Was Pablo Assis [Apis],[3] their chief, alive? I would like to know his whole history, life, death, and all, minutely. The Temecula ejectment will be one of the episodes in my story, and any and every detail in connection with it will be of value to me. I shall also use the "San Pasquale Pueblo History," and I have written to Father Ubach and to Mr. Morse, of San

Diego, for their reminiscences. You and they are the only persons to whom I have spoken of my purpose of writing the novel, and I do not wish anything said about it. I shall keep it a secret until the book is about done.

I hope very much that I can succeed in writing a story which will help to increase the interest already so much aroused at the East in the Indian question.

If you think of any romantic incidents, either Mexican or Indian, which you think would work in well into a story of Southern California life, please write them out for me. I wish I had had this plan in mind last year when I was in Los Angeles. I would have taken notes of many interesting things you told me. But it is only recently, since writing out for our report the full accounts of the different bands of Indians there, that I have felt that I dared undertake the writing of a long story.

I am going to New York in a few days, and shall be busily at work there all winter on my story. My address will be, "The Berkeley," corner Fifth Avenue and Ninth Street.

I hope you are all well, and enjoying the same sunshine as last year. Mr. Jackson is well, and would send his regards if he were at home.

Yours, always cordially,

Helen Jackson.

Printed in James, *Through Ramona's Country*, pp. 18–21; James, *Heroes of California*, pp. 367–70; and Lindley and Widney, *California of the South*, pp. 200–202.

    1. Michael Augustine Corrigan (1839–1902) was the third Catholic archbishop of New York.

    2. Junípero Serra (1713–84), a native of Majorca, became a Franciscan missionary in 1730 and emigrated to Mexico in 1749. President of the Baja California missions, he founded San Diego de Alcala in 1769 and eight other missions. HHJ's *Century* article was among the first to bring his story to national attention.

    3. Pablo Apis (d. 1853), later a prominent Temecula leader, was born at Guajome and raised at Mission San Luis Rey, where he was baptized on June 15, 1798. As representative of a group of Luiseño Indians, Apis was granted Little Temecula Rancho by Mexican authorities. However, in 1853 the U.S. Land Commission rejected his land claim.

TO THOMAS BAILEY ALDRICH

New York.

Nov. 24 — 1883

Dear Mr. Aldrich,

    I hate to "fess" — but I must — that I arrived here on Tuesday last, and instantaneously with utmost ignominy, "flopped" — Shade of Grant White[1] forgive me — but no other word expresses the thing you do, when in an hour, from being upright and strong, you became limp and flat— "flopped," with an attack of laryngitis, which has kept me in bed four days: and will keep me in the house a week: and what is worse, will rule my winter. I was foolish to stay in Colorado so long. It snowed: and I got bronchitis instantly: which was a bad beginning for the journey: so here I am setting out for my winter on the Atlantic Seaboard, in a very unseaworthy condition. This is why I am not coming to Boston now. It would be foolish. I must wait till April or May.

Another reason is that I am going to set to work immediately on a long story: and I do not want to break in on my work, till it is done. It will be three or four months hard work.— I want to ask you, confidentially, about its title. — Has anybody written a story called, "In the Name of the Law?" —The title is so good, it seems to me, it must have been used, I hope not. I want it. No other will suit my purpose. — My story is all planned; in fact, it is so thought out it is practically half written: it is chiefly Indian — but the scene is in Southern California, and the Mexican life will enter in largely. I hope it will be a telling book: — and will reach people who would not read my Century of Dishonor.

Do you remember, of course you do, Warners story of the Doe? — Do you think the story of two human beings, husband and wife, fleeing from place to place, to place, seeking a chance of life, and a home, and never finding it, could be told as simply and unsupportedly as that was, and be effective? — I think so. That is what I am going to try to do.

Do not speak of this. I shall tell no one but Warner and Gilder. I want to make sure of my title, however, and must ask about that.

I have just been luxuriating in the last no. of the Roman Singer.[2] How stupid of the world not to see what a rare sweet story it is. It is above heads. That is the trouble. E. P. Roe[3] hits 125,000 at first stroke. —

I read my own paper with fear and trembling: only one error however: but that, alas, stabbed me: for I knew it would not have been there, except that you felt sure I must have said it, and you did not therefore like to change the word. But how you must have wanted to!

Dear Mr. Aldrich, I haven't called a river "darling," these thirty years! Really I haven't.—

It was "daring."— Fancy how I felt when I read the sentence. To be seen, at fifty odd, bareheaded in the street, so to speak, — by which I mean, in plain print, — calling a river, a darling river![4] Do I not well to weep?

I am wondering what you thought of the Mormon paper:[5] — if you sent it back to Col. or if you sent the cheque instead, as I had asked. — I did not expect to come Eastward so soon when I wrote you. —

I send all that I may, to Mistress Aldrich, of my regard and my regret to still longer defer that visit. — Do you think she would care for a basket because it was Indian-made, though not fine nor beautiful? If so I will send her one, big enough to hold wood for your wood fire. —

Yours ever truly

Helen Jackson

ALS (MH, Aldrich Papers).

1. Richard Grant White (1821–85) wrote articles for the major periodicals, as well as novels and a twelve-volume edition of *The Works of William Shakespeare*.

2. "A Roman Singer" by F. Marion Crawford was serialized in the *Atlantic Monthly* (July–Dec. 1883).

3. An army chaplain during the Civil War, Edward Payson Roe (1838–88) became pastor of a Presbyterian church in New York in 1865. To raise money he lectured on various Civil War topics and established a writing career. Because of poor health, he resigned from his parish and turned to writing full time.

4. A reference to her article "O-B-Joyful Creek and Poverty Gulch," *Atlantic Monthly* 52 (Dec. 1883): 753–62. On p. 762 the creek was described as "darling."

5. A reference to "Women of the Beehive," which was eventually published in *Century Magazine* 28 (May 1884): 114–22.

TO HIRAM PRICE

New York.

Nov. 25. 1883

The Berkeley.

Hon. H. Price

Com. of Ind. Affairs.

Dear Sir,

I have been prevented by illness from sooner replying to your letter of the 19th.[1] — (Letter L. Case 31.) —

In regard to the reservations laid off in San Diego Co. Cal., I used the expression "laid off by guess," deliberately.[2]

The Surveyor who laid them off, a man named Wheeler,[3] is now in the Surveyor General's Office, San Francisco. It was he who showed to me the plats of the reservations; and he said that he himself laid them off by a map in San Diego County "as near as he could guess," to the tracts in which the Indian villages were.

The Agent or Inspector under whom Wheeler was working was a clergy-man. I think his name was Dryden:[4] but of this I am not sure.

On these plats, now in Wheeler's possession, — (or at any rate showed by him to me, last May, in the Surveyor General's Office at San Francisco, —) are marked, as I said, additional lines in color, showing what tracts should be added to the Reservation.

Mr. Wheeler told me, that he marked these lines, and recommended to the Agent that the additional tracts be asked for.

Except by means of these plats, and their additional lines I know of no way in which the Office can possibly gain any information in regard to the tracts which should be added to the present Reservation.

But whether these plats, and these additional lines are correct or not, I had no means of judging: and my opinion is that the only safe sure way of getting the desired information is by new surveys in every instance.

Yours truly
Helen Jackson

ALS (LR #21830—1883, SC 31, OIA, RG 75, NA).

1. For Price to HHJ, Nov. 19, 1883, see CoCC, HHJ I, box 2, fd. 5.

2. In "Report," p. 464, HHJ wrote; "All the reservations made in 1876—and that comprises nearly all now existing—were laid off by guess, by the surveyor in San Diego, on an imperfect county map."

3. In 1875 the Interior Department contracted with M. G. Wheeler, U.S. deputy surveyor, to survey the San Jacinto Mountains.

4. The Reverend D. A. Dryden was appointed as a special agent on Mar. 31, 1875, and was present during the 1875 Temecula eviction.

TO HIRAM PRICE

New York
Nov. 25, 1883
The Berkeley
Corner 5*th* Av. & 9th St.

Hon. H. Price
Com. Ind. Affairs
Dear Sir,

I wish to add a private and confidential supplement to my letter, this day sent, replying to the Office letter of the 19*th* inquiring of me in regard to the San Diego Co. reservations. (Letter L. Case 31.)

I was not favorably impressed by the surveyor Wheeler.

I said to him,

"How did you get at these boundaries of these reservations you laid off?"

"Well, I guessed at them, as near as I could."

"How did you know anything about the situation of all these Indian villages?"

"I had lived a good many years in San Diego Co. and knew in a general way where they were."

"Why did you not make surveys first, so as to be sure they were right, before having the lands set off?"

"That was just what I said to him.— (Dryden I think.)— but he was in a great hurry and said we'd get them set off anyhow, and then if they were not right we could get them altered."

I owe it to Mr. Wheeler, to state that Mr. Kinney was inclined to believe him to have been fair and right meaning in the transactions.

I do not. — If all these reservations had been laid off by "guess", I believe there would have been at least one, which would have happened right for the Indians and wrong for the whites! Whereas, as it is, I think it is hardly an exaggeration to say, that if they had been laid off with a view, 1stly. — to avoid giving the Indians good lands, 2dly. to leave the Indians outside bounds so that they would be at every body's mercy, they could not possibly have been better chosen and placed.

Moreover, at the time of the laying off of the Capitan Grande Reservation, both Wheeler and the Clergyman Agent, were staying in the house of Dr. Strong: the man who stole the best part of the Capitan Grande lands from the Indians, by first renting it, and then refusing to move off. See Exhibit I in my Report — and affidavit of Father Ubach.[1]

The Captain of the Capitan Grande Indians told us of his having had an interview with the Surveyor and Agent in Dr. Strong's house, and imploring them not to run their reservation lines up on the bare stony mountain.

New surveys, in charge of a clear headed, just minded man, one so strongly in sympathy with the Indians cause that he cannot be either bribed or hood-winked by the San Diego Co. settlers — are the only way by which these reservations can ever be straightened out.

Should such a survey be ordered, I would most earnestly request that it be done under the supervision of the Mr. Rust, whose appointment in Lawson's place, Mr. Kinney and I so strongly urged. He and Mr. Kinney are the only two men I know in all Southern California that I would trust absolutely in all matters affecting Indian interests. I am sure that Mr. Rust, from his passion for Indian archaeology, as well as interest in the Indians' welfare would be glad to assume charge of the survey, and accompany the Surveyor. I am not, of course authorized to speak for him, in any way, but my impression is that he would be glad to do this, simply for his expenses. I shall never cease to regret that he was not appointed Agent. It is not once in a million times that a man of his means, education, and standing could be found willing to accept the position of Indian Agent. I trust his name will not have escaped your mind, in case the place should become vacant again. He has bought a place in the San Gabriel Valley, and established himself there, for a permanent home for his family; and has already made some interesting archaeological discoveries in the region.

May I recal[l] to your mind, now the case of Miss Sheriff, the teacher in the San Jacinto Valley, at Saboba, whose salary was reduced $100. —

In a letter some time ago, received from you, you said that the case of Miss Sheriff would be made the subject of a special communication to me. But I have not yet received any letter in regard to it.

I feel exceedingly anxious in regard to the matter. As I wrote to you, her expenses there are necessarily great — as she is obliged not only to board, at a dear rate, but to hire a horse and buggy every day to drive five miles to her school. There is no place where she can possibly live, any nearer. The place where she does live is sadly unlike what she ought to have in way of food, and comfort. It was a marvel to me that she could endure it.

Her resignation would be an irreparable loss to the Indians. She is in many respects superior to all the other teachers in San Diego Co. — But I think she will be obliged to resign if the salary is not restored to its former figure.

I thank you for the copies received of my Report and I am greatly gratified and surprised that it was printed with so few typographical errors. — I will send to you before long, a list of 100 names to which I would be glad to have the office mail them as you kindly suggest. The remaining 75 I will mail myself —from here: but I think I shall delay doing that until such time as the Bill which you frame for the Mission Indians, is likely to come up in Congress. I want to place the Reports so as to result in newspaper mention which may reach Congress.

If you will kindly give me information which will enable me to do this, I think I can command some influence.

Yours truly
Helen Jackson.

ALS (LR #22018—1883, SC 31, OIA, RG 75, NA).
1. "Report," pp. 496–500; see HHJ to Price, May 5, 1883, note 1, above.

TO MARY ELIZABETH (SHERIFF) FOWLER

New York
Dec 1. 1883

My dear Miss Sheriff

I have written twice to Mr. Price about your salary, — but have received no answer, beyond the statement in one letter on another subject that the "case of Miss Sheriff would be made the subject of a special communication to me." As that special communication did not come, I wrote again two weeks ago, but cannot get an answer.

I still hope it will be all right, I made so strong a presentation of the facts in the case.

I had a letter from Mrs. Ticknor two weeks since, saying she must resign at end of the quarter. — I shall ask Mr. Price to give her a vacation. Her loss to those Cahuillas would be irreparable. I honestly do not believe there is one woman in a million that could endure life in that Cahuilla village. You haven't the least conception of it. It is lonely enough where you are — but it is a metropolis compared with that Cahuilla wilderness. Ten miles from a white person! — and such white persons at that. — If Mrs. Ticknor has to go, I do not believe any other woman can be found to take the place. I don't wonder Mrs. Ticknor is worn out.

Dear Miss Sheriff, I want you to do something for me. —

Get Will Webster[1] to tell you all about the jury in which he served after the killing of Juan Diego by Sam Temple[2] last Spring. — You can bring up the subject, in connection with my Report — Will will see that he is the young ranchman referred to. — I want to weave the incident into a story — and for that purpose I want to know all about the jury — & its proceedings —the Judge &c. — How do they get a jury together in those remote places —? Where did they meet — What did the Judge say? What did Sam Temple say? Was he sworn in presence of the Jury? — Was he kept prisoner — how long — where —

— What evidence did the Jury have *except* Sam Temples? — How many men on Jury?

Any & every detail you can get will be of value.

You will see Messrs. Brunson & Wells name in the Report — I hope the new Agent is a better man than Lawson — Brunson & Wells are appointed by the Atty. Genl. — to attend to all questions affecting Indians rights to lands. Tell the Captain this. — Goodbye —

Yours always affly—

Helen Jackson

The Berkeley, Corner 5th Av. & 9th St.

ALS (CSmH, HHJ MSS, HM 14214).
1. William B. Webster (1857–91) served on the coroner's jury impaneled to examine the case. Because the Indians had removed the body, the jury never reached a

verdict. Sam Temple then had a hearing before Justice Tripp, who ruled the shooting justifiable homicide.

2. Juan Diego, a Cahuilla Indian, was murdered by Sam Temple on Mar. 24, 1883, for stealing a horse. HHJ fictionalized this event in her novel *Ramona* in depicting the death of Alessandro, Ramona's husband.

Temple (ca. 1840–ca. 1909) arrived in the San Jacinto area around 1876 and worked as a teamster hauling timber. The killing of Juan Diego was not his only act of violence. The year before he had attacked a group of Chinese railroad workers with a pick handle; in May 1885 he was involved in a shootout, and two years later he was convicted of battery. See Brigandi and Robinson, "The Killing of Juan Diego: From Murder to Mythology."

TO THOMAS BAILEY ALDRICH

New York.
The Berkeley
Tues. Eve.
Dec. 4 1883

Dear Mr. Aldrich,

Is it really so bad as that? "The most difficult that come!" —

If you did but know how I have tried the last year to make them better. I have a hope you will find the Mormon paper legible.

I know what I have missed & am missing, in not being in Boston just now. — The lunches I could forego — & the receptions: they are high on my list of the abhored. But the "Dinners — plays — & readings" — and especially the "Heaven Knows What." — All those I sigh over. —

But I have got this "concern" as the Quakers say, on my mind of my story: — and I am almost foolish enough to feel that I hold my own body, in trust as it were, till I have got the book done. — I shall not be outside the door after four o'clock — nor outside my bed, after ten, till it is done. —

I find that it is all so predestined in my mind that nothing remains but the writing down — and I am writing 1000 to 1500 words a day, which, for me, is about miraculous. — If you find out that "In the Name of the Law" has been used, my heart will be broken — Mr. Warner says, — not — I hope he is right. —

In face of your piteous tale of the sixty unread Mss. how can I urge you to read mine! And yet I do exceedingly want it here if you are not going to use it — and as for the money, I have spent it already!

Yours ever truly
Helen Jackson.

P.S. You will like to see what a Gunnison Editor thinks of my last paper:[1] — he copies it entire — I'll never dare to go to Crested Butte again. I didn't suppose they "took" the Atlantic South or west of Pueblo, in Colorado. —

ALS (MH, Aldrich Papers).
1. A reference to HHJ's article "O-Be-Joyful Creek and Poverty Gulch."

TO WILLIAM HAYES WARD

[January 1, 1884]

Dear Mr. Ward,

Thanks for the cheque — & the papers. — Can you send me the "Justifiable Homicide in S. Cal."[1] I have no copy of that.—

A happy New Year to you & many of them.

I hope you will find time to come up & see me. —

I take lunch always at half past one — and would be delighted to have you lunch with me, any day: — Let me know the day before hand. —

I am sure you will be interested to know that I am at work on a story — which I hope will do something for the Indian cause: it is laid in So. California — and there is so much Mexican life in it, that I hope to get people so interested in it, before they suspect anything Indian, that they will keep on. — If I can do one hundredth part for the Indians that Mrs. Stowe did for the Negro, I will be thankful. — I have been considering it, and planning it for two years nearly — so there now remains little but the writing out: — and I hope to have it done next month. — I would like to consult you about the title. — "*In the Name of the Law*" — It is so good a title that I feel as if it must have been used before — but the literary friends I have consulted say, not. Have you ever heard of a story by that title?

Yours ever truly
Helen Jackson

The Berkeley
Jan. 1*st* 1884

ALS (CSmH, HHJ MSS, HM 14197).
1. HHJ's prose piece on the death of Juan Diego appeared in the *Independent* (Sept. 27, 1883) : 1–2.

TO HIRAM PRICE

[January 16, 1884]
Hon. H. Price

Dear Sir,

I have accepted your kind offer to mail for me, a number of the Reports on the Mission Indians; and forward herewith — a list of nearly 200 addresses to which I would like to have it sent.[1] —

If it is possible, I would like to know beforehand when the bill for the Mission Indians is likely to come up — that I may just at that time, give copies of my Report to newspapers here & elsewhere, — so as to get some paragraphs or articles written which may help the bill. —

I am sorry to see by your Report that you do not favor the purchase of lands for those Indians. I feel sure that if you had gone over the ground you would do so. —

Setting aside all question of the bands now living in villages on patented grants, there are hundreds of others for whom there is no prospect but starvation, in the comparatively near future, unless the Govt. steps in to give them some spot from which the whites cannot drive them.

If there is any way in which I can serve you, in regard to the framing of this Bill, I need not say that it will give me great pleasure to do so.

Yours truly
Helen Jackson

New York.
The Berkeley
Corner 5*th* Av. & 9th Sts.
Jan. 16 1884.

ALS (LR #1285—1884, SC 31, OIA, RG 75, NA).
1. The list included members of the WNIA and ministers, judges, newspaper editors, and friends, many of whom HHJ met during her Mission Indian tours.

TO MARY ELIZABETH (SHERIFF) FOWLER

New York
The Berkeley.
Corner 5*th* Av. & 9th St.
Jan. 20. 1884

Dear Miss Sheriff —

Your letter was exactly what I wanted — not a detail too much. —

I would also be glad of just such an account from Will Webster — if you could get it out of him. Are you still boarding there? —

I shall wait with the greatest interest the developments in the case of the Saboba village.

I believe that Brunson & Wells will do all that can be done to win the case for them.

I hope you are very well.

Remember me to the Websters — also to Mrs. Jordan when you see her. —

Could you not write out for me a full description of that "Feast for the Dead?" — I have no idea what it is. —

Remember me to the Captain — & to all the children. —

Tell Captain, that very many people in all the cities are thinking and talking about the Indians and wish to help them — and that though it takes a long time in a great country like this, to get any thing done, — and perhaps even he himself may not live to see things much better, yet his children will, — I saw an account yesterday of thirty five Indian children being brought to be put in school at Milwaukee. All the cities now have organized branch societies of the Indians Rights Association[1] — The work is progressing. —

Yours always cordially
Helen Jackson

ALS (CSmH, HHJ MSS, HM 14215).

1. The Indian Rights Association (IRA) was founded in Philadelphia in Dec. 1882 by Herbert Welsh and Henry S. Pancoast following their visit to the Great Sioux Reservation in Dakota the previous summer. Welsh's uncle, William Welsh, was the first chairman of the Board of Indian Commissioners. The association, with Herbert Welsh as executive secretary, established branches in major cities, sponsored investigative tours to reservations, undertook an extensive publication program, and maintained a full-time lobbyist in Washington, D.C. See Hagan, *The Indian Rights Association: The Herbert Welsh Years, 1882–1904.*

TO HIRAM PRICE

[ca. January 20, 1884][1]
New York
The Berkeley.
Corner 5th Av. & 9th St.

Hon. H. Price
Dear Sir,

A letter from Richard Eagan [Egan][2] Esq. of San Juan Capistrano, — a good friend of the Pachanga Indians, says,

"By an executive order dated June 27, 1882, certain lands in Tp. 8. S. 2 W. S. B. M. Cal. were set apart for the use of the Temecula Indians. They have several times since then, applied to the agent at San Bernardino, to have the boundaries of their lands defined — (for the reason that they are constantly troubled by trespassers) — but without success.

About 500 acres of this land specified in the order, in Secs 27 & 28 had already been disposed of to settlers.

The Capt. came to see me today, and stated that the Indians very much desire that a competent person be authorized to go there and show them the lands they are entitled to occupy. Can you not do something to assist them in this matter?" xx — .

These are the Indians described in My Report, in Exhibit *M*.[3] —

They were persuaded by Lawson to abandon their plan of getting their lands under the Indian Homestead Act, and to have them set off as a reservation instead. He promised them they should each have individual titles, if they would do this.

What his motive could have been, I am at loss to imagine.

I wrote to Mr. Eagan that, except under appropriation from Congress the Dept. could not — as I understood it, — order any such surveys: — and that a general appropriation would be asked for this winter.

He replies

"I have written to the Indians, advising them it will be necessary to await the action of Congress, in the matter, but it seems strange that the Dept. is so powerless in a little matter like the one referred to, as the cost of having a competent person survey and define the boundaries of the reservation should not exceed $50. — Were it not for the time necessarily consumed in going and coming I would have gone and set the boundary stakes some time ago, free of all charge to the Indians."

Have you no contingent fund, from which this could be done? I am sure these Pachanga Indians are in especial danger of being trepassed on. — They have made this little valley an oasis of cultivation — and the land is now made much more desirable by the opening of the San Diego Railroad, which has a station within six miles of their village.

If Mr. Eagan can be empowered to have this survey made, I will guarantee his good faith.

Yours truly
Helen Jackson

ALS (LR #1558—1884, SC 31, OIA, RG 75, NA).
1. Although undated, this letter, received on Jan. 23, 1884, was probably written about Jan. 20.
2. Richard Egan (1842–1923), a native of Ireland, came to San Juan Capistrano in 1868. He served as justice of the peace, ca. 1870–90, and was a Los Angeles County supervisor, 1880–84. In 1902 he assisted Charles F. Lummis and the Warner Ranch Commission in selecting a reservation site at Pala for the Indians of Warner's Ranch who were evicted on orders of the U.S. Supreme Court.
3. "Report," pp. 504–6, included a brief history of the Pachanga Indians with a short statement from the *San Diego Union* of Sept. 23, 1875, commenting on the ejectment proceedings against them.

TO ABBOT KINNEY

[January 17, 1884–February 2, 1884]

Dear Co.

. . . .

Feby. 2. Whether from the horrible weather, or from overwork I don't know, I collapsed for a week, and had an ugly sore throat and did no work. Now I am all right again and back at my table, but shall go slower. I am leading a life as quiet as if I were at Mrs. Kimball's — I go nowhere — am never out after 5 P.M. I am resolved to run no risks whatever till after I get this story done. I hope it is good. It is over one third done. Am pretty sure the 1st of March will see it done. Then I will play.

The weather has been horrible — snow after snow, after snow; raw and cloudy days, — I have sighed for Southern California.

But in the house I have been comfortable — have not once seen the mercury below 60 in my rooms. The apartment is sunny and light — 6th floor — east windows — all my "traps" as Mr. Jackson calls them came in well, and the room looks as if I had lived in it all my life.

Now, for yourself — What have you done? How are you running your home? — Who is at the Villa? Is Mrs. Carr well? My regards to her. Don't you wish you had carried home a wife? I am exceedingly disappointed that you didn't.

Miss Sheriff writes me that a suit is brought for the ejectment of the Saboba Indians. Let me know if you have heard of it — what Brunson & Wells says. I wrote to Wells a long time ago asking for information about the suit by which the Temecula Indians were ejected — but he has not replied.

What do you hear of the new agent?

I got Miss Sheriff's salary restored to old figure.

Abbot Kinney and Jackson were appointed as special Indian agents. (Pasadena Historical Museum)

I have just sent a list of 200 names to Com. Price to mail our report to. Of course you had copies. I feel well satisfied with it. Do not you? I wish they'd send us again somewhere. They never will. I've had my last trip as a "junketing Female Commissioner."

Do write soon; — and answer all my questions — and don't wait for me to reply, but write again. I am writing from 1,000 to 2,000 words a day on the story and letters are impossible, except to Mr. Jackson. Whether I write or not you know I am always the same affectionate old General.

Yours ever,

H.J.

Printed in James, *Through Ramona's Country*, pp. 329–30; and in Davis and Alderson, *The True Story of "Ramona,"* pp. 221–22. HHJ started this letter on Jan. 14 and finished it on Feb. 2. Additional omissions have been made from the original typescript.

TO AN INTIMATE FRIEND[1]

The Berkeley, *February* 5, 1884.

. . . I am glad you say you are rejoiced that I am writing a story. But about the not hurrying it — I want to tell you something. You know I have for three or four years longed to write a story that should "tell" on the Indian question. But I knew I could not do it; knew I had no background, — no local color for it.

Last spring, in Southern California, I began to feel that I had; that the scene laid there — and the old Mexican life mixed in with just enough Indian to enable me to tell what had happened to them — would be the very perfection of coloring. You know that I had lived six months in Southern California.

Still I did not see my way clear; got no plot; till one morning late last October, before I was wide awake, the whole plot flashed into my mind, — not a vague one — the whole story just as it stands to-day, — in less than five minutes, as if some one spoke it. I sprang up, went to my husband's room, and told him; I was half frightened. From that time, till I came here, it haunted me, becoming more and more vivid. I was impatient to get at it. I wrote the first word of it December 1. As soon as I began, it seemed impossible to write fast enough. In spite of myself, I write faster than I would write a letter. I write two thousand to three thousand words in a morning, and I *cannot* help it. It racks me like a struggle with an outside power. I cannot help being superstitious about it. I have never done *half* the amount of work in the same time. Ordinarily it would be a simple impossibility. Twice, since beginning it, I have broken down utterly for a week — with a cold ostensibly, but with great nervous prostration added. What I have to endure in holding myself away from it, afternoons, on the days I am compelled to be in the house, no words can tell.

It is like keeping away from a lover, whose hand I can reach.

Now you will ask what sort of English it is I write at this lightning speed. So far as I can tell, the best I ever wrote! I have read it aloud as I have gone on, to one friend, of keen literary perceptions and judgment, the most purely intellectual woman I know — Mrs. Trimble.[2] She says it is smooth — strong — clear. "Tremendous" is her frequent epithet.

. . . The success of it — if it succeeds — will be that I do not even suggest any Indian history, — till the interest is so aroused in the heroine — and hero — that people will not lay the book down. There is but one Indian in the story.

Every now and then I force myself to stop, and write a short story or a bit of verse; I can't bear the strain; but the instant I open the pages of the other, I write as I am writing now — as fast as I could copy! What do you think? Am I possessed of a demon? Is it a freak of mental disturbance? or what.

I have the feeling that if I could only read it to you, you would know. — If it is as good as Mrs. Trimble, Mr. Jackson, and Miss Woolsey think, I shall be indeed rewarded, for it will "tell." But I can't believe it is. I am uneasy about it; but try as I may — all I can —I cannot write slowly for more than a few moments. I sit down at 9.30 or ten, and it is one before I know it. In good weather I then go out, after lunching, and keep out, religiously, till five, — but there have not been more than three out of eight good days all winter, — and the days when I am shut up in my room from two till five alone — with my Ramona and Alessandro — and cannot go along with them on their journey are maddening.

Fifty-two last October — and I'm not a bit steadier-headed, you see, than ever?

I don't know whether to send this or burn it up. Don't laugh at me whatever you do.

Yours always,
H.J.

Printed in The Contributors' Club, *Atlantic Monthly* 86 (Nov. 1900): 713–14, as "How Ramona Was Written."

1. Banning, *Helen Hunt Jackson*, pp. 202–3, claims that HHJ wrote this letter to Higginson; and Odell, *Helen Hunt Jackson*, p. 211, also hints that he might be the recipient.

2. HHJ may have met Mrs. Mary Trimble, a New York Quaker, in California in the summer of 1882. The following Dec. she stayed with Mrs. Trimble in New York for several days.

TO EPHRAIM W. MORSE

New York.
The Berkeley
Corner 5th Av. & 9th St.
Feb. 7, 1884

Dear Mr. Morse,

Many thanks for your letter of June 22d. — The dates you give will enable me to get from San Francisco, the full report of the case.

Now there is one other matter I would like to know about in details: and Sheriff Hunsacker can give them to you: it is the case of the San Luis Rey Indians against Maj. Coutts to remove some sheep he had seized.

Mr. Hunsacker spoke to me of it, when I was in San Diego, but not seeing any practical use to be made of the facts, I took no detailed notes of the conversation. Now however I would like a full Report of the case. If any expense is involved in getting it, I will gladly pay it.

It makes me envious even to write the word San Diego, & think what sunny weather you are no doubt enjoying: The weather has been incredibly bad for two months: a succession of snow storms, ie. slush, mud: and sun only every third or fourth day.

With regards to Mrs. Morse & Mrs. Whipple, & many thanks for your trouble in looking up these matters for me.

I am, always cordially yours
Helen Jackson

ALS (CSf, Phelan Collection).

TO ANTONIO F. AND MARIANA CORONEL

New York, *February* 13, 1884.

Dear Mr. and Mrs. Coronel:

I am glad you gave me my choice of the pictures; for the two I have taken I like, and the other two I think very bad. Mr. Sandham can have them. I have taken the two which show the side-view of your faces.

I hope you are having better weather in Los Angeles than we have here. For three weeks we have scarcely seen the sun. Snows, rain, fogs, sleet, ice, have been our daily diet. It is far the worse winter I ever saw.

Mr. Jackson returned to Colorado last month. I look for him here again in March.

I am still at work on my story [*Ramona*]. It is more than half done.

I wish you would ask those Indian women, who made the lace for me, what would be in their Pala or San Luis Rey dialect, the words for *blue-eyes*. I want to have a little child called by that name in my story—if the Indian name is not too harsh to the ear. I often wish myself in Los Angeles, I assure you, in this horrible weather. Did you receive the copy of our report on the Mission Indians? I ordered it sent to you.

With many thanks for the pictures, and warm remembrances to you both and to Miss Mercedes,

I am always, yours truly,
Helen Jackson.

Printed in Lindley and Widney, *California of the South*, p. 203.

TO ABBOT KINNEY

[February 20, 1884]

Dear Co:

Your first letter made me wretched. If we had "been and gone" and got a rascally firm set over those Indian matters I thought we might better never have been born.

But your second reassures me.

I sent you one of the reports. You can get all you want, I think, by writing to Commissioner Price. I sent him a long list of names to mail it to. They said I could have all I wanted. Of course you can too. There is a bill of some sort, prepared and before Congress.[1] I have written to Teller asking for it, or sum and substance. He does not reply. None of them care for anything now, except the election.

. . . .

I am working away at the story — twenty chapters done. I'd like to consult you. Do you think it will do any harm to depart from the chronological sequence of events in my story?

For dramatic purposes I have put the Temecula ejectment *before* the first troubles in San Pasquale.

Will anybody be idiot enough to make a point of that? I am not writing history. I hope the story is good.

. . . .

I hope you are well and jolly. I'm awfully sorry you are not married. Good night. Always

Affectionately yours,

General.

. . . .

Printed in James, *Through Ramona's Country*, pp. 336–37; Davis and Alderson, *The True Story of "Ramona,"* pp. 223–24. Additional omissions not relevant to the Indians have been made.

1. On Jan. 10, 1884, the draft of a bill and a printed copy of "Report" were submitted by Commissioner Price to Secretary Teller, who sent them on to President Chester A. Arthur. On Jan. 14 the bill was submitted to Congress; it passed the Senate on July 3, 1884, but failed in the House.

TO HIRAM PRICE

New York.
The Berkeley
Corner 5*th* Av. & 9th St.
Feb 27. 1884

Hon. H. Price
Dear Sir,

I sent to the Ind. Bureau some weeks ago, a list of between 100 & 200 names of persons — to whom, — according to your kind suggestion — I would be glad to have our Report on the Mission Indians sent.

I have heard lately from two or three persons whose names I felt sure must have been on the list, that they had not received the Report.

Can you tell me, whether those lists were received, and the Reports sent?

And can you kindly send me, here, 50 copies more? I am continually asked for a copy, still, & I have only two left.

I learned by the last letter I received from the Dept. that a bill has been framed for the relief of the Mission Indians. If I could be informed when it is likely to come up, I could secure some valuable editorials bearing on it.

Can you send me a copy of it? or a resumé of its chief features to use in these Editorials?

Yours truly
Helen Jackson.

ALS (LR #4038—1884, SC 31, OIA, RG 75, NA).

TO THOMAS BAILEY ALDRICH

[March 10, 1884]

Dear Mr. Aldrich,

· ·

Since the 1st day of December, I have written, I suppose, over 200 letters — and 150,000 — or 160,000 words in my story — not to be called after all, "In the Name of the Law", but "Ramona." — I grudge giving up the other title: but I am advised strongly that it will be a mistake; — will "show my hand," so to speak — The story is done — I finished it last night, at 11 P.M. — the first time in my whole life, that I ever wrote anything more than a letter, in the evening: — but I could not leave off within ten pages of the end. —

I am in great doubt whether to print it first as a serial in the Century or Harpers; or bring it out as a book: — if it hits well as a serial, I strike my best blow, so: if not, I have thrown my weapon away. — Some day I shall write a long story without a purpose. — not a weapon, — and then I shall hope most earnestly that you will like it well enough to print it in the Atlantic. — but this one, is not *for myself.*

Yours always, — & gratefully this time,
Helen Jackson

The Berkeley
March 10. 1884.
P.S. — "The Women of the Bee Hive" will appear in the May Century. —

ALS (MH, Aldrich Papers). A section of this letter not related to Indians has been omitted.

TO AMELIA STONE QUINTON

New York
The Berkeley
April 2*d* — 1884

Dear Mrs. Quinton —

My story is done — 170,000 (or more) words. — It is called "*Ramona.*" —

It is to run as a serial in the Christian Union, beginning the 1*st* of May. It will take six months. —

— I am going to strike for the churches this time. I do not dare to think I have written a second Uncle Tom's Cabin — but I do think I have written a story which will be a good stroke for the Indian cause. —

Now the thing I want of you is, to please send me your list of *Secs.* & *Pres.s* of your branch associations: —

— The Christian Union will then send to them, mailed copies of the paper containing the advertisement of the beginning of this story — & I hope they will all subscribe to the paper for 6 mos. as a campaign doc. —

— The paper has paid me (for them!) — a large price for the story — a good deal less than half what I should have had for it in the Mags, — however — but I preferred this — 1*st* because the Mags. could not begin it for a year & a half — 2*d* to hit the religious element — 3*rd* to have only a weeks interval between the numbers. — I believe 100,000 readers of this sort will do more for the cause, than four times that number of idle magazine readers. — In the autumn I shall publish it in book form. —

Of course the paper is doing this to push the paper — not to help the Indian! — but each will react on the other — So I want to give them a good list. — I might take some off that list you sent me. I suppose — But I think the Branch Associations ought all to have the story to read as it comes out, — to read it at their monthly meetings: —

Is not this a good idea? —

Yrs ever —
H. J.

ALS (MA 4571, Pierpont Morgan Library, New York, New York; hereinafter NNPM).

TO WILLIAM H. RIDEING

[May 28, 1884]

Dear Mr. Rideing,

I had myself thought of that objection to the Underground R. R. story.[1] It would of course be offensive to a large proportion of your Southern audience.

So might the Indian story to some of your California and western readers.[2] Had you thought of that?

The old Quaker times, and the Colorado life, I can handle without fear of hurting anybody's feelings, and I think I will write both those stories this summer.

You will perhaps be surprised, however, when I say frankly in regard to the price you name, that it would not be equal to the rate at which I am elsewhere paid.

I have had, I suppose rather exceptional good fortune, in winning such recognition that the magazines & newspapers are willing to pay me very high prices for all the work I can do. I am never paid by the page, or by counted words: and the St. Nicholas,[3] for instance has just paid me $300 for a series of six little papers only about 1800 words long, & costing no labor whatever. The Century and Harpers pay me from $200 to $250 an article.

But two $250 articles in the Century would not cost me half the labor that I should be obliged to put into a story such as you require for the Companion.

You, as a trained & artistic literary worker can easily realize this. The short diversions, enforced separations & successions of incidents, the long list of "ruled-out" situations & incidents — altogether make up a series of conditions about impossible to fulfil, & requiring the carefullest labor. — Still, it is a pleasure to conquer difficulties, and sometimes, out of the very difficulties would come a greater success if they were triumphantly surmounted — &, as I frankly said to you, I would be very glad, for my own purposes as a writer, to gain the attention & liking of your great army of readers.

But I really ought not to do such a piece of work as one of these stories would be, under $500; and I should not care to undertake it, even for that sum, except for the advantage of getting a hold on your audience.

If you had asked me to set my own price, I should have said, for such a story, to be from 15000 to 18000 words long — (for it would be impossible to determine beforehand the exact length. A thousand words more or less might make or mar the whole thing, & I would never undertake to cut out a story pattern exact to a thousand words), — for such a story I should have said $600.

I hope this will not seem to you unreasonable. You must bear in mind that after all my work, & after the trimming, cutting & condensing my chapters as I should never dream of doing except to fit the Companion's measures, there will still remain the chance of your not taking the stories; in which case I shall have practically thrown away the three or four months work which put into my ordinary Mag. articles would have brought more money, besides being in better shape for publication in a volume.

But if you will pay $500 a story, in case they suit you, I will take all these risks, and will do my very utmost to make the stories as good as Mrs. Oliphants![4]

If I do, you will feel as strongly as I do that they are not dear at the price.

You know I have the strongest possible of motives for doing this: — the desire of a woman with a hobby, to gain for herself the widest audience possible.

I enclose to you a copy of my Report to the Int. Dept. on the Mission Indians. You can see from this, what materials I have for Indian stories; & whether you would be willing to run the risk of their being offensive to some white men!

I hope you & Mr. Ford[5] will find time to glance at my "Ramona" in the Christian Union.

Yours truly
Helen Jackson.

The Berkeley
May 28, 1884.

ALS (Helen Hunt Jackson Papers, Jones Library, Amherst, Massachusetts; hereinafter MAJ). Although this particular letter has little to do with HHJ's Indian crusade, it is included to give the reader a sense of the money that she commanded for her work.

William Henry Rideing (1853–1918) moved from his native England to Springfield, Massachusetts, becoming private secretary to Samuel Bowles of the *Springfield Republican*. Rideing later worked for Whitelaw Reid at the Tribune before joining the editorial staff of the *Youth's Companion* in Boston in 1881.

1. The underground railroad was an informal network that aided fugitive slaves to reach safety in northern states or in Canada. As many as fifty thousand slaves were rescued between 1830 and 1860.

2. A reference to HHJ's short article on Susette La Flesche, entitled "An Indian Girl's Definition," *Youth's Companion* (Feb. 5, 1885): 52.

3. *St. Nicholas* was a children's magazine published from 1873 to 1943. Mary Mapes Dodge (1838–1903) not only served as its first editor, but chose the name for the magazine.

4. Scottish-born Margaret Oliphant (1828–97) was the author of over one hundred books, including novels, history, and biographies.

5. Daniel Sharp Ford (1822–99), a printer by trade, bought the *Youth's Companion* in 1857 with a partner. The partnership was soon dissolved, and Ford served as editor and business manager of his magazine.

TO JOSEPH BENSON GILDER

[June 28, 1884]

Dear Mr. Gilder

I think the Continent people have moved their office, & I do not know their new address.[1] Will you kindly address this note for me?

I hope you are all well and flourishing, spite of the heat. — Here we are luxuriating in floods of rain — severe on the railroad people: but a delicious innovation on the usual parched summer.

I save your paragraph about Ramona. Thank you. — Who is your "Lounger?"[2]

Is it yourself? If so ask him whether "reduced to paper" is a correct expression. He said Ramona had been reduced to paper in a wonderfully short time: ie: he meant to say that: what he really did say, was that I had been reduced to paper: but it was evident that he meant the other. —

Now, I have heard of paper being reduced to pulp — persons reduced to poverty — statements or ideas reduced to writing: —but reduced to paper, I never did before see. — How is it? —

My regards to that inaccessible sister of yours.[3] —

Ever truly
Helen Jackson

Colorado Springs
June 28, 1884.

ALS (NN, JB Gilder Papers).

1. Possibly a reference to the *Continental Monthly*.

2. "The Lounger" was a section in the *Critic*. HHJ is referring to "The Lounger," *Critic* n.s. 1, no. 22 (May 31, 1884): 259, which described *Ramona* as "a novel with a purpose—a very excellent purpose," as well as "an exceptional work." The comment that intrigued HHJ was the following: "It was written at the Berkeley in this city last winter, when Mrs. Jackson was confined to the house by bronchitis; and though reduced to paper with astonishing rapidity, was found to require little or no revision."

3. A reference to Jeannette Leonard Gilder, who founded the *Critic* with her brother, Joseph.

TO HENRY LAURENS DAWES

Colorado Springs
Aug. 27, 1884

Dear Mr. Dawes —

Thanks for your kind letter. — The accident was not so bad as the news-paper said[1] — (it was very vexing that it got into them at all: we thought we had succeeded in keeping it out) —

I had no internal injuries whatever, — nor a bruise or a strain, except the breaks in the left leg: a strange thing, considering that I fell from top to bottom of my stairs! — But the breaks were bad enough — three places, badly smashed, as well as snapped. — However, the leg is doing well, and the doctors says, will ultimately be as good as ever: — So I have every reason to be thankful.

I am glad to hear that you are going to California to look after the Indians there. I do not know anything about the Round Valley Indians:[2] but I am sure they cannot be in such desperate need, — or so deserving, — of Government help, as the Mission Indians.

— I do implore you not to overlook the latter. It has been the greatest dissapointment of my life that all my work in investigating their state, and making that Report, has accomplished nothing, only yesterday I had a letter from Los Angeles, bringing a message from one village of them, which nearly broke my heart. I could never again go to see them. I tried as much as possible, to explain to them the great uncertainty of my being able to get anything done: but they could not believe me. The fact of the Government having sent out a woman to see what they needed, gave them great hope. It is cruel, that nothing has been done, for them. The man whom we wanted appointed as their agent, would have at least protected them from the sort of trespass described in this letter.[3] I am sick at heart, and discouraged. I see nothing more I can do, or write. — This is wrong I suppose. The people who have accomplished good in this world, have been people who were never discouraged and never sick at heart! — I send you a copy of my Report on the Mission Indians — also letters of introduction to Mr. Kinney my fellow worker — and to an old Mexican gentleman in Los Angeles[4] who can tell you a great deal, and who is worth seeing on his own account. — It is from him that the letter came, enclosing the message, I quote to you. —

Why will you not come by way of Colorado? — It will take you no longer: and if you have never seen our glorious scenery, will repay you. — The journey from here, via Denver & Rio Grande R. R. to Ogden, where you connect with the Cent[ral] Pac[ific] — is the most wonderful I have ever taken, in any part of the world. — It would give me the greatest pleasure to see you in my own house — and by the middle of Sept. I am *promised* to be able to stand with one crutch! As that is more than I can now do, with *two*, unless somebody is near to steady me. I am not very sanguine about it. — But I can go everwhere in my wheeled chair, & am perfectly well: & I cannot tell you what pleasure it would give me, to have you visit us. —

With warm regards to your wife and daughter, believe me,

Always cordially yours

Helen Jackson.

over. —

I shall write to Mr. Coronel to go to see the lawyers Brunson & Wells, in Los Angeles who were appointed at our request U. S. Attys. to attend to just such questions as this. I wish very much you could see these lawyers & see if they are really accomplishing anything.

It is heart rending to think of these poor creatures journeying up to Los Angeles, to send me this bootless message —and now waiting and watching for the answer. I wish you could see the Rincon village — the best cultivated lands we found — ditches, corrals, horses, cattle — they are an industrious people. —

The explanation of the strange phrasing of Mr. Coronels letter is, that he dictates in Spanish to a niece who is not very familiar with English.

Mr. Coronel speaks but little English: but you will enjoy talking with him, through his wife's interpreting. —

Extract from Mr. Coronel's letter

"Today the Captain of the Rincon Rancheria, was here at my house, Jose Luis Albanes [Albañas],[5] accompanied by two other Captains. They told me that the despoliation of their lands, which they occupy continues the same, and the destruction of their animals. They tell me that they went to see the Indian Commissioner, and complained to him, and asked his protection and what lands they could have for pasture. The Commissioner answered that he did not have the power to arrange those business. He marked out some public land for them to pasture their animals, but these have been occupied by sheep, & other animals & the Indians are not permitted to use them. They tell me that all they wish is for the Government to mark them out a place where they can live & be quiet.

Having told you my Commission which I think has no remedy and is useless to occupy yourself with it, but as they begged me so much to write this to the Queen (for that is what they call you) that I have been obliged to trouble and distract you from your many attentions.

They will wait for your answer in regard to this particular, and think of it, as their only salvation, or final sentence, as they wish to undeceive themselves, so as not to suffer so much vexations, and resign themselves to die in misery. I agreed with them that what you would answer, I should forward it to Father Ubach so as he could inform them of the result."

ALS (DLC, Dawes Papers).

1. On June 28, 1884, HHJ fell down her stairs and severely broke her leg.

2. The Round Valley Reservation, first established in 1856, was home to the Concow, Yuki, Pitt River, Potter Valley, Little Lake, and Redwood bands. Continual white encroachment and a worsening of the Indians' living conditions prompted Congress in 1884 to authorize an inspection of the reservation by a special Senate committee. Massachusetts senator Henry L. Dawes, as a member of the committee, submitted his official report in Feb. 1885. Aware that outside reformers might ameliorate the condition of the Indians, he recommended to the WNIA that they undertake missionary work at Round Valley. Round Valley became the association's second missionary station.

3. A reference to Horatio Rust.

4. A reference to Antonio Coronel.

5. Possibly a reference to the father of José Albañas, a well-known ceremonial leader at Rincon who died in Aug. 1941.

TO ANTONIO F. AND MARIANA CORONEL

Colorado Springs,
September 4, 1884.

My Dear Friends:

I am sorry to tell you that the bad news you heard of me was true. On the 28th of June I fell from the top to the bottom of my stairs, and broke my left leg—a very bad break; the large bone crushed in for about two inches, and the small bone snapped short. When they found me the leg was doubled at right angles between the knee and ankle. Mr. Jackson thought when he saw it I would never walk again; but, on the contrary, I am going to have as good a leg as ever. A great triumph for a woman of my age and weight. I am on crutches now, and very bad work I make with them, I assure you. I am too heavy and too much afraid. But I have a wheeled chair, in which I can go all about the house, and on the veranda, and I have had an exceedingly comfortable and pleasant summer in spite of the broken leg, and by New-Year's the doctor thinks I will be walking well.

The message from the Rincon Indians made my heart ache. I shall send it to the Indian Commissioner at Washington; but, as you say, we can not hope for much result from it. The firm of Brunson & Wells, lawyers in Los Angeles, were appointed last year, by our request, as United States attorneys, to act in all cases relating to Indian lands. It is a long time since I have heard from them. When I last heard, they hoped to save the Saboba lands for those Indians. It might be well for you to see them, and lay the case of these Rincon Indians before them. Say to Mr. Wells that I asked you to do so. You know that

Helen Hunt Jackson. (Courtesy of Jones Library, Inc., Amherst, Mass.)

the time of the presidential election is now near, and at such times no man cares for anything but politics. If Blaine[1] and Logan[2] are elected, I shall fear a sad four years for the Indians. Logan is an Indian-hater. I do not know what the Democratic party would be on the Indian question. It could not be worse than the other, and it might be better. The only message you can give to those Indians from me, is that I have sent a copy of their message to Washington, and that is all I can do. That my heart aches for them, and has never ceased to ache since the day I was in their village. That many good people are interested for their race, and are trying to accomplish something for their help; but the men in power in the Government change so often, it is hard to get anything done. And Congress (the great Council) will not give the money we ask for. If they could once be made to understand that everything depends on Congress voting the money for their relief, they would realize more that the officers of the Government are powerless to keep their promises. There are Indians starving to-day in Montana, because Congress last winter cut down the appropriations which the Indian Commissioner asked for for the year. You see when that is done, the Secretary of the Interior and the Indian Commissioner are utterly helpless. They have no way of getting money except by Congress voting it. I sometimes wonder that the Lord does not rain fire and brimstone on this land, to punish us for our cruelty to these unfortunate Indians.

Another Commission is coming out to California this autumn to look after the Round Valley Indians. One member of it is Senator Dawes, who is a good friend to Indians. I have begged him to go down also into Southern California and see the Mission Indians. If he does, he will call on you. I have given him a letter to you. I never received the portraits of Father Junipero you speak of having sent me. Did you send them to this place, or to New York?

Mr. Jackson is very well, and would desire his remembrances to you both if he were at home. But he is in Denver at present. With many thanks for your letter, and warm regards to you both, also to your niece,

I am always, truly yours,

Helen Jackson.

Printed in Lindley and Widney, *California of the South*, pp. 205–6.

1. James Gillespie Blaine (1830–93), twice a presidential candidate, was secretary of state under both James A. Garfield and Benjamin Harrison.

2. The Republican vice-presidential candidate in the 1884 election, John Alexander Logan (1826–86), also served in the Senate.

TO ABBOT KINNEY

[September 28, 1884]

Dear Co:

. . . .

I am thinking of coming to So. California as soon as I can hobble! I must fly from here before November, but I do not feel quite up to shutting myself in for the winter as I must in New York. So I propose to run across to your snug seashore — for two or three months of sunshine and outdoors — before going to New York. Do you not think that wise?

I wrote to Mrs. W[hipple][1] in San Diego — the only place I know in all California where there was *real* comfort. Also I like the San Diego climate best. But I learned to my great disappointment that she had gone to Los Angeles. The N's[2] urge my coming to a new hotel in San Diego — but I have a mortal dread of California hotels. Do you know anything of it? — And do you know where Mrs. W[hipple]'s house in Los Angeles is? If it is on *high* ground? . . .

. . . I shall bring my Effie[3] with me — too helpless yet to travel alone. Goodness! What martyrdom crutches are! While I was stationary in bed it was fun in comparison with this. But I am a sinner to grumble, I shall walk with one crutch and one cane, next week, the doctor thinks, and that is great luck for such a bad compound fracture as mine; and at my age. My weight is also a sad hindrance. If I weighed only 125 or so they say I could walk with a cane now. Ultimately — they insist — my leg will be as good as ever, and *no* lameness. I shall believe it when I see it! . . .

I had a letter from Mrs. C——[4] the other day. Strange, that disorderly chaotic woman writes a precise methodical hand, clear as type, characterless in its precison; and I, who am a martinet of ardent system, write — well— as you see! What nonsense to say handwriting shows character.

I have ordered a copy of *The Hunter Cats of Connorloa*[5] sent to you. You will laugh to see yourself saddled with an orphan niece and nephew. I hope you won't dislike the story. I propose in the next to make you travel all through Southern California with 'Susy [Jusy] and Rea' — and tell the Indian story over again. I only hope that scalawag C——,[6] of Los Angeles, will come across the story, and see himself set forth in it. He will recognize the story of Fernando, the old Indian he turned out at San Gabriel.

As you recollect the situation of lands at Saboba was there good land enough in the neighborhood for those Indians to get homes? The Indian appropriation bill passed in July has a clause enabling Indians to take land under homestead laws, with no fees.

What are Brunson and Wells doing? Anything? — What is the state of the Saboba matter? But I suppose you can think of nothing save politics till next Dec.

Write soon. I want to know about Mrs. W[hipple]'s house — if it is high, sunny, airy, etc.

Yours always,

General.

Printed in James, *Through Ramona's Country*, pp. 338–40; and Davis and Alderson, *The True Story of "Ramona,"* pp. 225–27. The deletions were made by James.

1. Mrs. D. J. Whipple ran a boarding house in San Diego on 10th and G streets. She later established a boarding house at Sixth and Pearl streets in Los Angeles.

2. More than likely this should be the "M's," a reference to the Morses of San Diego.

3. In her will HHJ gave her maid, Effie McLeod, $100 for each year she had lived with her. See HHJ to Helen Banfield, May 20, 1885, CoCC, WSJ I, box 1, fd. 5.

4. Probably a reference to Jeanne C. (Smith) Carr.

5. *The Hunter Cats of Connorloa*, a children's book written by HHJ, was a portrayal of Abbot Kinney at his home at Kinneyloa with his seventeen trained cats, who hunted gophers. The children, Jusy and Rea, were fictitious, but the eviction of the old Indian from San Gabriel was an actual incident. The villain in *Hunter Cats* was an attorney with a big ranch at San Gabriel—probably based on Alfred Beck Chapman.

6. This is more than likely Alfred Beck Chapman (1829–1915), who came to California with the military in the 1850s, retired, and settled in Los Angeles in 1859. He practiced law and was the city attorney for Los Angeles in 1863 and the Los Angeles County district attorney in 1868. He owned a 700-acre ranch at San Gabriel, where he pioneered in growing citrus. In 1871 he founded the city of Orange.

TO CHARLES DUDLEY WARNER

[October 2, 1884]

Dear C. D. W. —

You ought to see me on crutches — I have four different gaits — totally unlike each other —

Do you think an exhibition would "draw"? —

Day before yesterday I went to drive for the first time. A new Heavens & a new earth! — It was about worth while to have been shut up these months to get the sensation. —

Nobody but a desperdoe [*sic*] like me, would have managed to get into the carriage. I did it as I go up & down stairs, sitting down! —

It's astonishing what way there is, when there's a will. — It was a spectacle though — carriage driven up on sidewalk close to my gate — I sitting down *flat*

on its floor, backwards, & hoisting my 170 pounds of body in by my hands —
dragging the LEG after me! —

Even my good Effie couldn't help laughing.

— Now I shall drive every day.—

The Dr. says if I weighed only 120 or so, I could walk with a cane now. I
myself feel as if I should *never* feel safe without crutches under my arms. I have
got to learn anew the walking motion. — But I am a monstrously lucky woman
to get a leg again at all. — & I do believe it is ultimately to be as good as ever.

Just as soon as I can step, I am going to take Effie, & flee to San Diego, —
for two or three months of out doors & sunshine, before venturing into the
Atlantic seaboard winter. — If only our malignant October snows will hold off
till I can get away, I will be grateful. —

Did you see that some paper the other day, said in reviewing the Mag.s
"again we have an autocrat!" — [marginal note: # meaning you!] That was true
— I always turn first to the Drawer¹ — This last no. was simply delicious. —
You recollect when you first took hold of it, you wrote to me severely one day.

"Did you think I was doing it for fame!" — But you will compel fame out
of it — That first page will come to be looked for a great deal more than the
Easy Chair² — which between you & me, seems to be growing more & more
perfunctory.

I suppose you are not reading Ramona, or I should have heard from you
about it. — It is winning good praise, I think & I hope it will stir people up —
The next thing I shall do, will be a child's story, on the Indian Question! —
educate a few thousand children if I can, to grow up ready to be just: I grew up
with my sole idea of the Indian derived from the accounts of Massacres. It was
one of my childish terrors that Indians would come in the night, & kill us! —

Has that paper you read me last winter been published? If so do send it to
me — & I hear you had a grand thing in the N[orth] A[merican] Review — I
sent to our shops for it but they hadn't it. You might send me that too.

— I have done little this summer — a few bits of verses — & a story or two
— but nothing of account. — When I get to San Diego, I shall sit down &
work. —

My love to Mrs. Warner. What do you mean by your new house? It is not
possible you have left that heavenly grove?

— By the middle of January I hope to be in the Berkeley again — and Mr.
Jackson with me. We look forward to renewing our acquaintance then. — I
think I have not had twelve hours solid talk with him, since July 1st — He is in
Denver all the time, except Sundays — & people over run him as soon as he
gets here. — Now, he is off on a grand inspection of the whole road, with a

company of foreigners — English, Scotch, Dutch, — representing the foreign Stock & bondholders. — He will be gone ten days or two weeks— — and as soon as may be, after his return, I shall set off for Cal. — I hope by the 25*th* at latest.

If I do not, I am in danger of being caught by bronchitis, & kept here for weeks.

What "Toil & trouble" is to live.

Yours always
H.J.

Colorado Springs
Oct. 2. 1884.

ALS (CtHT-W, Warner Collection). Although this letter has little to do with HHJ's Indian crusade, it has been included to show her indomitable spirit and the retention of her sense of humor as she coped with her severely broken leg.

    1. "The Drawer" was an outgrowth of Fletcher Harper's Monday dinners when stories went around the dinner table. Whenever he heard a good one, he asked the teller to write it down and put it in the drawer of his office desk. Once a month the stories were gathered by the editor and worked into the department.

    2. "The Easy Chair" was the editor's department of *Harper's Magazine*.

TO HENRY C. BOWEN

Col. Springs
Oct. 15, 1884

Dear Mr. Bowen,

I saw the other day — in a commercial letter from Chicago — that there was so much too much wheat on hand this fall, that it was a serious problem how to deal with it — & that the farmers would probably sustain a serious loss from this overstocking of the market. —

In the same paper was a paragraph giving an account of the starving Piegan Indians! — dying at the rate of one a day, literally of starvation.[1] — Indians on a reservation — under charge of an agent. The reason they are dying thus, is that Congress reduced the appropriation for the Indian Bureau, — and the Dept. was simply without money to buy necessary supplies. —

The terrible antithesis of these two statements — these two conditions existing side by side with each other, in our land, has haunted me ever since, and I have tried, in the enclosed poem,[2] to set it in a strong enough light to strike home to people's consciences. —

If your Editor likes to print the poem, do you not think he might well call attention to the facts on which it is based, — by a short editorial note? — I hope he will feel like doing this — & I would be glad to see the poem in print, as soon as possible — while the point is most forcibly to be made. —

—Will you kindly tell me who is acting as Editor now? —

Many thanks for your cheque & note.

Yours ever truly

Helen Jackson

ALS (ViU, HHJ [7080-b]).

1. The Piegans, along with the Blood and Northern Blackfeet, made up the Blackfeet confederacy, originally from the upper Missouri and Saskatchewan River area. By HHJ's time, a majority of the Blackfeet had settled in Canada while others lived on a small reservation in northeastern Montana.

2. The poem "Too Much Wheat" appeared on the front page of the *Independent* (Nov. 6, 1884). An editorial on page 19 described the poem as having "strength" and presented the reader with background information on the famine among the Piegans juxtaposed to the overproduction of wheat.

"TOO MUCH WHEAT."

BY Helen Jackson (H.H.)

"Too much wheat!" So the dealers say.
Millions of bushels left unsold
Of last year's crop; and now, to-day,
Ripe and heavy and yellow as gold,
This Summer's crop counts full and fair;
And murmurs, not thanks, are in the air,
And storehouse doors are locked, to wait;
And men are plotting, early and late.
"What shall save the farmers from loss,
If wheat too plenty makes wheat a dross?"
"Too much wheat!" Good God, what a word!
A blasphemy in our borders heard.

"Too much wheat!" And our hearts were stirred,
But yesterday, and our cheeks like flame.
For vengeance the Lord his loins doth gird,
When a nation reads such tale of shame.
Hundreds of men lie dying, dead,
Brothers of ours, though their skins are red;
Men we promised to teach and feed.

O, dastard Nation! dastard deed!
They starve like beasts in pens and fold,
While we hoard wheat to sell for gold.
"Too much wheat!" Men's lives are dross!
"How shall the farmers be saved from loss?"

"Too much wheat!" Do the figures lie?
What wondrous yields! Put the ledgers by!
"Too much wheat!"

O, Summer rain,
And sun, and sky, and wind from West,
Fall not, nor shine, nor blow again!
Let fields be desert, famine guest
Within our gates who hoard for gold
Millions of bushels of wheat unsold,
With men and women and children dead
And daily dying for lack of bread!
"Too much wheat!" Good God, what a word!
A blasphemy in our borders heard!

Colorado Springs, Col.

TO HENRY TELLER

Col. Springs,
Nov. 14, 1884.

Dear Mr. Teller:

I have received letters from So. California touching two matters which I think worth while to lay before you, hoping you may be able to do something in each case.

The first is relative to Mrs. Ticknor, who was teaching in the Cahuilla Valley when I was there. In our report Exhibit C, p. 19, you will find an account of her school.[1] It was incomparably the best school we saw. Her control of her scholars remarkable, and her influence over the adults great. She speaks Spanish, and had lived in the neighborhood of these Indians for several years, with her husband, at whose store they dealt. Hence they knew and trusted her, and she knew and trusted them; and when she became a widow she took the school. She has two children besides herself to support. She had been a teacher in Pennsylvania before her marriage. I heard only praise of her in the region; when I was there she was so worn out, I begged her to take a leave of absence. Unforunately, instead of doing that, she resigned. She writes:

"I felt sure of the school again, as Mr. McCallum[2] appeared to regret my leaving very much, and repeatedly told me I could have a school again; said if I did not care for my old school I could have one of the two new ones he had authority to open. . . . I wrote him some time ago, I felt able and anxious to be at my work again, and in reply received a very curt note, saying that there were no vacancies, and if there were, there were others who ought to have it. I was much hurt and indignant at such treatment."

If it is within the province of the Indian Bureau to inquire into the reasons for this refusal and re-employ Mrs. Ticknor, I hope earnestly it will be done. She merits that much justice. I do not believe a teacher could ever be found who would or could do for the Cahuillas what she did.

The second matter is a letter from Don Antonio Coronel, of Los Angeles, one of the pioneer settlers there, a man to whom all the Indians go in their troubles. I copy the extracts from his letter on a separate paper, for easier reference.

Surely it is a gross inefficiency on the part of this agent, since there is a law firm in Los Angeles especially authorized to look after all land questions and disputes affecting Indians' interests, to say to these Indians that he can do nothing for them. No wonder they distrust all we say.

I also write to call your attention once more to the recommendation in our report, p. 13, for the purchase of the Pauma Ranch.[3] I was bitterly disappointed that the bill as prepared for the relief of the Mission Indians did not include this recommendation. Is it not possible to add it now? The Rincon Indians whose reservation lies just north of this ranch, are the best workers we saw. See p. 29 of the report. They are worse pressed on, annoyed, robbed, than any other Indians in the country. So also of the Pala and La Jolla Indians, surrounded on three sides by the Rincon, La Jolla and Pala reservations lies this Pauma ranch. You see the evident desirability of the purchase.

Yours always cordially,
Helen Jackson.

I leave for California to-morrow. Address Los Angeles, Corner Pearl and 6th streets.

Extracts from Mr. Coronel's letter.

"To-day the Captain of the Rincon Rancheria was here at my house. Jose Luis Albanes, accompanied by two other Captains. They told me that the despoliation of their land continues the same, and the destruction of their animals. They told me that they went to see the Indian Agent, and complained to him, and asked his protection, and what lands they could have for pasture, and the agent answered that *he did not have the power* to arrange those matters.

. . . They tell me that all they wish is for the Government to mark them out a place where they can live in peace, and be quiet. . . . They will wait for your answer in regard to this, and think of it as their only salvation, or final sentence, as they wish to undeceive themselves so as not to suffer so many vexations, and resign themselves to die in misery."

(The peculiarities of this English is in consequence of Mr. Coronel's dictating in Spanish, to a niece who only imperfectly understands English. He himself does not speak it.)

Typescript (LR #22736—1884, OIA, RG 75, NA). HHJ also included a letter to Mary Ticknor from a student at Cahuilla.

The following, not in Teller's hand, was written on HHJ's letter: "Write McCallum agent of Mission Indians and quote first four lines of page 2—and ask if this woman cannot be employed, and if not, why not. Say that Helen Jackson speaks very highly of her & of her efficiency as a teacher and urges her appointment."

1. "Exhibit C: The Cahuilla Reservation," in "Report," pp. 484–85, includes a lengthy description of the schoolteacher and her surroundings.

2. A reference to S. S. Lawson's replacement.

3. "Exhibit P., The Pauma Ranch," in "Report," pp. 512–13, includes two letters from Bishop Mora offering to sell the Pauma Ranch to the government for $31,000.

On Jan. 12, 1891, the "Act for the Relief of the Mission Indians in the State of California," largely based on the Jackson/Kinney report, became law. The final report of the commission established under this law recommended the purchase of Pauma Ranch. See R. V. Belt to John W. Noble, Dec. 19, 1891, LR #9299—1891, SC 31, OIA, RG 75, NA.

TO HENRY TELLER

(Private.)

439 Pearl Street,
Los Angeles,
Nov. 27, 1884.

Dear Mr. Teller:

I hear from the Poncas in Nebraska that some of the Indian Territory Poncas have been up there on a visit. The agent set the time for their return with the exception of Frank La Flesche,[1] uncle of "Bright Eyes;" he was to be permitted to make a long visit if he desired. The poor fellow was one of those who were bribed or threatened into going "willingly" to Indian Territory, and urged the whole tribe to submit. He finds that Standing Bear and his band are much better off than the Indian Territory band, having better horses, better farms and stock. Their share of the annuity is paid directly to them, and they have no agent or overseer. Being in the old home has made La Flesche homesick and he and his wife do not want to go back to Indian Territory at all. They want Joseph La Flesche,[2] Bright Eyes father, the leading man of the Omahas, to write to the Department for leave for them (Frank La Flesche and wife,) to remain with Standing Bear; but Joseph is afraid to interfere, and says: "as Frank made his bed, so he must lie."

I have written to the friend (Mrs. Goddard of Boston) who writes me all this, that I do not believe the Interior Department now would put any obstacle in the way of the Ponca Indian's remaining in his old home. Have I done wrong? I told her of the band of Cheyennes that you allowed to go north and settle, and advised her to advise Frank La Flesche to stay with Standing Bear and see what came of it. Since sending my letter off, it has occurred to me that there might be a possibility of getting from you a specific order that this Indian Frank La Flesche be permitted to join his people in Nebraska. What I would like to see, would be the hegira of all those "contented" Poncas from Indian Territory, back to Nebraska, and the order of the Department to let them stay, as a final settling of scores on one point, with that hypocrite, Carl Schurz.

I am praying daily that he is not rewarded by a Cabinet position again.

Yours always cordially,

Helen Jackson.

P.S. All I can learn thus far of this Indian agent here,[3] corroborates the impressions I expressed in my last letter. I earnestly wish it were possible to get rid of him, and put in the Mr. Rust we urged before. In him the Indians would have a warm friend. As it is, "an Indian in a contest with a white, is as helpless as a rat in a pit;" said Mr. Wells to me the other day. (Wells of Brunson and Wells).

Typescript (LR #23278—1884, OIA, RG 75, NA).

1. Frank La Flesche, or White Swan, was a half-brother to Joseph La Flesche, father of "Bright Eyes." In Nov. 1877, along with ten other Ponca chiefs, Frank had pleaded the tribe's case before government officials. He was part of another delegation to Washington, D.C., in Dec. 1880.

2. Joseph La Flesche (1822–89), the last recognized chief of the Omaha tribe, was the son of a French fur trader and an Indian woman. Aware that his children would have to live in the white world, Joseph encouraged them to adopt the dominant culture.

3. A reference to McCallum.

TO THOMAS BAILEY ALDRICH

Los Angeles
Dec. 1*st*, 1884

Dear Mr. Aldrich

Excuse this sheet off a blotter — (If you knew it was off the "Paragon Handy Tablet," would you respect it more?)

I have no other paper unpacked; — and I cannot wait, to tell you how much pleasure your line about Ramona has given me. — But I am not satisfied till you say, it has made your heart ache, as well as given your ear pleasure: — What I wanted to do, was to draw a picture so winning and alluring in the beginning of the story, that the reader would become thoroughly interested in the characters before he dreamed of what was before him: — and would have swallowed a big dose of information on the Indian Question, without knowing it. —

Every incident in Ramona, (ie. of the Ind. Hist) is true. A Cahuilla Indian was shot two years ago, exactly as Alessandro is — and his wife's name was Ramona — and I never knew this last fact, until Ramona was half written! What do you think of that for a coincidence? — And what do you think of this, also — that I wrote the whole of Ramona, at the rate of 2000 to 3000 words a morning — faster than I can write an ordinary letter — & I altered hardly a word to a chapter, on revising it.

It was an extraordinary experience, & I am not without my superstition about it. My ordinary habit of composition is slow: — 700 to 1000 words a morning, a very good days work: — there were days on which I wrote between 3000 & 4000 words in 3 1/2 to 4 hours — in Ramona! —

Mr. Niles has a copy of my Report to the Int. Dept. on the Mission Indians. — If you would take the trouble to ask him for it, & look it over, you would give me a real pleasure: and —if you are going to do me the great honor of reviewing Ramona — — you will find this Report a splendid help towards it.

Travelling on crutches was not so bad as I feared. — I made the journey with great comfort — & am revelling in open windows sunshine — flowers, — incredible for the 1st of December. This is probably as near a perfect winter climate as the Lord has thought it wise to let mortals enjoy. —

Presently, I am going to work again: — an Indian-Mexican story for the Youth's Companion is my highest ambition now! If I can get their half million of readers to listen to such a story, it will be worth while. —

My love to Mrs. Aldrich — — and thanks again & again to you, for telling me that you think Ramona "beautiful" —

— Praise from you or from Gilder, makes me feel young, spite of my gray hairs & crutches!

Yours ever
Helen Jackson

439 Pearl St.
Los Angeles.

ALS (MH, Aldrich Papers).

TO CHARLES DUDLEY WARNER

Los Angeles.
Dec. 25, 1884

Dear Mr. Warner —

I am confident you owe me a letter: — but if you owed me forty, I should still write all the same, to thank you for your notice of Ramona.[1] —

You have liked it better than I dared to hope — and felt it, which is better than liking it. I have been much cast down by the general run of the notices of it: — not that they did not praise the book — but nobody except you, & the N. Y. Tribune critic has seemed to care a straw for the Indian history in it. — I am sick of hearing that the flight of Alessandro & Ramona is an "exquisite idyl", & not even an allusion to the ejectment of the Temecula band from their homes. — one man said, "the language here & there is marred by shocking profanity — & we cannot commend it to those who would read nothing they could not read without a blush in the presence of their families or of ladies". —

This is the "Commercial Gazette" whatever that may be. Niles sends me the slips cut out & labelled.

The N. Y. Eve. Telegram says that it is "dull reading", — "all finish & no end", — "It is said that Lord Beaconsfield[2] upon receiving from the Queen a magnificent copy of Romola, intimated to a friend, his sense of the graciousness of Her Majesty, the genius of George Eliot[3] & the magnificient dullness of her story, a story which few persons have the courage to say openly they do not like. We suspect that something of the same feeling will accompany this highly elaborated romance of Helen Jackson's which may be described as all finish & no end". —

—Now what do you think of yourself for having praised such a story as that: —

"If he cannot stand what is good enough for me what a very superior young man, this superior young man must be!" —

Who is the Lit. Ed. of the Eve. Telegram? — Exit Ramona — I'll thank you warmer when I see you. —

— When? — I don't know, I fear not before April or May. I am *mired* — expressive but dreadful word: — My broken leg is pretty strong — So far as that is concerned I could walk now, with a cane — But the sound leg, has struck: — overworked ever since I got on my crutches last September — it has given out in the hip, & is lame & painful. I am ordered now to rest it all that is possible — & to make up my mind to be on crutches for months yet! —You see the horribleness of weighing 170. — If I had been of a decent size & shape, I should be walking very well, now. — However I am a lucky woman to get a leg at all. After such a terrible fracture — & I really am much more composed in my mind now that I have abandoned all the harassing effort to make progress in walking, & do each day a little more than the day before. — I am exceedingly well — Sleep eight hours — am rubbed down (massage) for two — eat for three — drive every afternoon, three more — and when you add that all up, what's left? Not much. — I ought to be more content than I am — but I am afraid for my life to grumble, lest a worse thing come upon me. —

I have been here a month — the last week rainy — but it is a soft warm summery sort of drizzle, which is delicious to drive in, after you have been dried up in Colorado, for months. — As for roses — & the rest — well you can't image it: — the people say there are "very few flowers just now" & then they proceed to idly snip off for you, your two hands full! — Los Angeles is just as rubbishy, barbaric, huddled, gay colored, as ever — the most un-American place in America —

— I am never tired, walking my horses up & down the streets, and gazing at the people. — I suppose they will begin to think I have something to sell presently! — or worse! —

I am sure I asked you to send me that lecture of yours — & you didn't. — And, really, it is a grievance that you have not written for so long. I hope & trust you are well. It makes me shudder to think of the weather which has closed in on everybody I love — In Colorado, merc. below zero — snow — miners on a strike — coal famine — & poor Mr. Jackson running the Denver & R[io] G[rande] railroad. — In N.York, snow & slush, & the East wind. —

Aren't you glad Gail Hamilton is not going to be President?[4]

And do you think Blaine was crazy when he withdrew his libel suit? —

— Goodbye — My love to Mrs. Warner — I hope she is strong & well — & I want very much to be told now about that new house. Yours always —

William Jackson.

439 Pearl St.

At Mrs. Whipples. —

P.S. Oh—I forgot. Merry Christmas! —

ALS (CtHT-W, Warner Collection).

1. Informing its readers that they were in for "an intellectual as well as an emotional pleasure," the *Hartford Courant* on Dec. 8, 1884, p. 2, described *Ramona* as "not a preachment nor a diatribe, but purely the work of an artist" with a story line that was "exquisite and sad but not hopelessly sad." The reader would find "an idyllic story and the literary charm of a refined style" as well as the "keenest sketches of many and varied characters." The review concluded: "What we lay special stress on now, is the thoroughly artistic manner in which the author has accomplished her task."

2. Benjamin Disraeli (1804–81), the first earl of Beaconsfield, twice served as prime minister of England. He was not only a statesman but a man of letters.

3. George Eliot was a pseudonym for English-born Mary Ann Evans Cross (1819–80), who was the author of numerous novels, including *Silas Marner* and *Middlemarch*, as well as essays and poetry.

4. Author Gail Hamilton was Blaine's secretary.

TO UNKNOWN

Los Angeles

Jan. 13 1885

Dear Mr. [?]

It is odd that on the same day on which I had mailed a note to Mr. Bowen asking him to tell me the name of the author of the Independent's notice of Ramona,[1] that I might write and thank him personally, your note should have reached me: — Something more than coincidence perhaps: — as yours must have been in the town before mine was written. —

No notice gave me so much pleasure as yours. None was so fully appreciative of the deep purpose of the book. —

Perhaps you have read my "Century of Dishonor?"

That failed to realize my hopes. I fear few have read it, except those that did not need to!

Then I thought if I could write a story so interesting that people could not put it down; — and weave into that story, the true history of some of the Indians' sufferings, — I might thus, as [St.] Paul says "haply convince some."

— But I fear the story has been too interesting, as a story —: so few of the critics seem to have been impressed by anything in it, so much as by its literary excellence, etc. etc. —

I am positively sick of hearing that "the flight of Ramona & Alessandro is an idyl" — & no word for the Temecula ejectment. — I do not know what to do next. — I am thinking of writing a child's story with the same motif as Ramona. — The children have more heart than grown up people. —

But I am taking up your time with my hobby — & all I meant was to say, again, thank you!

Yours truly
Helen Jackson

ALS (Frank Jewett Mather Autograph Collection, Leaf 34, Manuscripts Division, Department of Rare Books and Special Collections, Princeton University Libraries, Princeton, New Jersey). This is a collection of autographed letters, not necessarily to Mather but collected by him.

1. The review of *Ramona* appeared in the Dec. 18, 1884, issue of the *Independent*, p. 10; no author was listed.

TO UNKNOWN[1]

Los Angeles, Cal.,
Thursday, Jan. 22, 1885.

. . . .

I am gaining very slowly in walking, and am still on crutches, and I fear likely to be so for months. But if one must be helpless I know of no place in the world where one can bear it better than in Southern California. The hills are already green, as velvet, the barley many inches high, in some volunteer patches in full head, larks and linnets singing all along the roads, and all sorts of flowers in full bloom in the gardens; nevertheless it is cool enough to make a fire welcome, indeed needful, at night and in the morning; the perfection of weather.

I hope you have read my story *Ramona* and become converted by it (if you needed conversion) on the Indian question. I have, in this book, flung my last weapon! If this does not tell, I know nothing more to do. In my *Century of Dishonor* I tried to attack people's consciences directly, and they would not listen. Now I have sugared my pill, and it remains to be seen if it will go down.

Yours always cordially,
Helen Jackson

Excerpted in *Literary World* 17 (May 29, 1886): 184. This letter extract was proceeded by "A Recollection" of HHJ written by "J.," who probably was John Stevens Cabot Abbott (1805–77). The boarding pupils of the Abbott Institute, which HHJ attended, lived in the John Abbott home. In his recollection, "J." notes that "H.H." came to live in "our house in New York." For additional information, see Odell, *Helen Hunt Jackson*, pp. 38–43.

1. The recipient of the letter may have been Edward Abbott, editor of *Literary World*, 1878–88 and 1895–1903.

TO CHARLES DUDLEY WARNER

Los Angeles
Feb. 8. 1885

Dear Mr. Warner—

· ·

— Apropos of tomahawking however, I've just tonight got the Nation's review of Ramona.[1]

— I hope you have seen it. — I'd give a good deal to know who wrote it — —The assertion of the lack of consecutiveness in the bringing in of Alessandro's declaration of love to Ramona, shows that the reviewer had read that part of the story carelessly — — for it was expressly, & after long deliberation, my intention *not* to tell it baldly in the open narrative, but to bring it in, afterward, in Alessandro's resumé of the situation, as he is hiding by the chapel. —

— Nothing is more absurd of course than to ascribe hostile criticism to personal animus — but I cannot help the feeling that in this case there must be some such thing. It is impossible that a story which has had the good fortune to please such critics as Aldrich & you — & so many others, can have seemed to any man clever enough to be admitted on the staff of the Nation, so bad as he says Ramona is. —

If Howells[2] or James[3] or Bishop[4] wrote book-notices for the Nation, I should understand it! — of course I appear to them to deserve *tomahawking* —

Your new house — a music room — mantel of Saracemi tiles — my mouth waters! —

Of course I shall come if I can — but that is doubtful — I shall come to N. York in April —

— I will not risk coming before it is fairly warm — — but I believe I shall be on crutches, even then, & I see no signs, myself — of ever getting off them —

— What the N. York men may be able to do, remains to be seen: but to my mind, it appears as if my legs had "stuck" & successfully — for the rest of their lives. —

You wouldn't believe how used I have got to the crutches — & how well I am —

I lie in bed twelve hours — write two or three in the forenoon — drive all the afternoon — every day: — I can do everything I ever did, except walk — & if I never walk again — I know one thing — few people get as much out of one pair of legs, as I have already had out of mine! — Love to Mrs. Warner.

Yours & hers forever
Helen Jackson

. . . .

ALS (CtHT-W, Warner Collection). Only the portion of this lengthy letter relative to Jackson's Indian reform work is reproduced here.

1. This review, which appeared in the *Nation* 40 (Jan. 29, 1885): 100–101, outraged HHJ initially because she assumed the reviewer was a man; when she found out that the reviewer was a woman, she accepted it. In a Mar. 8, 1885, letter to Thomas Bailey Aldrich (MH, Aldrich Papers), HHJ wrote: "I've learned that it was a *woman* who wrote that notice of Ramona in the Nation: So, I don't care, a bit. While I thought it was [*Nation* literary editor Wendell Phillips] Garrison, I felt outraged. — He has never read the story himself. If he had, he would never have admitted the notice, I am sure. — I know something of the Nations list of 'lady reviewers', & I think I know now, who wrote it: — & the reasons. — She had had her grievance."

2. William Dean Howells (1837–1920) worked as a reporter and editorial writer in Ohio and served in the United States consulate in Venice, Italy, before joining the editorial staff of the *Atlantic Monthly*, where he worked from 1866 to 1881, becoming editor-in-chief in 1871. He is most known today for his novels, including *The Rise of Silas Lapham*.

3. Henry James (1843–1916) was a distinguished essayist, short story writer, and novelist, whose works included *Daisy Miller*, *The Portrait of a Lady*, and *The Bostonians*.

4. William Henry Bishop (b. 1847), whose novels were serialized in the *Atlantic Monthly* and *Harper's Magazine*, also wrote a volume of travel essays as well as numerous articles.

TO THOMAS BAILEY ALDRICH

Los Angeles
Feb 9. 1885

Dear Mr. Aldrich —

There have been such things printed as "A review of a review" —

— Don't you feel like doing a little tomahawking for me? —and also for the Atlantic, itself, and for everybody else, who has praised Ramona? — Of course you have seen the Nations review of it — it is not only an insult to the book &

to me, but to every one who has praised the book. — I cannot understand it. Nothing is more absurd than to ascribe hostile criticism of ones work, to personal animus: & yet it really seems, in this instance as if there must be some such thing behind so extraordinary a slapping in the face. —

There is one curious point about it — the accusation of the lack of consecutiveness in the narrative, as evinced by the scene with the Señora having preceded the declaration of love between Ramona & Alessandro; this proves that the reviewer glanced carelessly over that part of the book. Else he would have perceived that it was on purpose that I avoided the formal declaration, in the open current of the story, but brought it later in Alessandro's reverie in his resumé of the situation. I did this after deliberation: I have always an inexplicable repugnance to the writing the final denouement of courtship, "out loud". —

— It is impossible that a story which has had the good fortune to so heartily please such critics as Aldrich, & Warner, and Higginson — & the many others who have praised it, can have appeared to any man (clever enough to be on the Nations staff), so bad, as this man says Ramona appears to him. — I want exceedingly to know who wrote it.[1] — I have always felicitated myself on not having enemies — Perhaps I have been mistaken. —

I shall suggest to Niles to utilize this notice, & the N. Y. Telegram's (— the only unflattering ones which have appeared —) in a parallel column advertisement — putting opposite them the verdict of the Atlantic Critic, Pall Mall etc.

— The worst of that delicious bit of praise you gave me, in calling me a Murillo[2] —

— I am silly enough to shut my eyes sometimes with pleasure at recalling it, & try to dream what next I may paint to deserve it — the worst of that is, that so few Americans will know what "a Murillo" is was or "might be!" — Too severe? — No! — which I could prove, if I hadn't reached the bottom of my page.

Yours always,

Helen Jackson

ALS (MH, Aldrich Papers).

1. The reviewer was a woman. See HHJ to Warner, Feb. 8, 1885, note 1, above.

2. The *Atlantic Monthly* review noted: "The contrast extends to the treatment, for Mrs. Jackson shows a ripeness of art and a richness of color which make one feel that he has come unexpectedly upon a Murillo in literature." Bartolomé Esteban Murillo (1617–82) was a Spanish painter whose paintings of madonnas, saints, and street children were among his best-known works.

TO WILLIAM SHARPLESS JACKSON

March 29 — [1885]

Dearest —

I am sure I am not going to get well — & I want to bid you goodbye while my mind is clear. —

— At first, I did not want to die — I would have liked to do a few more of the things that I had planned — but now I am more than willing. — It is of no consequence about the few words more I could say — If Ramona & the Cent. of Dishonor have not helped — one more would have made little odds — But they *will* tell in the long run — The thought of this is my only consolation as I look back over the last ten years, & realize how I have failed to be to you what I longed & hoped to be. — But it is not too late yet, my beloved, for you to have wife & children & live the life that will satisfy your longings. —

It is the greatest hope of my heart that you will desire to marry our Helen[1] — She will make you a pure devoted loving wife, & a splendid mother for your children & will meet your wishes & views far better than I have done — I have left her the bulk of my property, feeling that it would be wrong for me to let my grandfathers money go away from his heirs, & that you do not need it.[2] I hope you will think this was right. — If you marry Helen, it will be a happiness to me, in whatever world I am in, to see her & her children heirs to all I had. — If you do not feel drawn to her, — let me implore you, darling, to marry some one else — *very soon* — do not live the life of a homeless tie-less man any longer than you must — — but be *sure*, this time, dearest to marry some one whose tastes & standards in all matters of living are like your own — Don't make a second mistake love — You will wonder I can write so calmly of this — I am writing as if I spoke to you from another world — Will — — You have never known how deep my realization has been of the fact that I was not the *right* wife for you: — much as I have loved you: — with a different woman & with children at your knees, you would have been a different man — & a happier one. —

— God will give it to you yet — & it was time! — I am glad to go for your sake, my beloved one. Forgive every pain & vexation I have ever given you, & only remember that I loved you as few men are ever loved, in this world, *nobody* will ever love you so well; — that you will feel, as the years go on — & I shall perhaps hear you say it to yourself, some day as I am watching you. —

Your Peggy,—

ALS (CoCC, WSJ I, box 1, fd. 5). Although much of this letter does not relate to HHJ's Indian reform, it is included because it reveals an interesting personal side to her relationship with Will.

1. A reference to HHJ's niece, Helen Fiske Banfield. In 1888 WSJ married Helen Banfield, and the couple had seven children. Helen Banfield Jackson committed suicide on Oct. 18, 1899, in Colorado Springs.

2. HHJ informed her niece that she would inherit the bulk of her property and hoped she would carry out all the provisions of the codicil she had drawn up but had not yet signed. See HHJ to Helen Banfield, May 20, 1885, ALS (CoCC, WSJ I, box 1, fd. 5).

TO HORATIO NELSON RUST

1600 Taylor St.
S[an]F[rancisco]
April 29 — 1885

Dear Mr. Rust,

I am too ill to write — sit up only half an hour a day — The malarial poison has resulted in a nervous prostration which it will take months to recover from — — the malaria itself is not thrown off either, so I expect to lie here helpless for months. — I saw Mr. Coronel a short time. He did not speak of any new Indian matters.

I can do nothing now, Mr. Kinney might. I have written to him.[1] He knows Sec. Bayard.[2] — I believe if you went to W[ashington] with letters from him, — with the influence you have there, you might get appointed as Agent for the Mission I[ndians] — That is all the hope I see. Sec. Lamar[3] is in earnest to do justice to the I[ndians] I am assured.—

If I get well I shall make a strong effort there. — But at the best that can be hoped for, it will not be before autumn that I can do anything.

It is the worst thing about illness, the irreparable loss of time.

Yours truly
Helen Jackson

Tell Mr. Kinney you have heard from me — & — I am too ill to write — cannot do any of the things he suggested in his last letter. —

ALS (CSmH, Rust Collection, RU 760).

1. HHJ's Apr. 1, 1885, letter to Abbot Kinney is reproduced in James, *Through Ramona's Country*, p. 343.

2. Thomas Francis Bayard (1828–98) was secretary of state in Grover Cleveland's first administration.

3. Lucius Quintus Cincinnatus Lamar (1825–1905) was a Mississippi senator who was appointed secretary of the interior by Grover Cleveland. In 1888 he became an associate justice on the Supreme Court.

TO SAMUEL C. ARMSTRONG

1600 Taylor St.
San Francisco
May 14. 1885

Dear Gen. Armstrong,

Thanks for your note of the 1*st* which has just reached me here.

Such proofs of the influence of words one has spoken for a cause near at heart, are very comforting.

It is so easy to feel that one's work is of no consequence.

I received the no. of your little paper containing Miss Goodale's notice of *Ramona*.[1] If I had not been ill, I should have written to thank her for it. I have been ill for three months — & am still confined to my bed, from a terrible malarial poisoning contracted in Los Angeles.

One or two other critics have said that Ramona was "inadequate as an presentation of the Indian Question." —

It is strange, to me, that any one could fail to see, that the story was not in the least introduced as a presentation of the general Indian question. — All I hoped, by it, was to call attention to the general Indian question, by rousing interest in the fates of one little band of Indians — about whom I had come to know enough in detail, to get a background & local coloring, for a story in which they should figure.

I wish I did know enough of the North West Indians — the Ind. Terr. Indians — the Indian wars — &c to get as clear a setting for a larger novel, covering the broad ground, as I have had for these poor little 3000 Mission Indians. —

But to do that, one must have lived on or near reservations, & been familiar with governmental relations in detail for years. — If poor Tibbles could have put into the brain of an experienced writer, all the material he had for that crude story of his, and then added his own enthusiasm we should have had a great story.[2] Perhaps some one may do it yet. — I believe that wonderful woman Alice Fletcher could do it[3] — Perhaps she yet may. I hope she has regained her health.

Yours very sincerely
Helen Jackson

ALS (Hampton University, Hampton, Virginia).

1. Elaine Goodale Eastman's review, "An Indian Love Story," appeared in the Feb. 1885 issue of the magazine of Hampton Normal and Agricultural Institute (now

Hampton University), *Southern Workman*. Eastman (1863–1952) began her teaching career at Hampton, then taught at one of the day schools on the Sioux Reservation before becoming the first superintendent of Indian schools for the Dakotas. She married Santee Sioux physician Charles Alexander Eastman in 1891. See Eastman, *Sister to the Sioux: The Memoirs of Elaine Goodale Eastman, 1885–91*.

2. Tibbles in his autobiography, *Buckskin and Blanket Days*, p. 235, remarked that he had hastily written a propaganda novel entitled *Hidden Power*. He quoted the following from the *Boston Transcript*: "His book can hardly be praised for literary excellence; yet despite that fact, it cannot help making a strong impression."

3. Anthropologist Alice Cunningham Fletcher (1838–1923) worked closely with the Omaha tribe, implementing allotment of their lands, as well as supervising allotment of lands on the Winnebago and Nez Percé reservations. In 1911 she collaborated with Francis La Flesche on *The Omaha Tribe*. See Mark, *A Stranger in Her Native Land: Alice Fletcher and the American Indians*.

TO HORATIO NELSON RUST

1600 Taylor St.
San Francisco
June 11 1885

Dear Mr. Rust,

I had already written to Washington before your note came: — I was too ill to write much — & I had but one channel through which to reach Sec. Lamar, but I sent a few memoranda which I am sure will be laid before him, & I hope may have some influence.

I should think it would be well for you to go to Washington — such men as Hawley[1] & Prof. Baird[2] would have influence I think — Mr. Kinney would know better what is best for you to do.— I most earnestly hope you will be appointed.[3] I am a little better — but do not yet sit up —

Yrs truly—
Helen Jackson

ALS (CSmH, Rust Collection, RU 761).

1. Joseph Roswell Hawley (1826–1905), a lawyer and newspaper editor, served in the U.S. Senate, 1881–1905.

2. Spencer Fullerton Baird (1823–87) was a zoologist who taught at Dickinson College before accepting a position in 1850 at the Smithsonian Institution in Washington, D.C., where Helen and Edward Hunt knew him well. The most important of his works were the zoological volumes of the Pacific Railroad surveys.

3. Rust was not appointed Mission Indian agent until Aug. 1889.

TO ANTONIO F. AND MARIANA CORONEL

San Francisco
1600 Taylor
June 27, 1885

My dear friends,

I am glad to see the accounts in the papers you have sent me of some farther movements in relation to the Mission Indians. —And I have been much cheered by an interview with Prof. Painter.[1]

If he really undertakes to get something done for those Indians, he will be worth more than all the Senators and Congressmen put together.

I hope he will return to Southern California, and visit the rest of the villages. He is thinking of it.

Have you yet been up the Verdugo Canon to get those two baskets I ordered from the old Indian woman there? —I fear she will think me a "lying white", if she does not get her money before long.—

I am sorry to tell you I am still in bed: the malarial symptoms seem to be over but it has left me in a state of nervous prostration, which nothing touches. I can eat literally nothing, and of course am very weak: — it has been a trying experience —and I fear I have months more of it yet to come. It is a year tomorrow since I broke my leg! My unlucky year. —

— I have been asked by one of the Eastern Magazines (a childrens magazine)[2] to write a poem, narrating some incident or legend in California life — if possible something to do with the Indians. I do not know anything which seems to me to be adapted to tell in a ballad; and I have wondered if in Mr. Coronel's storehouse of memories, he could not think of some old stories which would be suitable for the purpose. — If he can, and you would write them down for me, I would be greatly obliged to you. —

I hope you are all well —

Always faithfully your friend
Helen Jackson.

P.S. When you get those baskets, I would like to have them sent here by Express. There is no doubt that I shall have to lie here for many weeks yet, & I shall enjoy having them. Send with them, also, the flat one I gave you to keep. I'd like that, to keep work in, on my bed.—

ALS (Seaver Center, Coronel Collection). Reprinted in Davis and Alderson, *The True Story of "Ramona,"* pp. 181–83.

1. Charles C. Painter (d. 1895) was a Congregational minister who taught at Fisk University before joining the Indian Rights Association in 1883. Initially working from the Boston office, he became the association's Washington lobbyist. He frequently visited Indian reservations and wrote regular reports on what he saw. In Painter to Coronel, June 19, 1885 (CSmH, HM 38231), Painter mentioned having consulted with Jackson.

2. A reference to *Youth's Companion*.

TO MARY ELIZABETH (SHERIFF) FOWLER

San Francisco
1600 Taylor St.
July 17. 1885

Dear Miss Sheriff —

I was indeed glad to hear from you. I have wondered many times if you ever received the Christian Union last summer, with Ramona in it. I ordered it sent you. I hear it has caused much anger in San Diego Co. — It is well. — I am glad of it! —

This has been my malign year — the 28th of June 1884 I fell from top to bottom of my stairs at home — & broke my left leg —the worst possible break. — The 28th of June 1885 found me in bed here — having been ill since Feb. 14 with a terrible malarial poisoning contracted in Los Angeles where I had been for three months.

I am still in bed — very weak & ill. The Drs. say I will get well — but I myself do not expect to. —

I am profoundly touched by the message of the Capitan. To think that the poor souls should still believe in me, when nothing has been done for them! — Give him my grateful remembrances — and tell him, if you *can* — about Ramona: — tell him that over a hundred thousand people have read that story, & are sorry for the Indians — & that many good people are working to *try* to get justice done them by the Government: that I believe the new Secretary[1] is their friend — & the new President[2] too — & hope has not yet died in my heart, though the time is very long and bad men are in greater numbers than the good men, in the Great Council at Washington. — Prof. Painter who is the right hand man of the Indian Rights Association, of Phila. was here last week. I hope he has gone down South to visit the Mission Indians. —

I cannot tell you how glad I am to hear of your approaching marriage — I wish you would tell me more about it — where your home will be. — Mr. Fowlers business &c. — You have my heartiest good wishes & congratulations. — But who oh who will ever love the Saboba Indians as you do!

— Remember me to Mrs. Ticknor if you see her. I am glad she is back at Cahuilla. When you are in San Diego remember me to Mr. & Mrs. Morse. Tell them I have bitterly reqretted that I did not go to San Diego instead of Los Angeles. —

I wanted to be with Mrs. Whipple — & I had never known that there was such danger of malaria in L.A. —

— I have a lot of Harpers Weeklies &c — here — would you like them for the school? — Can I send by Express so you will surely get them? If so, what address? —

Yours always affectionately

Helen Jackson

ALS (CSmH, HHJ MSS, HM 14216). Copy also in CoCC, WSJ II, box 3, fd. 33.
1. A reference to Secretary of the Interior Lamar.
2. Grover Cleveland (1837–1908) served as the twenty-second and the twenty-fourth president of the United States.

TO [THOMAS WENTWORTH HIGGINSON?]

[July 27, 1885]

· ·

I feel that my work is done, and I am heartily, honestly, and cheerfully ready to go. In fact, I am glad to go. You have never fully realized how for the last four years my whole heart has been full of the Indian cause—how I have felt, as the Quakers say, "a concern" to work for it. My "Century of Dishonor" and "Ramona" are the only things I have done of which I am glad now. The rest is of no moment. They will live, and they will bear fruit. They already have. The change in public feeling on the Indian question in the last three years is marvellous; an Indian Rights' Association in every large city in the land . . . Every word of the Indian history in "Ramona" is literally true, and it is being reenacted here every day.

I did mean to write a child's story on the same theme as "Ramona," but I doubt if I could have made it so telling a stroke, so perhaps it is as well that I shall not do it. And perhaps I shall do it after all, but I cannot conceive of getting well after such an illness as this.

· ·

Printed in Higginson, "Helen Jackson," *Nation* 41 (Aug. 20, 1885): 151.

TO GROVER CLEVELAND

[August 8, 1885]

To Grover Cleveland
President of the United States
Dear Sir,

From my death bed I send you message of heart-felt thanks for what you have already done for the Indians.[1]

I ask you to read my Century of Dishonor.

I am dying happier for the belief I have that it is your hand that is destined to strike the first steady blow towards lifting this burden of infamy from our country, and righting the wrongs of the Indian race.

With respect and gratitude
Helen Jackson

Aug. 8 1885

ALS (NjP, General Manuscripts Miscellaneous: JA-JE, Folder: Jackson, H. H. 1830–1885, subfolder 2). Also reprinted in *Critic* n.s. 4 (Oct. 3, 1885): 167; *A Century of Dishonor*, p. 515; and Davis and Alderson, *The True Story of "Ramona,"* p. 81.

1. On Aug. 12, 1885, Helen Hunt Jackson died of cancer.

Bibliography

BOOK REVIEWS AND NEWSPAPER AND MAGAZINE ARTICLES CITED FULLY IN THE NOTES ARE not included, with the exception of Jackson's Indian-related articles in the *Independent*.

Most biographical data came from the following widely used sources, unless otherwise noted: *Appleton's Cyclopaedia of American Biography, Biographical Dictionary of American Territorial Governors, Biographical Directory of the American Congress, Biographical Directory of the United States Executive Branch, 1774–1971, Dictionary of American Biography*, T. W. Herringshaw's *Encyclopedia of American Biography of the Nineteenth Century*, Dan L. Thrapp's *Encyclopedia of Frontier Biography, History of the Bench and Bar of California, Merriam-Webster's Encyclopedia of Literature, The National Cyclopedia of American Biography, Notable American Women, The Twentieth Century Biographical Dictionary of Notable Americans, Who Was Who in America, Who Was Who in American Politics*, Carl Waldman's *Who Was Who in Native American History: Indians and Non-Indians from Early Contacts through 1900, Who's Who in the Pacific Southwest*.

RECORDS OF THE NATIONAL ARCHIVES

Record Group 75. Records of the Bureau of Indian Affairs.
Office of Indian Affairs, Letters Received.
Office of Indian Affairs, Letters Sent.

ANNUAL REPORTS OF THE COMMISSIONERS OF INDIAN AFFAIRS

United States. Department of the Interior. Office of Indian Affairs. *Annual Report of the Commissioner of Indian Affairs to the Secretary of the Interior for the Year*. Various years. Washington, D.C.: Government Printing Office.

MANUSCRIPT COLLECTIONS

Abbott Memorial Collection: Lyman Abbott Autograph Collection. Library, Bowdoin College, Brunswick, Maine.
Aldrich, Thomas Bailey. Papers. Houghton Library, Harvard University, Cambridge, Massachusetts.
Berg, Henry W. and Albert A. Collection. New York Public Library, Astor, Lenox, and Tilden Foundations, New York, New York.
Bowen, Henry Chandler. Collection. Huntington Library, San Marino, California.
Carr, Jeanne C. (Smith). Collection. Huntington Library, San Marino, California.
Chapin-Kiley Manuscripts. Special Collections and Archives. Amherst College Library, Amherst, Massachusetts.

Conway, Moncure D. Papers. Butler Library, Columbia University, New York, New York.

Coronel, Antonio F. Collection. Seaver Center for Western History Research, Los Angeles County Museum of Natural History, Los Angeles, California.

Curtis, George William. Papers. Staten Island Institute of Arts and Sciences, Staten Island, New York.

Cushman, Charlotte. Papers. Library of Congress, Washington, D.C.

Dall, Caroline. Papers. Massachusetts Historical Society, Boston, Massachusetts.

Davis, Richard Harding. Collection. Clifton Waller Barrett Library in the Alderman Library, University of Virginia. Charlottesville, Virginia.

Dawes, Henry L. Papers. Library of Congress, Washington, D.C.

Gilder, Joseph Benson. Papers. New York Public Library, Astor, Lenox and Tilden Foundations, New York, New York.

Hampton University Archives, Hampton, Virginia.

Holmes, Oliver Wendell. Papers. Houghton Library, Harvard University, Cambridge, Massachusetts.

Holmes, Oliver Wendell. Papers. Library of Congress, Washington, D.C.

Jackson, Helen Maria Fiske Hunt. Collection. Bancroft Library, University of California, Berkeley, California.

Jackson, Helen Hunt. Collection. Clifton Waller Barrett Library in the Alderman Library, University of Virginia, Charlottesville, Virginia.

Jackson, Helen Hunt. Manuscripts. Huntington Library, San Marino, California.

Jackson, Helen Hunt. Papers. Tutt Library, Colorado College, Colorado Springs, Colorado.

Jackson, Helen Hunt. Papers. Jones Library, Amherst, Massachusetts.

Jackson, William Sharpless. Family Papers. Tutt Library, Colorado College, Colorado Springs.

Johnson, Robert Underwood. Papers. Butler Library, Columbia University, New York.

Longfellow, Henry Wadsworth. Papers. Houghton Library, Harvard University, Cambridge, Massachusetts.

Mather, Frank Jewett. Autograph Collection. Library, Princeton University, Princeton, New Jersey.

Morse, Ephraim W. Collection. San Diego Historical Society, San Diego, California.

Personal-Miscellaneous (Helen Hunt Jackson). New York Public Library, Astor, Lenox, and Tilden Foundations, New York, New York.

Phelan, James D. California Authors Collection. San Francisco Public Library, San Francisco, California.

Pierpont Morgan Library, New York, New York.

Reid, Whitelaw. Papers. Library of Congress, Washington, D.C.

Rust, Horatio Nelson. Collection. Huntington Library, San Marino, California.

Scribner's Sons. Archives. Library, Princeton University, Princeton, New Jersey.

Special Collections, University of California, Los Angeles, California.

Twining, Alexander Catlin. Papers. New Haven Colony Historical Society, New Haven, Connecticut.

Warner, Charles Dudley. Collection. Watkinson Library, Trinity College, Hartford, Connecticut.

Whipple, Henry B. Papers. Minnesota Historical Society, St. Paul, Minnesota.

NEWSPAPERS

Boston Daily Advertiser, 1879–81.
Boston Evening Transcript, 1879, 1881.
Hartford Courant, 1879, 1880, 1881, 1884.
Hemet News, 1932.
New York Daily Tribune, 1879–81.
New York Evening Post, 1879–81.
New York Herald, 1881.
New York Independent, 1879–81, 1883–84.
New York Times, 1879–81.
Niobrara Pioneer, 1877, 1880–81.
Rocky Mountain News, 1880.
San Diego Union, 1875, 1883, 1887.
San Francisco Call, 1887.
San Luis Rey Star, 1883.
Santa Barbara Daily Press, 1882.
Springfield Republican, 1881.

MAGAZINES

Atlantic Monthly, 1881–84.
Century Magazine, 1883–84.
Christian Union, 1880–81.
Critic, 1884–85.
Harper's Weekly, 1881.
Nation, 1881.
Overland Monthly, 1885.
St. Nicholas, 1880.
Youth's Companion, 1885.

DISSERTATIONS AND UNPUBLISHED MANUSCRIPTS

Burgess, Larry E. "The Lake Mohonk Conference on the Indian, 1883–1916." Ph.D. dissertation. Claremont Graduate School, 1972.

Eastman, Elaine Goodale. "Spinner in the Sun: The Story of Helen Hunt Jackson." Unpaged typescript in the Sophia Smith Collection, Women's History Archive, Smith College, Northampton, Massachusetts.

Friend, Ruth E. "Helen Hunt Jackson: A Critical Study." Ph.D. dissertation. Kent State University, 1985.

Wanken, Helen M. "Woman's Sphere and Indian Reform: The Women's National Indian Association, 1879–1901." Ph.D. dissertation. Marquette University, 1981.

SECONDARY SOURCES

Adams, Mrs. Henry. *The Letters of Mrs. Henry Adams, 1865–1883,* pp. 489–503. Ed. Ward Thoron. Boston: Little, Brown, 1936.

Alexander, Carolyn Elayne. *Abbot Kinney's Venice-of-America.* Los Angeles: Westwide Genealogical Society, 1991.

Allen, Margaret V. *Ramona's Homeland.* Chula Vista: Denrich Press, 1914.

Anderson, Gary Clayton. *Little Crow: Spokesman for the Sioux.* St. Paul: Minnesota Historical Society Press, 1986.

Banning, Evelyn I. *Helen Hunt Jackson.* New York: Vanguard Press, 1973.

———. "Helen Hunt Jackson in San Diego." *Journal of San Diego History* 24 (Fall 1978): 457–67.

Board of Indian Commissioners. *Eleventh Annual Report of the Board of Indian Commissioners for the Year 1879.* Washington, D.C.: Government Printing Office, 1880.

———. "Third Annual Meeting of the Lake Mohonk Conference." In *Seventeenth Annual Report of the Board of Indian Commissioners for the Year, 1885.* Washington, D.C.: Government Printing Office, 1885.

"Book Reviews." *Overland Monthly* 2d s. 5 (March 1885): 330–31.

Brigandi, Phil, and John W. Robinson. "The Killing of Juan Diego: From Murder to Mythology." *Journal of San Diego History* 40 (Winter/Spring 1994): 1–22.

Byers, John R., Jr. "The Indian Matter of Helen Hunt Jackson's Ramona: From Fact to Fiction." *American Indian Quarterly* 2 (Winter 1975–76): 331–46.

Carillo, Fr. J. M. *The Story of Mission San Antonio de Pala.* Oceanside: North County Printers, 1959.

Carrico, Richard L. "San Diego Indians and the Federal Government: Years of Neglect, 1850–1865." *Journal of San Diego History* 26 (Summer 1980): 165–84.

Carter, Franklin Charles. *Some By-ways of California.* San Francisco: Whitaker & Ray-Wiggin Company, 1911.

Clark, Stanley. "Ponca Publicity." *Mississippi Valley Historical Review* 29 (March 1943): 495–516.

The Contributors' Club. "How Ramona Was Written." *Atlantic Monthly* 86 (November 1900): 713–14.

"Current Criticism: Something Very Rare." *Critic* n.s. 3 (January 10, 1885): 22.

Davis, Carlyle Channing, and William A. Alderson. *The True Story of "Ramona": Its Facts and Fictions, Inspiration and Purpose.* New York: Dodge Publishing Company, 1914.

Dobie, J. Frank. "Helen Hunt Jackson and Ramona." *Southwest Review* 44 (Spring 1959): 93–98.

Dorr, Julia C. R. "Emerson's Admiration of 'H.H.'" *Critic* n.s. 4 (August 29, 1885): 102.

Eastman, Elaine Goodale. "The Author of Ramona." *Classmate* (January 21, 1939): 6–7.

———. "An Indian Love Story." *Southern Workman* (Feb. 1885): 19.

———. *Sister to the Sioux: The Memoirs of Elaine Goodale Eastman, 1885–91.* Ed. Kay Graber. Lincoln: University of Nebraska Press, 1978.

Emerson, Ralph Waldo. *The Journals and Miscellaneous Notebooks of Ralph Waldo Emerson, 1866–1882.* Vol. 16. Ed. Ronald A. Bosco and Glen M. Johnson. Cambridge: Belknap Press of Harvard University Press, 1982.

Engelhardt, Fr. Zephyrin. *San Luis Rey Mission.* San Francisco: James H. Barry, 1921.

Garner, Van H. *The Broken Ring: The Destruction of the California Indians.* Tucson: Westernlore Press, 1982.

Goddard, Martha Le Baron. "A Century of Dishonor." *Atlantic Monthly* 47 (April 1881): 572–75.

Green, Norma Green. "Four Sisters: Daughters of Joseph La Flesche." *Nebraska History* 45 (June 1964): 165–76.

———. *Iron Eye's Family: The Children of Joseph La Flesche*. Lincoln: Johnsen Publishing Company, 1969.

Hagan, William T. *The Indian Rights Association: The Herbert Welsh Years, 1882–1904*. Tucson: University of Arizona Press, 1985.

Harsha, William Justin. "How 'Ramona' Wrote Itself." *Southern Workman* 59 (August 1930): 370–75.

———. *Ploughed Under: The Story of an Indian Chief*. N.p., 1881.

———. *Timid Brave: The Story of an Indian Uprising*. N.p., 1886.

Hayes, Rutherford B. *Diary and Letters of Rutherford Hayes: Nineteenth President of the United States*. Ed. Charles Richard Williams. 5 vols. Columbus: Ohio State Archaeological and Historical Society, 1924.

Hays, Robert G. *A Race at Bay: New York Times Editorials on "the Indian Problem," 1860–1900*. Carbondale: Southern Illinois University Press, 1997.

Hayter, Earl W. "The Ponca Removal." *North Dakota Historical Quarterly* 6 (July 1932): 263–75.

Higginson, Thomas Wentworth. *Contemporaries*. Boston: Houghton, Mifflin, 1899.

———. "Helen Jackson." *Nation* 41 (August 20, 1885): 150–51.

———. "Mrs. Helen Jackson ('H.H.')." *Century Magazine* n.s. 31 (November 1885): 254.

Hill, Joseph John. *The History of Warner's Ranch and Its Environs*. Los Angeles: private printing, 1927.

Hoig, Stan, *The Sand Creek Massacre*. Norman: University of Oklahoma Press, 1961.

Hufford, D. A. *The Real Ramona of Helen Hunt Jackson's Famous Novel*. 4th ed. Los Angeles: D. A. Hufford and Company, 1900.

Jackson, Helen Hunt (H.H.). "Captain Pablo's Story." *Independent* (October 25, 1883): 1–2.

———. *A Century of Dishonor: A Sketch of the United States Government's Dealing with Some of the Indian Tribes*. Boston: Roberts Brothers, 1888.

———. "A Chance Afternoon in California." *Independent* (April 5, 1883): 1–2.

———. "A Day with the Cahuillas." *Independent* (October 11, 1883): 1–3.

———. "Echoes in the City of Angels." *Century Magazine* 27 (December 1883): 194–210.

———. "The Fate of Saboba." *Independent* (December 13, 1883): 1–2.

———. "Father Junipero and His Work." *Century Magazine* 26 (May/June 1883): 199–215.

———. *Glimpses of Three Coasts*. Boston: Roberts Brothers, 1886.

———. "Justifiable Homicide in Southern California." *Independent* (September 27, 1883): 1–2.

———. "The Massacre of the Cheyennes." *Independent* (January 1, 1880): 2–3.

———. "A Night at Pala." *Independent* (April 19, 1883): 2–3.

———. "Outdoor Industries in Southern California." *Century Magazine* 26 (October): 803–20.

———. "The Present Condition of the Mission Indians in Southern California." *Century Magazine* 26 (August 1883): 511–29.

————. *Ramona*. Boston: Roberts Brothers, 1884.

———— (H.H.). "Standing Bear and Bright Eyes." *Independent* (November 20, 1879): 1–2.

————. "The Temecula Exiles." *Independent* (November 29, 1883): 3–4.

————. "The Wards of the United States Government." *Scribner's Monthly* 19 (March 1880): 775–82.

James, George Wharton. *Heroes of California*. Boston: Little, Brown, 1910.

————. *Through Ramona's Country*. Boston: Little, Brown, 1910.

Kappler, Charles J., ed. *Indian Treaties, 1778–1883*. New York: Interland Publishing, 1972.

King, James T. "'A Better Way': General George Crook and the Ponca Indians." *Nebraska History* 50 (Fall 1969): 239–56.

Kvasnicka, Robert and Herman J. Viola, eds. *The Commissioners of Indian Affairs, 1824–1977*. Lincoln: University of Nebraska Press, 1979.

Lindley, Walter, and J. P. Widney. *California of the South*. New York: D. Appleton and Company, 1888.

Mardock, Robert Winston. "Standing Bear and the Reformers." In *Indian Leaders: Oklahoma's First Statesmen*, ed. H. Glenn Jordan and Thomas M. Holm, pp. 101–13. Oklahoma City: Oklahoma Historical Society, 1979.

Mark, Joan. *A Stranger in Her Native Land: Alice Fletcher and the American Indians*. Lincoln: University of Nebraska Press, 1988.

Marriott, Katheryn E. "Helen Hunt Jackson in Santa Barbara." *Noticias* 28 (Winter 1982): 84–92.

Mathes, Valerie Sherer. "The California Mission Indian Commission of 1891: The Legacy of Helen Hunt Jackson." *California History* 72 (Winter 1993–94): 339–59.

————. "Helen Hunt Jackson: A Legacy of Indian Reform." *Essays and Monographs in Colorado History* 4 (1986): 25–58.

————. "Helen Hunt Jackson and the Campaign for Ponca Restitution, 1880–1881." *South Dakota History* 17 (Spring 1987): 23–42.

————. *Helen Hunt Jackson and Her Indian Reform Legacy*. Austin: University of Texas Press, 1990.

————. "Helen Hunt Jackson and the Ponca Controversy." *Montana, the Magazine of Western History* 39 (Winter 1989): 42–53.

————. "Helen Hunt Jackson as Power Broker." In *Between Indian and White Worlds: The Cultural Broker*, ed. Margaret Connell Szasz, pp. 141–57. Norman: University of Oklahoma Press, 1994.

————. "I Am Going to Write an Indian Novel, the Scene Laid in So. California . . ." *Journal of San Diego History* 42 (Spring 1996): 108–13.

————. "Nineteenth-Century Women and Reform: The Women's National Indian Association." *American Indian Quarterly* 14 (Winter 1990): 1–18.

————. "Parallel Calls to Conscience: Reformers Helen Hunt Jackson and Harriet Beecher Stowe." *Californians* (July–Aug. 1983): 32–40.

Mendoza, Patrick M. *Song of Sorrow: Massacre at Sand Creek*. Denver: Willow Wind Publishing Company, 1993.

Mott, Frank Luther. *A History of American Magazines 1850–1865*. 5 vols. Cambridge: Harvard University Press, 1957.

Nevins, Allan. "Helen Hunt Jackson, Sentimentalist vs. Realist." *American Scholar* 10 (Summer 1941): 269–85.

Norgren, Jill. *The Cherokee Cases: The Confrontation of Law and Politics.* New York: McGraw-Hill, 1996.

Odell, Ruth. *Helen Hunt Jackson (H.H.).* New York: D. Appleton-Century Company, 1939.

Painter, Charles C. *The Condition of Affairs in Indian Territory and California.* Philadelphia: Office of the Indian Rights Association, 1888.

Perdue, Theda, and Michael D. Green, eds. *The Cherokee Removal: A Brief History with Documents.* Boston: Bedford Books of St. Martin's Press, 1995.

Powell, Lawrence Clark. "California Classics Reread: Ramona." *Westways* 60 (July 1968): 13–15.

Priest, Loring Benson. *Uncle Sam's Stepchildren: The Reformation of United States Indian Policy, 1865–1887.* Lincoln: University of Nebraska Press, 1969.

Prucha, Francis Paul. *American Indian Policy in Crisis: Christian Reformers and the Indian, 1865–1900.* Norman: University of Oklahoma Press, 1976.

———. *American Indian Treaties: The History of a Political Anomaly.* Berkeley: University of California Press, 1994.

Quinton, Amelia Stone. "Care of the Indian." In *Woman's Work in America,* ed. Annie Hathan Meyer, pp. 373–91. New York: Henry Holt, 1891.

"Recent American Fiction." *Atlantic Monthly* 55 (January 1885): 130.

Schultz, Duane. *Over the Earth I Come: The Great Sioux Uprising of 1862.* New York: St. Martin's Press, 1992.

Schurz, Carl. *Speeches, Correspondence and Political Papers of Carl Schurz.* 3 vols. Ed. Frederick Bancroft. New York: G. P. Putnam's Sons, 1913.

"The Schurz Mystery." *Nation* 31 (February 24, 1881): 125–26.

Scott, Bob. *Blood at Sand Creek: The Massacre Revisited.* Caldwell: Caxton Printers, 1994.

Shinn, Milicent W. "The Verse and Prose of 'H.H.'" *Overland Monthly* 2d s. 6 (September 1885): 315–23.

Shipek, Florence Connolly. *Pushed into the Rocks: Southern California Indian Land Tenure, 1769–1986.* Lincoln: University of Nebraska Press, 1987.

Smith, Wallace E. *This Land Was Ours: The Del Valles and Camulos.* Ventura: Ventura County Historical Society, 1977.

Starr, Kevin. *Inventing the Dream: California through the Progressive Era.* New York: Oxford University Press, 1985.

Stellman, Louis J. "The Man Who Inspired 'Ramona.'" *Overland Monthly* 50 (September 1907): 2–5.

Street, Douglas. "La Flesche Sisters Write to St. Nicholas Magazine." *Nebraska History* 62 (Winter 1981): 515–23.

Svaldi, David. *Sand Creek and the Rhetoric of Extermination.* New York: University Press of America, 1989.

Tibbles, Thomas Henry. "Anecdotes of Standing Bear." *Nebraska History* 13 (October–December 1932): 271–76.

———. *Buckskin and Blanket Days.* Lincoln: University of Nebraska Press, 1969.

———. *The Ponca Chiefs: An Account of the Trial of Standing Bear.* Ed. Kay Graber. Lincoln: University of Nebraska Press, 1972.

Tourgée, Albion W. "Study in Civilization." *North American Review* 143 (August 1886): 246–61.

Trefousse, Hans L. *Carl Schurz: A Biography.* Knoxville: University of Tennessee Press, 1982.

Utley, Robert M. *Frontier Regulars: The United States Army and the Indian, 1866–1891.* New York: Macmillan, 1973.

Van Horn, Kurt. "Tempting Temecula: The Making and Unmaking of a Southern California Community." *Journal of San Diego History* 20 (Winter 1974): 26–38.

Vroman, A. C., and T. F. Barnes. *The Genesis of the Story of Ramona.* Los Angeles: Kinsley-Barnes and Newner Company, 1899.

Warner, Charles Dudley. "A-Hunting of the Deer." In *In the Wilderness,* pp. 54–81. Boston: Houghton Mifflin.

———. "H.H. in Southern California." In *Fashions in Literature and Other Literary and Social Essays and Addresses,* pp. 321–30. New York: Dodd, Mead, 1902.

Weber, Francis J., ed. *King of the Missions: A Documentary History of San Luis Rey de Francia.* Los Angeles: Timothy Cardinal Manning, n.d.

Wilson, Dorothy Clarke. *Bright Eyes: The Story of Susette La Flesche, an Omaha Indian.* New York: McGraw-Hill, 1974.

Woolsey, Ronald C. *Migrants West: Toward the Southern California Frontier.* Sebastopol: Grizzly Bear Publishing Company, 1996.

Wright, Mable Osgood. *My New York.* New York: Macmillan Company, 1926.

Index

(*Illustration pages are in **boldface***)
The following abbreviations are used:
HHJ   Helen Hunt Jackson
WSJ   William Sharpless Jackson
bio   reference to short biographical entry